MAR 1 1 2021

WHEELS *of* COURAGE

WHEELS

of

COURAGE

How Paralyzed Veterans from World War II
Invented Wheelchair Sports, Fought for Disability
Rights, and Inspired a Nation

* * *

DAVID DAVIS

CENTER
STREET

Nashville   New York

Center Street
Hachette Book Group
1290 Avenue of the Americas, New York, NY 10104
centerstreet.com
twitter.com/centerstreet

First Edition: August 2020

Center Street is a division of Hachette Book Group, Inc. The Center Street name and logo are trademarks of Hachette Book Group, Inc.

The publisher is not responsible for websites (or their content) that are not owned by the publisher.

Library of Congress Control Number: 2020935798

ISBNs: 978-1-5460-8464-8 (hardcover), 978-1-5460-8462-4 (ebook)

Printed in the United States of America

LSC-C

10 9 8 7 6 5 4 3 2 1

To Gene "Jerry" Fesenmeyer:
Thank you for sharing your story with me.

And to my sister, Margot Davis (1960–1986):
We miss you every day.

PROLOGUE

The Greatest Show on Four Wheels

March 10, 1948: A Wednesday evening in New York City. The illuminated marquee looming over the entrance to Madison Square Garden promotes the evening's featured attraction: BAS-KETBALL TONITE: KNICKS vs. ST. LOUIS BOMBERS.

Inside the world's most famous entertainment palace, a haze of cigarette smoke hangs over the basketball court, empty save for two referees in black-and-white-striped shirts with whistles around their necks. A ring of loudspeakers hanging from the rafters burbles with the sonorous tones of public-address announcer John F. X. Condon as he notifies the assemblage that an exhibition game between two teams of World War II veterans will precede the main event.

What the near-capacity crowd of 15,561 spectators is about to witness is the most unusual form of basketball since 1891, when Dr. James Naismith invented the sport with a pair of peach baskets and a soccer ball.

World War II had ended nearly three years previous, but the war was still uppermost in the thoughts of many Americans. More than sixteen million men and women—about 10 percent of the nation's population—had served in the U.S. Armed Forces during the war. American casualties (dead and wounded) totaled one million, a number that exceeded the population of all but five U.S. cities. Everybody knew somebody who had participated in the most destructive conflict in human history.

On the domestic front, the effort had been all-consuming. Americans bought war bonds, planted victory gardens, sent Red Cross parcels overseas to prisoners, rationed food and gasoline, conserved metal and paper, worked in munitions and aircraft factories, and memorized maps of the European and Pacific theaters. In the peace that followed, the public's interest in veterans' issues remained as high as the nearby Empire State Building. Moviegoers flocked to view *The Best Years of Our Lives*, *So Proudly We Hail!*, and *Thirty Seconds Over Tokyo*. Books about the war, from John Hersey's *Hiroshima* to Norman Mailer's *The Naked and the Dead* to James Gould Cozzens's *Guard of Honor*, were published to prize-winning acclaim.

The servicemen who took to the Garden hardwood that night were as extraordinarily ordinary as other veterans. They were the "mud-rain-frost-and-wind boys" that journalist Ernie Pyle celebrated in his Pulitzer Prize–winning columns from the front lines. They were "Willie and Joe," as sketched by Bill Mauldin in his Pulitzer Prize–winning cartoons. They were your brother, your husband, your neighbor, your best friend from high school, your boss. They came from Paterson, New Jersey; Billings, Montana; Needham, Massachusetts; Brooklyn, New York; and the Boyle Heights section of Los Angeles. They were GI Joes and Dogfaces, Buck Privates and Mud Eaters, Leathernecks and Grunts.

Except these veterans were different. All of them were permanently paralyzed from the waist down from injuries they'd incurred during the war. All of them were seated in slender metal wheelchairs. The home team was made up of patients at Halloran General

Hospital on Staten Island; the visitors traveled to New York from Cushing General Hospital in Framingham, Massachusetts.

When the game started, the chatter in the stands gave way to uneasy, muted murmuring. Halloran's Jack Gerhardt was speeding around the court like racecar driver Mauri Rose cornering at the Indianapolis 500 when he collided with another player and spilled out of his chair. Matrons gasped and dabbed at their eyes with handkerchiefs; crusty sportswriters complained that the smoke from their Lucky Strikes was causing them to tear up.

But after Gerhardt muscled his body back into his chair and demanded the ball, and after the Cushing crew brayed their displeasure at the officials—"Whatsamatta, ref, can't you hear either?"—the mood inside the arena relaxed, and the fans began to cheer and whistle as if they were witnessing a miracle.

Which, in many respects, they were. For millennia, paraplegia had been a death sentence that physicians were powerless to prevent. The life expectancy of soldiers with traumatic spinal-cord injuries during World War I was estimated to be about one year. But now, the wonders of modern medicine were promising hope, and paralyzed veterans like Gerhardt, a wiry paratrooper wounded at Normandy, could envision a future.

How that future would unfold was less clear. People with severe disabilities were usually shunted off to institutions or hidden away in private homes. The barrier-plagued society accommodated only non-disabled people. There were no curb cutouts at the street corners of most American cities, no ramps leading to the entrances of office buildings. There were no handicapped parking spaces or kneeling buses, no homes with accessible toilets, showers, and doorways.

That myopia extended to sports. Prior to World War II, playing sports was out of bounds for those with "crippled bodies," a common phrase from the era and one that encompassed amputees and polio patients. The Paralympics didn't exist. Neither did the Warrior Games or the Invictus Games. And, who in their right mind would consider racing the 26.2 miles of the Boston Marathon in a wheelchair?

It turned out that thousands did. From the paraplegia wards of far-flung army and navy hospitals came a radical experiment: wheelchair sports. What started out as a fun diversion within the rehabilitation process soon turned into something more: spirited competition, yes, but also an avenue toward an independent life, an affirmation of a future, a diminution of stigma.

When paralyzed veterans took wheelchair basketball out of hospital gymnasiums and into storied sports stadiums like Madison Square Garden, Boston Garden, Chicago Stadium, the Oakland Civic Auditorium, Los Angeles's Pan-Pacific Auditorium, St. Louis's Kiel Auditorium, and the Palestra in Philadelphia, they showed that they were not going to hide their condition behind closed doors. Their skill and moxie stirred a large section of the nation and, most importantly, they educated doctors, politicians, the media, business owners, and the general public about the latent value of people with disabilities.

Just days after the game in Madison Square Garden, *Newsweek* plastered on its cover a photograph of Jack Gerhardt holding a basketball while sitting in his wheelchair. Non-disabled athletes using wheelchairs challenged the paralyzed veterans for on-court supremacy, and these teams, including the Knicks, the Boston Celtics, the Harlem Globetrotters, and top-ranked college squads, were handily defeated. Hollywood came calling to make a film about the men, starring the actor who that very evening was mesmerizing the audience at a Broadway theater a few blocks away from the Garden: Marlon Brando.

During the war, servicemen and women in the Pacific and European theaters experienced the worst of humanity. They watched mortar bombs kill their buddies standing fifteen feet away, leaving behind only a pair of mud-encrusted boots. They witnessed the appalling horrors of the Nazi concentration camps after they freed tens of thousands of half-dead slaves. They saw the devastation wrought by the explosions of two atomic bombs.

Now the war was over. Paralyzed veterans had sacrificed their glorious youth for their country and for freedom. They were alive, but their bodies and souls were damaged. They wanted no sympathy or special treatment. They simply wanted the opportunity to regain their sense of wholeness and to take their rightful place in society.

This book tells the long-forgotten story of how three groups of courageous and unbreakable pioneers—paralyzed veterans from World War II; the doctors and physical therapists who created the rehabilitative treatments to keep them alive; and the educators and coaches who used sports to motivate them—came together to change their world and, in so doing, changed ours.

CHAPTER 1

The Boys

JOHNNY

On a January night in 1938, Dessa Tippetts hurried to her seat inside the cavernous gymnasium on the campus of the University of Wyoming in Laramie. The slim sophomore wore her dark brown hair in a fashionable bob with a side part. Her eyes sparkled with verve as she peered down at the basketball court and caught sight of her boyfriend, Johnny Winterholler, lining up for the opening tip-off.

Four thousand students, faculty members, friends, and local supporters—the largest crowd in the fourteen-year history of "Hell's Half Acre" gym—buzzed with anticipation. The Cowboys were facing the University of Colorado, undefeated in Big Seven conference play and led by Byron "Whizzer" White, the future Rhodes scholar who later became an associate justice of the U.S. Supreme Court.

White and the Buffaloes had traveled to Laramie the previous year and whipped Wyoming, even though Hell's Half Acre was "worth about ten points to us in every game," according to Winterholler's teammate, Curt Gowdy, who went on to fame as a broadcaster. "The thin air at seven thousand feet, which we took for granted, left them breathless after a while."[1]

Cowboys coach Willard "Dutch" Witte directed Winterholler to spearhead the attack, and Wyoming took the lead, 19–16, in a nip-and-tuck first half. They held the margin in the second half as Johnny handled the ball and milked the clock in a nervy display of floor management. He tallied nine points, while White fouled out with one point. The fans counted down the final seconds of the hard-fought upset, 44–39.

Johnny showered quickly, then hurried to meet Dessa outside the locker room. They walked together to the student union and joined center Lew Young and the rest of the team for an impromptu celebration. Johnny had ROTC duties early the next morning, so they agreed to call it a night.

He escorted Dessa to the entrance of the women's dormitory. They parted with a lingering kiss beneath the blackened sky that seemed to stretch to eternity, illuminated by a billion stars and the moon's golden trail. Johnny wasn't much for introspection, but as he strolled to his fraternity house on that Friday evening, he couldn't help thinking how fortunate he was.

Johnny had spent his boyhood dealing with tragedy and hardship. John's parents, Carl and Marie, were Volga Germans from Russia who immigrated to America in 1912. In all, Marie gave birth nineteen times, with fourteen of her children reaching adulthood. Johnny arrived in 1916, the second of the clan to be born in the United States. He and his siblings spoke German at home and English at school. During and immediately after World War I, at a time when hamburgers were renamed "liberty sandwiches," they faced scorn because of their familial roots.

When Johnny was twelve, Carl Winterholler was killed in an automobile accident. Marie married a laborer at a local steel mill. Johnny and his stepfather fought, and when things didn't improve between them, he was sent to live with an older sister in

Wyoming. "It was during the Depression," he recalled years later. "We had a big family, and I lived away from my folks because it was one less mouth to feed."[2]

The town of Lovell is located in northern Wyoming, just south of the Idaho border. With a population of about two thousand hardy souls when Johnny was a teen, the hardscrabble ranching community alternated between sixteen-hour days in the burst of summer and interminable winter nights.

Sports was Johnny's path to salvation. He excelled at baseball, but playing basketball with his brothers inside the heated school gym was a favorite winter pastime. When he wasn't involved in sports, he hunted deer and elk and fished for steelhead trout in the cool, shimmering mountain streams of the Big Horn Basin.

"[Moving to Lovell] was the beginning of my life," he said. "Things just seemed to come together."[3]

Johnny clerked in a clothing store, picked crops, and rough-necked in the oil fields during the Depression years. Anything for a few bucks. At age sixteen, he made seven dollars a day, pretty good money for that time, and contributed five dollars from every paycheck to support the household. Though still underage, he enlisted in the National Guard, and earned a citation for good horsemanship.

He met his life's enduring love in high school. Dessa Tippetts was the daughter of a local rancher and his wife, Heber and Permelia, who lived on a large farm of several hundred acres about two miles outside of town. They grew corn and sugar beets; their cattle and sheep grazed on federal lands in the Big Horn Mountains. Her family was among the local Mormon settlers, but the young couple's different religious affiliations (Johnny was raised Lutheran) didn't interfere with their budding romance.

Johnny admired her family's stability and deep community roots.

He and Dessa made for a striking couple dancing to "Pennies from Heaven" and "The Way You Look Tonight" at the chaperoned mixers. Dessa was serious-minded, but liked to laugh; they joked that she "only" had seven siblings. With brown eyes and brown hair and a dark complexion, Johnny reigned as the school's most celebrated athlete. The "can't miss" star was reportedly being scouted by the Boston Red Sox, the Washington Senators, and the St. Louis Cardinals, with their wizard of a general manager, Branch Rickey.[4]

Instead, Johnny and Dessa enrolled at the University of Wyoming in the southern part of the state. Agile and muscular, the five-foot, eleven-inch, 185-pound wunderkind turned into an all-conference selection in baseball, basketball, and football. Sportswriters needed to consult their thesauruses to describe his stylings on the gridiron: "elusive," "scampering," "slippery," "lightning-legged," "piston legs," "whirlwind," "swivel-hips." On the diamond, he batted .532 his junior season to lead the league and was called the "best defensive gardener" in the outfield.

Johnny majored in geology and worked at a men's clothing shop in Laramie. He and his younger brother pledged Phi Delta Theta. Within the fraternity, Johnny was known as a stern taskmaster. "Every young freshman that come in had to have an older man that kept him in line," said basketball phenom Kenny Sailors, who was later credited with introducing the jump shot to the then-earthbound sport. "I didn't take wearing a suit, coat, and a tie on Monday night [at dinner] too serious until I run into Johnny and he had a little paddle about [two feet long], and I took it pretty serious after I got hit a time or two."[5]

Winterholler paid for college with a scholarship from the Reserve Officer Training Corps (ROTC). He took compulsory classes in weapons training, held in the basement of Hell's Half Acre, and mastered drill procedures. What began as an obligation to pay for school grew into something more. During his senior year, Winterholler was elected captain of the Scabbard and Blade, the military honor society.

His ROTC scholarship came with an obligation. After graduation, Johnny was obligated to serve in the U.S. armed forces, which meant that he was unable to pursue a professional sports career immediately after graduation. He could only watch as his Colorado rival, "Whizzer" White, signed a lucrative contract with the Pittsburgh Pirates of the fledgling National Football League. (White later joined the navy.)

Johnny had planned to join the army, and perhaps the Army Air Corps, but due to an apparent misunderstanding, the appointment was not tendered. In an unusual move, University of Wyoming president Arthur Crane intervened on Johnny's behalf and sent an application for a commission in the Marine Corps directly to Major General Thomas Holcomb, the commandant of the Marine Corps.

"In spite of the praise that has been showered upon him [for his sports success], he is a quiet, modest and earnest young man," wrote Crane. "In school he has been entirely self supporting and in addition has helped two younger brothers...He is intensely interested in military matters, and I feel he should be an outstanding addition to your splendid Corps.[6]

"Because there will be an increase in our defense forces due to present conditions in Europe, I would consider it a compliment to our University and Corps of Cadets if Mr. Winterholler's application could be given favorable consideration," Crane concluded.[7]

Crane's letter was persuasive, and Johnny's application to the Marines was expedited. In the summer of 1940, after he and Dessa graduated from Wyoming, Johnny earned a commission as a second lieutenant. He was ordered to report to the Marine Corps Basic School at the Philadelphia Navy Yard for officers' training. There, he studied mapping and tactics, including perimeter defenses and the protection of platoon flanks. He learned precepts of leadership and how to command troops while maintaining discipline and morale under the harshest conditions. He reviewed the code of conduct during warfare, including the Geneva Convention of 1929, signed by the United States, which laid out conditions for the treatment of prisoners of war.

Winterholler completed Basic School in February of 1941 and was promoted to first lieutenant. He bade farewell to his family and to Dessa, who was staying on in Laramie to work at the student union.

Their parting visit was achingly brief. She tried not to cry but could not contain her tears. They promised to write each other often and vowed to marry when he could send for Dessa to join him.

On April 3, 1941, Johnny and others with the 1st Separate Marine Battalion left Mare Island Naval Shipyard, just north of San Francisco, aboard the USS *Henderson*. Their mission: to prepare for the defense of the Philippines in case war were to break out between the United States and Japan.

★ ★ ★

STAN

The first time Stan Den Adel hiked to the top of Mount Tamalpais, just north of the newly opened Golden Gate Bridge, the natural world overwhelmed his senses.

Towering redwood trees, native lupine wildflowers, cascading waterfalls, the crashing waves at Stinson Beach, a pack of lurking coyotes, the lingering scent of coastal sage. A red-tailed hawk surfed the airstream. Fog blanketed the Muir Woods below.

Stan had always relished being outdoors—he was one merit

badge away from earning the rank of Eagle Scout—but he'd never before experienced such rugged, wild majesty. He took a final panoramic gaze at the breathtaking vista before beginning his descent. He felt joyous to be alive.

Stan and his family were recent transplants to Marin County in California. His father, Franz, came from Pella, Iowa, a prairieland community founded by Dutch settlers, and had fought in Europe during World War I. His mother, Francis, was an orphan who taught school in Pella before meeting and marrying Frank (as he was called). They kidded that, with their similar first names—Frank and Francis—they were destined to be together.

They moved from Iowa to Oak Park, Illinois, ten miles west of Chicago's Loop, where Stan was born on August 9, 1923. He and his younger sister, Shirley, benefited from a family friend's benevolence and spent weekends exploring the city's cultural sights: the Art Institute, the Museum of Science and Industry, the 1933–1934 World's Fair.

The family left Oak Park at the tail end of the Great Depression. Stan graduated from high school in Tucson, Arizona, where he showed off his Chicago basketball skills (although he acknowledged that Shirley was the better athlete). When Frank found work as a haberdasher in San Francisco, they settled just across the bay in the town of Corte Madera.

There, Stan was smitten by the alluring woods that reached nearly into their backyard. He'd slip out of the house on Redwood Avenue in the morning or late afternoons after school and head toward Mount Tam. He timed his climbs to the summit and tried to beat his personal best.

The U.S. Forest Service hired him on a temporary basis as a forest-fire fighter and to eradicate invasive blackberry plants in Yosemite National Park. It was backbreaking labor of the most unglamorous sort, and he fell asleep every night exhausted. But he'd found his calling. He enrolled in Marin Junior College, determined to pursue a full-time job with the U.S. Forest Service.

It was the summer of 1941. Stan was eighteen years old, with a toothy grin below tousled brown hair and brown eyes. His future was as mapped out as the trails leading up to Mount Tam.

★ ★ ★

That summer, as baseball fans debated whether Ted Williams would break .400 and boxing aficionados speculated about Billy Conn's chances against heavyweight champ Joe Louis, much of the world was at war.

Germany's blitzkrieg had steamrolled Western and Central Europe and, allied with Italy, faced only a desperate, resolute Britain. The Soviet Union had invaded Finland and was annexing neighboring territories west of its borders, in accordance with its non-aggression pact with Germany. Japan was pursuing its long-standing conflict against China and threatening to subsume other nations and territories in the Far East.

The United States, though officially neutral, was preparing for war. Congress had passed the Selective Training and Service Act of 1940, signed into law that September by President Franklin D. Roosevelt. This led to the country's first peacetime draft and required all men between the ages of twenty-one and thirty-five (later revised to ages eighteen to forty-five) to register with local draft boards. To qualify, men had to stand taller than five feet, weigh more than 105 pounds, and possess at least half of their teeth.

In early 1941, Roosevelt signed the Lend-Lease Act. This allowed the United States to supply foreign nations—particularly Britain, but also the resistance movements in occupied countries—

with food, military equipment, and arms, while skirting existing neutrality laws. Defense spending soared, the U.S. Armed Forces readied more active-duty personnel, and factories began churning out planes, tanks, ships, munitions, and supplies.

Fighting Fascism in Europe with what Roosevelt called "the arsenal of democracy" was the president's top priority. But, with U.S. and Allied interests and colonies scattered across the Pacific, he couldn't ignore Japan's militarism in the region. Tensions between the two sides ratcheted up after Roosevelt froze Japanese assets in the United States and closed the Panama Canal to Japanese shipping. The Allies also imposed an embargo to cut off Japan's access to major sources of petroleum, steel, and iron. Japan responded by seizing control of French Indochina (known today as Vietnam) and signing the Tripartite Pact with Germany and Italy to form the Axis powers.

Roosevelt and his military aides considered the Philippines to be the strategic cornerstone of the Pacific. The United States had gained control of the archipelago (as well as Guam and Puerto Rico) after its victory in the Spanish-American War of 1898. Located just 1,800 miles from Tokyo, and situated between the South China Sea and the Philippine Sea south of Taiwan, the Philippines formed a buffer between Japan and the rubber- and oil-rich territories of Indonesia, Singapore, and Malaya, controlled by the Dutch and the British.

From his air-conditioned aerie atop the Manila Hotel, General Douglas MacArthur, commander of the U.S. Army Forces in the Far East, pooh-poohed the threat of war. "The Germans have told Japan not to stir up any more trouble in the Pacific," he told reporter John Hersey, maintaining that Japan had "overspent itself" with its campaign against China.[8]

"If Japan entered the war," MacArthur continued, "the

Americans, the British, and the Dutch could handle her with about half the forces they now have deployed in the Far East."

★ ★ ★

GENE

Gerald "Gene" Fesenmeyer shivered in the small bedroom he shared with two of his three brothers. It was five o'clock in the morning in the dead of winter in 1941. Outside it was dark as coal, but Gene knew the hogs were awake and eager for their chow.

He pulled on layers of clothes over his long johns, wrestled into his boots, and grabbed his hat. He hauled buckets of slop over to where the hogs were penned and filled up their trough. They greeted him with wet snouts and their usual breakfast-time clamor and then ignored him in their frenzy to get to the food.

He stared at their oversize bodies—the biggest were easily double his weight—while they munched and grunted content-edly. He swore quietly and returned to the house. A bowl of steaming oatmeal was his reward, and then he went out to finish the remainder of his morning chores.

Gene was fifteen years old. He was born and raised in Sham-baugh, Iowa, which he described as "a little know-nothing place" about five miles north of the Missouri state line. His father, Lester, farmed 160 acres with corn, wheat, and soybean crops. His mother, Bessie, cooked, sewed, washed clothes, and raised six children.

They lived in a big old farmhouse without insulation. Snow blew into the house in the wintertime and formed snowdrifts in-side the windows. There was no indoor plumbing. The outhouse was about one hundred feet off to the side of the house; no-body lingered there long when the temperature dropped below freezing. They took turns pumping water from the well.

In high school, Gene played basketball and ran track, and he skated on the Nodaway River when it froze. Otherwise, work defined his life. He milked the cows, shoveled out the manure, put down new bedding for the livestock, and made sure there was plenty of wood for the potbelly stove. He managed the team of horses and, during the spring and summer, labored from sunup to sundown alongside them: plowing, tilling, and planting. He picked corn by hand, throwing each ear into the family's wagon, and helped his father butcher the hogs in the yard.

After school, he had a part-time job at the hardware store in Clarinda, the nearest town (population 4,905). When he wasn't needed at his father's farm, he hiked several miles to Grandfather Fesenmeyer's spread and took care of his prize-winning Poland China hogs. One of them, nicknamed the "Black Bomber," was so enormous that six kids climbed on his back to pose for a snapshot.

Gene didn't mind the drudgery, even during the bitter winters, but lugging slop for the hogs that pushed him around was one task he detested. He told his siblings and his classmates that he would leave Shambaugh, population 270, as soon as he could. He wanted to do something, accomplish something. He planned to wait until after he graduated from high school to figure out his next step. Maybe he'd make it all the way to Chicago, nearly five hundred miles away.

Today, Saturday, offered brief respite from the daily grind. He had to work at the hardware store. Afterward, he was going to the movies at the Clarinda Theatre, "The Wonder Show Place of Iowa." The feature film was *Dr. Jekyll and Mr. Hyde*, starring Spencer Tracy, Ingrid Bergman, and Lana Turner.[9]

The date was December 6, 1941. Gene Fesenmeyer fingered the quarters in his pocket. He was ready for an adventure.

CHAPTER 2

Prisoner in the Philippines

Johnny Winterholler was part of the U.S. force sent to train the Philippine Army for battle. He was first stationed at Olongapo Naval Yard at Subic Bay in Luzon, the largest and most populous island of the Philippines. He had little time to play tourist in the "Pearl of the Orient."

He wrote home to Dessa at least once a week. He never commented about his military obligations except for a brief aside about doing some target practice with his pistol "to stay in shape for a future war or something."[1] Instead, he returned to one theme: his devotion to her.

"Dessa Darling: I love you so much, it hurts. All I do is think of you all day long. You're on my mind constantly. Sometimes I wish I weren't a Marine and just have you and never leave you. Don't ever get the idea my work means more than you. It doesn't. You come first then my job."[2]

Another letter mentioned how much he was looking forward to seeing her the following summer: "Honey, July of '42 can't come around soon enough to suit me. When that time comes you are coming here if humanly possible. I can't take a chance waiting another year after that. If I were to lose you then the fire would definitely go out...Honey, you and I are in for many good times if you will only be patient enough to wait for me. I know I can wait."[3]

On December 8, 1941, Johnny awakened at Cavite Navy Yard, located in Manila Bay, to news reports about the bombing of Pearl Harbor by the Japanese.

Later that day, with less fanfare but with similar devastating results, Japan turned its attention to the Philippines. Its Zero fighters destroyed scores of the B-17s and P-40s that made up the U.S. Far East Air Force as they sat parked on the ground at Clark Field and Iba Field.

President Franklin D. Roosevelt went before Congress and called the surprise attack "a date which will live in infamy." He asked for and received a declaration of war against the Japanese Empire. Three days later, Germany and Italy declared war on the United States.

The battle for control of the Pacific theater initially went badly for the Allies. Japan wrested control of the air and the sea and gobbled up Thailand, Burma, Indonesia, Malaya, as well as Shanghai and Hong Kong. Guam and Wake Island, both U.S. possessions, were also lost.

The grim news grew worse as Japanese troops invaded Luzon from the north and the south. Winterholler and the 1st Separate Marine Battalion manned the anti-aircraft defenses at Cavite. Their three-inch batteries and .50-caliber machine guns were woefully inadequate to defend against Japan's relentless air raids. They could only bear witness to the base's destruction. Fires spread out of control and consumed the barracks, the power plant, ammunition supplies, and the USS *Sealion*, a submarine.

As First Lieutenant Carter Simpson later wrote, "A toy pistol would have damaged their planes as much as we did."[4]

By Christmas, General Douglas MacArthur declared Manila an open city. He ordered his troops to retreat to the rough-hewn mountainous and jungle terrain of the Bataan peninsula. MacArthur withdrew his headquarters to Corregidor, an island situated two miles from the southern tip of Bataan. Winterholler and the 1st Separate Marine Battalion also evacuated to Corregidor, where they joined forces with the 4th Marine Regiment.

Known as "The Rock," Corregidor was nearly four miles long and a mile and a half wide at its broadest point. The tadpole-shaped island was a military fortress that protected the entrance to Manila Bay. Its imposing, if outdated, batteries featured coastal-defense guns and mortars, machine guns, and anti-aircraft artillery. Below ground was an elaborate network of bombproof tunnels built by the U.S. Army Corps of Engineers to house personnel, ammunition supplies, and hospital facilities, all of which were connected by a small electric railroad. As long as the U.S. forces could hold the Gibraltar of the East, Japan would not be able to use Manila as a base of operations.

MacArthur pinned his defense of the Philippines around hope: that promised reinforcements from the United States would arrive in time to stave off the enemy strikes. But with Roosevelt focused on the European theater, that support never came. Undermanned and undersupplied, with Japan's air, naval, and ground forces effectively surrounding his men, MacArthur's strategy was doomed.

As the Japanese closed in on the Philippines, Roosevelt ordered MacArthur to abandon his post and leave Corregidor. He and his family escaped to Australia on March 11. Once in Melbourne, MacArthur issued his famous proclamation: "I shall return."

The Battling Bastards of Bataan held on for another month. Approximately 78,000 troops, including 12,000 Americans, surrendered on April 9. That left Corregidor to the mercy of Japan, which displayed none. For twenty-seven days and nights, the Rock was kept under constant artillery fire and aerial bombardments that destroyed most of the island's defense capabilities, enervated morale, and depleted the supplies of ammunition, food, water, and medicine. When the ventilation system faltered, the stench of sweat, blood, and decaying human bodies became overwhelming.

American and Filipino troops huddled within the stifling underground tunnels. They cursed "Dugout Doug" MacArthur and fought on. Winterholler drove a truck full of torpedoes into the water so that the Japanese couldn't capture them. He helped the 4th Marines establish defenses against a beach invasion. When he learned that several wounded men were trapped in their anti-aircraft position, he gathered volunteers and moved the men to a more secure location.

For his heroism, he was awarded the Silver Star and the Bronze Star with a V for Valor device. His commendation was reported in newspapers from Honolulu to Asbury Park, New Jersey. "Those who are personally acquainted with Johnny are not surprised at a citation of bravery," sports columnist John Hendrickson wrote. "His character, undaunted courage, and outstanding ability as a leader of men have been outstanding characteristics of Johnny Winterholler in anything he has attempted in the past."[5]

Johnny and the approximately 12,000 other holdouts on Corregidor faced an enemy estimated at approximately 250,000. Half-starved and completely drained, beset by malaria, dysentery, and sleepless nights, they couldn't withstand the aerial shelling and artillery assaults that erupted in endless waves. "The island was warped by the force of firepower," according to historian John Glusman.[6]

Finally, they could endure no more. The surrender came on May 6, 1942, signed by General Jonathan Wainwright IV.

The Americans and the Filipinos had held out for four arduous months, an ordeal that cost the Japanese valuable time and resources. But for now, the Rising Sun ruled the Pacific, from the Aleutian Islands in the north to the Solomon Islands in the south—a stretch of nearly five thousand miles.

★ ★ ★

Immediately after the fall of Corregidor, U.S. Marine Corps Commandant Thomas Holcomb sent a Western Union telegram to Johnny's mother, Marie Winterholler. The bureaucratic language brought her little comfort:

> The commandant U.S. Marine Corps regrets to advise you that according to the records of this headquarters your son FIRST LIEUTENANT JOHN WINTERHOLLER U.S. MARINE CORPS was performing his duty in the service of his country in the Manila Bay area when that station capitulated. He will be carried on the records of the Marine Corps as missing pending further information. No report of his death has been received and he may be a prisoner of war. It will probably be several months before definitive official information can be expected concerning his status. Sincere sympathy is extended to you in your anxiety and you are assured that any report received will be communicated to you promptly.[7]

The first positive news about Johnny's whereabouts came in August. Helen Summers, one of the twenty-two nurses who had escaped Corregidor via submarine before the surrender, told Dessa that Johnny "looked very well and was very cheerful" while taking part in the beach defense.

Unbeknown to Dessa, his ordeal was just beginning. After their surrender, U.S. and Filipino troops were interned on the southern portion of Corregidor on a concrete-floored area located between the beach and its cliffs. For three days, they were given no food. Johnny was stripped of his possessions: a ring, a watch, and nearly $1,000 in cash.

The prisoners were taken to Manila and herded through the city by mounted Japanese cavalrymen. Johnny was part of a large contingent that was transported in an overcrowded and over-heated metal boxcar to the town of Cabanatuan in central Luzon, about eighty miles north of Manila, then marched five miles to POW Camp No. 1.

The heat was wretched. There was no working water supply within the barbed-wire prison. The POWs were packed into dirty and primitive huts. Their captors did not follow the guidelines put forth by the Geneva Convention for the humane treatment of prisoners; they did not provide adequate accommodations, food, or medical care.

Many Nippon officers felt only contempt for the prisoners in their charge. Under the command of Lieutenant Colonel Shigeji Mori, the guards meted out scant rations of rice for lunch and supper without meat or vegetables. Prisoners scrounged for something, anything, to eat: beetles, snakes, grass, discarded corncobs.

Mosquitoes, flies, roaches, and rats contributed to a maelstrom of illness: dysentery, beriberi, malaria, scurvy, night blindness. Medicines that might have saved lives—quinine, sulfa tablets—were withheld.

June and July were horrific months. As many as forty men died daily. Beatings for infractions large and small were common. When three officers were caught trying to escape, Johnny and the other captives were forced to watch their punishment. U.S. Army Lieutenant Colonels Lloyd Biggs and Howard Breitung and Navy civil engineer Lieutenant R. D. Gilbert were stripped of their clothing and tied to stakes with their hands behind their backs. Over the next forty-eight hours, they were beaten and whipped by Mori's men while exposed to blistering heat and typhoon-like rains. Filipino farmers passing by were forced to take part.

Finally, the three men were cut down, thrown into a truck, taken to a clearing, and executed. According to sworn statements from eyewitnesses, one of the three was decapitated.[8]

Winterholler and other officers were confined to their quarters because they had shared the same barracks as the would-be escapees. They were not allowed to bathe or use the make-shift outdoor toilets. Johnny's weight plummeted and his muscle strength deteriorated. He suffered from impaired hearing and beriberi, the latter caused by severe vitamin B-1 deficiency. He lost feeling in his feet. He later described this time as the "darkest and cruelest period during the internment."[9]

When he approached his captors and begged them to supply more food to the prisoners, he was told, "Think of your comrades who die on the battlefield. You should consider yourself fortunate to be alive."[10]

In October 1942, Mori sought volunteers to transfer to another POW camp. Figuring things couldn't get any worse, Winterholler signed up to leave Cabanatuan. He wasn't wrong, but only just.

He and a thousand other American POWs were put on a squalid ship designed to accommodate approximately three hundred men.

Two torturous weeks later, they arrived at Davao Penal Colony on the southeast coast of the island of Mindanao. It was here that Johnny Winterholler spent the last two months of 1942, all of 1943, and the first four months of 1944. Eighteen months in hell.

★ ★ ★

Davao Penal Colony, also known as DaPeCol, was a maximum-security prison set on a vast plantation. Major Kazuo Maeda ordered his prisoners—even those with malaria and temperatures of 103 degrees—to work in the surrounding fields and rice paddies from seven in the morning to six in the evening. He beat them when they fell.

Though the food was initially an improvement over what had been available in Cabanatuan, it didn't last. Soon, the Japanese cut back on the prisoners' rations. The crowded barracks, overrun by rats, boiled with the fetid stink of urine, feces, mud, and rot.

Lieutenant Colonel Richard Hunter, a veteran from World War I and the U.S. camp commander, selected Winterholler from the pool of officers to be the camp's provost marshal. Johnny was put in the difficult position of supervising the prisoners, some of whom were involved in pilfering and petty thievery inside the prison. He created a military police force to maintain order and conduct daily inspections. He also worked with the mess officer to set up a feeding system for the camp's two thousand prisoners. His hunting skills came in handy when he was given permission to shoot water buffalo to supply meat for the guards and then supervise the butchering.

"To portion out the diminishing supply of food and turn away a starving buddy who might have asked for a second helping of rice was tough," he later said.[11]

He also witnessed the daring escape of ten U.S. servicemen and two Filipino convicts from the supposedly escape-proof prison. According to author John D. Lukacs, Captain Austin Shofner of the 4th Marines considered asking Winterholler, a friend, to join them. They were hoping to connect with the Philippine resistance movement, with the ultimate goal of informing the U.S. government about the Bataan Death March and the inhumane conditions within the POW camps. Due to concerns about Johnny's declining physical condition, Shofner decided not to ask Johnny to accompany them.[12]

The helplessness the prisoners experienced was as mentally draining as the harsh punishments and the bleak environment. Some men, despondent, went stir crazy and attacked the guards; others shut down and ceased speaking. Most tried to cling to hope and talked ceaselessly about food: their most memorable meals, favorite restaurants, favorite foods, favorite desserts, favorite way to eat eggs, favorite Christmas and Thanksgiving feasts. Perhaps their happiest moment came with the arrival of Red Cross boxes filled with soap, sardines, chocolate bars, and other familiar goodies from home.

Johnny had always avoided cigarettes. But, in the concentration camp, he started smoking to pass the time and assuage hunger pangs. Amid the stench and the coughing of the men around him, he occasionally let his mind wander to sweeter memories: dancing cheek-to-cheek with Dessa, fishing and hunting with his brothers in Wyoming.

Not long after his arrival at Davao Penal Colony, the Marine Corps informed Marie Winterholler that Johnny's official status had changed. Her son was no longer missing in action; he was "in the hands of the enemy." The news that Johnny was a POW sparked cautious joy throughout Wyoming.

Dessa wrote to the Prisoner of War Information Bureau. Identifying herself as Johnny's fiancée, she requested permission to write him. Soon dozens of letters in her neat handwriting crossed the Pacific in care of the International Red Cross. She had no way of knowing if Johnny was actually getting her letters, but the mere act of writing them made her feel connected to him.

She wrote that she'd been promoted to manager at the student union in Laramie. She wrote about Marie's health and her family's farm in Lovell. She wrote that three of Johnny's brothers—Phil, Al, and Hank—were seeing action in the war.

The most astonishing, stop-the-presses news was about the University of Wyoming's basketball team. Led by Kenny Sailors, Johnny's fraternity brother, they went 31–2 during the 1942–43 season and won the NCAA championship in New York City. Two days later, the Cowboys defeated St. John's, the National Invitation Tournament winner, in a benefit game at Madison Square Garden that netted more than $24,000 for the American Red Cross's War Fund.[13]

The University of Wyoming was now the best collegiate basketball team in the land for the first and only time in the school's history. For his efforts, Sailors won the Chuck Taylor Award as the country's most outstanding college basketball player.

★ ★ ★

Dessa kept writing to Johnny even though she received no reply. She fretted about his fate as details of the cruel treatment of U.S. soldiers inside the Japanese POW camps began to circulate in the States. (These accounts were initially censored by the government so as not to alarm the American public.) There were multiple published reports that Johnny had taken part in the Bataan Death March. This was untrue, but Dessa had no way of knowing that.

Meanwhile, Johnny's health worsened. After developing malaria in the summer of 1943, he was placed for several months in the crude hospital for prisoners. He recovered enough to return to his barracks, but relief was only temporary.

During the night of March 20, 1944, Winterholler found that he could no longer move his legs. Minimal portions of rice and gruel, the lack of vitamins, protein, minerals, and other nutrients, and a series of infectious diseases with names that sounded like tropical drinks had desecrated the body of the finest athlete Wyoming had ever produced. The man with the "swivel hips" and "piston legs" did not have the strength to get out of bed, much less walk or stand unaided.

Doctors in the POW hospital diagnosed him with polio. It was later determined that blood vessels in his spinal cord had ruptured spontaneously, producing a hematoma that pressed against the spinal cord and rendered him paralyzed from the waist down. An operation to relieve the pressure likely would have averted permanent damage, but the inadequate facilities and the foul conditions at Davao Penal Colony made such a procedure impossible to consider.

When he didn't get better within a month, when he understood that his condition might be permanent, Winterholler readjusted his mental outlook. He didn't despair or succumb to self-pity. He didn't lament that he would not be able to roam the outfield for the St. Louis Cardinals.

He concentrated on surviving and on home as word spread via the bamboo telegraph that the United States was gaining supremacy over Japan. Johnny and the other prisoners could tell by the way the guards acted that the reports were probably accurate. The

U.S. military's island-hopping strategy in the Pacific that started at Guadalcanal was proving successful, with the Gilbert and the Marshall Islands, and then the Marianas, falling to American forces. Fleets of B-29 bombers were now capable of reaching Japan's major cities, including Tokyo and Osaka, and destroying factories, railroads, airfields, and bases.

With MacArthur pushing to regain the Philippines, the Japanese vacated Davao Penal Colony. They moved all of their prisoners to the north, either to Japan or to more secure locations in the Philippines.

On June 6, 1944, D-Day in Europe, Johnny was blindfolded, loaded onto a stretcher, tied wrist-to-wrist along with some 1,250 other prisoners, and taken by truck to Lasang. Wearing only a G-string, he was carried onto an old freighter called the *Yashu Maru*.

He was crammed into an airless coal bunker. Another prisoner, an army doctor named Calvin Jackson, stashed the secret diary he'd been writing inside Winterholler's loincloth, figuring the guards wouldn't search there.

Wrote Jackson: "I told [Johnny] if he messed up my diary he would be a goner." (Jackson's account, based on the smuggled diary, was published years later.)[14]

The hell ship meandered north equipped with two wooden buckets as a latrine for the exhausted and diseased prisoners. At Cebu City, they were transferred to another hell ship called the *Singoto Maru*. The circulation of a Red Cross box to each prisoner staved off hunger, but little else. Johnny watched Lieutenant Willard Weden collapse from heat prostration and die, one of many casualties on that journey. Another prisoner went mad and had to be chained to a post.

Nearly three weeks after leaving Davao Penal Colony, they arrived in Manila. They docked across the bay from where Johnny had been captured on Corregidor back in 1942. The POWs were taken to Bilibid Prison in the heart of the city.

Built by the Spanish in the nineteenth century, the facility had been condemned as unsanitary by the American authorities before the war. A twenty-foot-high cement wall covered with charged electrical wires encircled the penitentiary. Atop the wall stood Japanese soldiers holding machine guns. Along the walls were freshly dug graves.

Johnny was confined to the POW hospital. He had pneumonia and bedsores on his back and right hip; he was unable to control his bladder or bowels, and he had no feeling in his legs. After enduring a daily ration of approximately 840 calories for more than a year, he weighed 115 pounds, down from his playing weight of 185 pounds.

The struggle to live, to survive the atrocities, was a breath-by-breath process. One morning, he noticed that the sloughing crater of a bedsore on his hip was attracting a line of ants that were scurrying up and down his numb leg. He peered at the wound and saw that the rapacious army had eaten away the rotting flesh, leaving behind a clean wound.

He grimaced. Some good news at last.

In fleeting moments, he felt fortunate that he was so sickly. Prisoners who could walk were being shipped to Japan to work as slave laborers. Many of them died because the Japanese refused to carry flags or markers on their ships to signify that prisoners were on board. In one instance, when the USS *Shark* submarine torpedoed and sank an unmarked Japanese freighter in the South China Sea, nearly 1,800 POWs died (including Lieutenant Colonel Hunter, the camp commander at Davao Penal Colony).

Reprieve from almost certain death came in late October 1944, when General MacArthur led an amphibious invasion of the central island of Leyte. The naval and air fight that ensued in Leyte Gulf effectively destroyed the remnants of Japan's Navy and allowed U.S. forces to advance toward Luzon.

On February 3, 1945, artillery fire and aerial bombing heralded the onslaught of the U.S. Army. The 1st Cavalry Division were the first troops to enter Manila, followed closely by the 37th Division. MacArthur had finally returned.

Inside Bilibid, the prisoners watched their captors open the gates and flee into the city. The healthiest prisoners gathered together in the central courtyard to greet their liberators. Rear elements of the 37th Division arrived the next day, surprised to find that the Japanese had abandoned the prison and its approximately 800 POWs and 450 civilian prisoners.

Johnny lay on a stretcher in the hospital ward. He had been held captive for nearly a thousand days. He was covered in rags so worn that it was impossible to determine their original color. He could smell smoke from buildings that had been set afire by Japanese demolition squads. Manila was burning.

Next to him sat a stack of Dessa's letters, 154 of them, delivered by the Red Cross. Somehow, they'd caught up with him here, in this crumbling old penitentiary in the Pearl of the Orient.

Johnny stared at her familiar handwriting. He tried to imagine what she'd written him about over these many months. All the birthday celebrations, the Christmas and Thanksgiving holidays, the movies she watched, the friends she spoke to. He pictured her red-cheeked face against the starry Wyoming sky.

The letters sat unread. He wasn't ready.

CHAPTER 3

The Battle of the Bulge

Stan Den Adel was eighteen years old when Pearl Harbor was attacked in 1941. That moment irrevocably altered the trajectory of his life just as it changed the lives of so many other Americans. His dream of working in the great outdoors and pursuing a career as a National Park ranger was put on hold.

In early 1943, Stan was drafted into the army. He scored well on an aptitude test during basic training and was selected to enroll in the newly launched Army Specialized Training Program (ASTP). This was designed to teach a concentrated and accelerated curriculum to 140,000 of the brightest recruits, including future secretary of state Henry Kissinger, U.S. senator Bob Dole, authors Gore Vidal and Kurt Vonnegut, actor-comedian Mel Brooks, and New York City mayor Ed Koch.

"The Army has been increasingly handicapped by a shortage of men possessing desirable combinations of intelligence, aptitude, education, and training in fields such as medicine, engineering, languages, science, mathematics, and psychology, who are qualified for service as officers of the Army," General George C. Marshall noted.[1]

Stan enrolled at the University of California, Berkeley, to study medicine, assured that he would be able to attend Officer Candidate School after graduating from the ASTP. In addition to taking his regular course load, he was required to wear an army uniform and take five hours per week of military instruction. Many of his peers were already overseas in the thick of it, and Stan felt guilty whenever he strolled past the campus's eucalyptus grove and entered the Life Sciences Building, or when he grabbed coffee with pals Al Armstrong and A. K. George. He consoled himself with the thought that getting a college education and attending officer school would make him a valuable asset in the war effort.

Den Adel completed two semesters at Berkeley before the army abruptly changed course. The desperate need for combat replacement troops in Europe and the Pacific, as well as internal bickering within the War Department about ASTP's usefulness, led to the program's demise in early 1944. Stan never got the opportunity to go to Officer Candidate School.

Instead, he was ordered to report to Camp Cooke, some 250 miles south of San Francisco, and join the 11th Armored Division. From March until early September of 1944, Stan and fellow ASTPer Al Armstrong trained with the more experienced soldiers from the 11th Division who'd been conducting field exercises in Louisiana and the California desert before moving to Camp Cooke. Stan relished exploring the natural splendors of California's central coast, but he complained about the boredom. Patrol duty meant ensuring that Japanese spies didn't try to land on the beaches near Santa Barbara, a not-so-dangerous threat in the summer of 1944.

His stint at Camp Cooke was interrupted by the death of his father. Frank Den Adel had been working for the Western Ocean Division of the Army Corps of Engineers in Sausalito when he developed pneumonia and died. Stan was close to his father and mourned his sudden loss. He vowed to remember the one bit of career advice his father offered him: don't ever choose to be a banker.[2]

In September, Stan penned goodbye letters to his mother and sister and boarded a Pullman sleeper car for Camp Kilmer, New Jersey. En route to the embarkation hub, Stan and Al debated where they were going next: Italy? France? The Balkans?

His last moments on American soil were fleeting: peering up at the USS *Hermitage* from the pier, hearing his name called out loud, shouldering a stuffed duffel bag, walking up the gangway. He saluted the Statue of Liberty as it disappeared in the distance and the *Hermitage* joined a convoy of troopships.

Midway across the Atlantic, their destination became known: the harbor city of Southampton, England. From there they were shuttled to the village of Tisbury, which Stan described as a "two pub-sized town." They camped in Quonset huts in the woodlands of an old country estate and trained for their coming assignment in Europe.[3]

★ ★ ★

For the next two months, as the D-Day push by the Allies reached an ominous lull, Stan hiked daily in the rolling fields of the Salisbury Plain, a chalk plateau near Stonehenge, bursting in autumnal shades of red, gold, and green. He reveled in the thatched-roof cottages, the ruins of ancient castles, the tiny village pubs with their dartboards and strange-tasting brews. He could almost forget that the war was still raging.

His idyll lasted until mid-December. Stan and the 11th Division crossed the English Channel at around the same time that Adolf Hitler was mounting a desperate charge along the Western Front. Hitler aimed to smash the Allies in the Ardennes Forest, along a seventy-five-mile stretch in Luxembourg and southeast Belgium, before turning north to seize the port city of Antwerp. Hitler believed that, if the strike were to succeed, the war would turn in Germany's favor and, perhaps, force the Allies to the bargaining table apart from the Soviet Union.

The thickly forested terrain of the Ardennes seemed an unlikely site to stage such an attack, especially with winter approaching. But the element of surprise paid off when German troops and Panzer tanks penetrated a thinly held sector of the American line and created a significant "bulge" in their position.[4]

Hitler's ploy forced a hasty change of plans among the Allies. General George Patton, in command of the U.S. Third Army, raced north to attack Germany's southern flank. The 11th Armored was ordered to the front to support the counter-thrust.

Torrential rains and freezing temperatures greeted the troops upon their arrival in France. Stan spent the first night huddled inside a leaky pup tent outside of Cherbourg. He managed to snooze in the back of a half-track the next morning as the miles-long caravan of vehicles moved southward. It took several days for the entire division—thousands of soldiers and their rolling stock of jeeps, scout cars, tanks, 6x6 cargo trucks, mortars, cannons, antiaircraft guns, .50-caliber machine guns, and other assorted weaponry, plus ammunition and fuel—to assemble at the airport strip outside Rennes.

Stan and "C" Company were sent toward the city of Sedan, in France, and then into Belgium under blackout conditions. Their instructions were to stop the Germans from reaching Liège, where vital supplies of gasoline were stored. They spent the days after Christmas outside the village of Neufchâteau, probing and searching for the enemy on the main road linking Sedan and Bastogne.

The temperature plummeted. Many soldiers suffered from

frostbite. Others threw off their boots, wrapped their frozen feet in blanket strips, and stuffed them into overshoes. They covered themselves in white bedsheets for camouflage in the snow.

On New Year's Eve day, "C" Company escorted six tanks toward the village of Magerotte, northwest of Bastogne. The infantrymen, separated from one another by about ten feet, formed a skirmish line and entered a dense forest of mature pine trees standing in perfect rows. The forbidding woods were silent except for the sound of crunching snow underfoot.

A muffled pop broke the spell. "Shoe mine," were the whispered words that passed down the line. They re-formed and made sure to tread in the footsteps of the soldier directly in front of them.[5]

They exited the woods and headed warily down a sloping pasture near the hamlet of Acul. In the distance stood a prosperous-looking farmhouse. Without warning, the Germans rained mortar shells on them. Soldiers next to Stan were torn asunder by shrapnel. Warm blood spilled onto white snow. The word spoken now, loudly, was "Medic!"

Stan and A. K. George, his foxhole buddy, picked up a .30-caliber machine gun that had been abandoned and fired rounds at the enemy. Then they ran like hell for shelter. Sixty-ton German Tiger tanks opened fire and pummeled them. Dead soldiers draped the sides of burnt-out tanks.

In the chaos of battle, one platoon member carrying a machine gun on his shoulder had it catch on a snow-laden branch, triggering a burst of gunfire that killed a fellow soldier and wounded another.

They fell back to the surrounding ridge. Heavy snow was falling. Stan and A.K. chiseled into the ice-covered turf to dig a foxhole so deep that their helmets were slightly below ground level when they sat down facing each other.

Exhausted and near frozen, they realized that they hadn't eaten since breakfast—twelve hours earlier. Stan ducked out to forage and managed to scrounge a one-gallon can of frozen corned beef hash. They chewed on icy chunks of the pinkish stuff and shivered in the black night. Thus they rang in 1945.[6]

★ ★ ★

The Battle of the Bulge was costly. The Americans suffered approximately 75,000 casualties (killed, wounded, or missing), according to the U.S. Army Center of Military History, while Germany sustained some 100,000 casualties.[7] By the end of January, the Allies had closed the bulge and regained control of the Western Front. Patton and the Third Army soon breached the Siegfried Line, Germany's fortified defensive system built along its western borders, and drove toward the Rhine River. The Germans were on the run.

Stan and his squad celebrated the milestone with a private moment. Grimy and exhausted, sporting weeks' growth of facial hair, they left the front lines for the rear area and, for the first time since leaving England, took showers and shaved.

The respite didn't last long. On March 6, back in the fray, Stan was wounded when a machine-gun barrel swung around in its swivel and coldcocked him in the nose, knocking him out. His face, he recalled later, was left "a bloody mess." Medics stitched up what he described as an "inconsequential" injury, and he spent several days at a convalescent hospital in Metz, France. By now, he had earned his sergeant's stripes.[8]

He caught up with the rapidly moving "C" Company in Oppenheim, Germany, in time to cross the Rhine on a pontoon bridge and to storm into Bavaria. They met spasmodic and stubborn opposition: from isolated forays by Luftwaffe planes to intense, brief firefights with German soldiers in the villages they traversed.

When the 11th Armored Division entered the town of Zella-Mehlis, its soldiers found hundreds of foreign slave laborers forced to manufacture parts for Walther pistols and other small arms in a munitions plant. Stan celebrated alongside the newly liberated workers, who were joyous for their freedom and ecstatic to welcome their rescuers.

It was increasingly obvious that the war was winding down. Rumors abounded that the 11th Armored, by now the easternmost division of the U.S. Army, would soon meet up with its Soviet counterparts moving west. On April 28, news alerts announced that Benito Mussolini, the deposed Italian Fascist dictator, had been executed. Two days later, Hitler committed suicide inside his command bunker in Berlin. Most of the German soldiers they happened upon were prisoners marching desultorily. Stan started to believe that he was going to make it home unscathed.

On the morning of April 30, "C" Company took the lead on the road toward the village of Wegscheid on the German-Austrian border. A shot-up armored car, abandoned and still smoking, confirmed earlier reports that the Germans had maintained a strong presence in the vicinity. The 11th Armored knew it had a fight on its hands.

Artillery pounded the hilltop town for twenty minutes, and P-47 Thunderbolts bombed and peppered the enemy position. "C" Company dismounted from their half-tracks and left the protection of the forest to advance in a skirmish line toward a barren, upwardly sloping field leading to Wegscheid, perhaps one thousand yards ahead. Several tanks supported their right flank.

They stepped carefully. There was no resistance for two hundred yards. Then, from inside the damaged homes and cellars came nonstop automatic-weapon fire. Stan threw himself to the ground and prepared to return fire. But when he saw the tanks abruptly halt and reverse direction, he knew it was time to withdraw immediately.

Stan dashed pell-mell for cover as machine guns strafed the field. Just as he reached the woods, he was shot in the back.

He fell to the ground. He attempted to get up and resume running, except he found he could not move his legs. Time seemed to simultaneously stop and speed up. He heard his platoon lieutenant and squad leader call for help. His breath came in jagged bursts. He was trapped in place.

Stan felt himself being lifted up by his collar and dragged from danger. He watched himself being loaded onto a jeep and whisked to an aid station, then taken to a field hospital. He was shot up with morphine.

Inside a large tent, surgeons began removing bone fragments and shrapnel from his back. He felt no pain, but he was angry that they had to slice open his field jacket to operate on him. The darn thing was brand new![9]

Stan later heard that the 11th Armored took revenge by clearing out Wegscheid with a massive fusillade. A final push took them to Linz, in Austria, where they encountered the dead and the half-dead inside the Mauthausen concentration camp. Eventually, they met up with the Red Army. They had traveled approximately 1,600 miles—1,600 *combat* miles—since landing in Cherbourg in December, a phenomenal pace.

Exactly one week after Stan Den Adel was shot and left permanently paralyzed, Germany surrendered. On May 9, World War II in Europe officially ended.

CHAPTER 4

Okinawa

Gene Fesenmeyer was fifteen, still underage for the draft, when the Japanese bombed Pearl Harbor. He wanted to join the fight right away, so he signed up for the Iowa state guard. He followed every skirmish in the newspapers and watched the black-and-white newsreels at the movie theater.

"I was eager to fight," he said. "I wanted to get in there and kill. All we wanted to do was go kill Japs."

Gene skipped school to enlist in the Marine Corps Reserve in March of 1944. His parents had to sign a consent form because he was seventeen. At five-foot-nine and 131 pounds, with hazel eyes and a ruddy complexion, he looked even younger.

On June 26, 1944, the day he graduated from Clarinda High School, Gene grabbed his diploma and bounded from the stage to catch a Burlington Trailways bus for Omaha, Nebraska. He didn't want to be late for his induction ceremony. That same night, he departed for San Diego to undergo basic training.

Military life agreed with Gene: the uniform, the drills, the camaraderie, and particularly the three steady meals. He gained weight in camp. "The training for combat was easy," he said, compared to working from dawn to dusk on the farm in Shambaugh.

He completed an eight-week course as a rifleman, alternating between the M1 Carbine and the Browning Automatic Rifle (BAR). He was an excellent shot—all that time spent hunting with his brothers had paid off—and was assigned to carry a BAR into battle. Designed by firearms pioneer John Browning, the gas-operated BAR weighed a hefty twenty-one pounds. The load grew heavier with the dozen twenty-round magazines that Gene was expected to carry in a belt around his waist. But the BAR was also portable, reliable, and fully automatic.

In the dusty hills above Camp Pendleton, north of San Diego, Gene and three hundred other infantrymen from the 1st Division were training for one mission: the invasion of the home islands of Japan, with the first phase scheduled to begin in late 1945. Predictions of Allied casualties in what the military was calling Operation Downfall—and others were dubbing "planned Armageddon"—ranged from fifty thousand to one million servicemen.[1]

Gene was young, but he wasn't naïve. He recognized that his chances of surviving the operation were slim. "We would've been the guys who went in," he said later, "and we would've been killed. They were raising us as nothing more than cannon fodder. My war was [going to] end with one thing."

By the fall of 1944, Japan was resisting the inevitable with the desperation of a cornered bobcat. Places that few Americans had ever heard of before Pearl Harbor—Tarawa, Peleliu, Iwo Jima—became notorious for the enormous number of casualties sustained by both sides. As U.S. forces inexorably tightened their hold in the Pacific, Fleet Admiral William "Bull" Halsey described his tactics this way in a *Time* magazine cover story: "Kill Japs, kill Japs, and then kill more Japs."[2]

Gene and the Third Battalion of the 1st Marine Division

shipped overseas on the USS *Wharton* troop transport in November of 1944. En route, they stopped at Pavuvu, the largest of the Russell Islands. It had been the site of a ferocious battle with heavy fatalities and was now a jumping-off place for U.S. combat units in the Pacific. They moved on to Guadalcanal for large-scale field maneuvers and landing exercises.

Their immediate objective was to conquer Okinawa, the largest of the Ryukyu Islands, so that U.S. forces could use it as a staging base for the anticipated attack on Japan, located about 350 miles to the north. Preparation for the Battle of Okinawa, codenamed Operation Iceberg, resembled the planning for the Normandy Invasion on D-Day.

Commanded by Major General Pedro del Valle, the 1st Marines joined with other marines and army and navy personnel, nearly 200,000 strong, for the assault on the sixty-mile-long island, in what was to be the largest amphibious landing in the region. Gene was part of the newly created Tenth Army, consisting of army and marine ground forces, and headed by Lieutenant General Simon Bolivar Buckner Jr.

Admiral Chester Nimitz directed the opening phase of the offensive: Navy battleships and planes shelled Okinawa for days before the U.S. invasion on April 1, 1945. Doctors and nurses were prepared for the bloodbath that they knew would follow. At their disposal were "25,000 litters, 50,000 blankets, 7 billion units of penicillin, 30 million vitamin tablets, 100,000 cans of foot powder, and 100,000 iodine swabs," according to historian Albert Cowdrey.[3]

Gene watched the shelling from an attack transport ship. The night before the landing, those aboard feasted on a huge turkey dinner. "Fattening us up for the kill," the boys laughingly called their last meal, journalist Ernie Pyle reported.[4]

Going into combat for the first time, staring at the grim possibility of death, Gene's mood swung between confidence and nervousness, between bravado and despair. He busied himself with his gear: canteen, rain poncho, mess kit, first-aid kit, C-rations, helmet, knapsack, pick and shovel, socks. He cleaned his BAR and double-checked his machine-gun belts. He discarded his khaki uniform for green herringbone combat togs. He sharpened his bayonet. Then he tried to sleep on one of the narrow cots that were stacked four tiers high in the hold.

"It was April Fool's Day and Easter Sunday," he recalled. "You know you're in for a battle when you see six or seven hospital ships waiting out there in the harbor. You know somebody's going to get hurt."

★ ★ ★

They were prepared for "slaughter on the beaches," wrote Ernie Pyle, who accompanied them onto Okinawa.[5] Instead, their "Love Day" landing was unopposed along the Hagushi beaches on the west side of the island. They briskly advanced inland toward the Kadena Air Base with few losses. Within days, they'd reached the East Coast, effectively cutting the island into two.

It was when the marines turned south, toward Okinawa's strategically vital section, that they began to understand the enemy's tactics. Japanese troops had withdrawn from the central part of the island and amassed their defenses in the south, just beyond the capital city of Naha. The rugged hills and ridges around Shuri Castle provided the Japanese with excellent cover and observational positioning when the Americans pushed toward the well-entrenched, well-camouflaged maze of bunkers, caves, tunnels, and pillboxes.

"All hell broke loose," Gene said. "It was a shitting mess. You're right down there where it's either you kill or get killed. You keep firing that BAR till you run out of ammo. Then you're in deep shit."

Hours passed in a gory daze. Sniper fire came from all sides, echoed by the pop of a grenade primer cap, the rumble of incoming mortars and the whine of howitzers, machine guns rat-tat-tatting. Turning to yell something to the guy running alongside you only to see him get blown up, and his innards splashed across your uniform. The putrid stench of decaying corpses and rotting flesh. Nighttime patrols interrupted by bayonet attacks. Field-stripping and reassembling your weapon; sleep when you could grab some.

The BAR and its .30-06 cartridges were difference-makers in the jungle. "I was a killer," Gene said. "They would put me out in front of the lines with that weapon, and I was to guard the lines."[6]

Torrential rains deluged their foxholes, where mud, blood, feces, and maggots churned together into a gumbo of jungle rot and malaria. "It was combat from the very first," Gene said. "You were dug in in the ground, water up to your ass or up to your neck."

Shuri Castle was captured in late May amid heavy casualties. The Japanese retreated farther south with U.S. troops in relentless pursuit.

One late afternoon in early June, not far from Naha, Fesenmeyer was advancing carefully, alert for pockets of resistance. From behind a wall, he spotted an enemy sniper perched on the branch of a tree. His heart beating like a pounding drum, he gathered himself and jumped out from behind the wall to get a clear shot with his BAR.

At that moment, the sniper fired his Nambu .31-caliber

semi-automatic pistol. The bullet entered Gene's chest at an angle, between his left shoulder and his heart, and clipped one of his lungs before exiting through his spine.

"I made the mistake of trying to aim at him," he said later, "and you only make one mistake. I should've just sprayed him, and I didn't. I gave him a split second. Time so he could pull the trigger. He was quicker."[7]

He fell, blood spurting from his body. "As soon as I got hit, I remember hearing this Mexican kid yelling, 'Fessy's hit! Fessy's hit!'" he said.

Gene passed out. "I don't remember hitting the ground," he said. "A guy from the same squad—Harold Lemmon—he pulled me back behind that wall again. In the process he got shot through the shoulder and the neck. But he lived."

The sniper didn't. "About seven guys hit him all at once," he said. "They made hamburger out of him. He was dead before he hit the ground."

Gene was fortunate that the bullet struck him where it did. Two inches lower or two inches higher, and he probably would have died. He was also fortunate that, from the moment he was shot, he was passed through an elaborate evacuation chain aimed at preserving his life. He was given basic first aid to halt the bleeding before stretcher-bearers rushed him to a field hospital. Medics worked to stanch hemorrhages, apply dressings and sulfa drugs, and supply plasma and morphine.

When he woke up, he found himself in a dimly lit tent. He could feel surgeons digging pieces of lead from inside his body and dropping them into a pan. He recalled hearing one of the doctors say, "This boy's going to be paralyzed."

Gene didn't have the slightest idea what that meant. He had never heard of anyone being paralyzed.

Later, when the doctors bluntly informed Gene that he would never walk again, when he understood that his paralysis would be permanent, he broke down. "I cried like a baby because I wanted to go back [to combat]," he said. "Everybody was saying how lucky I was. Shit, how lucky can you get? You're laying there almost dead."

★ ★ ★

The eighty-two-day effort to capture Okinawa, the last and bloodiest battle in the Pacific theater, ended on June 21. Approximately 12,500 GIs, marines, and sailors were killed, including Buckner, the highest-ranking U.S. officer to die in the war. (Ernie Pyle was killed on Ie Shima, an island west of Okinawa.) The wounded numbered approximately 36,000, with additional noncombat injuries; thousands had to be evacuated for battle fatigue. Some 100,000 Japanese soldiers died, while 150,000 Okinawans perished or went missing.

Afterward, Buckner and the military brain trust were criticized for the high mortality rate. The American tactics had been "ultra conservative," wrote correspondent Homer Bigart of the *New York Herald Tribune*. "Instead of an end run we persisted in frontal attacks. It was the hey-diddle-diddle straight down the middle."[8]

The savage fighting and exorbitant casualties contributed to the decision to find an alternative to the invasion of Japan that Gene Fesenmeyer and many other marines and soldiers had trained for. Operation Downfall never materialized after President Harry Truman authorized the detonation of atomic bombs over Hiroshima and Nagasaki in August of 1945.

Truman, too, was criticized for deploying such destructive

weapons against largely civilian populations when, by numerous reputable accounts, Japan was likely to surrender. But the result of Truman's momentous decision was undeniable. Japan officially surrendered on September 2, 1945. World War II was finally over.

Gene Fesenmeyer survived Okinawa, but his own private war was just beginning. Until the day he died, he never forgot staring up at the tree where the sniper shot him, when the direction of his life forever changed.

Combat is "very exciting," he said. "You're right down there where it's either you kill or get killed. It's exhilarating until you get shot. That changed things a helluva lot."

CHAPTER 5

"An Ailment Not to Be Treated"

STAN

The bullet that struck Stan Den Adel in the lower back left him paralyzed, but it did miss his lungs. And, because the battle at Wegscheid was fought close to a main roadway, medics were able to evacuate him from the front line without delay. Doctors at a nearby field hospital treated his wound promptly and efficiently.

So much for the good news. The quality of his care sharply deteriorated from there. He was taken to an evacuation site—a circus-size tent set up next to a grass airstrip—where it rained constantly. For five days, Stan lay parked on soggy turf. He received no attention beyond that which he got from the aides who emptied his urine collection bottle and gave him food. He celebrated the end of the war while lying in discomfort on a government-issued litter.

Finally, he was brought to a U.S. Army hospital facility in Reims, France, not far from the little red schoolhouse where German officials signed the Instrument of Surrender on May 7. There, doctors discovered that Stan had a perforated chest wound—likely the exit point of the bullet—and that blood had accumulated and congealed there. When he was rolled onto his back so that the doctors could clean the area, Stan felt excruciating pain for the first time.[1]

His chest injury healed once it was cleaned and treated. But a more serious problem emerged: bedsores had formed because Stan had been kept in virtually the same position for days on end, with only a blanket between his body and the damp canvas litter.

The neglect continued. Stan was shipped to Bristol, a port city in England, to await a plane to fly him to an army hospital in California. He was scheduled to leave numerous times, but each time the trip was abruptly canceled without explanation. His weight plummeted, and his strength diminished. The pressure sores grew.

On June 26, he was taken by train to Glasgow, Scotland, and then carried onto a C-54 transport plane. First stop: Iceland, for refueling; then Newfoundland, for more fuel; then arrival at Mitchel Field on Long Island outside New York City. More time passed before Stan and other returning servicemen were put on a C-47 bound for the West Coast.

The interior of the plane was broiling hot. When they puddle-jumped to the various stops—Cincinnati, Chicago, Moline—passengers and crew rushed to the air-conditioned comfort of the PX, leaving behind Stan and his festering sores. By the time they reached Reno, he was the lone passenger. Finally, in mid-July, Stan was admitted to DeWitt General Hospital, near Auburn, California, on the edge of the Sierra Nevada range.

Nearly two and a half months had passed since he was shot. He had received no treatment for his injury except for the initial surgery and subsequent immobilization. He weighed less than one hundred pounds, down from about 160 pounds. Debilitating pressure sores tattooed his backside and hips.

His mother, Francis, had received a telegram from the army stating that Stan had suffered a "slight injury." Eager to see her son after a long separation, and believing that he wasn't too badly hurt, she made plans to visit him. After all, DeWitt General Hospital wasn't too far from Marin County.

Stan refused to allow her to visit. Instead, he wrote her and bluntly explained the situation. "I was shot in the back—right across back of lungs. Spinal cord was severed and I am paralyzed from about my last ribs down."[2]

He lay in bed, hapless and depressed. The natural wonders of Mount Tam seemed like a hallucination from another lifetime.

★ ★ ★

GENE

From the beach at Okinawa, Gene Fesenmeyer was taken on a stretcher and lifted onto a DUKW—a six-wheel amphibious truck affectionately called a "Duck"—with other wounded men. They loaded him onto a sling to put him on a hospital ship anchored off of Okinawa.

It turned out to be the wrong one. In a scene reminiscent of a Marx Brothers movie, his caretakers had to get him off the ship and return him to shore, and then put him on another DUKW. This one, eventually, delivered him to the aptly named USS *Mercy*, even as he was crying out in agonizing pain.

At one point, Gene noticed a chaplain lurking by his side. "I couldn't figure out what the hell he's doing there," he said later. "I kept waking up and there's this guy. Well, he was waiting for me to die. Everyone figured I was on my way out."

He was deposited on Guam, where he recovered for several weeks. He weighed less than one hundred pounds and felt more dead than alive. He finally wound up at the U.S. Naval Hospital at Aiea Heights, Oahu.

To prepare him for his flight to the mainland, medical personnel aspirated Gene's lungs daily so he could withstand the pressure inside the plane. Whenever the nurses stuck a long needle in him, without anesthesia, to suck the gunk out of his lungs, he'd grasp the bed frame tightly to prevent himself from yelping.

Afterward, attendants rolled his bed out onto the lanai (an outdoor patio). He faced the blue water and stared at an old hibiscus tree swaying in the breeze. He vowed that, if he survived, he'd find a way to live in paradise.

His lungs healed slowly. On the hospital plane from Hawaii, he was thrown from his cot. Doctors feared that he wouldn't be able to stand the pain, but he managed. Barely. Upon his arrival at the naval air station in Oakland, Gene was placed in a big ward with other servicemen who were paralyzed. They took one look at his stick figure, weighing in at seventy pounds, and placed bets on whether he'd live through the night.

"They were a bunch of wild ones," he said, "all Marines from other battles. They had been there, done that on Iwo Jima and as far back as Guadalcanal."

Lying in bed, trying to regain his weight and equilibrium, Gene developed huge pressure sores, and then pressure sores on top of them. Doctors told him they could do nothing, and that they were more life threatening than his initial injury.

Meanwhile, back home in Iowa, two marine officers went to the family farm to inform his parents that Gene had been wounded. The good citizens of Clarinda started the Fesenmeyer Fund to raise money for Gene's recovery. That didn't ease the constant pain and the spasms he endured.

"It was just bad pains in the worst places you can imagine," he said. "It started in the back and went through your groin. You'll be fine, and then all of a sudden the pain just shoots through you."

He was transferred to the Marine Corps base at Camp Pendleton in Southern California, where he had trained before going overseas. Then he was nineteen and eager to kill the enemy. Now he was twenty, gravely wounded, and facing an uncertain future.

"I knew I was bad off," he said. "There were guys dying from pressure sores and everything else," he said.

★ ★ ★

JOHNNY

After the U.S. Army's 37th Division liberated Bilibid Prison, Johnny Winterholler was taken to the University of Santo Tomas in Manila for emergency treatment, then to an army hospital on Cebu Island in the Philippines. The first thing he did, in a letter to Dessa, was to apologize for "three years of inactivity."

His letter did not detail what had happened to him. "It will suffice to say that it was tough and consequently many of us didn't do so well," he wrote. "I say us because, unfortunately, I must include myself. I shall not tell you the nature nor extent of my injury but I feel that now I could at least tell you I was injured. I feel that everything is going to be OK. So why alarm you with a lot of fancy medical terms."

What mattered most, he wrote, was that "I love you now more than anything in the world, and the past three years has only proven to me that I'm the luckiest guy alive. You and I have a 'heap of living' to do when I return and we shall start in as soon as possible. Ok?"

He concluded with two instructions: "Make the best batch of

fudge you have ever made, honey—I'm hungry," and "No word to Mother on what I have told you."[3]

When Winterholler's condition stabilized, he was evacuated to the States via a series of flights that took four interminable days. On March 9, 1945, he arrived at the U.S. Naval Hospital on Mare Island—his point of departure when he left for the Philippines in 1941.

As soon as she heard from Johnny, Dessa resigned from her job as director of the student union at the university. She left Wyoming for California, accompanied by her mother and Johnny's mother. Their reunion was emotional and sobering. The women were over the moon that he was alive, but they couldn't believe how emaciated he was; that he was no longer the lithe and athletic Johnny from before and that he couldn't walk.

Johnny and Dessa were left alone to talk over their future. There wasn't much to discuss. They'd vowed to get married before he was sent to the Philippines. Now that he was home, nearly four years since he'd left, they decided that they'd waited long enough.

On March 18, the high-school and college sweethearts were married in a brief bedside ceremony in the hospital, with their mothers, Marie and Permelia, in attendance. Johnny and Dessa held hands and stated their vows while he lay in bed and she stood alongside him in a stylish dress. There wasn't a dry eye in the room.[4]

His homecoming was made official with a trip to Wyoming to visit family and friends. When he got together with his three brothers—Hank, Phil, and Al—who'd also served in the Pacific and survived the war, the reunion of the "fighting Winterhollers of Lovell" made headlines.[5]

Johnny was frail and underweight; multiple bedsores festooned his lower torso. He was paralyzed below the Poupart's ligament, where the pelvis transitions to the lower limb in the groin area, leading to some bladder and bowel incontinence. He could move his legs, but he couldn't feel them.

And yet, he was alive. Johnny understood how fortunate he was to have avoided death while in captivity. The statistics were grim: approximately 40 percent of the 26,000 "U.S. Army and Navy personnel captured in the Philippines never returned," according to historian John Glusman, a shockingly high number compared to the European and Mediterranean theaters, where "the mortality rate for American POWs...was less than 1 percent."[6]

Johnny was determined to look forward. He was back in the States, together with Dessa. He'd handled plenty of tough times before. He resolved to stay positive, set lofty goals, and give the utmost effort to get better.

★ ★ ★

John Winterholler, Stan Den Adel, and Gene Fesenmeyer were among the approximately 2,500 U.S. servicemen who returned from World War II with spinal-cord injuries due to bullets, shell fragments, mine explosions, accidents, plane crashes, friendly fire, and other causes. This was a marked increase from previous wars. Indeed, the survival of these servicemen can be traced to unprecedented breakthroughs in modern medicine.

All vertebrate animals—reptiles, mammals, fish, fowl, amphibians—have spinal cords. The spinal cord in humans is a tubular column composed of neurons (cells) and nerve fibers (axons) sheathed inside the protective bony, membranous, and cartilaginous components of the spinal column. The spinal cord runs from the base of the skull to just below the rib cage; below that a bundle of peripheral nerves called the cauda equina (horse's tail) runs out through the gaps in the spinal column to the pelvis and lower limbs. The spinal column extends to the tailbone and is composed of some thirty-three interlocking bones called vertebrae: seven are located in the cervical (neck) area, twelve in the thoracic (chest) area, and five in the lumbar (lower back) area, along with five fused vertebrae in the sacral (pelvic) area, and another four in the coccyx (tailbone) region. The unfused cervical, thoracic, and lumbar vertebrae are linked together by intervertebral discs made of collagen and water. These discs act like shock absorbers for the spine, and together with the facet joints, allow for normal spinal motion while at the same time protecting the spinal cord within.

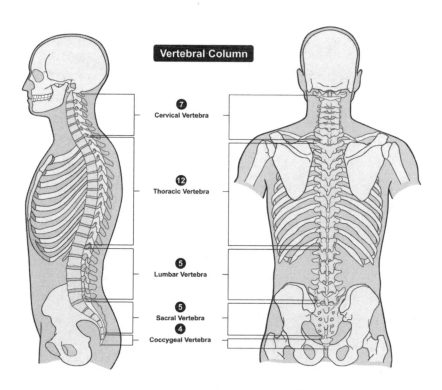

Vertebral Column

7 Cervical Vertebra

12 Thoracic Vertebra

5 Lumbar Vertebra

5 Sacral Vertebra

4 Coccygeal Vertebra

Together, the spinal cord and the brain make up the central nervous system—"control central" of the human body. If the brain operates like a computer, constantly receiving and processing data from our senses and internal organs, then the spinal cord functions like the information superhighway, helping to relay messages back and forth from the brain to the muscles, skin, and internal organs via the peripheral nervous system: the millions of nerves and sensory neurons that exit the vertebral column along the entirety of the spinal cord and extend to the body's periphery.

When healthy and intact, the spinal cord assists the brain to monitor and regulate nearly every sensory and motor function: from walking and talking to breathing and blinking; from kicking a ball and running to having sex and driving a car. (The optic nerve, for instance, transmits visual data from our eyes to the brain.)

Damage to the spinal cord disrupts the lines of communication between the brain and the body at or below where the injury occurred. Violent, blunt blows, such as tackling in football, usually do not sever the spinal cord, but damage to the spinal column, such as the fracturing or dislocation of vertebrae, may cause permanent disruption of the spinal cord. Penetrating injuries from knife and gunshot wounds can also severely injure or completely cut the spinal cord. Even less traumatic injuries and infections can cause bleeding and swelling in the spinal cord and bring about permanent nerve injury. Such injuries block sensory, motor, and reflex messages from the brain and may result in permanent paralysis. Peripheral nerves have the ability to heal, either with or without surgical intervention, but spinal-cord (central nerve) injuries do not.

Doctors have long used abbreviations to pinpoint the location of spinal-cord injuries. "C1" refers to an injury in the first vertebra of the cervical area, for example, while "S5" refers to the fifth vertebra in the sacral region. Typically, the higher the injury in the spinal column, the greater the resulting dysfunction. High cervical lesions, in the C1 to C4 areas, are the most severe and often involve the loss of movement and feeling in legs and arms, and maybe even the ability to breathe. People who have experienced what neurologists describe as a "complete" spinal-cord injury retain no motor or sensory function below the affected segment. Those with an "incomplete" spinal-cord injury may retain limited motor and sensory function below the level of the injury.

For millennia, spinal-cord injuries on and off the battlefield were considered a death sentence. The earliest surviving account of such an injury can be found in the Edwin Smith surgical papyrus, so named for the antiquities dealer who purchased the ancient Egyptian scroll in 1862. (Smith's papyrus is believed to be a copy of an original composition dated c. 2500 BCE.)

In what is considered to be one of the oldest surviving fragments of medical literature, the unknown author described two traumatic spinal-cord cases. The conclusion? Spinal-cord injuries lead to certain death and are "an ailment not to be treated."[7]

Physicians accepted this as doctrine into the nineteenth century. They often cited the two most famous incidents of spinal-cord injury to that point. There was the case of Admiral Horatio Nelson, the British naval hero whose "back was shot through" during the Battle of Trafalgar in 1805.

Legend has it that the ship's doctor told Nelson, "My Lord, unhappily for our country, nothing can be done for you." Nelson died shortly afterward.[8]

In 1881, an assassin's bullet lodged in the abdomen of President

James Garfield and rendered him paralyzed. The nation's newly elected president lay bedridden and in increasing pain for nearly three months. During that time, Garfield's body was assaulted by infection and sepsis until, mercifully, he died.[9]

The fate of most every patient with paraplegia was sealed not by the initial injury or blow, but by disease or infection. In the days before antibiotics were discovered, most patients developed urinary tract or kidney infections that proved fatal. Another common problem was the formation of decubitus ulcers, otherwise known as bedsores or pressure sores. Painful and toxic, they damaged the skin and, in severe cases, destroyed underlying fat and muscle tissue all the way to the bone.

The usual course of treatment was minimal: immobilize the patients and confine them to bed. Doctors rarely if ever attempted to get the injured out of bed or involve them in social, athletic, or vocational activities. What was the point? These "dead-enders" and "no-hopers," as they were typically labeled, were going to die soon anyway.

Patient care slowly improved with advances in anatomy and surgery in the latter part of the nineteenth century. The introduction of anesthesia, including nitrous oxide and chloroform, ushered in an era of painless surgery, while the discovery of the X-ray informed doctors about the location of the injury and the extent of the damage. Greater attention to sterilization and sanitary concerns (thorough handwashing and the use of surgical gloves, for example) reduced disease transmission within hospital wards, and the advent of the blood typing system made transfusions safer.

World War I expanded medicine's understanding of paraplegia simply because doctors treating wounded soldiers near the front lines, most notably neurosurgeons Dr. Harvey Cushing with the

U.S. Army and Dr. Otfrid Foerster from Germany, had the opportunity to observe and treat a sizable cohort of disabled soldiers.

Unfortunately, without antibiotics, they could do little to reduce the mortality rate. Cushing reported that 80 percent of servicemen with spinal-cord injuries died within weeks from infections caused by bedsores and/or catheterization. Overall, some 90 percent died within a year.[10]

Wrote British surgeon Sir Frederick Treves in the *American Journal of Care for Cripples* in 1917:

> There will be no more lamentable and pathetic figure than the soldier who . . . is paralyzed and left utterly helpless. . . . Here is a man in the very flower of his youth, bedridden for life, unable to move hand or foot, and dependent, at every moment of the day, upon the ministrations of others. . . . the mind is as vigorous and as alert as ever; the eagerness and independence of youth are still aglow in the brain; there are still the intense longing to do, the stimulus to venture, the desire to lay hold of the joys of life . . . this mental energy is associated with a body that cannot feel, limbs that cannot move, fingers without touch, and hands as listless as the hands of the dead.[11]

Cushing's efforts during World War I weren't for naught. One crucial lesson learned was that the chances of soldiers surviving their spinal-cord injuries dramatically increased the sooner they received medical attention. This knowledge led the military to institute a more effective evacuation system during World War II, starting with corpsmen giving basic first aid on the battlefield.

Other medical advances were proving beneficial for those with paraplegia. The discovery of penicillin in 1928, by Dr. Alexander Fleming in England, and the ability to produce large supplies of the wonder drug in the early 1940s, significantly reduced fatal bacterial infections without harming the body. Sulfa powder and tablets, derived from aniline dyes, arrived in the mid-1930s with the ability to stanch the spread of bacteria. The ability to collect, bottle, store, ship, and use vast amounts of blood and plasma helped doctors save lives near the front lines.

"It is paradoxical that through war, a concerted effort to annihilate man, we have learned more and better ways to preserve him," said Dr. Howard Rusk, who as the head of the Army Air Force's rehabilitation program was emerging as a leader in the treatment of people with disabilities.[12]

In other words, Stan Den Adel, Gene Fesenmeyer, Johnny Winterholler, and the 2,500 other paralyzed veterans from World War II were in the wrong place, but at the right time.

Their survival, while welcome, introduced a fresh set of concerns. Neither the military nor the medical community had considered, much less planned for, their survival. Doctors didn't know how to treat them—physically, emotionally, socially, or spiritually—because they had scant experience with paraplegia. No one could say if it was even possible for paralyzed veterans to live a "normal" lifespan. They were, at once, medical marvels and medical enigmas.

CHAPTER 6

The Munro Doctrine

Dr. Ernest Hermann Joseph Bors could not contain his anger and frustration. Bors was the assistant chief urologist at Hammond General Hospital, a newly built facility in Modesto, California. He noticed on his daily rounds that the paralyzed veterans in the hospital's various wings were tethered to their beds. Their life was marked by monotony: they stared at the ceiling, listened to music on headphones, smoked cigarettes, and wrote letters.

They were given no tasks or exercises, nor could they go anywhere unattended. They needed assistance just to move from room to room in oversize wooden wheelchairs that were as clunky as a Model T. They were the barely living tucked into white hospital sheets.

Slightly built, with "piercing gray-blue eyes that can spot a dirty glass connector on a urinary tube at 30 yards," according to *Paraplegia News*,[1] Bors wasn't just old school. He was old world. He was born in Prague in 1900, when Bohemia was part of the Austro-Hungarian Empire. His father was a physician; his mother's brothers were doctors. Bors recalled how, at age six, he sat at the kitchen table and listened to family members talk shop.

Bors went on to train as a surgeon and urologist at Charles

University in Prague. He married Olga Rudinger in 1925, shortly after she received her medical degree from the University of Prague. The Jewish couple fled the Nazi regime via Switzerland and landed in America in 1940. He obtained his medical license and taught at New York University's medical school while working at St. Luke's Hospital in Manhattan and St. Anthony's Hospital in Queens.

In 1943, Bors was commissioned as a captain in the U.S. Army Medical Corps. The following year, after receiving his naturalization papers, he was assigned to Hammond General Hospital, named in honor of William A. Hammond, the U.S. surgeon general appointed by President Abraham Lincoln in 1862.

Bors had seen only a handful of patients with paraplegia prior to his stint at Hammond. One case, from 1925, was imprinted in his mind: a man who had broken his back after falling down an elevator shaft. "My first impression was that we ought to operate," he later recalled. "My superiors sadly shook their heads. They said the case was hopeless; they said the man would die within three months of uremic poisoning [from kidney damage]—and he did."[2]

Upon his return to the States, Gene Fesenmeyer experienced this hands-off approach. "They didn't know how to take care of us," he said. "See, they believed that, if you had a spinal injury, you weren't supposed to get out of bed for a year. They wouldn't let us do anything. We were all screwed up every which way—physically, mentally, everything. I laid in that goddamn bed just rotting away."

Morale sagged. Stan Den Adel noted that, initially, he was consumed by anger, depression, and self-pity. If he couldn't even get out of bed, how could he envision a future for himself? He certainly didn't want anyone—including his mother—to see his poor condition.

In essence, Bors and other physicians were confronting two distinct but related issues. The first was the emotional shock the paralyzed veterans were experiencing about their sudden "new normal" condition. "Physical disability constitutes a threat to a way of life," Dr. Howard Rusk told journalist Jules Saltman. "The disability removes the individual from normal social experiences and from work situations—the two major sources of satisfaction and self-esteem . . . [resulting in] shattered ambitions and dreams."[3]

The second aspect, equally important, was the realization that each spinal-cord patient had incurred different degrees of physical damage, with consequences and complications that spanned the gamut of medicine: neurology and urology; respiratory and cardiovascular medicine; orthopedic surgery and plastic surgery.

Determined to find an effective therapeutic regimen for the paralyzed veterans, Bors turned to a singular touchstone: the only U.S. physician who had reported positive results treating spinal-cord injuries.

Like Bors, Donald Munro was born to be in medicine. His father, Dr. John Cummings Munro, was surgeon-in-chief at Carney Hospital in Boston. His mother, Mary, was the only daughter of Dr. Edward Robinson Squibb, the founder of the pharmaceutical company now known as Bristol-Myers Squibb. Munro attended Harvard College and Harvard Medical School. He served in France in the Army Medical Corps during World War I and, afterward, returned to Boston City Hospital as chief neurological surgeon.

Munro brushed with notoriety following a harrowing incident at a National Hockey League game in 1933. Toronto Maple Leafs winger Irvine "Ace" Bailey was hit from behind by Boston Bruins defenseman Eddie Shore. Bailey fell and hit his head on the ice. He started convulsing and was left unconscious with a fractured skull.

Munro was called in to operate. Two procedures relieved the pressure on Bailey's brain and saved his life, although his playing career was over. Newspapers across the United States and Canada praised the surgeon's skills.

At Boston City, Munro ran a small paraplegia ward in the mid-1930s. He showed that, with painstaking care, patients could survive the effects of their traumatic spinal-cord injuries. One significant step was to eliminate urinary sepsis through the use of tidal drainage. This was a mechanical method in which the bladder was filled with irrigating fluid and then emptied via a catheter inserted into the urethral tube inside the penis. Tidal drainage not only prevented bedwetting, but helped the patients regain continence.

Munro also devoted meticulous attention to preventing the formation of life-threatening bedsores. He demanded twenty-four-hour vigilance to ensure that sheets were consistently changed and the patient kept dry. He required that nurses stand watch and turn the patients' bodies every two hours to eliminate the formation of pressure sores.

The key to his system was holistic, multidisciplinary care before such terms were common. He assembled a team of doctors, surgeons, and therapists to treat each patient individually, with Munro retaining authority over the entire process.

Neurologists determined the location of the injury and the extent of the paralysis, while urologists concentrated on diagnosing kidney and bladder issues. Neurosurgeons were called on to sever the nerve roots of patients, so as to ease spasticity, or to perform laminectomies by removing bone fragments that compressed the spinal cord. Plastic surgeons repaired noxious bedsores with skin grafts. Physiotherapists were employed to guide patients through range-of-motion exercises to rebuild upper-body strength; aides and nurses massaged limbs and applied radiant heat to reduce spasms. Dietitians helped patients gain weight, while psychiatrists were available when patients experienced depression or anxiety.

Another of Munro's precepts was that the doctors could do only so much. The onus was on the patient to want to get better. "Rehabilitation is or is not within the patient himself," he told Saltman. "It is a spiritual attitude, not in the ecclesiastical sense, but rather as opposed to the physical. Without this spiritual urge within himself no patient can be truly rehabilitated, no matter what outside aid is made available; with it, extraordinary capacities come to light."[4]

Munro treated civilians, not servicemen, and his cohort was relatively small. But his success was unprecedented and easy to validate: his patients lived.

War-related spinal-cord injuries, often caused by explosions and gunfire, tended to be more traumatic than the injuries suffered by civilians. But Bors decided to follow Munro's cohesive approach. At Hammond, he insisted that the paralyzed veterans be moved together into one ward within the hospital, and demanded "complete administrative, medical, and professional control" over his charges. In so doing, he developed the "first unitary, comprehensive, continuing, multi-disciplinary SCI treatment and rehabilitation program in the United States," according to one of his former patients, George Hohmann, PhD, a paralyzed veteran from World War II who later became a psychologist.[5]

★ ★ ★

Sixteen million Americans served during World War II, representing more than 10 percent of the nation's population. Put another way: more than 40 percent of adult males were newly minted veterans.

Preparations for the return of this massive human army began well before the conclusion of hostilities. President Roosevelt signed the Servicemen's Readjustment Act into law on June 22, 1944, less than three weeks after the D-Day landings. The GI Bill of Rights has been described as "the last legislative act of the New Deal"[6] and "the most ambitious, extensive, and costly social program ever enacted following an American war."[7]

Commonly known as the GI Bill, it was designed to facilitate veterans' readjustment to civilian life by offering extended medical and hospital care; low-interest, insured loans for businesses, farms, and homes; stipends to pay for college tuition or vocational job training; and unemployment compensation of twenty dollars per week.

The Veterans Administration (VA) was the de facto authority over the GI Bill's treasure trove of benefits. Likewise, the VA administered the healthcare system put in place for the veterans. Beset by budget, staffing, and organizational woes, with an antiquated hospital system considered the backwater of American medicine, the VA was in need of an extensive overhaul. No one wanted a repeat of the Bonus March fiasco in 1932, when unemployed World War I veterans petitioned for early payment of their long-promised military service payout and were attacked and evicted by the U.S. Army under the command of General Douglas MacArthur. Traditional service groups such as the American Legion, the Veterans of Foreign Wars (VFW), and the Disabled American Veterans (DAV) questioned the VA's ability to handle the fresh wave of veterans and their dependents.

The VA's task was enormous. Some 650,000 Americans came home from the war with nonfatal injuries. They'd survived burns caused by kamikaze planes on carriers in the Pacific and frostbite while fighting in Europe. They'd broken bones parachuting from airplanes, stepped on land mines, and been shot by friendly fire. Mortar explosions had riddled their bodies with shrapnel; debilitating diseases and malnutrition had consumed them. They expected and were promised quality, lifelong medical care.

Before his death, President Roosevelt was concerned enough about "the physical and emotional condition of disabled men returning from the war" to write a letter to Secretary of War Henry Stimson urging him to ensure that "no overseas casualty [is to be] discharged from the armed forces until he has received the maximum benefit of hospitalization and convalescent facilities, which must include physical and psychological rehabilitation, vocational guidance, prevocational training and resocialization."[8]

In 1945, soon after Roosevelt's death, President Truman appointed General Omar Bradley as director of the VA. A star baseball player and classmate of Dwight Eisenhower at West Point, Bradley was known for commanding U.S. ground forces on D-Day. His reputation as a dedicated advocate for the common soldier was shaped in the columns of Ernie Pyle, who was impressed by Bradley's understated style during the Sicily campaign and, with some embroidery, dubbed him America's "GI General."

Bradley didn't want the job. He considered the position "inconsequential and demeaning"[9] for a general, according to biographer Steven Ossad, and complained that the physicians applying for jobs at the VA were the "dregs of the medical profession."[10] But he was loyal to his commander in chief and felt a moral obligation to take the job after having sent hundreds of thousands of young men into war. "I had heard the mournful cries of the wounded on the battlefield," he later noted. "In countless Army field hospitals, I had seen the maimed stoically enduring nearly unbearable pain."[11]

Under Bradley's watch, the VA embarked on an unprecedented building boom that produced the nation's largest network
of hospitals, located in places that benefited the most veterans,
with state-of-the-art design features. Bradley recruited Dr. Paul
Hawley, who had served as the chief surgeon in the European
theater during the war, as medical director of the VA. Hawley
stepped up the hiring of doctors and nurses, started a residency
training program, and mined the expertise of the nation's medical
schools to improve veterans' access to specialized care.

During the Potsdam Conference of 1945, as the Allies contemplated a new world order, Bradley met with Dr. Howard
Rusk about the homecoming veterans. Rusk was a strapping
Midwesterner who had joined the Air Force and served as chief
of medical services at the Jefferson Barracks Hospital outside St.
Louis. Rusk prodded Bradley and the VA to go beyond medical
and surgical services and offer a full menu of rehabilitation options
for veterans, from physical exercises to psychiatric counseling,
from vocational training to education opportunities.

If the first responsibility of medicine is prevention, and the second is care, then the third phase is "what happens after the fever
is down and the stitches are out," Rusk preached like a mantra.
"We realized it was not enough just to treat a man's physical
needs. We had to worry about his emotional, social, educational
and occupational needs as well. We had to treat the whole man.
And we also had to teach his friends and family how to accept
him and help him in his new condition."[12]

In 1945, rehabilitation medicine in America was as novel as
television. Rusk's advocacy of physical therapy for even the most
severely wounded veterans flew in the face of medical orthodoxy.
Critics charged that such services were a waste of government
dollars. In response, Rusk pointed to groundbreaking research

conducted at the Institute for the Crippled and Disabled in New York City (known today as the International Center for the Disabled), where Dr. George Deaver was demonstrating the folly of keeping injured patients on interminable bedrest or immobilizing their limbs for prolonged periods of time. This approach brought horrendous results: loss of muscle tone, blood clots, kidney and bladder stones, and bedsores, not to mention an overwhelming malaise. Deaver achieved superior outcomes by having his patients exercise and recondition their stiffened joints and muscles as soon as possible, albeit at a judicious and gradual pace.

Rusk was a true believer in and proselytizer of comprehensive rehabilitation. He wrote a weekly column for the *New York Times* for nearly a quarter of a century extolling its myriad health benefits. He was also a practical realist who argued that such innovation could actually save money. The faster and more completely the veterans healed, the faster doctors could discharge them from the VA hospitals. In the best possible scenario, these veterans would then be able to go out, find decent jobs, and start paying taxes.

Disfigured and paralyzed veterans also had to prepare themselves to face society's prejudice against and discomfort with disability. Individuals with physical and intellectual disabilities had been considered oddities since the dawn of humankind, their "otherness" blamed on everything from divine wrath to familial sin to character flaw. They were often ostracized and banished to institutions, where they were kept out of sight.

In the late nineteenth and early twentieth centuries, major American cities passed "ugly laws" that prohibited diseased, maimed, or deformed people from appearing on public streets. Eugenicists proposed to rid the world of people they believed were inferior.

In *Buck v. Bell*, the U.S. Supreme Court upheld a Virginia law that allowed states to sterilize "undesirable" inmates of public institutions. Justice Oliver Wendell Holmes Jr. wrote the majority (eight to one) decision in 1927, leading to as many as 70,000 forced sterilizations. "It is better for all the world if, instead of waiting to execute degenerate offspring for crime or to let them starve for their imbecility, society can prevent those who are manifestly unfit from continuing their kind," he opined before concluding, "Three generations of imbeciles are enough."[13]

The stigma of disability extended to the office of the president of the United States. In 1921, Franklin D. Roosevelt was a thirty-nine-year-old rising star in the Democratic Party when he was suddenly stricken with infantile paralysis, better known as polio. For the next few years, he withdrew from public life. But he was fortunate to have the financial resources and family connections to obtain the best medical treatment. He soaked in the soothing waters at Warm Springs, Georgia, and hired physiotherapists to help strengthen his upper body.

Roosevelt never regained the ability to walk unaided. He was fitted with heavy and painful braces that locked his legs in place at the waist and the knees; he could awkwardly lurch for short distances using a cane or a crutch while leaning on another person (often his son). In private, he employed a wheelchair to move about his office.

FDR didn't hide the facts of his illness. He was so pleased by his rejuvenation in Warm Springs that he purchased the spa and established a world-renowned polio rehabilitation center. (Warm Springs, however, was open only to white patients.)

Roosevelt recognized that disease can have lasting effects beyond scar tissue. After he won his first term as president, he took great pains to avoid being photographed or filmed in his wheelchair so as to "quiet the feelings of revulsion, pity, and embarrassment that his body provoked in others," according to biographer James Tobin.

"[A wheelchair] in Roosevelt's time was seen as something like a rolling prison," Tobin noted. "One was said to be 'confined to a wheelchair.' Wheelchairs were not for people leading normal lives. They were for sick people in hospitals and sanitariums. With an attendant always standing behind him, the man in a wheelchair was by definition not an independent human being who could care for himself. He was assumed to be sick."[14]

★ ★ ★

Dr. Howard Rusk's campaign touting the efficacy of rehabilitation medicine, along with Dr. Bors's work at Hammond General Hospital, buttressed the argument for creating separate units for veterans with spinal-cord injuries.

The VA selected Bors to oversee the nation's first spinal-cord injury ward, located at Birmingham General Hospital in Van Nuys, California. Six other SCI divisions were established at VA hospitals across the country: at Kennedy Hospital in Memphis, Tennessee; McGuire Hospital in Richmond, Virginia; in New York City at the Bronx Hospital and Halloran Hospital on Staten Island; Vaughan Hospital in Hines, Illinois, just outside Chicago; and Cushing Hospital in Framingham, Massachusetts, where Dr. Munro added to his already considerable responsibilities by working as a consultant.

Two naval hospitals—one in Southern California and one in New York—also devoted space exclusively to spinal-cord injuries.

It would take the dedication of doctors and nurses to handle the massive medical challenges surrounding paraplegia, many of which they'd never encountered before. And it would take the concerted effort of paralyzed veterans to take charge of their individual fates and reintegrate themselves into society. Their goals and their methods sometimes clashed, but together they would create a new paradigm for people with disabilities, one that would eventually extend from the VA hospitals to the civilian population.

CHAPTER 7

Birmingham Hospital

Stan Den Adel weighed about one hundred pounds. Pressure sores pockmarked his body. His hair was falling out, and he was certain he would be bald by Christmas. He had neither the strength nor the energy to leave his hospital bed at DeWitt Army Hospital.

Monotony and boredom were his bedside companions. Each morning, he was awakened at six to have his blood pressure, temperature, and heart rate checked, followed by a tray of lukewarm breakfast, the dressing of his wounds with a chlorine solution that brought back memories of his high school locker room, and a quick consultation of his chart by doctors and interns.

Afternoons and evenings were broken up by the delivery of meal trays and another dressing change. In the days before television was omnipresent in hospital rooms, he spent much of his days and nights sleeping.

That all changed for Stan and the other spinal-cord patients at DeWitt just before Thanksgiving, 1945, when they were loaded onto a hospital train and taken to their new home: Birmingham Hospital, located in the San Fernando Valley on 150 acres of farmland that had once been planted with carrots and lima beans. They were joined by paralyzed veterans from McCaw Army Hospital in Walla Walla, Washington; Bushnell Army Hospital in Brigham City, Utah; and Hammond General Hospital in Modesto.

There wasn't much between Birmingham Hospital and the nearest main thoroughfare, Ventura Boulevard, just endless fields of squash. Looking south, one could see an old MGM lot that contained long-abandoned movie sets. A weathered façade from *The Hunchback of Notre Dame* stood eerily in the distance.

At Birmingham, the spinal-cord injury center was part of a large complex of one-story units that fed into the main lobby, making it convenient for the patients to wheel themselves around. The grounds included a small theater, a gymnasium, and, eventually, an outdoor swimming pool in "an atmosphere that fell somewhere between a hotel and a hospital," according to former employee Linsey Deverich.[1]

Dr. Bors arrived from Hammond and was installed as the head of the VA's only spinal-cord unit west of Chicago. Stan and many of the approximately 220 other paralyzed servicemen under Bors's charge at Birmingham grew to admire the bow-tie-wearing chieftain they called "Pappy."

"He brought order and structure out of chaos," veteran Fred Smead said.[2]

Bors ministered to each patient, alert to their singular require-ments, and thought nothing of rushing to the hospital at three in the morning to comfort a sick or dying man. One journalist called him "Martin Arrowsmith come to life," in reference to the unconventional doctor from Sinclair Lewis's Pulitzer Prize–winning novel *Arrowsmith*.[3] In his office, Bors hung a framed copy of "The Serenity Prayer":

God, grant me the serenity to accept the things I cannot change,

Courage to change the things I can,
And wisdom to know the difference.

The veterans knew that the crusty, no-nonsense Bors cared
about them even when he scolded them for sneaking booze into
the ward or razzing the nurses. They tolerated his bleak bedside
manner during grand rounds performed before a well-trained
audience of interns, residents, and nurses.

"Well, well, back from the cemetery," he muttered to one
patient who'd shown marked improvement.

"Hello, Paleface," was his deadpan greeting to an African-
American veteran.[4]

Beyond worrying about his patients' physical woes, Bors's chief
concern was that the young men with broken bodies also had
broken spirits. This was especially noticeable in the earliest stages
of their recovery, when they were cycling through unfamiliar and
uncomfortable emotions: confusion, shock, anger, pain, grief,
and denial.

Some patients withdrew into themselves and refused to speak
to Bors or the staff psychologist or even their loved ones. It was as
if, seeing their own bodies irreparably damaged, they were paralyzed by their paralysis. At their lowest, Bors related, they would
"explode in temper and throw urine bottles [and] smash windows
with their canes. They felt hopeless, frustrated, bitter."[5]

Bors gained their trust by listening to them. He instituted
"gripe sessions" on the porches of the hospital, and encouraged
the paralyzed veterans to organize their own support group. He
fielded their endless questions and forthrightly answered them:
Would they be able to have sex again? Could they have children?
Was there any surgery that could regenerate their spinal cord and
allow them to walk again? What was their life expectancy? And

perhaps the most basic question of all: was it possible for someone with paraplegia to live a "normal" life?

"Most of all I had to learn patience," he later wrote, "to listen to, rather than to force Nature, to adjust rather than to attack, to observe, deduce and not to try to play Providence."[6]

★ ★ ★

Stan Den Adel's journey from darkness to light, from depression and despair to adjusting to a new and permanent normal, began with a simple perception. He noticed that the paralyzed veterans in the paraplegia ward who were doing all right, considering, were those who had accepted their fate, or at least had come to terms with it, and were intent on figuring out the next phase of their lives.

Every morning, he watched them plunk themselves into ungainly wooden wheelchairs to be taken outdoors by attendants to play a form of wheelchair volleyball (with a lowered net) that he could see from his window. They made lascivious wisecracks to the female nurses and called each other "Crip." Racy pinup photos of Veronica Lake, Rita Hayworth, Betty Grable, and Gene Tierney adorned the walls above their cots. The men graphically detailed their bowel disasters from oral laxatives and their leakage problems from catheters.

When one of them accidentally steered his wheelchair into a wall, the others lambasted the poor soul: "Hey, Crip, do you have a license to drive that thing?"

Den Adel couldn't help laughing. Being together with others who were facing the same disability, all of them figuring out how to accommodate and assimilate their altered condition, was enormously therapeutic. "Every day somebody did something we didn't know could be done from a wheelchair," he later wrote. "We shared our experiences with each other, speeding up the whole rehab process."[7]

The fact that Den Adel and the others were youthful veterans played a significant role in their healing. The physical culture of the armed forces kept them in good shape, which gave them an edge in the rehabilitation process. Once they regained a sense of equilibrium—once they adjusted to the "new normal"—many were thankful to be alive. They knew plenty of others who had been left behind permanently on the battlefield or who'd incurred equally damaging injuries. That didn't end their physical pain or salve their emotional trauma, but their sense of duty surely provided much needed perspective in overcoming their predicament.

His mother gave up her job in Marin County and moved to Southern California. Francis rented a little apartment close to the hospital and taught at a nearby private school so she could visit Stan as frequently as possible. Within eighteen months, her husband had died suddenly and her son had returned from the war a paralyzed veteran. But as soon as she entered Birmingham Hospital, she exuded positivity and showered Stan with love and encouragement.

"Our mother was always an upbeat, optimistic person," said Shirley Garthwait, Stan's younger sister. "She was not a worrier. I think she passed that on to Stan. At his lowest he had two choices: 'I'm either going to die or I'm going to get better. Do I want to say goodbye or see if I can get better?'"[8]

Thanks to a steady diet of nasty-tasting protein shakes, he gained weight. His brown hair grew back although, oddly, the new locks were curly, not straight like before. With his health stabilized, Stan underwent three major surgeries to close the gaping holes caused by the bedsores on his hips.

That freed him from the restriction of his hospital bed, and he threw himself into his rehabilitation chores with intense determination. His immediate task was to master the seventy-two activities required for daily living (ADL), a program conceived by Dr. George Deaver at the Institute for the Crippled and Disabled to help paralyzed veterans relearn a series of everyday, mundane tasks.

Den Adel started from the beginning: he sat up in bed by himself. This was not as easy as it may sound, given that his muscles had atrophied and the lower half of his body was dead weight. He grew dizzy and almost passed out from the exertion. He advanced to using a bedpan by himself; taking off his pajamas and putting on his clothes; eating with a knife and fork; using the toilet unaided; brushing his teeth and shaving; and so on.

He was timed for each test. As he got faster and more adept, his enthusiasm redoubled. Soon, he was swimming in the hospital pool and reporting to the gymnasium for physical therapy and grueling mat workouts. Bars were installed above his bed so he could stretch muscles that had long been inert and lift himself to a sitting position. His chest, arm, and shoulder muscles grew tauter. He ate his meals in the mess hall instead of picking at them while lounging in bed.

Den Adel's progress was so impressive that, in July of 1946, he and six other veterans with spinal-cord injuries were taken to San Francisco to participate in the first-ever exhibition on rehabilitation and physical medicine at the American Medical Association's annual convention. He demonstrated his ADL and wheelchair proficiency to the attendees and chatted with physicians who had never encountered, much less treated, someone with paraplegia.

The goal of the ADL was to prepare the veterans for an independent life outside the hospital. Finding a job was considered a crucial part of the process, but the prejudice ingrained among some employers proved to be an imposing hurdle. "Only a few companies had enlightened policies about hiring the handicapped," Dr. Howard Rusk noted. "Some companies didn't hire them at all. Others that had hired handicapped people during the war—when able-bodied labor was in short supply, and had capitalized on the public relations value of this wartime policy—were now firing them and replacing them with more able-bodied returning servicemen."[9]

In October of 1945, President Truman announced the establishment of the National Employ the Physically Handicapped Week to encourage private businesses to hire veterans with disabilities and bring "these people back into productive and useful citizenship."[10] The VA, the Surgeon General's Office, and the War Department rallied behind Truman and produced a series of short films on the topic with uplifting titles: *No Help Wanted, Voyage to Recovery, Half a Chance, Out of Bed into Action,* and *Toward Independence* (which won the Academy Award for best short documentary in 1948).

Complete with swelling music and jaunty narration, the films portrayed disabled veterans as model employees able to handle most every job, from teacher to architect to factory worker to X-ray technician. *Diary of a Sergeant* showed off the ability of double-hand amputee Harold Russell to tie his shoes and change a flat tire using his prostheses.

The films exhorted business leaders to look beyond the veterans' disabilities when hiring, noting that their "greatest handicap is you." The general public was told that the veterans were not looking for "a pity party," but instead wanted "a stake in the American future," just as every other citizen did.

Veterans with disabilities were informed that they could aspire to "a useful and independent life" so long as they followed their doctors' instructions. "You're getting better, you're looking forward instead of looking back," counseled one film. "You're going to be a better soldier and a better American."[11]

Stan Den Adel was featured in a VA production titled *What's My Score?*, a film about paraplegia and the ADL exercises. He was fortunate because the machine shop at Birmingham Hospital was falling behind schedule manufacturing braces for wounded veterans. Stan volunteered to help out and soon grasped the intricacies of the production process.

When an opening for a brace mechanic was listed, Stan applied for the position. He got the job and became the hospital's first full-time employee with a disability. He compiled a perfect attendance record as a brace-maker, and was hailed by hospital administrators as a "loyal and effective employee...in spite of disabilities considered to be permanent and total in extent." At a special ceremony held in the rec hall, he was saluted for showing that "in most cases, the handicapped person is a better worker and a more efficient and valuable employee than is the able-bodied worker."[12]

Pride was a crucial factor, Den Adel acknowledged. "There have been days when I didn't feel like going to work," he said. "Perhaps I had a fever. But I wanted to prove once and for all that we disabled veterans are worth employing, and I didn't want to spoil my record."[13]

★ ★ ★

Inevitably, disagreements arose between the injured veterans and the doctors in charge of their rehabilitation. The men sometimes felt like experimental subjects, little more than guinea pigs for their medical overseers to write about in prestigious scientific journals and to further their own careers. When Dr. Bors wanted to research the extent of sterility among the paralyzed veterans, they underwent uncomfortable tests and answered personal questions to help determine whether their reproductive cells could be stimulated.

One of the most contentious issues concerned ambulation. Bors and other physicians insisted that the paralyzed veterans learn how to use crutches and leg braces to walk. This would free them to venture places that were inaccessible to wheelchairs—which in 1946 was most places—as well as to climb steps and use public restrooms.

Getting around with crutches and braces was also perceived as more palatable to the public. Popular magazines published stirring dispatches from VA paraplegia wards that promised miracles: "We Will Walk" (*Saturday Evening Post*); "They Walk Again" (*Newsweek*); "Teaching the Crippled to Walk" (*Life*).[14]

Saturday Evening Post reporter Barrie Stavis watched Dr. William Kuhn, at a VA facility on the East Coast, harangue a patient who was reluctant to abandon his wheelchair. "Hey, Goldbrick, when are you going to get up out of that chair and stand on your feet?" said Kuhn, according to Stavis. "Stop living in an 'if' and 'maybe' world. Tomorrow you get out of that chair. Period. Tomorrow you stand on your own two feet. Period."[15]

Paralyzed veterans faced enormous pressure to step up and strap on. The ungainly braces, which extended from the heel to above the waist, weighed fifteen pounds each and took fifteen minutes to put on. They were uncomfortable when worn for long periods of time, and balancing on them was exceedingly difficult.

Den Adel persevered and became proficient enough to "walk" around the entire one-story hospital, a distance of about a mile and a half. Regaining his full, upright position after being in bed for a year gave him a tremendous psychological boost and allowed him to interact with others eye-to-eye. But, like many other paralyzed veterans, Stan decided to stick to the wheelchair as his primary means of locomotion.

The crutches were "downright dangerous except in a controlled environment," he noted. "Should one fall while using the crutches, it was impossible to get up without assistance—and then it took two people to help fellows like myself. Beyond that, it was impossible to carry anything while supported by crutches occupying both hands."[16]

★ ★ ★

For all the exercises that strengthened his upper-body muscles, and for all the activities that buoyed his spirits, it took two four-wheeled vehicles to truly liberate Stan Den Adel and other paralyzed veterans from the limitations of their disability.

The first was on display in the parking lot at Birmingham Hospital. There, a fleet of gleaming automobiles was lined up as if awaiting the start of the Indianapolis 500. They arrived after Congress authorized an assistance program that provided $1,600—then equivalent to about 85 percent of the retail cost of a new automobile—for the paralyzed veterans to purchase a car retrofitted with special adaptive equipment that allowed them to drive. The veterans were also given priority ordering rights ahead of the general public, a coveted edge in the postwar scramble for new cars.

Oldsmobile took the lead with its "Valiant Driving Controls" on models equipped with the Hydra-Matic transmission, the first transmission needing no clutch. A hand-operated brake-and-throttle system was mounted on the steering column; veterans simply had to push a lever to accelerate and pull it back to slow down. Other features that required foot or leg movements were moved or modified, and many drivers used spinner knobs to better control the steering wheel with one hand. (Oldsmobile also manufactured modifications for amputee veterans.)

Once Den Adel proved that he could operate the automobile, he took ownership of his mobility and autonomy. Having wheels in a society increasingly dependent on the automobile—particularly in car-friendly Southern California—was "by far the most effective rehabilitation tool devised to wean most of us from an institutionalized life [within] VA hospital wards," he noted.[17]

A different kind of four-wheeled conveyance proved to be equally useful in freeing paralyzed veterans from the binds of the hospital. Until the mid-1930s, wheelchair technology was an oxymoron. Wounded veterans (and civilians) who required such assistance had to rely on cumbersome, tank-like behemoths that weighed upward of 150 pounds. These chairs initially were made entirely of wood—including the wheels, until rubber was invented—and came with unmovable wicker backs and upholstered seats. Their oversize front wheels were so large that they couldn't fit through most standard doorways.

They were sitting chairs designed for permanent immobility: for patients cloistered in institutions and not expected to travel anywhere beyond the veranda, or for families who could afford to hire aides to push them. They were impractical for someone wanting to move around or live independently. The trite and offensive phrases "wheelchair-bound" and "confined to a wheelchair" were accurate.

Progress came because Herbert Everest yearned to escape those constraints. A graduate from the Colorado School of Mines, Everest was an experienced mining engineer and geologist. In 1918, he was fighting a fire inside a coal mine in Arkansas when he fractured his spine. He convalesced for several years after moving his family to the West Coast. When he tried to work again, he was frustrated by "the lack of a usable, folding wheelchair," he later said. "It just was not practical to tie the old hospital chair on the back bumper and go out on business errands."[18]

He fell into a dark depression. He was forty-eight years old. He couldn't support his family because no company would hire him. His future looked bleak until his wife happened upon a self-propelled, wooden wheelchair that he could fold and easily put inside the car. The contraption practically had to be rebuilt after each outing, but it brightened his mood. He had his freedom back.

The contrivance whetted Everest's appetite to create what he described as "a chair strong enough to stand the gaff"—meaning, a flexible chair that could withstand harsh treatment and handling. He enlisted the assistance of Harry Jennings, a non-disabled mechanical engineer, and a solution soon emerged that revolutionized mobility for people with paraplegia. Working together out of Jennings's garage in Southern California, they fashioned a comfortable, foldable wheelchair made of chromium-plated steel tubing.[19]

They shifted the two large wheels to the rear so that users could easily and comfortably propel the chair, and they placed two small casters in the front to provide greater stability and turning power. Lightweight, synthetic leather was used for the backing and the seat; with its cross-brace system, the twenty-four-inch-wide chairs could be folded easily and compactly to a width of ten inches. Each chair weighed about forty pounds, less than half the weight of the rigid-frame, oak-body models.

Everest and Jennings had cracked the code. They formed an eponymous business and filed patents for their design in 1936, just in time for the outbreak of World War II. Government contracts and positive word-of-mouth followed, and the company's manufacturing plant in Los Angeles soon couldn't keep up with demand. The E&Js were so popular among paralyzed veterans that there was a three-month waiting list after the war.

"I bought one for some astronomical sum," Gene Fesenmeyer said. "There weren't that many wheelchair companies back then. The E&J was considered to be the Cadillac. They were tons lighter. That made all the difference."

Combined, the adaptive cars and the foldable, lightweight wheelchairs unshackled previously home- or hospital-restricted paralyzed veterans. With some practice, Stan Den Adel could slide into his E&J by his bed at Birmingham Hospital, wheel himself out to the parking lot they dubbed "Oldsmobile Row," hoist himself into the driver's seat, fold up and stow the E&J in the back of the car, and cruise toward freedom and empowerment.

"We were no longer dependent on someone else to provide us transportation," he later noted. "Travel, education, recreation, romance, employment were all, for the first time since our injuries, within the realm of reality."[20]

Herbert Everest and Harry Jennings were practical-minded engineers intent on creating modern wheelchairs for those with paraplegia. When they etched their initials on the footboards of their wheelchairs, one aspect they didn't consider was whether their invention could be used for sports.

Stan Den Adel and other paralyzed veterans would do so, however. When they wheeled onto the basketball court in "the chair that adds the way to the will," they turned their E&Js into instruments of recreation and created a new paradigm for adaptive sports.

CHAPTER 8

Tip-Off

The way it started, Stan Den Adel recalled, was casual, unplanned, organic.

In early 1946, he and other patients from Birmingham's Ward C, all of them paralyzed veterans, would complete their mat exercises and then gather inside the gym to watch the action on the basketball court. The gym was a popular spot that spring, when a physical education instructor and basketball fanatic named Bob Rynearson was hired to oversee the sports program for veterans at the hospital.

Rynearson had organized a rec league for non-disabled servicemen and staff (including himself) as well as local teams around Van Nuys. Afterward, as the players toweled off, Stan and other paralyzed veterans would roll their wheelchairs onto the polished floor and take turns awkwardly lofting the ball toward the net, until a few of the men were alternately shooting and reaching skyward to halfheartedly defend against the shots, and trading jibes, and hooting when Kansas native Patterson "Pat" Grissom, wounded in March of 1945, flipped over his chair while driving for a layup.

What resonated with Rynearson were the expressions on the men's faces. They were excited, gleeful, engaged, and totally unselfconscious about their chairs. And, when they raced for the ball and passed it around, they showed a preternatural grace.

A thought struck Rynearson: why not use basketball, his favorite sport, as part of their rehab activity? He spoke to Den Adel and the others and invited them to a practice. "Maybe we can have some fun together," he said.[1]

Born in Salt Lake City, Bob Rynearson was a Valley boy. He'd grown up not far from where Birmingham Hospital was built, back when the hills and valleys stretching from the city of Los Angeles toward the foothills of the San Gabriel Mountains produced oranges and lemons, walnuts and apricots, olives and tomatoes, with a side helping of poultry and dairy. Farming was fast disappearing as the vast acreage of the Valley was divided and subdivided among movie studios, automobile and airplane factories, and the development of mile after square mile of single-family homes.

In this suburban playground, Bob played every sport. His father, George Arthur Rynearson, coached basketball, track, and gymnastics at Van Nuys High. The school was gaining a reputation for producing outstanding athletes, most notably future Hall of Fame quarterback Bob Waterfield and, later, Hall of Fame pitcher Don Drysdale. (Before entering the service in 1943, Waterfield married his Van Nuys High sweetheart, actress Jane Russell.)

Rynearson earned All-Valley first team honors in basketball. A true coach's son, he was a student of the game: learning proper technique, knowing the rulebook, drawing up offensive plays, devising defenses. He entered the University of California, Los Angeles, a straight shot ten miles down Sepulveda Boulevard, and played freshman basketball while majoring in business admin-istration and physical education and working part-time for Los Angeles's Department of Playground and Recreation.

War interrupted his college education; he would not graduate from UCLA until 1958. He worked as a sheet-metal fabricator and assembler at Timm Aircraft Corporation, in Southern California, from 1940 until May of 1944. Then he was shipped to boot camp at Farragut Naval Training Station in northern Idaho. Just before he was to have been deployed overseas, he was hospitalized with appendicitis. Instead of fighting in Europe, he assembled and repaired aircraft at the Puget Sound Naval Shipyard in Bremerton, Washington.

By then he was married to a dynamo named Frances; they met while they both worked as lifeguards. The couple bought a home in the community of Granada Hills, by the Santa Susana Mountains, and started a family. In April of 1946, at the age of twenty-five, Rynearson was hired as the assistant athletic director at Birmingham VA Hospital, in his hometown of Van Nuys, with an annual salary of $2,320.

★ ★ ★

Before World War II, sports was considered out of bounds for "crippled bodies," a term that President Roosevelt himself used. No organized wheelchair sports team or sports program existed for people with spinal-cord injuries.

A select few elite athletes had managed to succeed in spite of their disabilities. Mordecai Brown's right hand was mangled in a farming mishap when he was a child. "Three Finger" Brown became a Hall of Fame pitcher because his gnarled grip made the baseball spin violently when he hurled it toward the plate. Olivér Halassy was a one-legged amputee water polo player who helped Hungary win two gold medals and one silver medal at the Olympics. Amputee outfielder Pete Gray enjoyed a seventy-seven-game stint with the St. Louis Browns in the waning days of World War II. "The One-Armed Wonder" batted a not-so-wondrous .218. William "Dummy" Hoy, an excellent centerfielder with several major league teams, was one of several deaf ballplayers to play in the majors during the late nineteenth and early twentieth centuries.

They were the exceptions that proved the rule. That the athletes' nicknames—"Three Finger," "One-Armed Wonder," "Dummy"—blatantly referenced their disability is perhaps as noteworthy as their athletic skills.

After World War II, the VA brass under General Omar Bradley viewed recreation to be an essential part of the rehabilitation process for wounded servicemen. The objective was to boost morale and to "help the doctor get the patient well." Anything to keep the idle hands of young men busy.

The VA's Special Services division offered a full menu of canteen, chaplaincy, library, and sports activities. Their definition of recreation was as broad as the San Fernando Valley: at Birmingham there were table tennis and bowling tournaments; Monte Carlo nights; visits from sports celebrities and Hollywood stars; screenings of the latest movies; road trips to watch college football at the nearby Rose Bowl in Pasadena; instruction in art, chess, and music; drama and entertainment productions.

As assistant athletic director at Birmingham, Bob Rynearson's directive was to offer sports options to the veterans. He purchased volleyball nets, baseball gloves, and bows, arrows, and targets. A cavalcade of Hollywood stars passed their fedoras to raise funds to build an outdoor swimming pool amid the hospital's well-manicured grounds.

Paralyzed veterans offered a complex set of challenges when it came to sports. Sure, they could float and paddle around once they were assisted into a lake or pool. And, sure, archery was an excellent activity to increase their upper-body strength. But traditional athletic alternatives were seemingly not open to them because they couldn't walk, run, or jump. There was no history or culture of wheelchair sports to draw upon because, prior to the invention of the E&J, the clunky and intractable wheelchairs were unsuitable for sports.

Rynearson struggled to find a team sport that the paralyzed veterans could enjoy together. Attempts at wheelchair baseball and wheelchair volleyball met with partial success. Rehabilitation had its limits—or so it seemed—until the moment Rynearson saw Stan Den Adel and other paralyzed vets goofing around on the basketball court.

★ ★ ★

Baseball is known as the national pastime. Many have described football as our national religion. Neither of them boasts 100 percent American roots. Baseball originated from an amalgam of British games, including cricket and rounders, while football devolved from rugby and soccer.

Basketball is truly indigenous. *Life* magazine described it as "the only purely American major sport in the U.S."[2] It was invented in December of 1891 by James Naismith, a Canadian-born instructor in physical education at the International YMCA Training School (now known as Springfield College) in Springfield, Massachusetts. His boss, Luther Gulick, the head of the school's physical education department, gave Naismith, then thirty years old, two weeks to concoct a recreational activity that could be played indoors during New England winters.

Naismith made several false starts before settling on an original concept. He nailed a pair of peach baskets high above the floor on opposite walls of the school gymnasium and brought out an old soccer ball. The object of the game was simple: whichever team scored the most baskets during two fifteen-minute halves was declared the winner. A secretary typed up the thirteen rules of an invention Naismith dubbed "Basket Ball."

Basketball spread outside the YMCA like a well-orchestrated fast break. Requiring only a ball and two hoops, the sport appealed to everyone: "bluebloods and immigrants, farmers and city folk, girls as well as boys...There were all-Catholic teams, women's college teams, small-town teams, military teams, industrial teams, teams composed of theological seminarians, and colored teams and white teams," according to basketball historian Scott Ellsworth.[3]

The game, the rules, and the equipment soon evolved beyond Naismith's initial blueprint. String nets and iron rims replaced the peach baskets. Wooden backboards were hammered into place. The number of players was winnowed from nine per side to five, and dribbling was permitted. A company called Converse introduced the Chuck Taylor line of rubber-soled sneakers.

Global interest expanded after World War I. The South American championships arrived in 1930 and the European championships in 1935. A "demonstration sport" at the 1904 Summer Olympics in St. Louis, basketball made its official Olympic debut at the 1936 Berlin Games.

Naismith, then seventy-four, accompanied the U.S. contingent, composed primarily of players selected from the rosters of two Amateur Athletic Union (AAU) teams: the Universal Pictures squad from Hollywood and the McPherson Globe Refiners from Kansas. In Berlin, Naismith's adopted country defeated Canada, his birthplace, to win the inaugural gold medal in a game played on a muddy outdoor court in a driving rainstorm.

Final score: 19–8. The United States would not lose another Olympic basketball contest until 1972.

During World War II, every branch of the U.S. armed forces organized camp and base leagues. The service squads pulled together the regional strands of hoopdom into a red-white-and-blue mixture: Indiana farm boys playing alongside Jewish kids from Brooklyn playing alongside Ivy League grads from New England playing alongside Native Americans from tribal reservations in the Southwest.

Basketball reached its adolescence after the war, although it was still primitive by today's standards. The jump shot was a quirky maneuver that few players attempted, much less pulled off, and dunking the ball was unheard of. The twenty-four-second clock—which gives a team twenty-four seconds to put up a shot once it gains possession of the ball—hadn't been invented yet, so the games tended to be low-scoring, plodding affairs. Collegiate basketball was much more popular than the scattered professional and semi-pro industrial leagues.

At first blush, wheelchairs and basketball seemed a particularly unlikely combination. Height is an important factor in basketball, of course, and no one sitting in a wheelchair can boast about that. Basketball also demands constant motion: running, dribbling, rebounding, passing, playing defense, moving up and down the court. Even though the game's pace was slower in the 1940s than it is today, it was difficult to imagine that veterans with paraplegia could simultaneously control the forward, backward, and lateral trajectories of their chairs; avoid collisions with the nine other players on the court; manage all of the ball skills associated with the sport; and maintain balance without falling out of their chairs. Oh, and muscle the ball up to the rim and score, too.

Birmingham's cramped indoor gym raised numerous safety

issues. A dozen steel columns stretching toward the rafters lined the court, and bleachers extended almost to the out-of-bounds lines. Players had to be wary of slamming into these immovable obstacles or crashing into the cement walls mere inches beyond the baseline.

Rynearson could picture other cringe-worthy accidents, including overturned chairs and violent fender-benders. A paralyzed veteran might fracture his leg and not realize it because he couldn't feel anything below his hips.

But the more Rynearson watched the veterans in motion, the more advantages he saw. The court's smooth, flat surface was far superior for rolling wheels than dirt or grass fields, and the space was plenty large enough to accommodate ten wheelchair athletes. Basketball can be played year-round—indoors on hardwood and outdoors on pavement—and the upper-body contortions required for dribbling, passing, rebounding, and shooting the ball produced a sweat-filled workout in the upper chest, arms, and shoulders, precisely the areas of the body where people with paraplegia most need the exercise.

What persuaded him to move forward were the veterans themselves. Rynearson was a true believer in the value of rigorous sports; that training to defeat an opponent motivates athletes to strive to get better, even if that opponent is only himself. He also recognized that veterans who'd played sports on their high school, college, and service teams missed the competition. They not only wanted to play basketball; they needed to play basketball.

As for the prospect of injuries, the veterans could only guffaw. "I was shot during the war. I'm paralyzed for life and wearing a diaper. You think I'm worried about getting hit by a basketball?" was a typical refrain.

Rynearson configured a set of ten rules for the new game:

the four-wheeled equivalent of Naismith's "13 Rules." His goal was to maintain the pace of two-legged basketball without jeopardizing the players' safety, and to align as closely as possible to Naismith's original vision. That way, the players would only need to make minimal adjustments, and spectators could readily understand what they were watching.

His most perceptive insight was that the wheelchair, which he called "the means of ambulation,"[4] should be considered as the natural and integral extension of the player's body. Common-place, incidental contact between opponents' chairs was tolerated, but deliberately ramming an opponent's chair was prohibited and resulted in a personal foul.

Players were allowed two pushes on their wheels while in possession of the ball, after which they were required to pass, dribble, or shoot. Continuous dribbling was permitted, although the men found that dribbling and steering the chairs simultaneously was tricky business. Free throws were taken with the back wheels on the foul line. Teams were allowed twenty seconds to advance the ball from the back to the front court, and players were limited to six seconds in the free-throw lane area.[5]

Crucial decisions concerned whether to lower the rims from the standard height of ten feet and whether to shorten the distance from the free-throw line (located fifteen feet from the backboard). The veterans opposed this and characterized such changes as demeaning and condescending. Their viewpoint prevailed.[6]

Rynearson relinquished recruiting chores to wide-smiling Stan Den Adel. He didn't have to do much arm-twisting to wrangle the first set of players. Their ages ranged from twenty-two to forty-one; several were married, but most were single. They hailed from California, Idaho, Iowa, Colorado, Oklahoma, and points in between, and had been wounded in the European and the Pacific theaters. Most were army veterans, with a smattering of navy men and marines.

Pat Grissom gave up his farm deferment to join the 3rd Infantry Division; he was wounded by enemy fire in Worms, Germany. Kay Kentner was born in Samoa, and graduated from Montebello High School in Southern California before joining the navy. He was wounded aboard the USS *Boston* in the Admiralty Islands in October 1944. Jess Rodriguez went overseas with the Army's 34th Infantry Division and fought in Tunisia and Sicily; he was wounded at Cassino, Italy, by enemy machine-gun fire.

Ed Santillanes was an all-city baseball player at Jacob Riis High School in Los Angeles, with aspirations to play for the University of Southern California. He was injured near the Rhine River with the 65th Infantry Division when the jeep he was driving on patrol hit a roadside mine and rolled several times, with Santillanes pinned to the steering column.

"It was just fun getting out there to play basketball," he said. "The hardest thing was trying to dribble while you're in a wheelchair. You didn't just put the ball in your lap and take off like a bat out of hell. We made it part of our rehab. It was about exercising."[7]

★ ★ ★

Rynearson saw progress at every practice. The veterans grew adept at maneuvering their chairs with one hand while passing the ball with the other. They figured out how to set screens with their chairs that blocked their opponents and allowed teammates to get open and score. They discovered favorite spots on the court where they could shoot with a decent percentage. They learned how to quickly hoist themselves back into their chairs after they'd spilled to the floor.

It was time, Rynearson realized, to let them loose against another team. He didn't have to look far to find a worthy, if mismatched, foe.

On November 25, 1946, he arranged for the paralyzed veterans to play their first game. Led by Den Adel, Grissom, and Santillanes, they rolled onto the court at the Birmingham gym. Their opponent? A squad of doctors from Birmingham Hospital using wheelchairs they borrowed for the occasion. Rynearson himself donned the black-and-white-striped referee's shirt.

The veterans dressed informally, as if they were going to the corner store. They wore plain white T-shirts and long trousers. Most players were using leg bags, which attached to catheters to collect their urine, so the long pants offered some measure of concealment. Leather shoes protected their feet.

The spectators, scattered in seats around the gym, could tell immediately that four-wheeled basketball was very different from the two-legged version. The high-pitched squeak of rubber sneakers was replaced by the muted whirling of rubber tires tracking across the court. The clash of bodies in the air contending for a rebound gave way to a pileup of wheelchairs beneath the basket.

What remained the same was the swish of the ball cutting cleanly through the net, the musky aroma of sweaty athletes, the shrill whistle of the referee, the one-on-one and the five-on-five configurations and improvisations that make basketball an athletic form of chess.

And, it didn't take a coach's son to see that the competition itself, what today is regarded as the first organized wheelchair basketball game ever played, was a mismatch. The veterans took advantage of their experience manipulating their wheelchairs to score the first six points. They let up and held an 8–6 advantage at halftime, then poured it on in the second half while blanking the doctors.

"'Plegics Win Wheelchair Game, 16 to 6," was the headline in *The Birmingham Reporter* newsletter.[8]

"Call it the most unusual basketball game ever played— or the first time in the United States that paraplegics have entered competitive sports in wheelchairs—or simply say it was an action-packed, fast-moving and exciting contest," read the report, accompanied by a black-and-white action photograph. "Birmingham hospital...again proved that men paralyzed from the waist down are not doomed to a restricted life of inactivity if they have the will to overcome the handicap."[9]

A brief article about the game and the "spine-shattered" vets appeared shortly afterward in the *Los Angeles Times*. "The way those plucky lads jockey their wheelchairs around the premises reminds one of the Sunday drivers on the Arroyo Seco Speed-way," wrote columnist Braven Dyer, in a jocular reference to the name of the city's first freeway. "The vets made the medics look like a bunch of palookas."[10]

Rynearson was especially pleased that the players emerged unhurt (except for the doctors' pride). He immediately sched-uled contests with other non-disabled teams who were willing to play in borrowed wheelchairs. The vets defeated the doctors in a rematch, 21–7, then whipped the hospital's squad of correc-tive physical rehabilitation therapists. They beat the John Lloyd Sporting Goods team, 33–16, and outlasted Goldwater Tailors, 28–26, in triple overtime. They even journeyed from the hospital to play: they claimed victories at the Long Beach Auditorium, the Pan-Pacific Auditorium, and the Shrine Auditorium.

Their audacity and renown drew fans to gyms across the Southland. "We got tired of having people stare at us just because we were sitting in these chairs," Den Adel said. "Now they watch us because we are doing something. We're beating the able-bodied teams right off of the floor, and we proved to be faster, better shooters [and] had more stamina and toughened hands. The crowds loved it."[11]

And so did their doctors. "The patient's desire to play basketball or water polo, bowling or archery, is making his mental and physical rehabilitation a voluntary pleasure," Dr. Bors said.[12]

★ ★ ★

Across the country from Van Nuys, some three thousand miles away, paralyzed veterans at Cushing VA Hospital in Framingham, Massachusetts, were assembling the first wheelchair basketball team on the East Coast.

Named in honor of Dr. Harvey Cushing, the pioneering neurosurgeon who performed heroic work on the front lines during World War I, Cushing Hospital featured more than two miles of enclosed, heated hallways as well as three recreation halls. Dr. Donald Munro, whose novel treatment of civilians with paraplegia greatly influenced how Dr. Bors approached the rehabilitation of paralyzed veterans, supervised Cushing's neurosurgery department and its approximately four hundred paralyzed veterans.

Munro placed sports under the care of the hospital's athletic director, George Radulski, the former captain of the Boston University football team. Radulski first used the basketball itself as a workout tool: he played catch with paralyzed veterans as they lay in bed to strengthen their upper-body muscles, akin to exercising with a medicine ball.

In 1946, around the same time that Birmingham's team was forming, paralyzed veterans took to the Cushing gym and started playing wheelchair basketball under the supervision of Radulski and physical instructor Roe Laramee.[13]

Cushing's team boasted an array of skilled athletes. Sharp-shooting forward Dick Foley was a prized minor-league prospect with the Brooklyn Dodgers before the war, but he never got a chance to catch a game for the Olean Oilers. He parachuted into Holland with the 542nd Parachute Raider Battalion and was felled by mortar shell fragments that severed his spine.

Foley was joined by Greg Seymourian, injured at Anzio, Italy; Don "Red" Kratzer, a former Penn State football player who lost the use of his legs while serving with the 68th Tank Battalion; sparkplug Joe Villa, wounded in Europe in late 1944; and Manny Leonardo, who fought with the 7th Armored Division in Europe.

Their brand of ball evolved differently than Birmingham's. Players were permitted to race down the length of the court, holding the ball in their lap, without having to dribble or pass after two pushes on their wheels. And even incidental contact involving wheelchairs was whistled and called a foul.

The team's twice-a-week scrimmages became so popular that the court was overrun with participants. "Sometimes we have to have ten men on a team," Radulski said. "Everybody wants to get into the game. [It's] the best kind of physical therapy. The men are exercising hard, painlessly."[14]

On December 5, 1946, Cushing's team of paralyzed veterans ventured into Boston Garden for their first game outside the hospital. Their opponent was none other than the Boston Celtics.

Boston and other big-city teams (including New York, Chicago, St. Louis, Philadelphia, and Toronto) had recently formed a new professional league, the Basketball Association of America (BAA). Celtics owner Walter Brown was embracing all manner of promotions, including wheelchair basketball, in his team's maiden season.

That night, the Celtics—coached by John "Honey" Russell—were preparing to face the Detroit Falcons in a BAA showdown. Apparently, they overlooked their preliminary foe. Cushing's paralyzed veterans easily whipped the green-shirted pros, who were inept in their borrowed wheelchairs, 18–2, and would have blanked them except for a blind overhead toss by the Celtics' diminutive guard Mel Hirsch, who'd served in the army as a navigator with the "Thirsty 13th" transport squadron in the South Pacific.

Boston was awful their first year—their record fell to 3–12 after their loss to the Falcons—and the *Framingham News* joked that Cushing's thrashing "proved right the fellow who said of [the Celtics] after they had dropped several previous contests: 'Why, a team in wheelchairs could beat these guys.'"[15]

The Celtics demanded a rematch, and Cushing was happy to oblige. Two nights later, on the fifth anniversary of the attack on Pearl Harbor, Boston hosted the New York Knicks. The pros again borrowed wheelchairs, as well as a few players from the Knicks, and took on Cushing at halftime. The veterans prevailed again—and then the Celtics lost again to the Knicks.

In 1949, the BAA merged with the National Basketball League and created a new league: the National Basketball Association (NBA). The formation of the NBA halted the disharmony within the professional basketball ranks and, in so doing, created a solid foundation for James Naismith's invention to grow into the modern era.

The wheelchair version of basketball was just getting rolling, too, and already the first rivalry within the sport was being seeded. Paralyzed veterans from Birmingham and Cushing hospitals were squabbling even before they'd played a game against each other. Both teams claimed to be the true originator of wheelchair basketball; both teams claimed that their set of rules should be the sport's standard.

When Birmingham and Cushing—Los Angeles and Boston—finally met on the court, in the winter of 1948, their simmering feud would make newspaper headlines. And how their tussle over the rules was resolved would profoundly affect the development of the fledgling sport.

CHAPTER 9

Naval Hospital, Corona

When Gene Fesenmeyer was driven to the main entrance of the Naval Hospital at Corona, he thought he'd been admitted into heaven. He couldn't believe that the magnificent clubhouse and the lush grounds were part of a hospital. The expansive property looked more like a millionaire's fantasy wonderland come to life.

Which, in fact, it was. Rex B. Clark has been described variously as a scalawag, a racist, a genius, and a visionary who married into money. His wife was Grace Scripps, the daughter of publishing tycoon James Scripps, founder of the *Detroit News*. Clark didn't get along with his father-in-law, and he moved with Grace to Southern California to make his own fortune.

Just after World War I, he purchased fifteen square miles of inhospitable agricultural terrain about fifty miles east of downtown Los Angeles. There, he set about creating a farming community for poultry ranchers near the community of Corona. He named the town Norco, for north of Corona.

Clark changed course after discovering pockets of hot mineral water amidst the alfalfa fields. By 1926, he was showing off plans for a $1.5 million luxe spa that he hoped would lure the

Hollywood elite and other well-heeled visitors from Los Angeles. He purchased Pasadena's Oak Knoll Nursery for $30,000 and transported its entirety—plants, shrubs, trees, soil, and tools—to Norco. Construction costs ballooned past $4 million. Three years later, in a grand opening studded with movie stars and sports heroes, Clark unveiled a stunning showpiece that he christened the Norconian Resort Supreme.

The Norconian more than lived up to its grandiose name. Architect Dwight Gibbs designed the Spanish Mediterranean-style clubhouse, complete with a spacious ballroom, lounge, indoor baths, ornate Catalina tiles, elegant painted ceilings and murals, and hand-forged, wrought-iron chandeliers. Surrounding the building was an oasis for the rich and leisured: a sixty-acre lake, an eighteen-hole golf course created by the prominent Scottish golf course architect John Duncan Dunn, swimming and diving pools, hiking trails, horse stables, a private airfield, and a casino.[1]

Business boomed. Buster Keaton, Joe E. Brown, Babe Ruth, James Cagney, and Gary Cooper came to golf, gambol, and gamble. Olympic gold-medal swimmer Duke Kahanamoku splashed in the mammoth pool; Amelia Earhart practiced her airplane landings; and film director E. Mason Hopper used the Norconian to shoot *Their Own Desire*, starring Norma Shearer and Robert Montgomery, with a screenplay co-written by Frances Marion.

Clark's timing, however, was awful. The stock market crashed less than a year after the resort opened, plunging the nation into the Great Depression. Business sputtered; the celebrities vanished. Clark divorced Grace and married his longtime mistress. The Norconian closed, opened again, until what was now dubbed "Rex's Folly" was shuttered for good in 1940.

President Franklin Roosevelt authorized the purchase of the

Norconian for $2 million in a deal that closed right before the attack on Pearl Harbor. The U.S. government handed over the property to the navy, and Los Angeles-based architect Claude Beelman was retained to convert the Norconian into a hospital complex. Separate nurses' quarters, administration and patient wings, a chapel, a gymnasium stocked with the latest apparatus for corrective exercises, and a theater were added to the original buildings at an estimated cost of $15 million. The boathouse was turned into an officers' club.

As it turned out, the spa facilities and the mineral springs that made the Norconian such an attractive resort were ideally suited for rehabilitation purposes. Survivors from Pearl Harbor were among the first patients to be admitted, and then veterans with tuberculosis. Shortly thereafter, Corona was selected to be the West Coast center for the treatment of veterans with spinal-cord injuries, primarily navy sailors and marines who had served in the Pacific theater.

First lady Eleanor Roosevelt toured the hospital and came away impressed by its grandeur. "The grounds have been well landscaped and, as you go in, you think you are in an attractive hotel, which must be a pleasant atmosphere for the convalescent boys," she wrote in "My Day," her syndicated newspaper column. "There is an indoor swimming pool and individual baths, where the patients can have the benefit of hot sulphur water. I should think there are great possibilities for therapeutic treatment of all kinds."[2]

★ ★ ★

Gene Fesenmeyer arrived at Corona in horrible condition. He described himself as "all knees, elbows, and eyeballs" because he'd lost so much weight. He was wracked by severe nerve pain and plagued by bedsores. "I had just as well give it to you straight," he wrote in a letter to his parents. "I'll never be any better."[3]

He did get better, albeit slowly. Attendants plunked him in an old wooden wheelchair and rolled him outside, where he had a view of the foothills. He soaked in the sun wearing just his pajama bottoms and sunglasses, while the scent from the orange groves wafted overhead. He was fed ample portions of raw steak for protein and, as he gained weight, doctors began to treat his bedsores.

"I had pressure sores on pressure sores," he said later. "That was worse than the bullet wound. Lots worse. It wasn't pain exactly. You're laying there in bed. You were just rotting away, is what it amounts to. Time didn't mean much to us."

Gene credited Dr. Gerald Gray with nursing him back to health. Gray had attended the University of California at Berkeley and Harvard Medical School before returning to his native Oakland to practice plastic surgery in the city's Pill Hill neighborhood (so named for the many hospitals and doctors located there). Gray's wife was Patricia "Patsey" Virginia Clark, an equestrian who'd grown up in comfort on a 470-acre estate in San Mateo County known as House-on-Hill. Patsey's mother was Celia Tobin Clark, an heiress to the Hibernia Bank fortune who had married and divorced Charles Walker Clark, the eldest son of Montana's "copper king."[4]

During World War II, Dr. Gray donated his professional services as a "dollar-a-year man" for the navy. Always fashionably dressed in a well-tailored suit, with touches of distinguished silver in his neatly parted dark hair, Gray moved with his wife and their growing family to Corona. They bunked at the sprawling Fuller RanchO, across the Santa Ana River, about two miles from the hospital, in horse country that suited Patsey.

His duties included performing reconstructive surgery on veterans who'd sustained facial wounds. Gray rebuilt their noses, mouths, and ears to restore functionality and to improve their appearance. He also worked on burn victims who'd been injured aboard exploding vessels or who'd been exposed to leaked oil that was set ablaze. Like the veterans with paraplegia, these veterans were the first generation to survive their horrific wounds, thanks to penicillin, albumin, topical dressings, and other advances in burn treatment. Gray tended to their injuries with skin grafts, a painstaking method of transplanting healthy skin tissue from uninjured areas of their bodies to the damaged areas.

Gene Fesenmeyer went to Gray because he had developed an enormous pressure sore on the end of his sacrum, near the tailbone. He recalled that four hundred stitches were required to close it. "Doc Gray saved my life," he often said. "I wouldn't have made it without him."

He embraced his second chance and vowed to live life to the fullest. The townsfolk of Shambaugh and Clarinda had chipped in to raise funds for him. Gene used the money to purchase a Cadillac convertible equipped with hand controls. When he felt better, he drove across country to visit with family and friends in Iowa.

The long driveway leading to his parents' farmhouse was a muddy track. He had to park the car by the paved road, but couldn't negotiate the path with his E&J wheelchair. His brother Fred drove the tractor out to meet him, deposited Gene and his wheelchair in the tractor bed, and carried him home. As the mud splattered up from the big tractor, they laughed and laughed.[5]

His father excused him from having to get up at five in the morning to feed the hogs. But Gene discovered that the old homestead didn't suit his new condition. The winter was numbingly cold; transporting himself to the distant outhouse required the sort of advance planning that the Allies had used on D-Day.

"Wheelchairs and snow don't mix," he concluded.

On nights that Gene and his brothers went out drinking, he'd drive through town at around midnight blowing the car horn as a personal greeting. The mayor of Shambaugh came out to speak with his father and politely asked him to refrain from making so much noise.

Another time, he ran his car off the road with two other veterans aboard as passengers. A passerby who saw the accident called a wrecker to pull them to safety; thankfully, no one was hurt. Not long after that, Gene "hauled ass" for the sunny climes of Corona, surrounded by capable doctors and nurses and by fellow paralyzed veterans who knew exactly what he was going through.

★ ★ ★

In early 1947, Dr. Gray drove to Van Nuys to consult with Dr. Bors about the treatment of paralyzed veterans after they were discharged from the hospital. Later, inside Birmingham's sweatbox gym, he watched Bob Rynearson's team play wheelchair basketball. He was amazed at the veterans' grace and agility when they ran the offensive plays that Rynearson had devised and impressed when they worked together on defense to protect the rim. He saw violent spills and near-instant recoveries, and heard the players trade insults that reverberated against the gym's concrete walls.

At Corona, Dr. Edward Lowman, a physical medicine and rehabilitation specialist, ran the hospital's vibrant athletic program, with assistance from the staff physiatrist, Dr. Rodney Chamberlain. The navy used the hospital as a backdrop for the five-minute film *Voyage to Recovery*, which featured some of the innumerable sports options available to the veterans. Former patients described making informal, casual attempts at playing wheelchair basketball as early as the fall of 1945.

But the action Dr. Gray witnessed at Birmingham was different. The game was spirited, the men engaged. This was about competition: let the best man win, and on to the next shot and the next play.

Gray consulted with Rynearson and asked him how he'd organized the sport and scheduled games against other teams. Rynearson gave Gray a printed list of his thirteen rules, and the plastic surgeon hurried back to Corona with one desire: to spread what he called "the gospel of wheelchair basketball."[6]

He requisitioned several basketballs and, after receiving permission from the navy to allow wheelchairs on the shiny floor of the new gymnasium, passed word that a wheelchair basketball team was forming.

His first recruit was a patient whom Gray had grown quite fond of.

★ ★ ★

Johnny Winterholler had been transferred to the Naval Hospital at Corona from Mare Island in November of 1945. Dessa rented a place nearby so that she could be close to her husband and his doctors.

Things were looking up for Johnny. He was put on a high-calorie diet and given vitamin supplements to help him regain some of the weight and strength he'd lost during captivity. Dr. Gray repaired the ulcerated areas of his body and helped with his general rehabilitation efforts. He also collected several thousand dollars in salary that had accrued during his time in the camps.

Johnny succeeded in achieving one of his immediate goals: he learned to walk using leg braces and "Canadian crutches" (which are shorter than regular underarm crutches).

"Johnny Walks Now," read the headline in the *Salt Lake Tribune*.[7] Another story exulted, "He is now able to take 25 steps with the aid of crutches."[8] But like many other veterans, Johnny found that he preferred using a wheelchair as his primary means of getting around.

He told Dessa that he wanted to forget the Philippines "because that phase of my existence is behind me and a new one is beginning."[9] He rarely, if ever, spoke about his POW experience, even privately to family members, a reticence that was common among veterans of his generation.

Memories of the war intruded in ways expected and unexpected. Many journalists kept reporting that Johnny had survived the Bataan Death March, the details of which had finally reached the general public. He repeatedly denied this, but outlets printed the falsehood anyway.

Having been held captive for three years, Johnny had to file a detailed report with the Armed Forces bureaucrats about his captivity. He was called to testify to the War Crimes Office about the atrocities he had witnessed and, specifically, about the torture incident at Cabanatuan.[10] (In 1947, Shigeji Mori, the implicated officer, was found guilty and sentenced to confinement at hard labor for life. Much to the prisoners' dismay, Mori and other Japanese war criminals were eventually pardoned and released.)

Johnny's past kept colliding with the present. He and Captain John Burns had both been attached to the 1st Separate Battalion.

They grew to be close friends before they were captured on Corregidor and imprisoned in the Philippines. They hadn't seen each other in three years until the day Burns returned to his room at Corona to greet his new roomie: Johnny Winterholler, sitting in a wheelchair.

Neither man uttered a word for at least two minutes until Winterholler broke the ice. "Don't you recognize me, John?" he asked.

"I recognized you all right," Burns replied, "but I was just so surprised I couldn't speak."[11]

Burns was readying to resume his career in the marines. Johnny had to figure out a different path. He officially retired from the marines in December of 1946 with 100 percent disability. During his internment, he had received several promotions; the final one came by virtue of the Silver Star.

Colonel John Winterholler was now thirty years old. He was getting stronger by the day, but he was also approaching a crucial crossroads. Where were he and Dessa going to live? How was he going to make a living?

Those questions went unanswered for now. After Dr. Gray persuaded him to join the wheelchair basketball team at Corona, Johnny found temporary solace in the gym, the place where he'd enjoyed his greatest moments before the war.

When Johnny had stood close to six feet tall, dribbling the ball and shooting were as natural as walking. He'd moved around the court by instinct, with an unmatched fluidity of motion. Playing basketball in a wheelchair required a different approach. He had to learn how to simultaneously steer his wheelchair while moving and handling the ball. Once he figured out the angles of the game, once he understood that he had to rely on the muscles in his chest, shoulders, arms, and wrists for passing and shooting, he transformed into the four-wheeled "Spider" of Corona.

"Johnny was the star immediately," Gene Fesenmeyer said. "He got his weight back a little bit from being in prison. He had a beautiful build on him. He was a real athlete, as strong as could be. He could shoot that sucker."

Gray turned over the coaching reins to William O'Connell. The lieutenant from South Dakota had spent five years with the marines, seeing action in the Mediterranean and the Pacific. He received a Purple Heart after being wounded in the Solomons.

O'Connell didn't require a wheelchair; he got around on crutches. The players nicknamed him "Wild Bill," because he was "a crazy sonofabitch," Fesenmeyer said. "At Corona, he'd get drunk and go jump into the lake."

O'Connell recruited the rest of the squad from the pool of paralyzed veterans at Corona. "Pistol Pete" Simon, twenty-two and a rugged sort from Baton Rouge, Louisiana, had been a radioman with a squadron of Martin Mariner patrol bombers when he was wounded. Louis Largey had joined the marines for the Pacific campaign; the tank commander contracted polio while assigned to duty in China after the war.

At twenty-one, Fesenmeyer was the youngest member of the team. "Hell, I wouldn't have done it except for Doc Gray," he said. "He got us playing. I wasn't too good because I was too damn little. Doc Gray had to put lead weights on the front of my chair so I wouldn't flip over backwards."

They acquired a mascot, Donald Jeffries, a thirteen-year-old patient with paraplegia whose father was a naval officer, and a nickname that captured their spirited grit: the Rolling Devils.

The hour-long practice sessions were devoted to ball handling, shooting, wheeling, and retrieving loose balls. O'Connell used a blackboard to diagram plays, and then the veterans would go through them on the floor. They got the hang of moving their chairs backward and forward, suddenly and quickly, while scanning the floor and passing the ball.

They found that, with its unceasing flow, wheelchair basketball was as demanding as the two-legged version. "Some of the men tired quickly and a few had to be withdrawn from practice," O'Connell said. "[The game] is very rough and exciting. Wheelchairs moving at full speed collide and cause many upsets and thrills. It is the one game that leaves as excited and bewildered a crowd as any sport I have ever witnessed."[12]

As O'Connell whipped the team into shape, Dr. Gray contacted Rynearson and challenged Birmingham to a game. Rynearson accepted and brought the Birmingham boys to Corona.

They met on February 26, 1947, inside the sparkling new gymnasium. The game marked the public debut of the Devils. More important, this was the first-ever contest featuring two organized wheelchair basketball teams. All previous games involving the paralyzed veterans at Birmingham and at Cushing hospitals had featured non-disabled opponents using wheelchairs.[13]

There was some good-natured, service-related joshing among the players before the tip-off, what with Birmingham representing the army and Corona representing the navy and the marines. The visitors didn't realize that they enjoyed a huge advantage over the home team: Corona took the court without its best player, Johnny Winterholler, because he was unavailable to play that evening.

Birmingham initially had a tough time penetrating the Devils' defense because "they were up against a team that could handle their chairs," Rynearson later noted. Birmingham led only 5–1 at halftime.[14]

Rynearson counseled them during the break, and the second half told a different story. Resorting to what he described as "tricks learned from the experience of having played a number of games," Birmingham took charge and cruised to a 21–6 victory, with Stan Den Adel pouring in twelve points.

"Did we take a licking!" Dr. Gray said.[15]

Corona had practiced "only a few days for the game and displayed remarkable ability at the new sport," Rynearson observed. "The return game promises to be a good one and the Tars [sailors] threaten to down the undefeated Birmingham patients."[16]

O'Connell used the ignominious defeat on their home court to push the team members to avenge themselves. He positioned Winterholler at center to take advantage of his game-management skills and named Noel Smith, a former navy pilot from New Orleans, as captain.

They gained valuable experience by playing six matches against non-disabled teams in borrowed wheelchairs, including games against the hospital staff and doctors, and won them all easily. Corona fashioned an aggressive style: pushing the ball on offense, hounding the opposition on defense, unafraid of contact.

"You'd play against some team, and you'd beat the shit out of them, and then go get drunk afterwards," Gene Fesenmeyer said. "Then, the next morning, you gotta get up and play basketball again, just like a regular team would."

Elizabeth "Betty" Kinzer, a navy nurse assigned to Corona, noticed how wheelchair basketball, and the Devils' victories, boosted morale. "The patients seemed more confident, as though they had somehow proved to themselves if not yet to anyone else that they could succeed at something, and that maybe, if they really tried, they might be able to make some kind of a life for themselves after their discharge from the hospital," she recounted in her memoir.[17]

Less than two months after their first meeting, Birmingham hosted the rematch with Corona. Coach O'Connell and the

Devils piled into their cars for the long ride to Van Nuys, this time with Johnny Winterholler in uniform.

Birmingham had not seen the likes of the "Spider" before. His presence in the lineup changed everything. Again, the contest was one-sided, but this time the navy and the marines trounced the army, 41–10. Kent McKnight, a navy veteran who doubled as the team's publicist, led the way with seventeen points. Winterholler controlled the tempo and tallied eleven. The pupils had drubbed the teachers.

Playing the game was as effective as taking penicillin, according to Dr. Gray. "The things that [wheelchair basketball] has done for our players is astounding," he related to Rynearson. "Some of the boys were completely sunk before taking up the sport...It has given the boys a very definite feeling of being back 'in the swim' again; in fact, it has even made prima donnas of two or three. Ordinarily, I don't like that, but in this case, I love it."[18]

The paralyzed veterans who aren't on the team "follow our career with intense interest and some of them anticipate the time when they too will be able to play," Gray continued. "I've never seen any one thing make such extraordinary changes in the mental outlook of these men as this basketball."[19]

"This basketball" was so useful that Dr. Gray decided it was time to spread the gospel of wheelchair basketball beyond Southern California.

CHAPTER 10

Road Trip

Seventy years later, at the age of ninety-two, Gene Fesenmeyer could still recall details about the two rollicking road trips the Rolling Devils made in the spring of 1947.

Boarding a C-47 military transport plane with his teammates and flying up to the Alameda Naval Air Station. The police escort that shepherded the team into Oakland. Staying at Dr. Gray's horse ranch in nearby Walnut Creek and being thrown into the pool by his teammates. Going to a nightclub, with a showgirl reserved for him, and watching comedian Redd Foxx, "the dirtiest, funniest sonofabitch we ever heard," according to Gene.

And, last but not least, whipping the Oakland Bittners, one of the top-ranked basketball teams in the nation, in front of thousands of exultant fans. "We kicked their ass," he said.

Dr. Gray's personal connections led to the Devils making two trips to the Bay Area. First, he scheduled contests against two college basketball teams. Thanks to Corona's association with the navy, the team flew in comfort in a transport plane at a time when commercial airlines were not equipped to handle travelers with paraplegia and their wheelchairs.

The Devils looked snappy in their satin uniforms and red

jackets as they faced the varsity basketball team from Saint Mary's College. The four steel pillars that flanked the sidelines at dimly lit Kezar Pavilion in San Francisco's Golden Gate Park didn't slow the Devils' full-steam-ahead, zip-jerk-spin offensive stylings.

They crushed the Gaels of Saint Mary's, 28–10, with Winterholler chipping in sixteen. "Not our best game," coach O'Connell sighed. "Why, ordinarily we roll up 30 or 40 points."[1]

"Those kids get around like in the dodge-'em concession out at the beach," said Gaels football coach Jimmy Phelan. "And those chairs really took a beating... They figure the chairs can always be replaced; no taxpayer can object to this item!"[2]

The Devils then ventured across the Bay to play the University of California at Berkeley, Dr. Gray's undergraduate alma mater. Before 5,000 curious patrons at the men's gym, they outpaced the Golden Bears, 35–19.

"We would have to play a number of games before we'd be able to cope with them," coach Clarence "Nibs" Price said, "and then we couldn't be sure of taking their measure."[3]

The Devils returned to Corona, where they reeled off seven consecutive wins against non-disabled teams before they again flew north. Their next opponent was the Oakland Bittners, the semi-pro team owned by Lou Bittner, a local tax and insurance entrepreneur. His namesake squad was in its prime, having won the American Basketball League championship in March before losing in the national AAU finals to the mighty Phillips 66ers squad.

Lou Bittner's players were older than the college boys—many of them had served in the war—and they were much more talented. Their offense revolved around Jim Pollard, a high-flying forward in the days when dunking the basketball was a rare occurrence. The "Kangaroo Kid" led Stanford to the NCAA championship in 1942 before powering the Coast Guard team from nearby Alameda in the Service League. (He later starred for the Minneapolis Lakers in the NBA and was inducted into the Naismith Memorial Basketball Hall of Fame.)

The *Oakland Tribune* sponsored the Devils-Bittners matchup and set about hyping the contest with daily dispatches. Reporters at the newspaper employed linguistic gymnastics to explain paraplegia and wheelchair basketball to their readers. The sport was "designed to aid in the recuperation of veterans who are rigid from the waist down." The visitors are "boys who didn't 'walk away' when the war was over," and are considered "the whirling dervishes of wheelchair basketball." This game was the "vehicle cage championships."[4]

Wrote sports editor Lee Dunbar: "A number of people...look upon the Rolling Devils as a freak outfit playing basketball in a highly distorted manner. But if you think those lads from Corona can't play the game you have another think coming."[5]

The *Tribune* printed numerous photos in the week preceding the game. Here's Gene Fesenmeyer demonstrating the best way to pick up a loose ball while seated in a wheelchair. Heartwarming pictures of Lieutenant Louis Largey and his wife and daughter accompanied the story about how "Tank" was awarded the Silver Star and credited with more than three hundred kills in seventy-six hours during the battle at Tarawa.

Tickets for the 3,000 reserved seats at the Civic Auditorium were priced at $1.50, with general admission going for $1. Casey Stengel, the manager of the Oakland Oaks minor-league baseball team (who would parlay his success with the Oaks to land the managerial job with the New York Yankees in 1949), was chosen to assist the promotion by officiating a wheelchair free-throw shooting contest at halftime.

The Bittners were sent wheelchairs before the contest, and they practiced at the Athens Athletic Club in Oakland to mixed results. Players on both teams mingled at a pregame banquet and listened to Pinky Tomlin sing his smash tune, "The Object of My Affection." The next day, the Devils were guests of Stengel's in the ballpark as Casey's Oaks, headed by aging outfielder Vince DiMaggio, beat their cross-Bay rivals, the San Francisco Seals, in Pacific Coast League action.[6]

The basic question leading to the game was this: how would one of the best non-disabled teams in the world respond to playing basketball in wheelchairs? Coach O'Connell predicted an easy victory for the Devils. "We hope to give the Bittners the same medicine we handed to the Bonita All Stars last Wednesday in our 20th straight win," he crowed. "Our offense wasn't up to par, but the score of 31–5 indicates our defensive ability."[7]

Dr. Gray was equally confident, although more understated. "[The Devils] have too much experience on wheelchairs," he said. "And besides, the Bittners will find the Devils are one of the best hustling teams they've met this season... Wouldn't be a bit surprised if the Bittners remember them for a long time."[8]

On the night of May 26, a thunderous storm didn't prevent some 8,000 spectators from making their way to the Oakland Civic Auditorium, hard by Lake Merritt, east of downtown Oakland. Many of those who stayed home listened to the radio broadcast on KLX.

Gene Fesenmeyer was primed. When the Devils were introduced, "I flipped my wheelchair up off my two back wheels, flew down the ramp from the dressing room onto the floor, did a couple whip-arounds and took a bow," he later said. "Everyone went wild."

Before the opening whistle, a quartet of veterans who had been imprisoned during the war came onto the court to greet Johnny Winterholler. The four former POWs—Jack Stevenson, Earl Johnson, Ernie Lynch, and John Bridges—loomed over Johnny in his wheelchair, all of them beaming as they posed for photographs at mid-court. The sellout crowd rewarded them with a standing ovation. This was followed by the playing of "The Star-Spangled Banner," with an escort of marines to present the flag.

Perhaps Winterholler, described as a "hunk of dynamite on wheels" with an "uncanny shooting eye" by *Tribune* reporters, was inspired by the pre-game festivities. His twenty-two-point onslaught singlehandedly outpaced Oakland's entire roster.

Largey was the defensive star; he stuck to Pollard like a brand new product called Elmer's Glue-All. The "Kangaroo Kid" managed two points, and the Devils romped over the Bittners, 38–16.

The wheelchairs were the great equalizer. It was the Devils who enjoyed unfettered mobility, moving freely and scoring at will, while the non-disabled all-stars were limited in their movements and frustrated with the results. The Bittners had "great trouble in steering their chairs in the right direction," reported the *Tribune*. "When they took their hands off the chair it went in the opposite direction."[9]

Fans felt sorry for the Bittners, recalled Gene Fesenmeyer. "They weren't used to the chairs, and so when they got shoved they'd just tip over," he said. "The crowd laughed like hell."

Afterward, Mrs. Lou Bittner presented coach O'Connell with an enormous trophy. Net receipts of $2,800 went to the paralyzed veterans of Corona for the purchase of braces, wheelchairs, and crutches.

The *Tribune* produced a rousing fifteen-minute film about the Devils that highlighted their activities, social and athletic, during their travels. Shot in sixteen-millimeter with sound, the film showed the cheerful young men mugging for the camera and scoring on the court. The newspaper's promotion department sent the movie to VA and civilian hospitals to publicize the sport and to boost the morale of others with paraplegia.

Wheelchair basketball was proving to be a potent elixir, both for the players and the spectators. They were the "No. 1 sports sensation of 1947," according to *Wyoming Daily Eagle* newspaper columnist Larry Birleffi,[10] while writer Elsie Robinson used her nationally syndicated column "Listen, World" to extol the Devils' efforts. "It is one thing to stop a bullet and lie for months hospitalized," she wrote. "It is another and infinitely harder thing to gather up the shattered fragments of your spirit and force them to quicken again. They had done all this and now they were out in their wheelchairs challenging America, licking almost every team they met.[11]

"The real contest was a matter of spirit rather than of the flesh," she continued. "We are given to doubt the American way of life in these bewildered times. But here was as fine an exhibition of clean sportsmanship and courage as America has known in many a day and here, invisible but triumphant, was the faith and decency that carried it on and that is our hope in the future."[12]

★ ★ ★

In almost no time, news about the emerging phenomenon of wheelchair basketball spread by word of mouth to paraplegia wards in other VA hospitals. Dr. Gray sent a copy of the rules to the paralyzed veterans at Hunter Holmes McGuire Hospital in Richmond, Virginia. Described by the *Orlando Evening Star* newspaper as "a far cry from mere arm-chair athletes" and a team for whom "legs don't mean a thing," the red-shirted Charioteers were soon defeating the likes of the University of Richmond's varsity football team.[13]

The VA hospitals in New York flourished as a wheelchair-basketball hotbed. Two brothers who'd served in the marines, Al and Peter Youakim (the latter was wounded by shrapnel during the Bougainville campaign with the 3rd Division in the Pacific), organized a team among the paralyzed veterans at St. Albans Naval Hospital in Queens.

A team representing the veterans at Halloran Hospital on Staten Island recorded a string of victories against non-disabled clubs and prepared to take on the veterans at Cushing Hospital for East Coast supremacy. And, at the VA hospital on Kingsbridge Road in the Bronx, paralyzed veterans from ward 3-D wheeled into action as the Bronx Rollers.

When Gene Fesenmeyer and other vets from Corona were transferred to Vaughan Hospital in Hines, Illinois, they took the game with them. "We showed them how to play," Gene said. "They started the team and seemed anxious to learn all the rules."

The Hines Gizz Kids immediately reeled off twenty-seven consecutive victories against non-disabled opponents, including a win over Max "Slats" Zaslofksy and the Chicago Stags of the Basketball Association of America. The team's unusual nickname derived from the slang word for the catheter that drained urine from the bladder and was considered a crucial element in the life-preserving treatment of paraplegia. Paralyzed veterans called the devices "gizmos" (pronounced with a hard "g").

Naming themselves the Gizz Kids represented an inside joke at their own expense—and was another example of the coarse, sometimes profane, and deeply morbid sense of humor that many paralyzed veterans employed to cope with their condition.

This was a way to "own" their disability, as it were, like calling themselves "crip" and "gimp."

As they racked up victory after victory over non-disabled opponents, wheelchair basketball players were upsetting previously held notions of the limitations of paraplegia. Here they were, wheeling around basketball courts in front of the public and the media, not hiding away in some institution. Here they were, displaying athletic skills that were far superior to those of their non-disabled opponents. Here they were, traveling in an airplane and suffering no ill effects.

Their scrappy, take-no-prisoners attitude paralleled efforts away from the gym to take control of their fate and reintegrate into a society that was largely ignorant, apathetic, and downright hostile to the unique needs of people with paraplegia.

In the summer of 1946, a veteran with quadriplegia at the Bronx VA hospital named John Price began tapping out stories about himself and his brethren on a special electric typewriter donated by the Red Cross. The first issue of *The Paraplegia News* was a four-page newsletter with a simple motto: "A paraplegic is an individual." *PN* quickly became the national voice and conscience for paralyzed veterans across America.[14]

In the summer of 1944, Fred Smead was riding in a jeep in the small town of Torigni-sur-Vire in northwestern France. He'd landed on Omaha Beach in July and was chasing retreating Germans while on patrol with the 35th Infantry Division when a two-story building collapsed on the vehicle. The wall crushed three of his vertebrae and severed his spinal cord. He was eventually transferred to Birmingham Hospital, where he came under the care of Dr. Bors.

Smead became an outspoken advocate for the rights of paralyzed veterans. He scored an early victory when he traveled to

Washington, D.C., and lobbied to correct an existing bill that allocated service-related compensation for hospitalized veterans. A veteran who was single, with no dependents, and a patient inside a VA hospital received only $20 per month (or $0.68 a day). Smead's testimony pushed Congress to boost that allowance to the maximum amount of $360 per month.

With enthusiastic support from Dr. Bors, Smead and other patients at Birmingham decided to form a group exclusively for paralyzed veterans. They appreciated the existing traditional organizations that lobbied on behalf of U.S. veterans—including the Veterans of Foreign Wars (VFW), the American Legion, and the Disabled American Veterans (DAV)—but they wanted a separate, independent outfit that would address their specific concerns.[15]

"Because we were so seriously disabled, we felt that the other veterans' organizations could not give us adequate attention," according to paralyzed veteran Gilford Moss. "In short, we would be swallowed up and forgotten."[16]

Lloyd Pantages, a discharged patient at Birmingham and the son of movie theater magnate Alexander Pantages, used his connections to persuade famed divorce lawyer Jerry Geisler to draw up the necessary documents for the group to incorporate. Paralyzed veterans around the country followed Birmingham's example and, with prodding from Price, joined together in a nonprofit organization called the Paralyzed Veterans of America (PVA).

In February of 1947, the PVA welcomed some three hundred members from seven VA paraplegia wards to its first national convention, a three-day affair held inside Vaughan Hospital outside Chicago. Vena Hefner, who had been injured in a motorcycle accident while serving with the Women's Army Corps (WAC), was the sole female attendee. Approximately thirty veterans with quadriplegia were wheeled into the gymnasium on beds to attend the meeting.

At its second convention, held later that year at McGuire Hospital in Virginia, the PVA forced the Hotel John Marshall to change its segregation policy and allow African-American veterans to attend the banquet.

Atop the PVA's to-do list was obtaining government assistance for paralyzed veterans to purchase wheelchair-accessible homes, equipped with wide doors and hallways, ramps instead of stairs, and bathroom spaces and fixtures to accommodate their disability. The PVA also launched the National Paraplegia Foundation to raise money for medical research into spinal-cord injuries and diseases and to collaborate with doctors to find a cure for paraplegia.

These efforts, like those of the wheelchair basketball teams, would eventually benefit all those with paraplegia, including those who never served in the military. "With continued evidence of what a disabled man can accomplish, not only will many be given renewed hope and confidence, but the public, business and industry will be made to realize that the disabled— with a little help and understanding—can be useful, valuable and self-sustaining citizens," Fred Smead later stated.[17]

★ ★ ★

In June of 1947, not long after returning from their successful road trips to the Bay Area, the Rolling Devils scheduled a charity exhibition against college players in Sacramento. Johnny Winterholler tallied twenty-two points in the Devils' 43–14 victory over the Sacramento All-Stars; proceeds from the game went to support Bob Moore, a marine who fell victim to a booby trap in Pacific action. The next day, Governor Earl Warren presented team members with scrolls bearing the California state seal.

The Devils were invited to perform at the world basketball tournament, sponsored by the *Chicago Herald-American* newspaper, considered to be professional basketball's foremost showcase. Dr. Gray mentioned an "eastern campaign" to Bob Rynearson: "[Playing in] Madison Square Garden has always been our boys' goal, especially since defeating the Oakland Bittners."[18]

Instead, on June 15, 1947, fans were greeted with this headline in the *Los Angeles Times*: "Veteran's Wheelchair Team Will Hang Up Basketball Togs."[19]

Reports that the Rolling Devils were disbanding, published in dozens of newspapers across the country immediately after the game in Sacramento, surprised their followers. They were recognized as the world's best wheelchair basketball club, with an undefeated record after avenging their opening-game loss to Birmingham. Coach O'Connell was said to have been fielding requests about appearances from as far away as the Philippines and South America.

The abrupt breakup of the Devils happened because of the way the U.S. military designed its hospital system. Naval Hospital Corona was an active-duty hospital. Its charge was to care for the wounded until they were ready to return to their unit, transfer to a VA hospital (like Birmingham or Cushing hospitals), or go home.

Two years after V-E Day and V-J Day, when there was no urgency to restock the battlefield, marines and sailors were being released in droves from Corona. Several of the Rolling Devils, including Gene Fesenmeyer and "Pistol Pete" Simon, were shuttled to VA hospitals to continue their rehabilitation. Others returned to their families and their hometowns. Those who decided that they preferred California's temperate climate settled on the West Coast.

Johnny Winterholler was preparing for life after the marines, although he sometimes found it difficult to keep up with the latest trends in the fast-paced, postwar society. Many women were entering the workplace, and families were saving up for the next big thing: a television set. A baby boom was underway— every couple he and Dessa knew had a child or two in tow—and he tried to figure out why the young girls were swooning over a lanky singer named Frank Sinatra.

His number-one priority was to find work in a profession where his wheelchair would not be considered a liability. He enrolled in the Sawyer School of Business in downtown Los Angeles to take classes in accounting and business administration. He and Dessa were discussing their future plans—should they go back to Wyoming to be near family and friends?—when a job opportunity came along that was too good to pass up.

Dr. Gray was moving his family back to Oakland and reopening his plastic surgery practice. He needed an office manager to handle the billing and insurance details and asked Winterholler if he would be interested. Johnny readily agreed. He and Dessa would start life anew in the Oakland area, with the added security and comfort of having Johnny's personal doctor in the vicinity.

There's no evidence that Johnny Winterholler ever played wheelchair basketball again. He was the sport's first superstar, and lending his prominence to the Devils was exceedingly helpful in the embryonic dawn of adaptive sports. If he had continued, if he had formed a team among paralyzed veterans (and civilians) in the Bay Area, he might have been remembered as the Michael Jordan of wheelchair basketball.

But he no longer needed the game. After the athletic heights he had attained at Wyoming, he felt no urgency to prove himself again. All he wanted to do was enjoy his life with Dessa. And, now that he had a job, perhaps they could build their dream home and start a family.

Dr. Gray, meanwhile, was consumed with a vision. He wanted to create communities for those affected by paraplegia, veterans and civilians alike, where all the buildings were designed for the comfort of the residents, with convenient medical care, employment, and recreational opportunities. The campus would be a kind of wheelchair users' utopia, he avowed, and he began seeking donors to fund the project.

"Doc Gray used to bring that up," Gene Fesenmeyer said, "that he wanted to start a place like that. A regular town where paraplegics lived and married and worked. A place for wounded vets."

Gray found an influential ally in U.S. Army Air Forces Major General Uzal Ent, who had led the Ploesti oil field raids in eastern Romania during the war. In 1944, Ent himself was paralyzed when the B-25 bomber he was piloting crashed. While he was hospitalized, he called for those with paraplegia to be organized into a colony. In his spare time, he designed and built leg braces for paralyzed veterans like himself that were vast improvements over the cumbersome models the VA was using in the paraplegia wards.[20]

Ent's death in 1948 halted momentum for such a program, and Dr. Gray had to abandon his quixotic dream. A version of his vision did emerge in Needham, Massachusetts, where a number of paralyzed veterans from Cushing Hospital settled in a small community of accessible homes.

Oakland Tribune reporter Phil Norman, who'd covered the Rolling Devils–Bittners game, offhandedly promoted another idea. "[Wheelchair basketball for paralyzed veterans] has served as something both recreational and educational to the Devils," he wrote, "and should grow into something of a standard to all handicapped people."[21]

Norman's words proved prophetic. Thanks to the publicity generated by events like the Rolling Devils' groundbreaking road trips, the spread of adaptive sports beyond the VA hospitals was on the horizon. It would be left to the Devils' only true rival, the paralyzed veterans at Birmingham Hospital, to take wheelchair basketball to the multitudes.

CHAPTER 11

Rolling across America

The breakup of the Rolling Devils left Birmingham as the lone wheelchair basketball team west of the Mississippi River. Coach Bob Rynearson had no trouble scheduling exhibition games against non-disabled teams willing to use wheelchairs—these often doubled as fund-raisers for the PVA—but these opponents weren't their equals.

How many times could they meet, and beat, the likes of Marty's Food Center, Bond's Stove Works, Goldwater Tailors, and Whittier Chevrolet?

Local journalist John Old was a former basketball referee who wrote a sports column for the *Herald-Express* newspaper, Hearst's afternoon tabloid in Los Angeles. He'd witnessed the positive reactions the Birmingham players received whenever they played and, like other reporters covering the team, believed that they should emulate the Devils and showcase their inimitable brand of basketball outside sleepy Van Nuys.

After yet another exhibition game, the Birmingham players were asked a simple question: "How would you like to play in Madison Square Garden?"

The veterans laughed it off, but then the wheels started

turning, and the possibilities were discussed: "Madison Square Garden ... to show all these people what we can do ... impossible, all the complications of a trip ... well, it wouldn't hurt trying ... we might play the paraplegic centers on the way."[1]

They sent an inquiry to Garden officials: would they be interested in booking a wheelchair basketball team? The reply came back, "Sorry, our schedule for the season is filled."[2]

Their dream might have died then and there. But after meeting with Old and popular sportscaster Bob Kelley, the voice of the Los Angeles Rams of the National Football League (which had relocated from Cleveland in 1946), the veterans and the journalists devised a new plan: crisscross the country and play the wheelchair basketball teams from the paraplegia wards of other VA hospitals. The vets would take care of booking the games; Old and his newspaper pals would try to raise the funds.

The logistics of organizing a barnstorming trip involving a dozen athletes with paraplegia and their wheelchairs and their doctors and aides were mind-bogglingly complex. Would hotels be able to accommodate them? What if there was a medical emergency and one of the players was severely injured or even died? And how in the world were they going to pay for this? The cost to send the players to Memphis, Chicago, and New York City, with attendants, was estimated to be $10,000 (equivalent to roughly $100,000 today).

The more the players mulled over the idea, the more they embraced its potential. Competing against fellow paralyzed veterans would test their hoop skills, with bragging rights the prize. They'd be able to publicize the mission of the nascent PVA and to create awareness about paraplegia research. And, successfully undertaking an arduous trans-continental circuit would demonstrate to the public and the news media that America's paralyzed veterans could handle most any situation. Indeed, almost as revolutionary as a bunch of paralyzed veterans playing basketball in wheelchairs was a bunch of paralyzed veterans traveling around the country.

Team captain Stan Den Adel and Pat Grissom reached out to fellow veterans within the PVA to organize a slate of games. Kelley contacted his connections to get the word out, and Old used his column to plead for donations, emphasizing that this was a "nonprofit, all-expense-paid junket for a group of helplessly crippled combat veterans, whose greatest pleasure in life is playing basketball."[3]

Their cajoling did the trick. Crooner Bing Crosby, theatrical producer Blevins Davis, and the Hollywood Turf Club chipped in money for the cause. The Military Order of the Purple Heart and the American Legion signed on as sponsors and helped arrange for transportation and lodging in the various cities. Gaps in the travel schedule were plugged with exhibition games against non-disabled teams.

Since the players were technically patients within the VA, all that remained was for coach Rynearson to get the official authorization from Major General Carl Gray, the head of the VA, whom President Harry Truman had appointed to replace General Omar Bradley. With financial backing secured, and with enthusiastic support from Dr. Bors and Birmingham's medical staff, the veterans believed that this was a no-brainer.

They were dead wrong.

In early February, just days before the wheelchair cagers were scheduled to leave California, Major General Gray (no relation to Dr. Gerald Gray) turned down their request. The VA's chief medical director, Dr. Paul Magnuson, insisted that the journey would be "too long and too hard on the patients in that condition."[4]

"Boy, were we excited," Den Adel later recalled. "Then, deep gloom."[5]

Sports columnist Claude Newman slammed the "VA boneheads who turned thumbs down on the expedition." Wrote Newman: "I can see no sane or sensible reason for the Veterans Administration being opposed to the flying trip."[6]

Birmingham played one last card: an appeal to the commander in chief of the United States. Eight team members wired President Truman and urged him to "come to our rescue." They had taken the court "without a single injury or setback traceable to basketball in our two seasons of play," they said, and emphasized that the tour was about more than sports.

"The issue is much bigger than our small group, as this project, which carries the endorsement of all California veterans' groups, not only serves to boost our rehabilitation by keeping our competitive spirit alive but also serves as a great inspiration to other helplessly crippled veterans, our buddies still in the hospital," the wire said.

They also requested that Rynearson and other aides be permitted to go with them. "We have appealed in vain to high officials in the Veterans Administration at Washington for immediate leave without pay of three Birmingham staff members to accompany us in order that we will have the same expert care we have had in our previous games."

The wire concluded with a heartfelt plea: "Please help us, Mister President."[7]

Den Adel figured they'd find a sympathetic ear in Truman, who was readying for the upcoming presidential campaign against Republican Thomas Dewey. The president had long positioned himself as an ally of veterans and, particularly, disabled veterans, while emphasizing his own military experience. He'd joined the

Missouri National Guard in 1905 and rejoined when the United States entered World War I. Once they were mobilized and shipped to France, he assumed command of Battery D of the 129th Field Artillery Regiment and saw heavy action in the Vosges Mountains and in the Meuse-Argonne Offensive along the Western Front.

Truman had also initiated National Employ the Physically Handicapped Week to prod businesses to offer jobs to people with disabilities, including veterans. Once the event proved successful, he established the President's Committee on National Employ the Physically Handicapped Week to authorize funds for promotional efforts, including movie trailers and billboards. (Its charge was later expanded to include employment for people with non-physical disabilities.)

In 1947, Truman appeared on the cover of *Handicap* magazine, dressed in his trademark white summer suit and matching shoes, beaming alongside two patients from Birmingham, Gerald Kopp and Leo Ladouceur.[8] After the pair finished one-two in the first national bowling tournament for paralyzed veterans, they were flown to Washington, D.C. with Dr. Bors to shake hands with the president and General Omar Bradley and to show off their skills at the two-lane bowling alley in the West Wing.

The meet-and-greet marked "the first time that such prominent recognition has been given by the White House to the athletic program in the nation's V.A. hospitals," the *Birmingham Reporter* newsletter noted.[9]

But Truman decided to pass the buck to Colonel Robert Landry, the president's recently appointed Air Force aide. Landry, who had served with the 8th Air Force during the war, under the command of Lieutenant General James Doolittle, sided with the VA hierarchy and against the team. The president refused to overrule his decision.

Time was running out. Los Angeles Air Service pilots John Hanson and Bill Steimer, on standby with a chartered plane at Lockheed Air Terminal, patiently awaited their orders.

The players didn't take long to deliberate. They'd come too far to give up. Their decision to defy President Truman and the VA was unanimous. They checked themselves out of Birmingham Hospital so that they were no longer considered to be hospital patients and phoned the news to the pilots.

Because of the VA's intransigence, Bob Rynearson and other staff had to remain in California, even though they knew the players and their medical conditions best. As someone who had "thought, talked, dreamed, eaten and slept wheelchair basketball since its inception," Rynearson was deeply disappointed that he couldn't accompany his players on the historic journey.[10]

Reporter Old took charge of the team and handed off public relations duties to Texas Earnest Schramm Jr. "Tex" Schramm had been born in nearby San Gabriel, California. He went on to study at the University of Texas and then—during the war— served in the U.S. Army Air Forces. He joined the front office of the Rams, working alongside sportscaster Bob Kelley, and drew on his network of journalist pals to generate media interest in the Birmingham tour.

Dr. Harold Edelbrock, a local urologist, and three aides were brought on to accompany the team. Carl Knowles, a UCLA basketball standout and member of the gold medal–winning 1936 U.S. Olympic team, was chosen to fill in as coach.

Old contacted an employment agency to hire a registered nurse. Peggy Stapleton said that she had never flown in a plane before, but she had once worked in a hospital with spinal-cord-injured patients. She got the job; she was the lone woman on the trip.

★ ★ ★

On the morning of February 18, 1948, on a clear day that was perfect for flying, eleven paralyzed veterans and eight staff gathered at the Lockheed Terminal in Burbank. Outfitted in gleaming team jackets and seated in matching Everest & Jennings wheelchairs, Stan Den Adel and ten teammates—Louis Palmer, George McReynolds, Jack Heller, Bob Blakesley, Lee Barr, Charles Davison, Ron Wallan, Joe Lawson, Dean Camblin, and Jess Rodriguez—posed for press photographers on the tarmac. Their average age was twenty-five.

Getting on the plane presented the first challenge. There were no ramps to the main cabin, and the stairs leading to the doorway were too narrow for their chairs.

So they improvised. One by one, the players wheeled onto a long, solid wood plank. A forklift scooped them up and hoisted them skyward, like pieces of cargo. Then, with the help of the attendants, they were squeezed into the cabin, followed by their collapsible chairs.

The men handled the awkwardness with typical macabre humor. "Do not drop," one player joked as he was carried to his seat. "Use no hooks."[11]

Their first scheduled game, in Denver, was canceled because of the delay dealing with the VA. They flew to Amarillo, Texas, en route to the opening game in Kansas City, and learned that, while wheelchair basketball had taken them out of the shadows in Van Nuys, the rest of the world was appallingly ignorant about their disability.

Hotel managers had to take doors off their hinges so the veterans could access the bathroom. Curious crowds gathered wherever they went. One incredulous bystander whispered to the nurse, "What's wrong with these boys?"[12]

Pat Grissom had arranged to visit his family before meeting up with the team in Kansas City. He drove from California to Syracuse, Kansas, in his modified automobile, and then caught a train to Kansas City.

When he wheeled himself into the depot, he discovered that there were no elevators in the station. The only way to travel from below ground to the street was by escalator. The stationmaster had to clear the machine of people and switch it off. Grissom then wheeled backward onto the steps, with the back pair of wheels on one level and the front set on another. The escalator was turned back on, and up went Pat, gripping tightly to the handrail. Upon safely reaching solid ground, he shook the stationmaster's hand.[13]

The basketball part of the tour launched on February 19, when some 1,200 spectators braved chilly winds and crammed into Kansas City's St. James Recreation Center. There, they watched Birmingham blitz the non-disabled Municipal League champs, 52–8, as Dean Camblin, wounded while serving in the Medical Corps, not only tallied the game's first basket but also secured game-high honors with twelve points.

Police greeted them in Chicago and escorted them to the Morrison Hotel in the Loop. The night before the game, they took in the Ezzard Charles–Sam Baroudi bout at Chicago Stadium. Charles knocked out the twenty-year-old in the tenth round in what one reporter described as "legalized slaughter."[14]

Baroudi later died of a brain hemorrhage from the blows, sending a sobering message that the veterans knew well from the war: life can be taken away in an instant.

The team returned to Chicago Stadium the next evening to play the Northwestern University "B" team before a crowd of 16,000 fans. The students proved unable to roll their chairs and simultaneously execute plays, nor could they keep up with Birmingham's crisp passing and relentless hustle. They pitched their first shutout, 10–0, in a truncated exhibition during halftime of the Northwestern–Indiana University varsity matchup.

First-time observers of wheelchair basketball were flabbergasted by what they were seeing. The nonstop slashing and attacking, the hair-raising spills, the rough-and-tumble verve: the game was different, yes, but it was also thrilling and inspiring. And, after the novelty wore off, the focus shifted to the players rather than their disability.

"When a wheelchair overturned, the veteran righted it himself, crawled back in and got back into the battle with a shout," reported the *New York Times*. "They crashed into each other and into poles [and] stanchions with an abandon that few able-bodied athletes would have permitted themselves."[15]

At the team's next stop, in Buffalo, local blue laws threatened to derail a game that was booked for Sunday afternoon. A phone call to Governor Thomas Dewey in Albany saved the day, and the rout was on: a 52–14 victory over a pickup squad of non-disabled veterans, with Jack Heller, injured in the European theater, surprising everyone by scoring sixteen points.

In Boston, they were warmly received at the annual Washington's birthday reception, hosted by Governor Robert Bradford in the Old State House. Their next opponent, the team of paralyzed veterans from Cushing Hospital in nearby Framingham, did not embrace them so hospitably.

Birmingham arrived in New England amid a deluge of press clippings proclaiming it to be the world's first wheelchair basketball team. Dick Foley and his Cushing teammates grumbled that they should receive equal credit for originating the sport. And, for all the published reports about Birmingham's trailblazing matches against Johnny Winterholler and the Rolling Devils, the Clippers pointed out that they, too, had played against another team of paralyzed veterans.

In December of 1947—about ten months after Birmingham's historic first game against the Rolling Devils—Cushing traveled to New York to play the paralyzed veterans from Halloran VA Hospital on Staten Island, in what is considered to be the third-ever game between two wheelchair basketball teams involving athletes with paraplegia.

The Clippers also resented that the rules devised by Bob Rynearson—the so-called "western rules"—were receiving such acclaim. Cushing played under the "eastern rules," where all contact between the players and their chairs—even incidental touches—was verboten. The Birmingham players felt that this disrupted the natural rhythm and flow of the sport.

At Cushing, players possessing the ball were allowed unlimited pushes on their wheels, versus the two-push maximum stipulated by Rynearson. Birmingham proponents argued that the "Cushing pushing" gave the offense an unfair advantage and removed some of the teamwork inherent in the sport. Games devolved into "ten wheelchairs [going] down the floor in a mad, freewheeling charge," according to UPI sports reporter Oscar Fraley. "Then it's every man for himself and Normandy was never like this!"[16]

Newspaper accounts hyped the Birmingham-Cushing tilt as the "world wheelchair basketball championship." The Californians readied for the contest under the assumption that they would compromise on the rules, with one half of the game played by eastern rules and the second half played the western way.

The hosts refused to yield. The game took place on the Clippers' home floor using their rules before a whooping crowd that jammed the hospital gym. The sole aspect of the scene that was familiar to the visitors were the many veterans in wheelchairs who flanked the court to watch the contest. They watched one man in a body-and-shoulder cast use his free arm to push a buddy's chair. A half dozen veterans were stretched flat on their stomachs on cots.

Cushing took advantage of the eastern rules that allowed for full-court gallops, with the ball teetering on their laps, and grabbed an overwhelming 7–0 lead at halftime. Paul Hogan, a Lowell High School standout who had been wounded at Saint-Lô in northwestern France in 1944, led the Cushing attack, aided by Dick Foley and Don Kratzer, as Cushing stretched its lead to 12–0 after three quarters.

Nothing Birmingham countered with seemed to work: not the three-man zone defense they set up to stop the rampaging Clippers; not riding the ref about the mounting number of fouls. The final margin: 18–7.

Boston Herald sportswriter Will Cloney, who moonlighted as the director of the Boston Marathon, wrote that Cushing "wheeled around the court in their chromium-spoked chariots and threw [in] baskets that would have had a Boston Garden crowd popeyed."

With its victory, Cloney noted, Cushing had "staked claim to the world wheelchair championship."[17]

The trouncing stung. Birmingham lost because of the "namby-pamby eastern rules," captain Den Adel told the *New York Times* after the team landed at LaGuardia Field for its games in the metropolitan area. "Their rules don't permit the wheelchairs to touch. We're used to a good tough game on the West Coast."[18]

Birmingham was next slated to meet Halloran's team of paralyzed veterans at their gym on Staten Island. According to the hosts, a representative from Birmingham presented them with an ultimatum to play the game under "half western rules and half eastern rules." Halloran politely declined.[19]

"They would not grant us this courtesy after we had traveled 3,000 miles to play, so we called the whole thing off with them," Den Adel countered.[20] "Man, [the crowd] wants to see a basketball game, not a waltz," he groused.[21]

Old hastily arranged a game against the Bronx VA team, with one half played under western rules and one half under eastern rules. Birmingham prevailed over the Rollers, 29–22. They didn't get to fulfill their dream of playing in Madison Square Garden, but St. Nicholas Arena—less than a mile north on Manhattan's Upper West Side—and an appreciative audience that included five hundred patients with paraplegia from local hospitals provided a comfortable alternative.

In their free time, the players wheeled down Broadway and around Times Square and ventured into nightclubs. Bob Blakesley and Louis Palmer left their rooms at the Hotel Woodward to check out nearby Rockefeller Center. They rolled their chairs onto the famous ice rink and took a few spins before escaping unharmed. Later, they caught up with "alumni vets" from Birmingham who were training for budding careers as watch repairmen at the Joseph Bulova School of Watchmaking in Queens.

The team flew south to face off against the paralyzed vets from McGuire Hospital in Richmond. The sport was still new to the McGuire crew, and their rawness showed as Birmingham romped, 31–9. "A little more experience," Den Adel commented diplomatically, "and they should have a fine ball club."[22]

Next stop: Washington, D.C., where politics and lobbying took precedence. They donned suits and ties and rolled through the marbled hallways of the Capitol to confer with Representative Edith Nourse Rogers (R–MA), the chair of the Veterans' Affairs

Committee. Rogers was a passionate advocate for veterans, starting with her work for the Red Cross in World War I and continuing with her efforts to create the Women's Army Corps and to fight for passage of the GI Bill.

Over lunch at the House restaurant, the Birmingham veterans expressed support for pending legislation to provide federal funding for paralyzed veterans to build accessible homes. Rogers voiced her approval, but warned about the political obstacles the measure faced. She promised to update them on the bill's chances.

There was time for more basketball. They routed students from Catholic University, 65–13, with Dean Camblin registering twenty points in just one half, then throttled a team from Cincinnati's Xavier University, 16–0. "I'll stick to the regular game after this," one player muttered. "These guys are too good."[23]

One game remained: a matchup against the paralyzed veterans from Kennedy VA in Memphis. The visitors chuckled after hearing that the city had changed the name of the street where the hospital was located from "Shotwell Road" to "Getwell Road," presumably so as not to upset the patients and their visitors.

At the pregame banquet, the hosts gently taunted their guests: "Y'all are a swell bunch of fellows, but it's too bad that you've come all this way from California to get beaten."[24]

The swell bunch of fellows from California took their revenge, prevailing 27–9 before a crowd of more than one thousand fans at Ellis Auditorium. Exhausted but happy, they reveled in the Southern hospitality offered by a bevy of Memphis belles before boarding the plane for California.

A homecoming appearance at the Pan-Pacific Auditorium, Los Angeles's storied arena, capped off the season. Prior to a game between the Oakland Bittners and the 20th Century Fox team,

Birmingham defeated USC's basketball squad, led by future Hall of Famer Bill Sharman, 32–18.

All that was missing was a nickname for the team. They'd played every game on the tour in shirts emblazoned with the initials PVAAC—Paralyzed Veterans Association Athletic Club—which didn't easily roll off the tongue. Birmingham VA was too plain vanilla. Coach Rynearson asked the players to think of something evocative, like the Rolling Devils, before the start of the next campaign.

★ ★ ★

In the span of a few weeks, the team had defied the VA hierarchy and the White House, traveled around the country playing a sport they'd invented, and lobbied Congress for federal housing assistance and medical research.

Yes, they were weary, but they'd accomplished what they'd set out to do. They now embodied many identities: paralyzed veterans, pioneering wheelchair athletes, political activists, and role models for people with disabilities.

The statistics were impressive: 6,000 coast-to-coast miles traveled over fourteen days; a won-loss record of 8–1, including one stretch of five games played on consecutive nights in five different cities; 291 total points scored, led by Dean Camblin's sixty-four points; and an estimated 30,000 spectators, including many wounded veterans. Equally impressive: zero injuries.

Thanks to the efforts of publicist Tex Schramm, who went on to become the general manager of the NFL Dallas Cowboys and is now enshrined in the Pro Football Hall of Fame, Birmingham's tour turned wheelchair basketball into a national phenomenon. Articles about the sport and photographs of the players filled the pages of newspapers and magazines; newsreel footage was shown in movie theaters around the country.

This wasn't too surprising given that, immediately following the war, before the victory glow that radiated across the land was diminished by the drumbeat of the Cold War, reporters exhaustively covered the "veteran beat": their readjustment into society, the GI Bill of Rights, jobs, medical care, housing, and segregation in the Armed Forces.

Chest-thumping patriotism often leaked into the reportage, and certain topics—most notably, the psychic damage that afflicted many veterans during war, known then as "battle fatigue"—were taboo in mainstream publications. But with the cost of veterans' care and benefits estimated to have exceeded $1.4 billion in 1947 alone, these issues profoundly affected every citizen.

The approximately 2,500 paralyzed veterans who were "salvaged from the war" constituted a distinct niche for journalists of every stripe. *Popular Mechanics* weighed in on wheelchair basketball as the "new therapy for paraplegics," while reporter Lester Rodney of *The Daily Worker*, the Communist Party newspaper, championed the housing-aid bill for paralyzed veterans and questioned why it was stalled in Congress. *Women's Home Companion*, a glossy monthly devoted to recipes and decorating tips, sent a reporter to profile the men in the spinal-cord units of the VA hospitals and concluded, "They're still the same inside." The general-interest *Coronet* magazine published Lulu Laird's tantalizing tell-all entitled, "I Married a Paraplegic: What Is It Like to Be the Wife of a Paralyzed Vet?"[25]

Neatly packaged stories about wheelchair basketball highlighted the veterans' bravery in overcoming their injuries. Most of the stories glossed over the ugly, tedious aspects involved in rehabilitation—from the stench of the battlefield hospital and the despair within the VA wards to the protracted exercise routines and the unrelenting pain of muscle spasms—to concentrate on positive results. "Shrapnel, gunshot wounds, or field accidents had cut their spinal cords and rendered their legs useless," *Newsweek* noted. "But sheer grit, patience, and expert medical care had lifted them from hopeless invalidism to confident independence."[26]

"What these [men] have done takes more courage, in a way, than any they were called on to display against the enemy," the *New York Times* editorialized. "They had to conquer themselves. They had to learn laboriously to adjust themselves to this new condition...The years to come are not going to be wasted in vain regrets, in sitting on the sidelines of life. They are going to be participants."[27]

"One would think that they would shrink from public appearances," columnist Claude Newman wrote in the *Valley Times* newspaper. "No, sir, they want to get out and show the public what can be done when a man has intestinal integrity and perseverance. You know when you see such men that as long as Americans have such spirit on the sports front and in other things that democracy as we know it is safe."[28]

The upbeat tone notwithstanding, many stories brimmed with ignorance and condescension about paraplegia and disability. The players were described as "pedally handicapped" and "veterans who failed to walk away from the war."

One story explained: "They play in wheelchairs because they have no other mode of transportation."

This was "invalids' basketball" against "whole-bodied opponents," while another concluded: "They'd love to be able to run, these kids. But they left their locomotive powers on the battlefields of World War II."[29]

Examples of unenlightened newspaper headlines abounded.

"Legless Five Wins Game," read one, implying that the players' legs had been removed. Another baldly stated: "Wheel-Chair Basketball Gets Laughs," while others proclaimed, "Useless Legs—But Busy Hands" and "Crippled Vets Love Sports."[30]

Wrote one jokester: "Imagine the game of basketball played with players moving over the court in midget autos. Impossible? Well, maybe with midgets, yes, but not with wheelchairs. And who wants to play basketball from a wheelchair? Paraplegics, that's who."[31]

Added another: "If you've ever seen donkey basketball, wheel-chair basketball is a first cousin."[32]

The demeaning language obscured the straightforward message that the players themselves wanted to deliver. "We are not helpless," one paralyzed veteran told *Newsweek* magazine. "Don't let anyone consider us so. We want to be known as men who happen to be paraplegics, not as paraplegics who once were men."[33]

CHAPTER 12

The Mecca

Just days after the Birmingham team departed New York City and concluded its cross-country jaunt, paralyzed veterans from Cushing and Halloran hospitals faced off in the mecca of basketball: Madison Square Garden.

Tex Rickard, the late boxing promoter, had built the famed arena in 1925 for his hockey team, the Rangers, but by the mid-1940s the Garden was best known as a basketball hub: home to the National Invitation Tournament (NIT), college basketball's premiere showcase; Ned Irish's New York Knicks of the BAA; regular visits by the Harlem Globetrotters, the sport's most recognizable team; and frequent college hoops doubleheaders.

After having denied Birmingham's request to play there, the Garden's about-face decision came not long after Halloran and Cushing clashed for the first time, on December 19, 1947. Playing on their home court on Staten Island, Halloran prevailed, 20–19, after Jack Gerhardt fueled a late rally in the seesaw battle. Gerhardt led all scorers with ten points, while Dick Foley and Paul Hogan tallied six apiece for the visitors.

Broadway and nightlife scribe Ed Sullivan attended the contest. In "Little Old New York," his widely read column in the *Daily*

News, he described the "neck-and-neck game" as the "most re-markable sight of the entire past twelve months."[1] Sullivan, who was three and a half months away from debuting his Sunday night variety show on TV, took credit for suggesting to Ned Irish that the Garden book a game of wheelchair basketball.

Perpetually seeking ways to boost attendance, Irish scheduled the Halloran-Cushing rematch as a preliminary to the Knicks–St. Louis Bombers BAA game at the Garden. Sullivan urged his readers to attend and predicted that the exhibition, sponsored in part by the eastern division of the Paralyzed Veterans of America, would be "one of the great spectacles of 1948, because the cour-age of the paraplegics is a great American saga, nothing less."[2]

His column helped sell thirty thousand dollars worth of ducats. It didn't hurt ticket sales that Birmingham's cross-country road swing had generated countless newspaper articles. Nor did it hurt matters that Halloran and Cushing were eager to renew the burgeoning rivalry.

During their first game, a Halloran player overturned his chair before quickly reseating himself. "Right away they started yell-ing, 'Ringer,'" laughed Syd Schiller, who had been wounded in Germany with the Third Division. The powerfully built center boasted that, for the upcoming game, Halloran was perfecting a "flying wedge" to penetrate Cushing's defense, using pivot plays and screens.[3]

Halloran didn't need any trickery. Its roster was loaded with talent, starting with co-captain Gerhardt, who had been wounded while fighting with the 82nd Airborne Division; forward Marty Slitzky, a 30th Infantry Division casualty in Europe; Selig Bosh-nack, a Purple Heart recipient for his service in the Battle of the Bulge; and Salvatore "Sam" Panepinto, paralyzed after he was thrown from a jeep while stationed in Germany.

"[Gerhardt] can move upcourt just as fast as any college man can run," said Matty Begovich, a well-respected referee who'd played on St. John's famed "Wonder Five" team. "He has marvelous co-ordination in stopping, feinting and cutting. He's a great athlete."[4]

Halloran built a loyal fan base by beating a slew of local, non-disabled collegians. They steamrolled Wagner College, St. John's (whose team included future Hall of Famer Dick McGuire), St. Francis, St. Peter's, Hofstra, and Manhattan College. They also downed the undefeated Violets from New York University, 38–26, denying future Hall of Famer Dolph Schayes and future U.S. Olympic gold medalist Ray Lumpp. In its only other game against paralyzed veterans, Halloran romped over the Charioteers from McGuire Hospital, 31–13, at the Palestra in Philadelphia, behind Gerhardt's game-high fourteen points.

Four days later, on March 10, 15,561 curious basketball fans flocked to the third iteration of Madison Square Garden, located in Midtown Manhattan between 49th and 50th Streets, its un-assuming entrance on Eighth Avenue sandwiched between the neon-lit storefronts of Adam Hats and Nedick's hot dog joint. Those few households in New York with black-and-white tele-vision sets, a technological marvel in 1948, could view the game on WCBS-TV; others awaited the newsreel footage that would be shown in coming days in movie theaters.

New York City mayor William O'Dwyer acted as official starter for a crowd that included Assistant Secretary of the Navy Mark Andrews and incoming Assistant Secretary of the Army Tracy Voorhees. Sitting courtside were 150 veterans in wheelchairs, after the removal of the entire first row of seats around the court. Beneath the glare of lights and a cloud of cigarette smoke, the Garden had "the stark quality of a George Bellows lithograph," *Newsweek* magazine reported.[5]

Halloran wheeled onto the court in navy-blue-and-white jerseys to warm applause. The royal-blue-and-orange-clad Cushing players received an equally appreciative greeting. The game began under east coast rules.

Although many New Yorkers had read about the Birmingham team's visit, only a handful of spectators had ever seen wheelchair basketball. Many of them cringed at the vicious crashes and held their breath when players whizzed down the court at breakneck speed. Concern turned to admiration after Gerhardt took charge and started tossing in buckets from inside and outside the paint; they roared with delight as Halloran's relentless pressure stifled Cushing's attack en route to a 12–9 edge at halftime.

This was "hell on wheels . . . speedy, big-league basketball, with no quarter asked and none given," according to *Newsweek*.[6] Gerhardt and Cushing's Manny Leonardo topped all scorers with eight points apiece, but Halloran pulled away in the fourth quarter to triumph comfortably, 20–11. (Much of the crowd stuck around to watch Ephraim "Red" Rocha and Belus Smawley lead the Bombers over the Knicks, 82–73, much to Ned Irish's dismay.)

Gerhardt instantly became the poster boy for paraplegia and wheelchair basketball when he adorned the cover of *Newsweek* soon after the game. Photographer Ed Wergeles, who'd shot for the army's *Yank* weekly during the war, snapped the color portrait of the twenty-two-year-old infantryman dressed in a PVA singlet, right arm cocked with a basketball, while sitting in an E&J wheelchair and wearing a pair of well-worn brown brogue shoes.

Beneath the photograph was the headline: "Paraplegics: The Conquest of Unconquerable Odds."

★ ★ ★

Birmingham's unprecedented road trip and the debut of wheel-chair basketball at Madison Square Garden did not go unnoticed among the sports aficionados at the Helms Athletic Foundation in Los Angeles.

Paul Hoy Helms was just a youngster when his mother died during childbirth. He was raised by relatives, including Major League outfielder William "Dummy" Hoy, his deaf uncle, who inspired Helms's lifelong love of sports. Helms made his fortune after launching an eponymous bakery and delivery service that supplied bread to athletes during the 1932 Los Angeles Olympic Games.

Shortly afterward, he funded the Helms Athletic Foundation under the leadership of former semipro baseball player Willrich "Bill" Schroeder. The organization made its reputation by assembling panels of sportswriters and experts to select national champions and All-Americans in various sports. In 1948, Helms Hall opened on Venice Boulevard, next to the bakery, as a sports museum–cum–library featuring Schroeder's collection of memorabilia, trophies, and books.

When the Birmingham veterans returned from their barn-storming adventure, the Helms Foundation declared them the national wheelchair basketball champions for the 1947–48 season. Stan Den Adel, Pat Grissom, Louis Palmer, Jess Rodriguez, and the other players each received a commemorative medal, and coach Bob Rynearson was presented with a silver trophy to be used as a challenge cup for future competitions among the teams of paralyzed veterans.

Schroeder acknowledged that Birmingham had been defeated by Cushing, but he pointed out that Birmingham was the only one to play the four other paraplegia units. Their 45–5 record, most of which came at the expense of non-disabled teams over the previous two seasons, was also cited.

Their archrivals in Framingham did not receive the news well. Dick Foley and the Cushing crew protested that, since they'd handily whipped Birmingham, they deserved the honor. That stance irked the Halloran players, who argued that, since they'd defeated Cushing twice and McGuire once, they were the champs. Both sides wondered whether Helms officials were suffering from West Coast bias.

The spat was settled by Harry Schweikert, the acerbic sports columnist for the PVA's *Paraplegia News*. Schweikert was wounded twice in France and received a battlefield commission to first lieutenant for the attack on Nuremberg in 1945. Paralyzed after the war in a motorcycle accident, he played wheelchair basketball for various teams while moonlighting as co-owner of the Ichiban Tavern in Union City, New Jersey, near the eastern offices of the PVA.[7]

Schweikert was an unapologetic booster of sports for paralyzed veterans (and civilians) because he'd experienced its recuperative powers. As the first journalist to write extensively about wheelchair sports, he considered himself to be an even-handed arbiter. In the quandary about which team deserved the national title, he ruled in favor of Birmingham.

He praised the team for hitting "the jackpot with a tour of the U.S. in their own plane," and chastised Cushing and Halloran for their grousing.[8] "I believe Cushing violated an unwritten law of sportsmanship by not agreeing to [play half the game under western rules]," he wrote. "I believe Halloran violated it even further by indignantly refusing to play [Birmingham] at all—with the temperamental remark that California, as challenger, should play under eastern rules."[9]

Schweikert also celebrated the announcement that Bob Ryn-earson's Birmingham squad had acquired a nickname. The team is "hereby christened and shall now and henceforth be known by all cagers, by all sportswriters, by all people of the quint courts, and especially by all of those on C Ramp, as the 'Flying Wheels,'" Schweikert proclaimed in *Paraplegia News*.[10]

The catchy moniker, which Rynearson attributed to a sugges-tion from one of his players, Ernest Kossow, spotlighted a team in perpetual motion, on the court and through the air. That the Flying Wheels would become as synonymous with wheel-chair basketball as the Celtics and the Knicks would become with professional basketball was a prediction that even Harry Schweikert didn't dare make in 1948.

★ ★ ★

Stan Den Adel's rehabilitation at Birmingham was going swim-mingly on all fronts, including off the court. He'd found himself smitten by Peggy Stapleton, the last-minute replacement nurse who had used her annual leave to care for the players on the cross-country tour.

When the trip was over, Stan asked the brown-eyed nurse if he could call her for a date. She gave him the phone number at the home she shared with her mother and went back to work at a hospital in West Los Angeles.

What neither Stan nor Peggy knew was that the phone was broken and did not accept incoming calls. He kept dialing the number and getting a busy signal. He figured he was getting the proverbial cold shoulder. But once the problem was fixed, the two connected.

On October 8, 1948, Stan and Peggy were married in the

chapel at Birmingham Hospital. Bob Rynearson served as best man. Stan donned his braces and crutches for the wedding so that he could navigate unaided down the aisle to the altar. It was, he said later, the last time he ever used the darn things. From then on, he was sticking to his E&J wheelchair. After the ceremony, acclaimed movie director John Ford (*Stagecoach*, *The Grapes of Wrath*) hosted a reception for the happy newlyweds and their guests at his ranch in nearby Reseda.

The intimate relationships that developed between paralyzed veterans and their nurses and aides often led to romance and even marriage. One of Stan's teammates, Ray Mitchell, wounded by a land mine with the infantry, met the woman who would become his wife, the former Annette Olsen, when she was a nurse at Birmingham. Cushing's Manny Leonardo married Patricia Ann Price, the nurse who had cared for him. His teammate, Dick Foley, was introduced to his wife, Sheila, when she volunteered with the Gray Ladies wing of the Red Cross.

Both parties welcomed the arrangement. These women understood what they were getting themselves into and were well aware of their partners' physical limitations. "Peg was very supportive of Stan," said his sister Shirley. "Being a nurse, she knew how to care for people in that situation."[11]

Women who married paralyzed veterans were often questioned about their choice of partner or, worse, faced insults and slurs. Arthur White, a paralyzed veteran at Halloran Hospital, was returning home from a PVA meeting with his wife, a former lieutenant in the Army Nurse Corps, when a neighbor reportedly shouted at her, "You can't get a real man, so you got one three-quarters dead," according to the *New York Times*.[12]

The neighbor was arraigned on a charge of disorderly conduct.

Couples who'd married before the war had to adjust to the

husband's new condition. They also had to deal with the widespread assumption that spinal-cord injuries caused permanent impotence (inability to achieve an erection) and infertility (inability to conceive a child) in the men. Dr. Bors at Birmingham was among the first to study the sexual function of individuals with paraplegia and to counter that misconception.

Writing in the *Journal of Urology*, Talbot acknowledged that spinal-cord injuries often disrupt the sex lives of the paralyzed veterans, from orgasm to fertility to self-image, depending on the severity and location of the injury. But in the limited survey he conducted, Talbot was optimistic that, with time and rehabilitation, "for many of them the door to reasonable gratification or even paternity need not be arbitrarily closed."[13]

When Lulu Laird married her husband, Bob Laird, a paralyzed veteran who was treated at Birmingham Hospital, she admitted that she had to ask herself: "Would I be nurse or wife?" Her answer: "Today, I am a wife—make no doubt about it . . . As Bob's wife, I am a very happy woman."[14]

Not every coupling succeeded. Gene Fesenmeyer met his first wife while rehabbing at Corona. Jane Carney was the daughter of a nurse at the hospital who was highly impressed by his wheelchair basketball skills and his new Cadillac. The marriage didn't last long. Gene blamed this on his in-laws' expectations during the baby boom in the United States. "She had a lot of people telling her, 'You could do better,'" he said. "Her family hated my ass because everyone wants to have grandkids." As he put it: "I'm sterile, but I can have sex."[15]

Couples that couldn't have children often pursued other options. Johnny and Dessa Winterholler adopted two children, a girl and a boy. Cushing's Dick Foley and his wife adopted two boys.

Stan and Peggy Den Adel adopted a girl. By then, Stan was

confident that he could support his family. He received full disability pay to the tune of $360 per month. His job at the hospital brought in a decent salary. He even worked as an extra in the 1950 Warner Bros. noir mystery *Backfire*, starring Gordon MacRae and Virginia Mayo, filmed on the Birmingham campus.

Den Adel was saving his money to build his dream home in the suburbs. Patients at Halloran Hospital had broached the idea of lobbying for government-funded homes for paralyzed veterans. They noted how challenging it was for them to leave the conveniences available in the hospital and move into ordinary homes and apartments that didn't address their disability: ramps instead of stairs, widened doorways, conveniently placed light switches and fixtures, showers with seats, and lowered bathroom basins and mirrors.

In collaboration with the American Institute of Architects, they completed blueprints for a four-room house, including an ideal garage, and then constructed a full-scale model on the hospital grounds.

"We don't want to live in hospitals all our lives," Halloran's Syd Schiller said. "Naturally we'd like homes. My family lives three flights up and everybody's crowded as it is, so where do we go?"[16]

Proposed federal legislation to provide such housing to the veterans, estimated to cost about $20,000 per home, brought together odd allies. Senator Joseph McCarthy (R–WI) sponsored an early version of the bill, while the Communist *Daily Worker* newspaper backed the concept. Traditional veterans' groups, as well as VA chief Omar Bradley and Republican Party stalwarts, opposed the measure.

Support gained momentum when seventy-five PVA members rolled into New York's Grand Central Terminal in their wheelchairs and obtained thousands of signatures in a petition campaign.[17] Representative Edith Nourse Rogers helped secure passage of a compromise bill, Public Law No. 702, signed by President Truman on June 19, 1948. It granted paralyzed veterans up to $10,000 to obtain adaptive housing designed to their specifications. By 1951, the VA had approved a total of seventeen million dollars for 1,880 veterans to build homes under P.L. 702, according to the PVA.[18]

If their E&J wheelchairs and hand-operated cars gave them mobility, and if playing basketball brought them a renewed sense of pride, then ownership of a comfortable, accessible home represented stability and a singular oasis for paralyzed veterans.

Den Adel used his grant to build a home on a two-and-a-half-acre spread in Granada Hills, in the San Fernando Valley, so that he could live independently with Peggy and remain close to his doctors and his job at Birmingham. The redwood and stucco home was constructed without a staircase or step; Stan could access every room, as well as outside, without leaving his wheelchair. The bathroom was built large enough so he could turn around in it in his E&J and easily lower himself into the spacious bathtub.[19]

Many other paralyzed vets from Birmingham followed suit. Pat Grissom built his own place in Northridge, while Gene Fesenmeyer settled in Woodland Hills.

When Johnny and Dessa Winterholler moved north to Oakland, they first rented a small apartment. Then they scouted for sites convenient to Dr. Gray's office in Oakland and his ranch in Walnut Creek. They purchased a half-acre lot in Lafayette, between the two places, for $5,100 and designed a single-level, ranch-style home that was built around Johnny and his wheelchair and included extra-wide doorways and special bathroom fixtures.

★ ★ ★

More than one million African Americans served during World War II in every branch of the military and in every theater of operations. Their units were segregated, and their potential for career advancement severely constricted. Black enlistees were often slotted into support roles, despite performing well in the field when given the opportunity.

And, while the GI Bill helped many white veterans buy homes, secure loans, and pay for college, African-American veterans were not able to benefit fully or equally. Black Americans were unable to enroll in segregated universities in the South and were denied low-cost mortgages when they tried to purchase homes in the growing suburbs.

After blacks and other servicemen of color (including Japanese Americans) had fought courageously to topple a totalitarian dictatorship built on the swamps of ethnic bigotry, it was clear that change was past overdue. If the United States was going to promote lofty international ideals of equality and freedom, Americans would have to address discrimination and injustice at home.

In July of 1948, one month after signing Public Law 702, President Truman abolished segregation in the U.S. military. Executive Order 9981 stated that "there shall be equality of treatment and opportunity for all persons in the armed services without regard to race, color, religion or national origin."[20]

Many officers and cabinet members were furious at Truman for integrating the military—most notably Secretary of the Army Kenneth Royall, who was forced to retire because of his opposition. Only gradually did military units and hospitals begin to integrate during the Korean War.

Quietly, one aspect of military life had already desegregated. The paraplegia wards within the VA hospitals treated servicemen from all backgrounds. Vaughan, the Bronx, and Birmingham were among those facilities known to treat black patients alongside white paralyzed veterans, as did the Naval Hospital at Corona.

This was not an entirely altruistic endeavor. African-American paralyzed veterans had nowhere else to turn because blacks-only hospitals did not have adequate resources for the treatment of paraplegia.

Wheelchair basketball, too, opened the gym doors to non-white veterans with paraplegia. Joseph Jordan was paralyzed when the jeep he was riding in skidded off a wet highway and struck a mine-field in northern France. He was hospitalized at McGuire Hospital in Virginia, and became an original member of the Charioteers. (Jordan later earned his law degree and argued successfully before the U.S. Supreme Court to overturn Virginia's poll tax.)

Another pioneering black wheelchair player, Maurice Brooks, was paralyzed when he was shot in the spine in Germany. The Chicago native rehabbed at Hines and, while attending the Joseph Bulova School of Watchmaking in New York, joined the school's team. Two Latino players with paraplegia, Jess Rodriguez and Gil Ortiz, were mainstays on Birmingham's original teams, while Norman Harris was the first African-American ballplayer on the Flying Wheels.

Truman's Executive Order 9981 marked a breakthrough, but it came too late for the likes of Jackie Robinson. The brother of U.S. Olympic sprinter Mack Robinson, Jackie lettered in four sports at UCLA between 1939 and 1941: football, basketball, baseball, and track. He was among the most gifted athletes this country has ever produced, but no major professional sports team signed him to a contract because of his skin color.

In 1942, when Robinson was drafted into the army after Pearl Harbor, the U.S. military was as segregated as professional sports (with the exception of boxing). There were scant few black officers, but thanks to the intervention of heavyweight champ Joe Louis, Robinson was admitted to Officer Candidate School at Fort Riley, Kansas. He was assigned to the 761st Tank Battalion, the original "Black Panthers," at Camp Hood, Texas.

During training, Robinson refused a white bus driver's demand that he give up his seat and move to the back of the bus. He was court-martialed for insubordination and, after a trial, acquitted of all charges.[21]

In October of 1945, after he received his honorable discharge, Robinson signed a contract with the Brooklyn Dodgers organization. He played for the minor-league Montreal Royals in 1946. The following spring, he stepped from the Brooklyn Dodgers dugout at Ebbets Field to smash Major League Baseball's decades-old color barrier.

The NFL had integrated in the fall of 1946, when Kenny Washington and Woody Strode, two of Robinson's teammates at UCLA, took to the field for the Los Angeles Rams. In the summer of 1948, Don Barksdale, the son of a Pullman porter and another UCLA standout, became the first African American selected for the U.S. Olympic basketball team. Barksdale later joined the NBA after the league integrated in 1950.

Jim Crow did not disappear with the signing of a presidential decree and the signing of professional sports contracts, of course. But it's also true that the integration of the armed forces and professional sports helped change public perception about race just as the burgeoning civil rights movement was gaining momentum.

In the same way, exhibitions of wheelchair sports and news

reports about accessible housing did not vanquish societal prejudice and ignorance surrounding disability. But the presence of
the paralyzed veterans on the basketball court, and their demands
for much-needed benefits, helped usher in a more enlightened
era just as people with disabilities were beginning their arduous
fight for equal rights.

This was a time of change, a time to reconsider stereotypes and
prejudices, a time when ability—not disability or skin color—
shone like a beacon.

CHAPTER 13

Stoke Mandeville Games

On the hottest day in London in thirty-seven years, King George VI stood in his crisp, dark naval uniform in the Royal Box at Wembley Stadium and proclaimed open the fourteenth Olympiad of the modern era.

The 1948 Olympics were the first Summer Games in the twelve years since the propaganda whitewash of the "Nazi Olympics" in Berlin (and followed the canceled 1940 and 1944 editions due to the war). Germany and Japan were barred from the games because of their "aggressor" roles in the war, while the Soviet Union declined to participate for ideological reasons.

Exhausted Londoners were in dire need of distraction and cheer. The times were "Make Do and Mend," with strict rationing of food, clothing, fuel, and essential supplies. The belt-tightening extended to the Olympics, which became known as the "Austerity Games." With just two years to prepare and no money to build fancy new venues, Olympic organizers converted the greyhound racing track at Wembley into a cinder track for athletic events. There was no Olympic Village to accommodate the competitors. The men bunked in Royal Air Force and Army camps, while the women boarded in college dorms. The athletes used public transportation to get to their events, and the hosts humbly requested that visiting teams supply their own food.

"I have to admire the English people," said Ray Lumpp, an Army Air Force veteran who played guard for the gold medal–winning U.S. basketball team. "Everything they had, they shared with us."[1]

On July 29, 1948, under a blazing sun, some four thousand athletes representing fifty-nine countries marched around the Wembley track during the opening ceremony. Many in the short-sleeved crowd of nearly 90,000 spectators wept when 7,000 pigeons were released into the sky. "The flash of wings was like a snowstorm on that brilliant summer afternoon," the *Wembley News* reported.[2]

The loudest cheers were reserved for the resolute host nation's athletes and coaches who, as dictated by tradition, entered the procession last. They roared "like 700 lions," recalled British diver Peter Elliot,[3] as flag-bearer and fencer John Emrys Lloyd swept past the Royal Box and dipped the Union Jack to the King and the Queen.

One member of Britain's team was excluded from the procession. Jack Dearlove was the coxswain for the men's eight in the rowing competition. When he was eleven, his right leg had been amputated after he fell off a bicycle and was run over by a truck.

Dearlove did what kids often do: he adapted. He learned to get around on crutches and led an active life, which included marriage and three kids. At the ripe age of thirty-seven, he was a mainstay with the Thames Rowing Club, which won the Grand Challenge Cup at the prestigious Henley Royal Regatta.

Before the opening ceremony, Dearlove was informed that he would not be allowed to join the procession. His disability was apparently so dispiriting that officials prevented the audience (and TV viewers, too, as the BBC's broadcast coverage marked the first time the Olympic Games were shown on home television) from glimpsing his disability. Instead, he watched the proceedings from the stands as his teammates basked in the spotlight.[4]

Dearlove put aside his personal humiliation once the competition began. His ability in the boat remained unassailable; he guided England to the silver medal behind the Cal Berkeley crew representing the United States.

★ ★ ★

On the same day that the world's greatest amateur athletes gathered at Wembley, a different kind of contest commenced outside the market town of Aylesbury, located about forty miles from the stadium.

The inaugural Stoke Mandeville Games featured two teams of sixteen paralyzed veterans from the war, including two women, who competed in exactly one sport: archery. Patients from Stoke Mandeville Hospital and the Royal Star and Garter Home for injured servicemen rolled their wheelchairs to the hospital's neatly manicured front lawn and shot at targets placed some fifty yards distant.

After several rounds of shooting, Star and Garter defeated their hosts to win the Archery Shield Trophy. Then they enjoyed trays of homemade cakes and sandwiches and sipped tea and pints of beer with the doctors, nurses, and attendants. The Royal Air Force band supplied musical entertainment.

No one observing the festivities that afternoon would have thought to link this modest endeavor with the grandeur of the Olympics, however limited they were by the economic constraints of postwar England. No one could have foreseen that the Stoke

Mandeville Games would grow to become the Paralympics, the premiere sports competition for athletes with disabilities.

No one, that is, except for the man who ruled over Stoke Mandeville's spinal-injury center like a despot.

Dr. Ludwig Guttmann was forty-nine years old. He was a pint-sized figure with a small paunch, twinkling blue eyes behind rimless glasses, a thin mustache, and a thick, guttural accent. *Daily Mail* reporter Pat Williams described him as "a cross between Alfred Hitchcock and a pixie."[5]

Guttmann was a German-born neurosurgeon who possessed an extraordinary medical mind and an academic and professional résumé that ran for pages. He was also an ambitious self-promoter who achieved worldwide fame while revolutionizing the field of paraplegia. His treatment precepts broke with orthodoxy and influenced scores of physicians and researchers who visited Stoke Mandeville to study his methodology. His work and his writing hold sway even today, some forty years after his death.

Ludwig Guttmann was born in 1899 in the small town of Tost in Upper Silesia (now part of Poland). When Guttmann was a youngster, his Orthodox Jewish family moved to the coal-mining town of Königshütte, where he worked as an orderly at the local hospital—emptying bedpans, bathing patients, assisting in the operating room—while awaiting his call-up for World War I.

Guttmann observed his first spinal-cord injury when a well-built miner broke his back and received what was then state-of-the-art treatment. Four attendants held the injured man in the air in a supine position, Guttmann recalled, "two pulling on his legs and two on the upper limbs with the aid of towels fixed under the patient's armpits, while the surgeon reduced the fracture forcibly with his right fist from below. The patient was then put in a plaster cast and . . . screened off from other patients."[6]

Doctors told Guttmann that the patient would be dead within six weeks. Sure enough, he expired in five weeks. The picture of the hapless, deteriorating coal miner "remained indelibly fixed in my memory," Guttmann recalled in an unpublished memoir.[7]

Guttmann tried to enlist in the German Army, as his father had, but he was excused because of illness. He began studies at the University of Breslau, and earned his medical degree from Freiburg University in 1924. He was thinking of specializing in pediatrics when a friend suggested that there might be an opening in the neurology department at the hospital in Breslau. The encounter altered the professional course of his life.

Neurology is the branch of medicine that treats disorders of the nervous system, including spinal-cord injuries. The chief neurologist at Breslau hospital was Dr. Otfrid Foerster, already a legendary figure in the nascent field. (He treated Vladimir Lenin after his debilitating stroke.) Foerster had, coincidentally, worked at the hospital in Königshütte during World War I and was one of the few doctors who'd treated soldiers with spinal-cord injuries.

Guttmann worked first under and then alongside Foerster for most of the next decade. He studied pain pathways and the symptomatology of spinal-cord injuries, and detailed the sensory and motor loss that people with paraplegia sustain at each vertebral level, from the upper cervical (neck) area to the sacral (tailbone) segments. Guttmann also learned how to work eighteen-hour days, something his wife, Else, was forced to accept.

Foerster routinely hired Jewish doctors like Guttmann, but the rise of Adolf Hitler ended that practice. Guttmann and other Jewish physicians and nurses were dismissed from their jobs and forbidden from treating Aryan patients. Guttmann was offered various positions abroad. At one time he held a visa to go to

America. But believing that "this Nazi business could not last longer than two or three years," as he noted in an oral history with the Imperial War Museums, he stayed put.[8] He took one of the few posts he was allowed to take under the Nazi regime: chief neurologist and neurosurgeon at the Jewish Hospital in Breslau, where he oversaw a seventy-five-bed unit and a staff of unpaid Jewish doctors.

His thinking about the Nazis changed after the night of November 9, 1938—better known as Kristallnacht—when Jewish-owned homes, businesses, and schools were vandalized, and thousands were arrested, tortured, and sent to concentration camps. Guttmann contacted the British Society for the Protection of Science and Learning, an organization that helped foreign scholars escape persecution. The society secured visas for Guttmann, his wife, and their two children as well as a small grant for him to do research in neurosurgery at the Radcliffe Infirmary in Oxford.

Before departing, Guttmann bade farewell to his father. It was the last time he saw him alive. Bernhard Guttmann died in the Theresienstadt concentration camp, north of Prague, in 1942. Ludwig Guttmann's eldest sister died at Auschwitz, as did her husband and other members of his family.

Dr. Guttmann and his family sailed to Dover on March 14, 1939. They were greeted by rain, sleet, and wind as they took their places in a long immigration queue. An officer noticed the children, ages ten and six, shivering in the cold, and called them forward to process their papers. The gesture restored Guttmann's "confidence in humanity," he said. "That was England."[9]

Hitler's condemnation of Jewish scientists and doctors had real-life ramifications. During the years before and after World War I, Germany had gained a vaunted reputation for sophisticated scientific and medical research. That hub of knowledge was undone once scores of Jewish physicians and scientists fled their homeland and the Nazis. The "brain drain" exodus included more than a dozen Nobel laureates, the physicists who went on to develop the atomic bomb for the United States, and a biologist who helped unravel the antibacterial effects of penicillin.

Just when Germany most needed the skills of Dr. Ludwig Guttmann and many others, its leaders exiled them, ignored them, or murdered them.

★ ★ ★

Ludwig Guttmann had grown accustomed to directing hospital staff and performing surgeries. But at Oxford, he was relegated to conducting experimental research on nerve regeneration in animals. Meanwhile, his children mastered the intricacies of the English language much more quickly than he did.

That sense of frustration changed abruptly when Allied forces began planning the invasion of Western Europe to open a second front. Dr. George Riddoch, chair of the Peripheral Nerve Injury Committee for the Medical Research Council in England, anticipated the arrival of numerous patients with spinal-cord injuries during and after the D-Day assault. In preparation, Riddoch called on Guttmann to review the existing facilities for spinal-cord injuries in England.

Guttmann's well-researched memoranda, recently uncovered among Riddoch's papers, detailed his concerns about the subpar and outmoded practices he observed. He rejected the conventional, hands-off "recumbency" approach, where patients were immobilized inside plaster casts, confined to their beds, and hooked up to morphine—a process that generally doomed them to death by infection within six months.[10]

Instead, echoing the enlightened tactics employed by Dr. Donald Munro in Boston, Guttmann advocated for the comprehensive care of paralyzed patients. A person with paraplegia should not be considered "merely as a neurological, orthopedic, urological, or plastic surgical case," he argued, "but as an individual." It was the job of doctors "to treat a human being and not a disease."[11] He called for isolating the paralyzed veterans in specialized units and incorporating exercise and activities into their rehabilitation.

Impressed, Riddoch asked Guttmann to run a new spinal-cord center at Stoke Mandeville Hospital, located in Buckinghamshire County, under the auspices of the Ministry of Pensions. Guttmann accepted with one stipulation: he demanded total authority over every aspect of the unit.

Riddoch acquiesced. The national Spinal Injuries Center opened with twenty-six beds in February of 1944, about three months before the D-Day invasion.

Guttmann started at Stoke Mandeville without an office. The equipment was outdated and inadequate, and the doctors, nurses, and physiotherapists were unfamiliar with paraplegia. As for the first wave of patients who were admitted, Guttmann found their condition to be "in a very shocking state," with rampant pressure sores, urinary tract infections, and depression the norm. Many were snugly wrapped in plaster shells from head to heel.[12]

He threw himself into the job. There were many weeks he commuted by bus from his home in Oxford to Aylesbury on Monday morning and didn't return to his family until the weekend. His around-the-clock perfectionism—and what some critics described as an obstinate temperament—didn't win him many friends initially. He was viewed suspiciously because he was an outsider—Jewish and, worse, a foreign alien with a thick German accent. He challenged conventional thinking by stating that, with proper care, patients with paraplegia could recover and, with training, secure steady employment. His goal, he liked to say, was to convert "helpless, hopeless, paralyzed patients into tax-paying citizens."[13]

No detail was too small. He demanded that thirty metal bedpans be replaced with rubber models because the latter didn't produce pressure sores. He helped design the Stoke Mandeville Turning and Tilting Bed, an electrical device that obviated the need for nurses to manually turn the paralyzed veterans every two hours. His observations about autonomic dysreflexia (AD)—which more commonly occurs when the blood pressure of patients with a spinal-cord injury at or above the sixth thoracic (T6) vertebra (located approximately at the bottom of the shoulder blades) spikes suddenly—enabled doctors to understand and treat this life-threatening syndrome. By the end of 1944, the unit had more than doubled in size to more than sixty beds.

Veterans had little choice but to submit to Guttmann's gruff ministrations. A lavishly illustrated story that appeared in *Picture Post* magazine showed Stoke Mandeville's "lucky patients" as they received physical therapy. Headlined "Making New Men," the article revealed that "one secret of Dr. Guttmann's success is to make the patient want to get better, and do things for himself. When he begins to take an interest in his progress, and particularly when he begins to plan for his new life when he leaves hospital, success is sure."[14]

Albert Bull, an army chaplain who was paralyzed during the invasion of Sicily, recalled being embarrassed when Guttmann stopped by his hospital bed and "insist[ed] on relating the awful state of my bowels" to the assemblage.

"He drove his staff and patients ruthlessly," Bull said. "Some could not take it and were treated with short shrift. But as I look back I know we needed to be bullied. It is so easy to sit back, feel sorry for yourself and allow others to do everything for you."[15]

Another veteran told Guttmann that he was going to give his young wife a divorce because he believed she'd find marriage to him unsatisfying. Guttmann scoffed at the notion and counseled the husband to return home.

"One day I received a terse telegram: 'Twins, Sir'!" Guttmann related. "Altogether he has had four children."[16]

A paralyzed veteran visiting from the United States compared Guttmann to Bors. "He is much like Dr. Bors," he wrote in *The Cord*, "excitable, blowing up one minute and coming back five minutes later as if nothing had happened, and vitally concerned with paraplegia and assisting paraplegics and spreading what he called 'The World Paraplegic Movement.'"[17]

★ ★ ★

Like his American counterparts, Guttmann was a true believer in the healing power of sports and exercise. Guttmann ordered Quartermaster Sergeant Instructor Thomas "Q" Hill, on loan from the army, to put the patients through rigorous physiotherapy regimens. Hill played catch with veterans using a medicine ball to build up their shoulders, arms, and chest muscles, and he introduced darts, billiards, skittles (a form of bowling), and rope-climbing.

Archery was considered the ideal sport because the former servicemen could aim their bows and shoot their arrows from a seated position, thereby "strengthening, in a very natural way, just those muscles of the upper limbs, shoulders and trunk, on which the paraplegic's well-balanced, upright position depends," Guttmann said.[18] Archery was also an activity at which they could compete on equal terms with non–disabled athletes and women could compete on equal terms with men.

Guttmann's first experiment with team sports was wheelchair polo. He and "Q" sat in wheelchairs and, using shortened walking sticks as mallets, whacked around a weighted ball while trying to prevent the other man from scoring.

"Judging from my own and my opponent's difficulty in maneuvering the chair and keeping our legs still in position, a sport was about to be created in which the paraplegic was clearly less handicapped than the able-bodied," he concluded. "[A]ny wheelchair team of able-bodied players was hopelessly beaten by the paraplegic polo-teams."[19]

Wheelchair polo never caught on. One major obstacle was the equipment—that is, the wheelchairs. The sleek E&J models had yet to cross the Atlantic; Stoke Mandeville patients were consigned to well-padded, high-backed chairs that were akin to brown leather armchairs on wheels. While sturdy and comfortable, they weighed more than twice as much as the E&Js. These antediluvian devices were designed for the days when attendants pushed people with paraplegia onto veranda porches, not for self-propelled, fast-motion recreation.

In 1945, Guttmann began to experiment with another team sport: wheelchair netball. Again, he seated himself in a chair to play for the doctors' team against the patients. Again, the patients defeated the non-disabled team.

Netball is a cousin of basketball. The game is played with seven players per side; each is restricted to prescribed zones on the court. No dribbling is allowed. A ring and a net, placed at the top of a freestanding stanchion, constitute the goal; the ring is smaller in diameter than a basketball hoop. Backboards are not used.

The sport was rarely seen or played in the United States, but it was embraced in England (and Australia) as the women's version of James Naismith's invention. The wheelchair netball played at

Stoke Mandeville was a hybrid version. Netball's ring and net were used, but the restrictive zones were eliminated, giving the game more of a free-flowing flavor. It swiftly became the rage at the hospital in spite of the antiquated wheelchairs, with women competing alongside the men on the hospital's makeshift outdoor court.

Guttmann took credit for introducing to the world what he dubbed as "wheelchair basketball." This was probably an inadvertent error, either due to his ignorance about the differences between netball and basketball or his adjustment to the subtle peculiarities of the English language. Even today, websites devoted to adaptive sports inaccurately state that Guttmann "invented" wheelchair basketball. It's more accurate to say that he began experimenting with wheelchair sports as part of the rehabilitation process at Stoke Mandeville at roughly the same time that wheelchair sports, and specifically wheelchair basketball, were being developed in U.S. paraplegia wards.

No matter the exact terminology, Guttmann preached the benefits of sports at every opportunity. He decided to turn the Stoke Mandeville Games into an annual event, and invited cabinet ministers, royalty, and prominent sports officials and athletes to observe the action. On his travels abroad, he urged other nations to get involved. He published a magazine devoted to spinal-cord research called *The Cord*—with glossy advertisements for Guinness ale and Johnny Walker Scotch—that featured long articles about the competition.

"The idea [of games]," he wrote, "is to distract the patient's attention from his disability, to keep the man's intelligence and concentration lively, to promote a good blood circulation, to keep his healthy limbs supple, and to invigorate the body."[20]

His embrace of wheelchair sports was savvy public relations on

Guttmann's part. He understood that his adopted country relished its role as the progenitor of modern sport, having birthed soccer, cricket, tennis, golf, and rugby, and exported these and other pastimes to far-flung outposts of the globe, including the United States. English sportsmen were quick to point out, accurately, that the Wenlock Olympian Games, an annual event initiated by Dr. William Penny Brookes in 1850, inspired Anglophile Pierre de Coubertin to revive the Olympic Games in 1896. Gents perusing copies of the *Times of London* inside the city's most exclusive clubs still harrumphed that the Battle of Waterloo was won on the playing fields of Eton.

Guttmann was equally shrewd to align the Stoke Mandeville Games with the Olympic Games. It was surely no coincidence that he launched the competition on the opening day of the 1948 London Olympics. An early SMG logo featured three interlocking wheels (from a wheelchair), reminiscent of the five interlaced rings of the Olympic emblem.

The second Stoke Mandeville Games, in the summer of 1949, grew to seven clubs and thirty-seven paralyzed men and women. Wheelchair netball was added to the program, with three teams competing on the outdoor court. In what is believed to be the world's first wheelchair netball tourney, veterans from Lyme Green Settlement in Cheshire won the crown. (A woman identified as Margaret Webb played for Stoke Mandeville's team and took the court along with nine men.)

That afternoon, after tea was served, Guttmann proclaimed that, one day, what he called the "Grand Festival of Paraplegic Sports" would become "truly international and...achieve worldwide fame as the disabled men and women's equivalent of the Olympic Games."[21]

He would not be wrong.

CHAPTER 14

Gizz Kids

The Flying Wheels refused to stay grounded.

In early 1949, Bob Rynearson and Birmingham's wheelchair basketball team doubled down for a cross-country encore. Tour manager John Old had little trouble raising $15,000 to finance the journey after gossip columnist Hedda Hopper drummed up support from her Tinseltown connections. Gregory Peck ($50), John Ford ($350), Red Skelton ($100), Jimmy Durante ($100), and Walt Disney ($250) were among the donors, as were the Hollywood Stars and the Los Angeles Angels minor-league baseball teams.

In a grand coup, Hopper persuaded billionaire tycoon and aviator Howard Hughes to furnish a TWA airliner for the occasion. (Hughes happened to be the company's principal stockholder.) The veterans had shivered through a series of frosty flights the previous year. This time they were better prepared; they wrapped themselves inside "snuggies"—described in *Paraplegia News* as "a woolen sack, matching their uniform, which was drawn up around legs and hips and zippered at the side."[1]

The Wheels warmed up by defeating a group of U.S. Olympic basketball players, including Frank Lubin and Art Mollner from the Universal Pictures squad, and a team that featured movie stars John Wayne and Sonny Tufts. They revamped the roster, too, promoting Gil Ortiz, injured in the Pacific with the 154th combat engineers, and Nessim "Turk" Behmoiram, wounded in the Philippines with the 136th Infantry Regiment, to the varsity. George McReynolds, paralyzed while with the 90th Infantry Division, captained the squad in place of Stan Den Adel.

All of the publicity produced by their first expedition had inspired a boomlet of wheelchair basketball teams to develop in their wake. A group of Kansas City, Missouri–based veterans watched the Birmingham boys in action and decided "we'd like to form a team of our own," said team captain Bob Miller, who was injured on Omaha Beach on D-Day while serving with the 149th Combat Engineers. "We used our own wheelchairs in the first few [times] that we gathered out on an open basketball court on a playground."[2]

Sponsored by the American War Dads organization, the Wheelchair Bulldozers moved beyond the original mandate of paraplegia and filled out their roster with players who had experienced other disabilities. Joe Lawrence and Ray White were bilateral amputees, Lawrence having lost both legs below the knee on Okinawa, and White incurring his injury from a land mine in Germany. Doug Keaton, a high-school hoops hotshot, had contracted polio.

"We are proud to assist in extending the benefits of wheelchair basketball to the afflicted ones who share in it," Miller commented, "and particularly to the youths whose leg disabilities were caused by disease, accident, or other impairment that left them able to play this game…In performing this service for all leg-handicapped individuals who play or attend wheelchair basketball games, we feel that we are applying this sport to what will be demonstrated to be truly its most worthy purpose."[3]

175

Post–polio patients from New Utrecht High School in Brooklyn got together to start a team called the Whirlaways. The Rolling Gophers comprised veterans from Minneapolis and St. Paul; one of their top players, Jim McGarry, was a double amputee whose legs had been crushed in a railroad accident when he was a kid. The Jersey Wheelers, based in Paterson, was another "hometown" team of paralyzed veterans that also allowed amputees onto the squad. Dick Maduro, injured in a motorcycle accident, was organizing the Free Wheelers in the Tampa–St. Petersburg area with a roster of paralyzed veterans, single and double amputees, and post-polios.

Adding post-polios, amputees, and civilians to the cadre of paralyzed veterans expanded the talent pool for wheelchair sports. The grim reality was that the number of spinal-cord injuries that occurred away from the battlefield far exceeded the number of paralyzed veterans. Polio (also known as infantile paralysis) remained an ever-present danger in the late 1940s and early 1950s, when epidemics crippled tens of thousands of children and young adults. And there were the many casualties of everyday life: car, truck, and motorcycle crashes; accidents while diving, cycling, hunting, and participating in other pastimes; workplace-related injuries.

"While the three-and-a-half-year time span of World War II had produced about seventeen thousand amputees among servicemen," Dr. Howard Rusk wrote in his autobiography, "it had also created a hundred and twenty thousand amputees among our civilian population."[4]

The new teams clamored to meet the famous Wheels. "We will play anywhere at anytime and have five extra chairs," wrote William Young of the Evansville Rolling Rockets, a team made up of paralyzed veterans in Indiana, in a letter sent to Birmingham

Hospital. "We are undefeated and have had good crowds. We have uniforms."[5]

Timothy Nugent, an instructor of rehabilitation and physical re-education at the Galesburg Division of the University of Illinois, invited the Flying Wheels to play in a wheelchair basketball tourney the first week of April.

"Three wheelchair teams have already entered in the tournament," he wrote in a letter sent to Howard Hughes, in care of the mogul's RKO movie studio. "We would like to have your team participate in order to give this program a truly national flavor."[6]

By the time Hughes's office forwarded the letter to Bob Rynearson, the Wheels had already left California. Their second jaunt introduced wheelchair basketball to Texas, Oklahoma, and Michigan. They lost to Bob Miller and the Bulldozers in Kansas City before the "dozen Joes who gave their legs to Uncle Sam during the war," as they were described by the local newspaper, whipped the Oklahoma City University football team, 41–6, in an exhibition played before the semifinal games at the AAU national tourney.[7]

The East Coast swing was a disaster, as the Wheels renewed their acquaintance with six PVA-affiliated teams: paralyzed veterans from Cushing, Halloran, Bronx, St. Albans, McGuire, and Kennedy hospitals. With another season of experience, these squads were vastly improved, and the visitors managed wins only against McGuire and Kennedy. The Wheels blamed their crowded social calendar for the lowly 2–4 record: "Must have been the nite life!" was their excuse.[8]

On their return to Los Angeles, they celebrated with Hedda Hopper at the Barclay Kitchen, a hangout for Hollywood's movers-and-shakers. She swooned over them and related to her readers, "I never had a gayer evening. What stories! The boys are carefree, have no worries, and you'd never know they were handicapped...The party was stag except for Hopper. They're the best beaux I've found in a long time."[9]

★ ★ ★

The Wheels' second trip enhanced the growth of the sport and prodded the players to think beyond one-off exhibition games. The Halloran team took steps to organize a league of PVA-affiliated teams. McReynolds, the Wheels' captain, expressed interest in arranging a national tournament for all wheelchair basketball teams in the country, including non-veterans, on the same scale as those held for non-disabled cagers, like the well-known AAU and NIT tourneys.

Instead, it would take the forceful—some would say abrasive—personality of a non-disabled twenty-four-year-old doctoral student to jumpstart the transformation of wheelchair basketball from a rehabilitation tool geared exclusively toward paralyzed veterans at VA hospitals into a competitive sport for people with all manner of disabilities, with standardized rules for the teams, trained officials, a formal league, an annual national tournament and, eventually, international competition, and a wheelchair basketball hall of fame.

Timothy J. Nugent was born in Pittsburgh in 1923. His early years were traumatically chaotic. His father, a businessman, was hearing- and sight-impaired; his beloved youngest sister progressively lost her sight. Nugent himself had heart ailments that required multiple surgeries and kept him from playing ball and climbing trees. At different stretches in his youth he lived with an aunt and family friends. He basically raised his younger brother and two sisters because, he later related in an oral history, "Dad was never home."[10] In all, he attended eight grade schools and two high schools before graduating.

Nugent used athletics and a gritty resolve to surmount this tumultuous upbringing. He played football and ran track at Rufus King High School in Milwaukee, and set the school's high jump record. During two summers, he lifted two hundred-pound forgings, transforming himself from a "skinny little runt" into a muscular young man built "like a bull."[11]

He entered La Crosse State Teachers College in Wisconsin as a physical education and health major before enlisting in the army in 1943. He served with both the 99th Division and the 1st Division, and was awarded the Bronze Star for combat duty in Europe. A leg infection introduced him to the way military hospitals treated battle-wounded servicemen. After the war, he earned his bachelor's degree from La Crosse and began graduate work in educational psychology at the University of Wisconsin.

In the fall of 1948, Nugent was hired to create a comprehensive educational and rehabilitation program for students with permanent disabilities on the Galesburg campus of the University of Illinois. He took the job figuring he'd write his doctoral thesis about the experience and then return to Wisconsin to start his career. The concept itself was radical: "the integration of disabled students into a mainstream college campus, beginning with disabled veterans under the auspices of the Veterans Administration, but also including civilians with disabilities eager for a college education," according to disability rights historian Fred Pelka.[12]

Square-jawed and bespectacled, with a shock of red hair, Nugent threw himself into the job so zealously that he never returned to finish his dissertation. By the time he retired in 1985, after a thirty-seven-year career at the University of Illinois, he was recognized as the "Father of Accessibility," an internationally renowned expert not only in wheelchair sports but in myriad fields related to disability: education, legislation, transportation, housing, and architecture.

In the aftermath of World War II, only a handful of universities were opening their doors to paralyzed veterans, most notably UCLA in Southern California, where some twenty-five PVA members from Birmingham Hospital, including Stan Den Adel, were enrolled.

The Galesburg site began as a U.S. Army hospital. Declared as surplus in 1946, the hospital was converted into a branch of the University of Illinois, attracting hundreds of veterans covered by the GI Bill and other government-assistance programs. The sprawling campus was ideally contoured for wheelchair access, even during winter: sixty one-story, well-ramped brick units connected by heated, covered corridors, with convenient mess halls, laboratories, medical facilities, a gym, and an enormous indoor swimming pool.

Nugent was determined "to make it possible for people with severe disabilities to go to school and benefit from all the facilities provided, be they curricular or extracurricular," he later said. "The idea was to go to regular classes from the beginning. We didn't want special treatment. We attacked everything at once—therapy clinics, counseling, and sports—but concentrated on facilities that first year."[13]

Galesburg's first student with paraplegia was a married veteran named Harold Scharper. The staff sergeant had been wounded four times while fighting in Sicily and elsewhere in Italy with the Third Division's 15th Infantry unit. The last injury, at the Anzio beachhead, left him paralyzed. He mended at Hines VA hospital and attended the PVA's first national meeting there before enrolling at Galesburg, with support from the American Legion. A handful of other paralyzed students, most of them veterans, and one of them a woman, joined him.

Nugent found that the residents of Galesburg, a sedate community best known as the birthplace of poet-biographer Carl Sandburg, needed to be educated about the potential of those with disabilities. "We went out to [the Harbor Lights Supper Club] in the north end of Galesburg," he told Fred Pelka. "I [came] in with Harold Scharper and his wife. His wife was an attractive able-bodied lady, and I remember a couple of couples sitting at the bar, and one of the women turned around and asked, 'They don't allow those people in here now too, do they?' And she said it loud enough that Harold's wife heard it, and it was one of the worst fights that I ever had to break up."[14]

Central to Nugent's rehabilitation philosophy was physical re-education. "I realized very quickly...that they needed more than clinical therapy and more than counseling—they needed an opportunity to be alive and to sense a feeling of achievement and belongingness," he later said. Sports "helped [them] to overcome self-consciousness and it helped to develop self-confidence on the part of the individual with a disability," he maintained. They "have benefited in that they have been able to experience physical, emotional and social therapy through the sport—give vent to their frustrations and their energies and what not."[15]

Or, as he put it, "Why have a bicep if there is no use for it?"[16]

Adaptive bowling was his first attempt at recreation. Nugent and his students built a newfangled ramp that allowed them to bowl from their wheelchairs. The team of students with paraplegia was nicknamed the Squatters, while the amputees were called the Stompers.

His next foray was to follow in the tracks of the Flying Wheels and start a wheelchair basketball team. He raised money through the local chapter of the American War Dads to buy ten E&J wheelchairs and three basketballs, and the Chicago *Daily News* donated five chairs from its veterans' fund.

The student-athletes on the world's first collegiate wheelchair basketball team were primarily paralyzed veterans like Hal Scharper, with a mix of post-polios. Unlike Dr. Ludwig Guttmann, Nugent did not permit his female students to play organized wheelchair sports; they were consigned to the less-enlightened duty of wheelchair cheerleading.

Nugent's basketball team dubbed themselves the Gizz Kids, a nickname taken from the short-lived team at Hines VA hospital. In this case, "Gizz Kids" carried a double meaning. The first meaning was obvious to college basketball fans in and around the cities of Champaign and Urbana, where the main campus of the University of Illinois is located, about 150 miles south of Chicago.

The Fighting Illini teams of the early 1940s drew exuberant crowds to George Huff Gymnasium, thanks to a wondrous amalgamation of fast-breaking scoring and strangulating defense from the homegrown starting five of Gene Vance, Jack Smiley, "Handy Andy" Phillip, Ken Menke, and Art Mathisen. An offhand remark about the quintet's speedy stylings by WGN broadcaster Jack Brickhouse resulted in a memorable label: the Whiz Kids.

The 1941–42 squad won the Big Ten Conference and qualified for the NCAA tournament. The 1942–43 edition went undefeated in the Big Ten and finished with a 17–1 record, their only loss coming to the army service team stationed at Camp Grant. They were the odds-on favorite to win one of the two college basketball tourneys, the NIT or the NCAA, but before postseason play tipped off, three of the Whiz Kids were inducted into the army.

Coach Doug Mills decided that the team would not participate in any tournament without the missing players. "We were
shooting for the national championship and Uncle Sam changed
all that," Gene Vance later recalled.[17] (Johnny Winterholler's
alma mater, the University of Wyoming, ended up winning the
NCAA title that year.)

Gizz Kids surely echoed Whiz Kids, but it also referred to
gizmos, the slang word for catheters. "Gizz Kids" thus was
appropriate for basketball zealots, while also delivering a wink
and a nudge to people with paraplegia. There were "many inside
jokes about dribbling," according to Nugent.[18]

Coached by Nugent, the "galloping Gismos" easily won their
first three games against non-disabled teams, including a team featuring Ken Menke, one of the original Whiz Kids. The competitor
in Nugent wasn't satisfied watching his team roll over opponents
unaccustomed to wheelchairs. True competition, he believed,
occurred when equals were matched. "If you've got a team, what
good is it if there isn't somebody to play?" he asked.[19]

And so, like Bob Rynearson, Dr. Gerald Gray, and Dr. Ludwig
Guttmann before him, Nugent faced the daunting challenge of
organizing sports competitions for people with disabilities where
no such competitions had existed previously. In practically re-
inventing the wheel, he sought answers to questions that few had
previously contemplated: How do you arrange transportation
for the players and their wheelchairs—and train referees who've
never seen, much less played, wheelchair sports? How do you find
quality facilities while persuading gymnasium owners that rubber
tires and overturned wheelchairs won't damage their polished
hardwood floors? How do you attract sponsors and spectators?
How do you generate media coverage?

Equal parts ambitious and quixotic, opportunistic and prophetic,

Nugent decided to host a novel undertaking: the world's first wheelchair basketball tournament, to be held on the Galesburg campus. His opening gambit was to invite the PVA-affiliated teams from the East Coast, but his entreaties were rejected because of the cost and distance. His overture to the Flying Wheels, sent via Howard Hughes's office, came too late for Birmingham's barnstorming crew.

Undaunted, Nugent worked the phones and found interest closer to home. Bob Miller's Kansas City team, renamed the Rolling Pioneers, agreed to participate, as did William Young and the Evansville Rolling Rockets. One of Nugent's students, Don Swift, mentioned that the team of paralyzed veterans from Hines Hospital had re-formed as an independent outfit called the Chicago Cats, and they signed up.

The Rolling Gophers from the Twin Cities, a team from Hannibal, Missouri, and Nugent's Gizz Kids rounded out the six-team bracket.

In April of 1949, when the teams gathered at Galesburg, Nugent was ubiquitous. He welcomed the visitors, most of whom were paralyzed veterans, and settled them in the women's residence halls. He hired the referees and tutored them about the sport; booked the city's spacious National Guard Armory (with reserved seats going for three dollars, the equivalent of more than thirty dollars today); wrote and printed a program that included brief profiles of each player; arranged for the games to be broadcast over radio station WGIL in Galesburg; hobnobbed with coaches and players; fixed bent spokes; and tightened the screws holding the footrest adjustments.

Experience determined the outcome at the double-elimination tournament. Kansas City, riding a fifty-four-game victory streak, swamped the Chicago Cats, 51–11, and then downed the youthful Gizz Kids, 26–18, to reach the finals. Their opponent was Minneapolis and their thirty-game unbeaten skein, after the Rolling Gophers humbled Hannibal and the Gizz Kids.

The red-hot Pioneers defeated the Gophers, 27–16, in a bruising affair, to capture the inaugural National Wheelchair Basketball Tournament. Guard Jim Tomlinson, who became paralyzed when a wooden backstop overturned and struck him while he was playing service baseball, led the victors with fourteen points.

Wheelchair cheerleader Shirley Sayers distributed the trophies—the Gizz Kids overturned Hannibal, 25–16, for third place—and a check of $225, representing the net proceeds from ticket sales, was donated to the National Paraplegia Foundation, the PVA's research wing. Nugent's fourteen-page post-tourney report named an All-American team, compiled individual and team statistics, and included a financial statement.

The hastily arranged affair wasn't exactly March Madness on wheels. With all six teams hailing from the Midwest, a national tourney it wasn't. Only the local newspaper in Galesburg covered the event in depth.

But from this modest undertaking, Nugent, like Ludwig Guttmann in England, predicted a lofty future for wheelchair sports that few others could fathom. "This is a small beginning of a Great thing to be," he wrote with liberal use of capital letters, "not only much wanted but much needed…in the future to be a function of a NATIONAL WHEELCHAIR BASKETBALL ASSOCIATION."[20]

★ ★ ★

Before Nugent could organize a second tournament, much less contemplate the formation of a national wheelchair basketball league, the State of Illinois announced that it would close the Galesburg campus after the spring semester of 1949. That left the educational future of a dozen students with disabilities, most of them paralyzed veterans, in jeopardy.

Nugent rallied the troops and led a convoy of more than thirty students, including fifteen students in wheelchairs, to appeal to Governor Adlai Stevenson to keep the campus open. "Crippled Students Fight College Closing," read the headline from the Springfield *Citizens Tribune* newspaper.[21]

Stevenson refused to meet with them, and Nugent scrambled to save the rehabilitation program. He called dozens of institutions across the country to see if they would take in the students, only to be rejected by every one of them. "We had the fear that our fledgling program was going to come to an end," he told Fred Pelka.[22]

The tide turned after representatives of the Veterans of Foreign Wars, the American Legion, and the Disabled American Veterans voiced support for the students. Their pressure proved to be decisive. Nugent was given permission to transfer the program, and the Gizz Kids basketball team, to the university's main campus at Urbana-Champaign.

Twelve paralyzed veterans, one woman and eleven men, joined him for the fall semester in 1949. Conditions were less than ideal. Nugent received no salary from the state or the school, relying instead on contracts with the VA and the state's Division of Vocational Rehabilitation to fund treatments and services. His office was in a tar paper–covered shack that was war surplus. His students slept in similar shacks, eight to a unit. Potbelly stoves kept them warm through the long, cold Midwestern winters.

But the program thrived thanks to Nugent's single-minded vision and enthusiasm. Even so, he upset faculty, administrators, and parents with what one observer described as his "mailed-fist treatment."[23] Another compared him to "a dark cloud always in a hurry."[24] He once boasted that he knew his students "better than they know themselves, for I know what they can do—not what they THINK they can do. They don't have any excuses, and they aren't allowed any."[25]

Hundreds of young men and women with disabilities graduated under his watch, often with advanced degrees. Many alumni later became national leaders in the fight for disability rights. They alternately adored him or loathed him, depending on the hour. Nugent didn't much care. His form of tough love required his students to achieve functional independence.

Sharon Hovey, paralyzed in the legs, back, and trunk, was left alone in her room as part of Nugent's "functionality week" orientation program required of incoming students with disability—dubbed "Hell Week" by its participants. "I thought he was the cruelest man I had ever known," she later said. "Why, anyone could see I couldn't do things for myself. But he left me there for ten days in a row. At the end of that time I was furious—but I was functional."[26]

Though few people outside of the Urbana-Champaign community noticed, Nugent was fighting for innovations that were universally accepted years later. He collaborated with Greyhound to modify passenger buses with hydraulic lifts to transport his wheelchair students around the campus. He built accessible toilet stalls in the restrooms, used scaffolding planks to fashion entry ramps for classroom buildings, and badgered the university to make sidewalk curb cutouts.

Sports remained Nugent's prideful domain. He started an indoor wheelchair football team and used grant money to fit wheelchairs with pneumatic tires, which boosted the chairs' responsiveness and handling on the court. Between semesters, he packed the Gizz Kids and the cheerleaders into a caravan of cars to play other teams and put on wheelchair basketball and square dancing demonstrations for the public. His escapades and his students attracted reams of positive and sympathetic press for the university—and Nugent made sure that school administrators saw every last newspaper clipping.

★ ★ ★

At the close of the 1949 wheelchair basketball season, the L.A.–based Helms Athletic Foundation reviewed the records of the PVA teams before awarding the national title to the Bronx VA team. Paced by Van Rensselaer Brooks and Charles Turi, the tight-knit squad from ward 3-D reeled off twenty consecutive wins over a two-year stretch. They'd come out best in inter-PVA games, with a 7–2 record, and had easily handled the Flying Wheels, 36–24, during the latter's tour.

At the hospital on Kingsbridge Road, overlooking the Harlem River, the Bronx boys had a secret weapon. One of the staff physicians, Dr. Arthur Abramson, was a world-renowned expert on rehabilitation. He was also a paralyzed veteran. During the Battle of the Bulge, while serving with the Medical Corps, he had been wounded by a sniper's bullet.

After rehabbing at Halloran Hospital, he was installed as the chief of the Bronx VA's physical rehabilitation service. He conducted experiments on himself, once ingesting doses of curare to determine if the muscle relaxant reduced spasticity (it didn't). Another of his studies confirmed that, without exercise, bones and muscle atrophy.

The Helms's decision resulted in an unsatisfying split. The

Bronx VA and the Kansas City Rolling Pioneers both claimed the title of wheelchair basketball champs. The Bronx team was made up exclusively of paralyzed veterans, and their record was based on the games they played against other paralyzed veterans. The Pioneers included amputees and post-polios. A panel of sportswriters who'd never played the sport determined one crown; the other was determined in a *mano a mano* tournament created by a non-disabled faculty member who coached one of the teams.

Columnist and veteran Harry Schweikert praised Nugent's efforts in the pages of *Paraplegia News*, but he made a point of distinguishing between the two versions of the sport. "[PVA teams are] still amateur ball-playing. The 'Gizz Kids' . . . are professionals; their national tournament has no bearing on ours. The National P.V.A. Basketball Championship rests firm on its laurels. It is wholly for physical and morale profit, and not monetary."[27]

Nugent's version ultimately prevailed. But just as he'd faced opposition to his education and rehabilitation program for students with disabilities, first in Galesburg and then in Urbana-Champaign, the process to organize and regulate wheelchair basketball would not be easy.

CHAPTER 15

And ... Action!

In April of 1949, producer Stanley Kramer and actor Kirk Douglas drove to the San Fernando Valley to screen *Champion* for the paralyzed veterans at Birmingham. The noir box-office smash about an ambitious, scrappy fighter who stops at nothing to reach the top turned Douglas into a movie star and earned six Academy Award nominations, including Best Actor for Douglas.

Birmingham's proximity to the Hollywood studios made celebrity sightings a regular occurrence at the hospital. Stan Den Adel recalled that everybody who was anybody went to the hospital to pass out cigarettes, entertain the troops, and hobnob with the injured servicemen: Spencer Tracy, Claudette Colbert, Van Johnson, Dorothy Lamour, Hoagy Carmichael, Dinah Shore, Cary Grant, Olivia de Havilland, Bob Hope, Bing Crosby, and Van Nuys's own Jane Russell.

Bette Davis, who headed the Hollywood Canteen Foundation, helped raise $25,000 to build Birmingham's outdoor swimming pool. Gregory Peck, Jennifer Jones, and Lionel Barrymore toured the ward when producer David Selznick held the world premiere of *Duel in the Sun* in the rec hall. Cuban-born bandleader Desi Arnaz, who was stationed at Birmingham with the army's Special

Services, utilized the talents of his wife, Lucille Ball, and a bevy of leggy starlets for a weekly variety show. Count Basie and his big band made a red-hot appearance that was broadcast over the Armed Forces Radio Service.

During the war, acclaimed director John Ford produced documentaries for the Navy and the Office of Strategic Services, the predecessor of the Central Intelligence Agency. After resuming his career in Hollywood with *They Were Expendable* (1945), based on the exploits of a navy PT boat squadron in the Philippines, Ford bought a ranch in the San Fernando Valley and built a pool, tennis and badminton courts, and a bar. Pat Grissom remembered driving out to "The Field Photo Farm" with carloads of paralyzed veterans from Birmingham and indulging in weekend barbecues, square dances, and outdoor parties stocked with ungodly amounts of booze.

Stanley Kramer was just beginning to see his name appear in bold type. He had spent the war years in anonymity, producing short training and orientation films for the Army Signal Corps in Queens. He worked with an aspiring screenwriter named Carl Foreman; they shared a mutual distaste for the frothy, unambitious fare churned out by Hollywood's all-powerful studio system.

Kramer and Foreman yearned to make "message" movies— that is, films with a social conscience that questioned the status quo. "Stories that had something to say," Kramer described it.[1] After the war, funded by a windfall from a failed film project, Kramer rented a small office on Cahuenga Boulevard in Los Angeles and set up an independent production company called Screen Plays Inc.

He and Foreman scored their first hit with *Champion*, based on a short story by journalist-humorist Ring Lardner. The duo next teamed on *Home of the Brave*, a 1949 drama about racism in the military that grossed a tidy $2.5 million and was selected as one of the year's top ten films by the National Board of Review of Motion Pictures. The thirty-five-year-old Kramer was touted as a wonder-boy independent producer, able to deliver profitable, bold features with up-and-coming talent on shoestring budgets.

His timing was excellent. Hollywood had spent the war years buttressing the Allied effort with popcorn propaganda: dozens of spirited, patriotic tales made in close cooperation with the military. Films like *Wing and a Prayer* (1944), *The Purple Heart* (1944), *The Sullivans* (1944), *Thirty Seconds Over Tokyo* (1944), and *Guadalcanal Diary* (1943) extolled American heroism with gung-ho music, dramatic voice-overs, buddy-buddy bonding, heartfelt endings, and the nonstop consumption of cigarettes.

In the war's aftermath, with television encroaching on Hollywood's stranglehold on nighttime entertainment, the studio system was starting to unravel. A generation that had witnessed war's unspeakable horrors—from Pearl Harbor to the nuclear bombs detonated over Japan to the Nazi concentration camps—was unafraid to seek out edgier, mature material that confronted the complexities of postwar America. These films tackled anti-Semitism (*Gentleman's Agreement*, 1947, directed by Elia Kazan), mental illness (*The Snake Pit*, 1948, directed by Anatole Litvak), alcoholism (*The Lost Weekend*, 1945, directed by Billy Wilder), racial intolerance (*Pinky*, 1949, directed by Kazan), and surviving polio (*Never Fear*, 1949, directed by Ida Lupino).

Hollywood also gingerly explored the challenges that many returning veterans were facing. *Pride of the Marines* (1945) starred John Garfield as Al Schmid, a real-life marine dealing with the loss of his sight during the Battle of Guadalcanal. *Till the End of Time* (1946) showcased the confused outlooks of three veterans attempting to reintegrate into their communities. *Submarine*

Command (1951) confronted the psychological scarring from battle fatigue, known today as post-traumatic stress disorder. (*Let There Be Light*, a raw documentary about World War II veterans with shell shock, directed by John Huston and produced by the Army Signal Corps, was suppressed for years by the army because of its sensitive material.)

The most acclaimed of the bunch was *The Best Years of Our Lives* (1946). Directed by William Wyler, *Best Years* chronicled the discomforting postwar homecomings of three servicemen. One of the three characters is Homer Parrish, played by Harold Russell, who was himself a wounded veteran.

Russell lost his hands in an explosives accident on D-Day, when he was instructing a demolition squad with the 13th Airborne Division at Camp Mackall in North Carolina. Both arms were amputated below the elbow, and he was fitted with two metal hooks. He was the subject of a twenty-minute Army Signal Corps documentary entitled *Diary of a Sergeant* (1945), which depicted his arduous rehabilitation at Walter Reed Army Hospital in Washington, D.C.

Wyler was impressed by *Diary* and created a substantial role in *Best Years* for Russell, who had no previous acting experience. In the film, Homer is consumed by his disability. He refuses to accept that his next-door sweetheart, Wilma (played by Cathy O'Donnell), wants to marry him.

Best Years swelled to a schmaltzy, upbeat finale—spoiler alert: Homer and Wilma tie the knot—while also capturing the emotional turmoil of the three veterans. The film collected seven Academy Awards, including Best Picture and Best Supporting Actor for Russell's performance. (He also received a special Oscar for "the hope and courage he brought to his fellow veterans.")

★ ★ ★

At Birmingham, after the screening of *Champion*, Stanley Kramer was introduced to Dr. Bors and several of his patients in the paraplegia ward. Intrigued that "each one of [the veterans] was living a story more remarkable and important than *Champion*," Kramer drove to his office and, according to his wife, told screenwriter Foreman, "This is a story that needs to be told."[2]

Kramer may also have been persuaded by the success of *Toward Independence* (1948), director George L. George's thirty-minute "staged" documentary about the rehabilitation of paralyzed veterans. Produced by the U.S. Army and intended primarily for the veterans themselves, *Toward Independence* won the 1949 Academy Award for Best Documentary (Short Subject) approximately one month prior to Kramer's visit to Birmingham.

Once Dr. Bors, Birmingham hospital officials, and the veterans agreed to participate in Kramer's film project, Foreman began driving to Van Nuys to get acquainted with the paralyzed veterans of ward C. Austrian-born Fred Zinnemann, who had recently guided Montgomery Clift in his film debut (*The Search*), was chosen to direct. Kramer tapped Bruce Church, a wealthy lettuce grower from Salinas, for financing (the total cost was a modest $539,000).

Zinnemann and Foreman earned the veterans' trust by hanging out with them for hours and listening to their crude banter about sex, urine bags, and fulgurating fistulas. They talked with "Turk" Behmoiram about his burning nerve pain and watched the Flying Wheels, just back from their second cross-country trip, scrimmage in the gym. They observed Dr. Bors on his daily rounds as he strolled from bed to bed and alternately berated his patients and coaxed them to health.

Foreman modeled the film's central character, Ken "Bud" Wilocek, on the battlefield experience of Ted Anderson, a captain in General George Patton's Third Army. In March of 1945, Anderson was leading a combat patrol across the Rhine River at the small German town of Dörscheid when a German sniper shot him through the neck.

"I tried to get up," he later recalled. "My legs wouldn't move . . . I just couldn't move."[3]

One soldier died trying to drag him to safety. Two others were wounded while rescuing him. Anderson woke up in a hospital in Paris to discover that he was permanently paralyzed in one arm and both legs. His injury occurred just two weeks after he'd earned a Silver Star leading a similar patrol across the Moselle River.

A smolderingly handsome man whom his wife described as "a combination of James Garner and a young Tyrone Power,"[4] Anderson rehabbed at Birmingham and remade himself into a passionate advocate for disability rights. Typing with one finger, he wrote articles for *Paraplegia News* and corresponded regularly with John F. Kennedy and Joseph McCarthy, two World War II veterans who'd recently been elected to Congress. He was elected president of the Birmingham chapter of the PVA in 1948, replacing Fred Smead.

"My story is a bitter tale of combat shock, spinal cord surgery, and endless nerve pain," Anderson wrote. "Sheer, unadulterated pain. Nerve pain—the worst pain in the world. It is a story of wanting to die . . . of being afraid to live."[5]

He acknowledged that he'd wrestled with his conscience before agreeing to allow his story to be turned into a movie. "Paraplegics have only bitter contempt and hatred for anything or anybody who attempts simply to arouse public sympathy for the paralyzed veteran," he told reporter Darr Smith. "We dislike intensely any exaggeration, misrepresentation, or exploitation of the fact that we sustained spinal cord injuries in combat. We want only to have our story told in clean, unmistakably authentic language that the public can understand."[6]

Anderson said he had faith in the filmmakers because they promised realism, not exploitation. "We intend to use the word 'urine' on the screen for the first time," Kramer told UPI reporter Aline Mosby. "The fertility of paraplegics varies, and we will try to tell about that. Kidney stones and bed sores are problems to these boys. Their wives, sweethearts, and parents desert many of them. The boys drink a lot and sometimes get into accidents in their specially-made cars."[7]

The key to the film was casting the lead role. Press reports leaked that Kirk Douglas was going to land the coveted part. Kramer had other ideas. He was attracted to a twenty-five-year-old roughneck who had never made a movie before, much less starred in one, but whom all of Hollywood was touting as a can't-miss star.

Marlon Brando had been a virtual nobody when he was cast as Stanley Kowalski in the theatrical production of Tennessee Williams's *A Streetcar Named Desire*. Brando's performance electrified Broadway audiences and critics alike; studio chieftains were waving big-money offers at Brando and his ripped T-shirt that far exceeded the amount Kramer was prepared to offer.

Kramer's edge was that the part of Bud Wilocek, the paralyzed veteran, would test the hulking actor like no other. He sent Brando a twenty-page treatment written by Foreman, tentatively titled *The Courage of Ten*. Brando loved the concept and the offer of a one-picture deal for $50,000. He turned down roles in a forgettable movie called *St. Benny the Dip* and in French director Claude

Autant-Lara's adaptation of Stendhal's *The Red and The Black* to make his big-screen debut in a movie now titled *The Men*.

Two non-disabled character actors, Richard Erdman and Jack Webb (the latter of *Dragnet* fame), were cast as fellow paralyzed veterans on the ward. Academy Award–winning actress Teresa Wright (Ellen) and Everett Sloane (Dr. Brock) were cast as Bud's romantic interest and the physician based on Dr. Bors, respectively. (Wright had earned praise for her role in *The Best Years of Our Lives*.)

Three paralyzed veterans at Birmingham—Anderson, Grissom, and Herbert Wolf—were hired as consultants. Zinnemann cast another forty-five paralyzed veterans at Birmingham as extras, including one Japanese-American veteran and one African-American veteran. Arthur Jurado, an Air Corps lieutenant who survived the war unscathed only to break his back in a plane crash en route to the States, landed a hefty supporting role. (Gossip columnist Hedda Hopper described Jurado, who was twenty-seven years old, as "a Mexican boy from Los Angeles.")[8]

"My thought was that, if we could make these men play themselves, we could get far greater impact from them than from a group of actors, no matter how talented, who would have had only brief time for preparation," Zinnemann wrote. "And to put an actor into a wheelchair on short notice and to tell him to act like a paraplegic seemed like a rather doubtful proposition."[9]

Which was presumably why Brando, with his Method acting background, signed up for the role. He arrived in Los Angeles in the fall of 1949 and immersed himself in the routines of the paralyzed veterans in order "to learn as much as I could about these men," he said.[10] He had himself "admitted" to Birmingham under the guise that he was a paralyzed veteran who was transferred from St. Albans Naval Hospital.

Pat Grissom, who headed the PVA's local chapter, took Brando under his wing and introduced him to the veterans on the paraplegia ward. The actor spent several weeks "just studying everything they do," Brando said later.[11] He sought to integrate their physical limitations into his character's essence so that he could learn to manipulate a wheelchair as naturally as they did.

"I wanted to see how they got in and out of their chairs, the manner in which [they] crawl from one place to another," Brando said. "Paraplegics—they do the most amazing things. Races without their chairs. I seen guys walk on their hands. They can do one-armed pull-ups. They can do everything."[12]

Grissom gave his protégé high marks. "Sometimes he forgets and throws the upper part of his body into his pushing," he said. "You'll notice we always lean back, because we don't have much balance."[13]

"We had to teach him how to be a paraplegic," Ed Santillanes recalled. "We had to keep saying, 'Stop moving your legs. Don't cross your legs and don't stand up.' He did a good job."[14]

"Every once in a while I forget and lean down and scratch my ankle," Brando admitted. "A paraplegic never scratches his leg. There is no feeling there."[15]

Brando also sought to grasp what he called "the psychological effects their injuries had had on them, and the whole process of readjustment and rehabilitation."[16] He leaned on Ted Anderson, who related the "complete despondence" he'd experienced initially, feeling that he had "lost everything" and "didn't want anything to do with people."

Eventually, Anderson said, "I became readjusted but never reconciled to my fate."[17]

Anderson's words stamped Brando's portrayal. "I don't guess anybody can know how you feel, knowing half your body is

numbed or dead—temporarily 'adjusted,' forever unreconciled,"
Brando said. "I feel a great sense of responsibility to the boys out
there. If they're satisfied, I don't care if the picture is a flop or
not—and me with it."[18]

★ ★ ★

Brando occasionally slept in an extra room at Grissom's home in
Granada Hills. They played long games of poker and gin rummy,
and went out carousing with Anderson, Ray Mitchell, Pete
Simon, and Behmoiram. One of their favorite haunts was Roy
Harlow's Pump Room, located on Ventura Boulevard in Studio
City. The place was just far enough from Birmingham Hospital to
allow the men to relax and enjoy themselves, and its extra-wide
doors and open seating area accommodated their wheelchairs.

An incident at the Pump Room starring Brando has taken on
mythic proportions. One night, according to Richard Erdman,
as they were drinking and swapping tales, an older woman
approached their table.

"She said, 'You guys are paraplegics, aren't you? That means
you can't walk?'" Erdman later recalled to author-screenwriter
Jon Zelazny. "Somebody said, 'Yeah, that's right.'"

"That's too bad," she said. "You know, if you men had a
true belief in God, you could get right up and walk out of
here." Now Marlon piped up: "Don't bother us, lady. You
got your problems, we got ours." He was pretty tough with
her, and the guys liked that. But it only made her focus on
him the more. "You, of all of them, you look like you could
do it. Do you even *want* to walk?" He said, "Yeah, I wanna
walk!" "Then you have to imagine the power of God."

She was getting all worked up. "Just imagine His strength surging through your legs right now. You can stand!"

So Marlon struggled and struggled up out of his chair. He got to his feet, tottering—she was yelling, "You did it! You did it!"—and he fell back down. Well, the entire place was dead silent now; everybody was watching, and the woman kept badgering him to try it again...until Marlon suddenly leapt up, danced a jig in the middle of the floor, and ran out of the place! The guys were laughing so hard they almost fell on the floor, and the woman just stood there in shock.[19]

The content of *The Men* was no laughing matter, of course. In the film's opening sequence, Brando's character, Bud, is shot in the neck and wakes up permanently paralyzed. "I was afraid I was gonna die," he says in a voice-over that echoed Ted Anderson's own words. "Now I'm afraid I'm gonna live."

Distraught over his fate, Bud refuses to follow Dr. Brock's orders and quarrels with fellow veterans on the paraplegia ward. Much of his angst revolves around his relationship with his fiancée, Ellen (Wright). He initially refuses to see her because he doesn't want her pity or her tears.

When he allows Ellen to visit him, he tries to scare her away. He angrily whips off the bedsheets to reveal his lower body and snarls, "All right, I'll give you what you want. You want to see what's it's like? All right, look! I said look at me. Now get a good look...Is that what you want?"

Bud's outlook improves when he accepts that he'll never walk again. Then he begins the laborious process of healing himself. That includes arduous physical therapy that allowed Brando to flaunt his impressive upper-body physique while exercising alongside the equally impressive Jurado. Brando bowls from a wheelchair and, for a quick moment, is shown playing a vigorous game of wheelchair basketball.

Bud comes around and agrees to marry Ellen, although her parents are against the idea and refuse to attend the wedding. Ellen and Bud exchange their vows in front of many real-life paralyzed veterans at Birmingham, including Stan Den Adel, Pat Grissom, and "Turk" Behmoiram. Bud walks upright down the aisle, with the aid of crutches and braces, in a scene that recreated Stan's actual wedding with Peg.

Filmed on location at the hospital and at a Hollywood sound-stage, the overall tone of the film is far bleaker than the earnest *Best Years of Our Lives* and its climactic wedding. In *The Men*, Bud and Ellen separate almost immediately after getting married. They reconcile at movie's end, but given Bud's anguished recovery, their future is anything but guaranteed.

The hustle of Kramer's publicity ace, George Glass, resulted in a flurry of sympathetic articles that boosted the film's prospects. *Life* magazine, then the nation's preeminent print and picture publication, ran a three-page profile about Brando, with photos of "The Brilliant Brat" hanging out with his grandmother and her small dog at his aunt's two-bedroom bungalow in Eagle Rock in the northeast area of Los Angeles.[20]

Pictorial features in *Look*, *Screen Guide*, and the *New York Times* showed Brando looking sultry and playing wheelchair basketball. Hedda Hopper breathlessly chattered that he'd fallen for actress Shelley Winters "like a rabbit taking to a lettuce patch."[21] *Variety* reported that the producers had to construct special ramps to accommodate the veterans' wheelchairs for the scenes filmed at the Motion Picture Center studios in Hollywood.

On July 20, 1950, New York's Radio City Music Hall hosted the world premiere of *The Men*. Kramer believed that "we were on our way to automatic riches," and was encouraged by the mostly positive reviews.[22] "In an industry that lives by the box office, the film is remarkable, first of all, for tackling a touchy subject: the salvage of war-wounded paraplegics, men hopelessly paralyzed from the waist down," *Time* magazine opined. "More remarkable, the subject has been handled with frankness, taste and dramatic skill. The result is realistic, unsentimental and emotionally powerful."[23]

New York Times critic Bosley Crowther hailed Kramer as "a new Hollywood genius" who made "'A' movies on 'B' budgets." Noted Crowther: "Sports events in which paraplegics in their wheel-chairs have played normal teams have been held to accustom the public to the capacities of these 'immobilized' men, and in many other ways their abilities as participants in society have been revealed. But nothing yet demonstrated has so fully realized and portrayed—at least, to the public's comprehension—the inner torments, the despairs, the loneliness and the possible triumphs of a paraplegic as this picture does."[24]

Paralyzed veterans were pointedly critical about the film's veracity. "Hollywood clichés were unfortunately not avoided, particularly in the ending of the film," wrote PVA founding member Robert Moss in *Paraplegia News*. Still, Moss felt that *The Men* was worth the wait. "I saw the picture four times and was never bored by it...Don't miss it—and don't let anyone else miss it either!"[25]

Ted Anderson concurred, calling it "a movie we all feel eminently well done, and the paraplegics are hard to please when it comes to stories about themselves." He had one misgiving: "The dialogue's the way we talk, too, except they had to take out the cuss words."[26]

Despite Brando's presence, the reams of publicity, and the

favorable reviews, *The Men* sank at the box office. Pundits blamed the lack of on-screen chemistry between Brando and Wright, a casting miscue exacerbated by Zinnemann's decision to cut a subplot involving Ellen and a non-disabled suitor that clarified her resolve to marry Bud. Ukrainian-born composer Dimitri Tiomkin's overwrought soundtrack didn't help matters.

Perhaps the film's biggest obstacle was its inopportune release. A film with a decidedly anti-war message entered theaters just as America was entering the Korean War. "Designed as a postwar picture it was suddenly facing a prewar mentality," Zinnemann noted. "No wonder that people whose sons, husbands and fathers were going to fight could not bear to watch a movie such as ours. It folded in two weeks. It was a noble failure."[27] (Foreman earned an Academy Award nomination for Best Screenplay and won the Writers Guild of America award for "best written film concerning problems with the American scene.")

Still, as the first major Hollywood film to depict the condition of paralyzed veterans, *The Men* was a bold breakthrough. The conservative mores of the times demanded that the film refrain from showing explicit sexual content or having the characters curse. Those vérité touches would have to wait for the Vietnam era, with movies like *Born on the Fourth of July*, based on Ron Kovic's searing memoir, and *Coming Home*, starring Jane Fonda and Jon Voight.

Marlon Brando cashed his $50,000 paycheck and left his E&J wheelchair behind. He went off to make the cinematic version of *A Streetcar Named Desire*, the movie that made him an icon. Stanley Kramer, Carl Foreman, and Fred Zinnemann next teamed up on *High Noon*, the classic Western starring Gary Cooper. All of them received Oscar nominations.

Ted Anderson had watched them shoot *The Men* from his

wheelchair and found the experience unsettling. He was struck by how the artifice of filmmaking reduced the moment his life permanently changed to a staged re-enactment: "The scene ends, I look around the set. The cameramen start moving equipment. The prop man is collecting the weapons. I watch an actor rise from the dust and head back toward the dressing room, walking."[28]

Hollywood and the movie's burst of publicity didn't change Anderson. He remained a popular leader within the Paralyzed Veterans of America and continued to write extensively about paraplegia. He lobbied for the housing benefits of Public Law 702 and advocated for an attendant allowance for people with service-related spinal-cord injuries. He was married for a time and helped raise a daughter.

He lived for thirteen years after he was wounded in the war, in constant pain and with only partial use of his right arm. In 1958, he took his own life by stabbing himself in the chest.[29]

Hollywood didn't show that ending.

CHAPTER 16

Bulova Time

On a tree-lined street in the Woodside section of Queens, a redbrick schoolhouse fronted by four stately white pillars bustled with activity. A steady stream of World War II veterans rolled their E&J wheelchairs up the paved ramp to the one-story building and entered through the extra-wide doorway.

Inside, they found amenities designed for their comfort and safety: electric-eye–controlled doors, cork floors to prevent those using crutches from slipping and falling, a double-entrance safety elevator, an exercise room, two movie projection rooms, and medical facilities with a doctor and nurse in attendance.[1]

Welcome to the Joseph Bulova School of Watchmaking, a vocational institute that operated at no cost to the paralyzed veterans. The students came from every VA paraplegia ward in the country to learn the science of watchmaking and repair and to acquire training for a career that was thought to be ideally suited for paralyzed veterans in wheelchairs.

The Bulova Watch Company was founded by Josef Bulowa, a young immigrant from Bohemia. In 1875, he opened a small jewelry store in Lower Manhattan and began designing and manufacturing his own line of pocket watches and wristwatches under his Americanized name.

His son, Arde, succeeded him as the firm expanded into electric clocks. Arde also invested in radio stations in the industry's infancy, a venture that made him a multi-millionaire. The company prospered with pioneering marketing stratagems. Bulova produced one of the first nationally broadcast radio commercials and one of the earliest television ads. The latter lasted fewer than thirty seconds, reportedly cost nine dollars, and aired before a Brooklyn Dodgers–Philadelphia Phillies game in 1941. The snappy catchphrase: "America runs on Bulova time."

With lucrative defense contracts, Bulova had geared up to meet wartime demands at its factories in Queens and on Long Island. The company manufactured A-11 "hack watches" that could be synchronized to the second, as well as munitions, precision equipment, aircraft instruments, military fuses, and timing devices. During the war, Arde's brother-in-law, Harry Davis Henshel, served as a lieutenant colonel in the Twelfth Army Group under the command of General Omar Bradley.

Arde began strategizing about the rehabilitation of American veterans while the war was still raging. Through the company's philanthropic arm, he set up the charitable Bulova Foundation and explored opening a school for veterans. He waited to break ground on the brick-and-mortar facility until he received commitments from 750 jewelers and stores that they would employ his graduates.

In the summer of 1944, New York City mayor Fiorello La Guardia laid the cornerstone of the new building at 40-24 62nd Street, near one of Bulova's plants. The inscription read: "To Serve Those Who Served Us." The school opened its doors the following summer, just before the war's end, with murals in the front lobby illustrating the sweeping history of timekeeping. A swimming pool, a dormitory, and a gymnasium were added later.[2]

The founding of the school, wrote Dr. Howard Rusk in the *New York Times*, was "as important to the handicapped as V-J Day was to all of us in the services, because it opened an entirely new vista in thinking for the disabled."[3]

Bulova hired Howard Beehler, president of the Horological Institute of America, to serve as the school's dean, and to set up the first instructional branches at two army hospitals: Walter Reed Hospital in Washington, D.C., and Newton Baker Hospital in Martinsburg, West Virginia.

Working with the VA, Bulova recruiters sought out those veterans with the requisite finger dexterity, mechanical aptitude, and patience for the intricate craft. They boasted of the almost unlimited business opportunities that awaited the veterans who completed the training and emphasized that "a man does not have to be an athlete to repair watches," according to company executive Stanley Simon.[4]

Paralyzed veterans were among the earliest recruits. They typically began their studies while hospitalized, then transferred to the school after they were discharged from the hospital. They lived in apartments adapted for them by the New York City Housing Authority. During the year-long course, students learned the painstaking art of reading blueprints, the technique for working with precision grinding and polishing tools, peering through a loupe, and handling minuscule parts and screws.

Bulova supplied everything the students needed to succeed— including a set of tools and equipment (worth approximately $850) upon graduation. Their degrees carried value; the school was chartered by the state's Board of Regents. Befitting his postwar position as head of the VA and his close relationship with the Bulova family, General Bradley handed out diplomas to the twenty members of the first graduating class and called upon other companies to endorse President Truman's "hire the handicapped" initiative.

The school didn't ignore the veterans' desire for recreation, an especially necessary ingredient after six hours of classes. Bulova hired Benjamin Lipton, a non-disabled veteran, as a rehabilitation consultant to assist and counsel wounded servicemen as they transitioned to civilian life. Lipton was also charged with touring the VA hospitals to scout for possible enrollees and to plug the school's program.

Born on Manhattan's Lower East Side, Lipton was educated at Alfred University, in western New York, and earned his master's in public health from Columbia University in Manhattan. He served in the Army Medical Corps during the war and then held a commission as major in the reserves. After the war, while training convalescent soldiers for the VA, Lipton caught Bulova's attention by touting the therapeutic value of sports for the paralyzed veterans.

"Having a job, while basically important for these people, is not enough," he told wheelchair-basketball scholar Robert Szyman. "Concentrating on athletic excellence adds another dimension to their lives... [and we've found that] those persons entering competitive sports make the fastest adjustment."[5]

Short and compact, with a slight paunch, Lipton was inspired by the notoriety of the barnstorming Birmingham team and the success of the nearby Halloran squad on Staten Island. Their exhibitions led to the "growing recognition of the untapped potential resources of the disabled," he later wrote. "If a disabled person could summon the strength, courage and skill to actually play basketball," he continued, "there would be few limits to his capabilities if he were properly trained in a suitable field of employment."[6]

In the winter of 1949–50, thanks to Arde Bulova's largesse, the company established a wheelchair basketball team called the Watchmakers. Lipton volunteered as coach. To learn the nuances of the sport, he sat himself in a wheelchair and played alongside the veterans. He spent hours shooting baskets. "I learned very quickly it was a different game from that position," he told reporter Geraldine Baum, "and it wasn't an easy one."[7]

Lipton took care of every detail. He handled the scheduling arrangements and, when they played at places without ramps, bodily carried the men up and down the stairs. Once, when the Flying Wheels were grounded due to bad weather, Lipton summoned his "Minute Men." They carpooled, drove several hours, and replaced the Wheels for an exhibition game.

Their roster constituted a distinctive amalgam. They were primarily World War II paralyzed veterans, with several amputees and post-polios mixed in. They were air force, army, navy, marines; they were infantry, engineers, and amphibious forces. They'd rehabbed at every VA hospital in the land.

Flight navigator John "Jack" Buhs, shot down over Germany and imprisoned for months, came from Cushing. Selig Boshnack, an original member of Halloran's team, was injured while serving with the 29th Division in Germany. Navy Aviation Machinist Mate Felix Radleigh was severely wounded after kamikaze attacks on the aircraft carrier USS *Ticonderoga* in January 1945; he eventually underwent more than one hundred war-related operations at various hospitals. Maurice Brooks was shot in the spine in Germany, reportedly while capturing an AWOL serviceman; he rehabbed at the Hines paraplegia ward before enrolling at Bulova.

Arde Bulova's commitment to the wounded veterans was singular. He was also a savvy businessman. The founding of the Watchmakers marked the first time that a major U.S. corporation sponsored a sports team composed of people with disabilities. They became highly visible, rolling advertisements for the Bulova brand.

The players didn't complain. Unlike most other wheelchair basketball teams, they didn't have to worry about raising money to purchase equipment and uniforms or to rent gymnasiums for practices and games. They even had a built-in cheering section: the company's sales force came out to their games to root for them.

★ ★ ★

Stan Den Adel didn't accompany Pat Grissom, Gil Oritz, Louis Palmer, and the rest of the Flying Wheels on their third annual cross-country tour in the winter of 1950. Instead, he stayed in Southern California and recuperated from another operation.

As Dr. Bors, Dr. Guttmann, Dr. Rusk, and others were discovering, the aftercare for patients with paraplegia didn't follow a circumscribed, beginning-middle-end trajectory. Stan and other paralyzed veterans were wont to experience complications, from acute pain to bladder stones to pressure sores to high fevers, sometimes requiring extensive surgery, sometimes just routine maintenance.

Recovery, it seemed, was going to be a continuous and life-long endeavor. "I've had something like eighty operations," Gene Fesenmeyer recalled.

Gene Haley, a stocky long-range shooter who was injured while stationed with the U.S. Navy in Qingdao, China, replaced Den Adel as captain. Under coach Carl Knowles, who again filled in for Bob Rynearson, Haley and center Ray Mitchell, a lieutenant with Company K, 338th Infantry and a business major at UCLA, developed into a high-scoring duo that carried the offensive load.

The Wheels opened by trouncing non-disabled students from Amarillo College, 38–20. They followed that with a nail-biter over the Kansas City Pioneers, 19–18, snapping the seventy-game winning streak of the reigning National Wheelchair Basketball Tournament champs.

Their next scheduled game, in Chicago, was canceled. Tour director John Old called Frank Leahy, the coach of the University of Notre Dame's undefeated football squad, to see if they would play the Wheels. Leahy agreed to the match as a preliminary to the Notre Dame–Marquette basketball game.

By the time the Wheels arrived in South Bend, 5,000 spectators were jammed into the fieldhouse. The court was soon cluttered with capsized chairs belonging to Leahy's behemoths, including Steve Oracko and Jim Martin (both veterans themselves). Offensive guard Bob Lally managed a field goal for the home team, and Martin a free throw, as the Wheels stomped the Fighting Irish, 35–3.

The crowd stood and cheered the veterans with one minute left in the game, according to *New York Herald Tribune* sports columnist Walter "Red" Smith. One minute after the last player exited the floor, the mob was still standing and yelling.[8]

Next up were their archrivals from Cushing Hospital and their lineup of familiar faces. Manny Leonardo, Dick Foley, Greg Seymourian, Walter Maguire, and Joe Villa warmed up for the main event with an intra-squad scrimmage before the Boston Celtics–Rochester Royals contest at Boston Garden (in what was the first season of the NBA).

This time, California and Massachusetts clashed at the Boston College gym before a capacity crowd. The Wheels exacted sweet revenge on this chilly evening, defeating Cushing for the first time in three attempts, 28–22, as Haley and Mitchell combined for eighteen points.

The Wheels were so jubilant that they scarcely needed their plane to fly to New York for the next three games. They jumped on Halloran and ran up a 12–0 halftime advantage before cruising to a 30–24 victory, with Haley and Mitchell's thirteen points neutralizing Jack Gerhardt's game-high fourteen. Then they throttled the Bronx, 25–21.

Their third contest pitted the Wheels against the Ben Lipton–coached Watchmakers at the castle-like Ninth Regiment Armory on West 14th Street. Bulova's backing was not enough for the Watchmakers to overcome their inexperience against the more seasoned PVA squads (although Harry Schweikert declared them the "best dressed team on the courts" for their fancy duds).[9] This night was no exception: thanks to Maurice Brooks's quiet strength, Bulova kept the game close before falling, 29–28, to the Californians.

The Wheels concluded their eleven-city, six-thousand-mile airborne tour with a win over the non-disabled Thomas Tinkers squad in Lubbock, Texas, before 1,300 spectators. They finished 9–1, their only loss coming to the Kennedy Hospital team in Memphis, 31–22. The Deadenders gloated that they'd evened the score after losing to the Wheels the previous year.

Once the Wheels' plane hit the tarmac in Los Angeles, debate began to rage among the paralyzed veterans regarding which PVA team would be awarded the national wheelchair basketball title by the Helms Athletic Foundation. Halloran players argued that they'd beaten every team except the Flying Wheels and owned the highest scoring average (32.5 points) in inter-PVA contests.

The Wheels contended that they'd beaten every team except Kennedy, and that the Deadenders hadn't played all of the PVA-affiliated teams. Kennedy claimed the title because of its decisive triumph over the Wheels.

Helms officials met to determine the 1949–50 champion. Bill Schroeder declared the winner was…no one. The voters "gave up" reaching a decision, he told journalist Harry Schweikert, because judging the different teams' strengths and weaknesses was "too difficult."[10] The no-outcome result showed the folly of the system and appeared to some observers to demonstrate a lack of respect for the players and their competitive spirit.

Wheelchair basketball was not yet five years old, but already its growing pains were apparent. The doctors and rehabilitative specialists at the VA who encouraged paralyzed veterans to play wheelchair basketball did so with clear limits. Their main duty was to help their patients heal from their war injuries and then, when they were physically and psychologically prepared, to help them leave the hospital and re-enter civilian life. If sports could aid in that effort, great.

Bringing civilians into the mix, however, was outside the VA's purview. This coincided with an edict from the VA that barred patients from playing competitive sports at sites charging admission. Technical Bulletin 6-60, its formal name, also prohibited patients who participated in competitive sports from being absent from the hospital for more than forty-eight hours.

TB 6-60 was meant to "prevent unscrupulous exploitation of paraplegic teams as profit-making entities," according to wheelchair-sports historian Stan Labanowich. In reality, the VA directive threatened to "deprive the veterans of the opportunity to change public attitudes toward all disabled by denying them experiences in playing before large crowds."[11]

Veterans and PVA officials protested the implementation of TB 6-60 and urged the VA to lift the virtual ban on wheelchair basketball as a competitive sport. They argued that the games boosted the morale of the men while helping to educate the public about the ability and potential of disabled veterans. Further, the money from admission charges to the games didn't line the players' pockets. Rather, the funds were used to finance the PVA chapters and to defray expenses: travel, wheelchairs, balls, officials' fees, and more.

"We have pretty strict rules to keep it on an amateur basis," said Bernard Shufelt, president of the PVA.[12]

Their arguments went nowhere. If the veterans wanted to continue playing wheelchair basketball after they were discharged from the hospital, they couldn't count on much assistance from the VA. They had to start from scratch or join "hometown" teams, like the Jersey Wheelers, often with teammates from their hospital days. That added an extra layer of responsibilities— finding a coach, raising money to buy uniforms, renting practice facilities, promoting their games—even as they were adjusting to life outside the hospital.

★ ★ ★

The immediate beneficiary of the TB 6-60 edict was Timothy Nugent and his effort to organize a wheelchair basketball league among veterans, civilians, and students.

In the spring of 1950, as the Gizz Kids were settling into their new digs in Urbana and Champaign, Nugent waged a persistent letter-writing campaign and made numerous long-distance telephone calls to recruit teams to play in the second National Wheelchair Basketball Tournament. Much to his dismay, only five teams entered the tourney, held in Hannibal, Missouri.

The two-hour drive to Hannibal was convenient for the St. Louis Rolling Ramblers, a "hometown" team of veterans and civilians backed by the American War Dads. Coached by Joe Gorke, the Rams played their first game in 1948 prior to a tilt between the St. Louis Bombers and the Red Auerbach–coached Washington Capitols of the BAA.

Their debut was less than auspicious. They were trounced by the Kansas City Pioneers, 32–14, before a partisan crowd at the St. Louis Arena. But they hadn't lost since, even defeating Nugent's Gizz Kids, 29–26, in February.

On Wednesday and Friday nights, the Rams practiced at the Police Gym. There, Gorke discovered a budding star in co-captain O. G. Polster, a right-leg amputee after being hit by an explosive on Okinawa. Andy Zika, a left-leg amputee from shrapnel wounds while serving with the 3rd Army in Germany, was a valuable forward, while Washington University sophomore Jimmy Greenblatt, a post-polio, brought youthful energy and an effective left-hook shot.

"We're a lot better now," said guard Jim "Buzz" Schlitt, paralyzed while fighting with the 103rd Infantry Division near the Maginot Line in northeastern France. "We'll give [the Pioneers] a good scrap."[13]

At the Admiral Robert Coontz Armory in Hannibal, the Rams did more than that. They downed the host Rockets, then avenged their only loss by defeating the Pioneers, the defending champs, to reach the finals. Their opponent was Nugent's Gizz Kids, who'd advanced by beating the Chicago Cats, made up of former patients at Hines Hospital.

During the finals, the two teams were never separated by more than four points. They were tied 6–6 after one quarter. St. Louis took a 12–10 advantage at the half and led 20–16 after three periods. The Gizz Kids trailed by two points with less than one minute to go when the Rams' Ralph Walker, whose right thigh was shattered when the destroyer he was stationed on hit a mine near Borneo, iced the game with an overhand shot.

Final score: 24–20, St. Louis. Polster tallied a dozen points, while Don Swift, an accounting major paralyzed in the European theater, scored eight for Illinois.

Between games and at night, Nugent fraternized with the players to promote the National Wheelchair Basketball Association (NWBA) as the governing body of wheelchair basketball. An organized league in conjunction with the annual championship tournament, he argued, would improve competition; bring order to the loose confederacy of independent outfits; reconcile the different sets of playing rules; present a united front to the non-disabled world; and allow paralyzed veterans to continue playing ball after leaving the VA.

Nugent's passion carried the day, along with his belief that wheelchair athletes didn't just want to play, they wanted to compete to be the best. He was also practical. In accordance with the self-determination philosophy that he taught to his students, he let the players themselves, mostly veterans, take on important leadership roles within the NWBA hierarchy.

Bob Miller, the captain of the Pioneers, was elected NWBA president, while the Rams' Jim Greenblatt became vice president and Don Swift of the Gizz Kids was voted secretary. Nugent was named technical advisor, which gave him vast authority over both the league and the tournament. (His title later morphed to commissioner.)

Miller of the Pioneers was a true believer. "[Wheelchair basketball] has brought to the minds of people that 'cripples' are no longer content to be thought of as helpless persons, to be kept in behind closed doors," he noted in the *NWBA Bulletin* news-letter. "The NWBA is the best way that I know of for keeping wheelchair basketball a unified, functioning sport of the disabled, and this to me is a must if it is to remain one of our sources of expressing ourselves to the public."[14]

Much remained on Nugent's to-do list. A study of the different rules was undertaken and a comprehensive rulebook written that, for the most part, followed the western rules as originally outlined by Bob Rynearson. Nobody knew quite what to do about the Flying Wheels, the most famous team in the land, but one that operated independently from distant Los Angeles. And, by open-ing the gymnasium doors to civilians and people with disabilities other than paraplegia, a different challenge loomed. Would it be possible to ensure a level playing field if the participants them-selves came to the court with very different physical abilities?

★ ★ ★

In April of 1950, paralyzed veterans from Birmingham Hospital gathered at the headquarters of the Los Angeles Breakfast Club, in the neighborhood of Los Feliz, for their annual dinner. Ronald Reagan, the president of the Screen Actors Guild, served as master of ceremonies.

Reagan had recently wrapped work on *Storm Warning* (re-leased in 1951), co-starring Ginger Rogers and Doris Day, with much of the filming done in Corona, not far from the Naval Hospital. Wearing a bow tie, Reagan cracked corny jokes, intro-duced eighteen entertainment acts and performers, and posed for photographs with Pat Grissom and Ted Anderson. The pair told Reagan to watch for Grissom's cameos in *The Men*, which was due to be released in theaters that summer.[15]

The 450 veterans in attendance celebrated another successful road trip by the Flying Wheels, and another year above ground, with copious laughs and imbibing. All seemed right with the world.

One week later, President Truman dropped a bombshell in their midst by ordering the immediate closure of Birmingham Hospital. Dr. Bors and the paraplegia ward were to be transferred to a distant location in Southern California—the Long Beach Naval Hospital—with the VA to take charge of all operations. Approximately 1,200 patients were affected, two hundred of them paraplegia patients.

The veterans and nearly every San Fernando Valley resident were outraged. Grissom, Stan Den Adel, Gene Fesenmeyer, and many others had built (or were completing) specially designed homes in the area, using federal funds and their own money, so they could live and work outside the hospital confines yet remain close enough to consult with Dr. Bors at Birmingham. They'd formed a tight-knit community with an upbeat spirit that buoyed their dreams for the future. Such a disruption derailed those hopes and jeopardized their well-being.

Grissom and Anderson publicly lambasted Truman, calling the decision "politics of the basest sort on the part of the President with complete disregard of the health and welfare of paraplegics and tubercular patients."[16] Den Adel complained about Long Beach's clammy weather and worried that he'd have to look for another job.

They enlisted California's political powerbrokers to join the fight. Representative Richard Nixon (R–CA), who was readying to seek a Senate seat, noted that the sloping terrain of the Long Beach site was tricky for wheelchairs to negotiate without an assistant. Governor Earl Warren offered his support to the veterans:

"I think it would be a great mistake to move the hospital from Birmingham, where the patients are so happy."[17]

Friends, family, and concerned community leaders raised $5,000 to send Grissom, George Hohmann, and Bernard Rose (a tuberculosis patient) to Washington, D.C., to urge Truman to rescind the order. Hohmann had been shot mid-chest in 1944, when he was with the 102nd Infantry Division in Germany. (He managed nevertheless to throw a smoke grenade to enable his artillery crew to zero in on the target.) He was one of the paralyzed veterans from Birmingham who enrolled at UCLA, where he met his future wife, Pauline, in a class they shared. He was working on his PhD in clinical psychology.

The slender, curly-haired veteran from Texas told reporters that he lived fifteen minutes from Birmingham because he needed to go there at least three times a week. "Like the night I woke up at midnight with a temperature of 105," he said. "I rushed to my car and down to the hospital. They said it was nephritis—a serious kidney disease. They got it quickly or I might be pushing up daisies by now."[18]

Traveling to Long Beach for outpatient treatment entailed "a round-trip of 115 miles," he said. "And it's right through the heart of Los Angeles. What paraplegic is going to make that trip three times a week?"[19]

The three men pleaded their case to Truman's vice president, Alben Barkley, and with Carl Gray, administrator of the Veterans Administration. They wheeled themselves to the fence surrounding the White House in hope of gaining a face-to-face meeting with the president.

Unswayed by their protest, the president spent the Memorial Day holiday on the Potomac aboard the presidential yacht.[20]

Dr. Bors moved to Long Beach and took charge of the

paraplegia unit in the new facility, which he described as a "semi-permanent barracks."[21] Many of the paralyzed veterans who were his patients, including Grissom and Den Adel, decided to stay in their homes in the San Fernando Valley. For periodic checkups, they saw doctors at a VA facility in West Los Angeles. If they needed to consult Dr. Bors, they had to make the long drive south.

Bob Rynearson, a VA employee, also transferred to Long Beach. He helped members of the Flying Wheels regroup in their unfamiliar surroundings. There was no gymnasium on campus, so baskets were installed in a recreation hall that had been converted for practices. All of their games were played in high school gyms away from the hospital grounds. Inexperienced recruits took the place of the veteran players who remained in the San Fernando Valley.

Rynearson's presence ensured that the Flying Wheels would not be grounded. They all agreed that they'd overcome harsher setbacks.

CHAPTER 17

Korea

On June 25, 1950, less than a month after the Birmingham Hospital patients were moved to Long Beach, more than 60,000 North Korean troops crossed the 38th parallel into South Korea, marking the first armed conflict of the Cold War. The peace that followed World War II had lasted less than five years.

The roots of the war dated back to 1910, when Japan annexed Korea and brutally ruled over the peninsula for the next thirty-five years. After Japan's surrender to the allies in 1945, Korea was divided into two nations along the 38th parallel: the Soviet Union–backed northern half, known as the Democratic People's Republic of Korea, and the Republic of Korea in the U.S.-backed southern half.

President Truman committed air, ground, and naval personnel to aid South Korea, under the auspices of the United Nations. As North Korean forces quickly captured Seoul and drove south toward the port city of Pusan, Truman appointed General Douglas MacArthur, based in Tokyo while overseeing the occupation of Japan, to head the UN Command.

MacArthur countered with a bold, amphibious landing at Inchon, behind enemy lines, and UN forces recaptured Seoul and advanced to the 38th parallel. But his decision to push deep into North Korea, with the goal of unifying the peninsula, was a poorly conceived miscalculation. That incursion brought China into the conflict, and Mao Zedong unleashed his People's Volunteer Army in support of North Korea and its leader, Kim Il Sung.

Ferocious attacks and counterattacks, without a turn-the-tide victory, devolved into a dug-in stalemate along the 38th parallel. By the summer of 1951, Truman had fired MacArthur for insubordination and commenced negotiations to end the "police action." Talks between the warring nations continued after the election of Dwight D. Eisenhower as president.

An armistice was reached on July 27, 1953. No peace treaty was ever signed. Its indecisive resolution remains one of its most defining features. "A difficult, draining, cruel war had ended under terms no one was very happy with," concluded historian David Halberstam.[1]

Wedged between what became known as the "Good War" of World War II and the long-lasting Vietnam War, the Korean War has been called the "forgotten war." But the approximately 5.7 million American men and women who served in Korea between 1950 and 1953—and, especially, the 1.78 million who served in theater—never forgot: the troops who defended the Pusan Perimeter and those who landed at Inchon, the soldiers who endured the subzero weather at "frozen Chosin" and those who survived the offensives in and around Seoul. Some 34,000 U.S. troops died during battle, with approximately 103,000 wounded.[2]

Nearly 600,000 veterans from World War II also served in Korea, according to the VA, either on the battlefield or behind the lines. Many of them resented being "called away from their civilian jobs," according to Halberstam, "and told to serve in a war overseas for the second time within ten years, when all too many of their contemporaries had been called for neither."[3]

Cushing Hospital's John Power noted in *Paraplegia News* that the war provoked "a number of seemingly futile questions" among ex-GIs. "Was World War II just the semi-final? Are the lives that have been sacrificed, the wounds suffered, the tremendous sums of wealth spent all to go for naught?"[4]

From his wheelchair in Oakland, retired colonel John Winterholler did his part. During the conflict, Winterholler coordinated two blood-drive campaigns for the Red Cross. Hundreds of pints of collected blood were shipped to Travis Air Force Base, about fifty miles northeast of Oakland, and then to Korea to aid the troops. The remainder was processed into plasma.

He was inspired to help, he said, because of his personal experience in the war. He was told in the POW camp at Davao that, although he needed spinal-cord surgery, doctors were afraid to operate without blood and plasma on hand to treat the shock associated with the procedure.

"I feel a responsibility to see that blood is available in Korea whenever it is needed," he told the *Oakland Tribune*. "I know firsthand how important it is."[5]

One of the most valuable lessons military doctors had learned during World War II was the importance of treating injured servicemen as quickly as humanly possible. In Korea, this concept evolved into the creation of the first Mobile Army Surgical Hospital (MASH) units. The tent-based, truck-borne facilities, staffed with surgeons and nurses, were situated close to the front lines, often just beyond enemy artillery range. Their introduction helped reduce the fatality rate for the military wounded to 2.5 percent, down from 4.5 percent in World War II, according to surgeon and medical-military historian Dr. Michael Baker.[6]

The poorly paved roads and the mountainous terrain of Korea led to another innovation: medical evacuation by helicopter (or medevac). Sergeant Carl Cash was fighting with the 5th Marines, 1st Marine Division, when he was shot in 1951. The bullet hit him in the right side, ricocheted off his backbone, and went into his lung.

Paralyzed from the waist down, he was dragged from the battlefield. Medics gave him a shot of morphine, and then he was placed across the back of a jeep. The jeep broke down in the middle of a river, where Cash remained until a passing truck pulled out the jeep. Finally, a helicopter managed to drop down on nearby dry land and take him to safety.[7]

Cash and other veterans from Korea returned to a more indifferent America than the one that had enthusiastically greeted returning World War II veterans. Perhaps that was because the country was war-weary. Perhaps it was because the conflict involved a relatively small segment of the population in an isolated region of the world, in contrast to the all-out global effort summoned during the 1940s.

The paralyzed servicemen who came home from Korea experienced physical and mental obstacles similar to the ones that the paralyzed veterans from World War II had faced. But they navigated those challenges with less public fanfare and media attention. The sense of wonderment about surviving paraplegia was replaced with a "been there, done that" attitude. There was no Hollywood interest, as with *The Best Years of Their Lives* and *The Men*.

The "newbies" did enjoy the advantage of being able to lean on the World War II veterans in dealing with their injuries. Elder statesmen from the PVA returned to the paraplegia wards to offer advice about employment, sex, marriage, medical treatment, and wheelchair sports.

"You are going to live and probably have a normal life span or close to it," wrote PVA charter member Robert Moss in an open letter to Korean War veterans published in *Paraplegia News*. "Your symptoms may vary from day to day and infections may pop up at any time. You should avoid becoming a hypochondriac, which has happened to some extent to a lot of us, but at the same time, you should have a healthy concern for your body."[8]

That included taking advantage of the benefits of recreation. After he survived his medevac exodus, Carl Cash was treated at the U.S. Naval Hospital in Yokosuka, Japan. The Purple Heart recipient rehabbed at McGuire VA Hospital in Richmond and began to adjust to his new condition.

The bullet that had entered his lung and would remain there for the rest of his life didn't slow him down. Cash went back to school to earn his business degree. He joined the Charioteers team and went on to be elected to the National Wheelchair Basketball Association Hall of Fame.

Bill Johnson enlisted in the air force to fight in Korea. He was injured while hitching a ride back to Scott Air Force base near St. Louis. He recovered in the care of Dr. Bors in Long Beach, then joined the Flying Wheels. Johnson was an instant star, and his presence re-energized the Wheels during the 1950s and 1960s. He, too, was later enshrined in the NWBA Hall of Fame.

Brooklyn-born Carlos Rodriguez served in the Army's 187th Airborne Infantry Regiment. He'd been in Korea for two months when he was wounded by mortar and machine-gun fire at Inchon. He rehabbed at Valley Forge Army Hospital before joining the Whirlaways team. He later served as president of the Paralyzed Veterans of America.

Alonzo Wilkins was coming home from Korea when the ship he was aboard ran into stormy conditions mid-Pacific. He fell and was flung against the railing, which left the army veteran permanently paralyzed. He rehabilitated and then enrolled at the Bulova School of Watchmaking with designs on learning the trade.

Ben Lipton persuaded Wilkins to get involved in sports, and he turned himself into a four-wheeled superstar. He was not only selected to join the NWBA Hall of Fame, but he was the first individual inducted into the U.S. Wheelchair Athletic Association's Hall of Fame.

★ ★ ★

In the winter of 1951, Gene Haley, Louis Palmer, and the latest edition of the Flying Wheels embarked on their fourth annual cross-country tour. Excitement over their presence was palpably diminished. Neither Ed Sullivan nor Red Smith nor Dr. Howard Rusk wrote about them; only *Paraplegia News* columnist Harry Schweikert covered their trip in depth. They did not rekindle their rivalry with Halloran because the Staten Island hospital had suffered a similar fate to the one in Birmingham and was being closed, despite protests from PVA members.

The Wheels seemed to have lost their usual pizzazz, a casualty of their reorganizational move to Long Beach. They lost to the Kansas City Pioneers in overtime, then were embarrassed by their longtime rivals from Cushing Hospital, 49–19. They flew to New York City and beat the undermanned Bronx Rollers, 31–20, before falling to the Bulova Watchmakers, 32–25, and the Jersey Wheelers, 30–24. Their annual foray to Memphis to play the Kennedy Deadenders also ended in defeat, 31–19.

Long Beach conceded that this was the year for New England PVA—as the Cushing alumni now called their team—to shine. Coached by Bill O'Connor, who moonlighted as a talent scout for the Brooklyn Dodgers, the core of paralyzed veterans from Cushing—Greg Seymourian, Manny Leonardo, Joe Villa, and Dick Foley—followed the Flying Wheels into New York and swept the competition, downing the Bronx Rollers, 57–54, behind Walter Maguire's twenty-eight points; defeating the Jersey Wheelers, 41–20; and then beating Bulova, 40–26.

New England emerged as the first PVA wheelchair basketball team to finish the season undefeated against the other PVA teams. For their efforts, the Helms Athletic Foundation declared them PVA champs for 1951. The well-deserved recognition also paid tribute to the outsize role they had played in launching the sport back in the mid-1940s.

In late March, New England rode their hot streak to the Midwest, where Tim Nugent was hosting the third annual National Wheelchair Basketball Tournament on the University of Illinois campus at Urbana-Champaign.

Nugent's efforts to set up a national league and tournament were paying off. For the first time, four eastern teams entered the single-elimination playoff: New England, the Watchmakers, the Brooklyn Whirlaways, and the Jersey Wheelers. Representing the Midwest were Nugent's Gizz Kids (on their home court), the Kansas City Pioneers, the Hannibal Rockets, and the St. Louis Rams, the defending champs.

Ben Lipton's Bulova team was scheduled to fly out first class, but poor weather prevented their departure. They survived a thirty-hour travel ordeal and arrived for their first-round match with just enough time to eat. Their opponent was St. Louis, riding a two-year, thirty-five-game winning streak. The blue-and-gold-clad Rams easily clocked the weary Watchmakers, 32–20.

The Jersey Wheelers took an unscheduled flight and touched down at five a.m. on game day. They downed the Gizz Kids,

27–25, despite having to deal with the distraction of the university's wheelchair cheerleaders, who were "not short in the department of pulchritude," according to the NWBA's newsletter.[9] Meanwhile, the Pioneers defeated Hannibal, 28–20, and New England doubled up the Whirlaways, 32–16.

In the semifinals, the PVA champs couldn't find the range against the physical Pioneers. Only Walter Maguire, with eight points, was on target as New England shot a lowly .209 from the field. They kept the game close until Kansas City, led by ten points from Bruce Officer, a post-polio player, ended their magical season with a narrow 21–20 decision. St. Louis beat Jersey, 36–22, in the other semifinal, with O. G. Polster scoring eleven for the victors.

The final matched Kansas City, winner of the 1949 NWBT, against St. Louis, winner of the 1950 NWBT. Polster paced a balanced attack with ten points, and the Rams routed the Pioneers, 42–24, to claim back-to-back titles and a three-column golden trophy.

Jack Gerhardt and the Wheelers took third place, and Gerhardt, Bulova's Maurice Brooks, and Rams stars Polster and Jimmy Greenblatt were among those picked for the All-Tournament team. Proceeds from the tournament were earmarked for the PVA's National Paraplegia Foundation.

New England PVA's "paper title" offered some consolation, but this marked the final time that the Helms Foundation awarded this honor. Now that the sport had evolved from its roots among paralyzed veterans, now that Tim Nugent's NWBT was a successful enterprise, such an exercise was no longer necessary.

In wheelchair basketball, the PVA has "contributed something to society that will last permanently," Harry Schweikert wrote in *Paraplegia News*.[10] He was prescient, as usual, and paralyzed veterans would continue to play a significant role in the evolution of wheelchair sports. But moving forward, the U.S. champion would be determined exclusively at the NWBT.

Nugent's concept of a structured league for wheelchair basketball continued apace in the winter of 1951–52. Six proven teams formed the Eastern Division of the NWBA: the Jersey Wheelers, the Bulova Watchmakers, the Brooklyn Whirlaways, the Queens Charioteers, the Bronx Rollers, and the New York Spokesmen (made up entirely of post-polios). Harry Schweikert was named president of the division. Their records during the regular season would determine which teams qualified for the national tourney.

The same eight teams from the 1951 NWBT returned the next year, with two-time defending champion St. Louis the over-whelming favorite. The Rams were playing at home, with the tourney based at the Kiel Auditorium, and the nucleus of their lineup—featuring Polster and Greenblatt—was intact. During the regular season, they'd lost just one game, when the Gizz Kids snapped their streak of forty-three consecutive wins, 35–26.

St. Louis defeated New England PVA, 41–22, in the first round, then locked into a battle royal against the Brooklyn Whirlaways in the semifinals. Former heavyweight boxing champ Jack Dempsey applauded a cringe-worthy matchup that featured a whopping thirty-four personal fouls and numerous technical fouls. The teams were never separated by more than three points; the contest was tied at 25 with thirty seconds remaining, when St. Louis's Andy Zika nailed a short field goal to send the Rams to the finals.

Their opponent? The Gizz Kids, who'd crushed the Bulova Watchmakers, 49–22, and the Jersey Wheelers, 45–28.

Before the tip-off, the Illinois wheelchair cheerleaders were upstaged by the Rams' mascot: O. G. Polster's pre-kindergarten daughter. She stepped to the center of the floor, waved her arms for a yell, dropped her gum on the floor, nonchalantly picked it up, and retreated to the sidelines. One thousand spectators cheered her every move, while TV cameras recorded the antics.

Her nervy display inspired St. Louis. The Rams' defense clamped down on the high-scoring visitors, who shot an awful .178 from the field. Polster was held to seven points and Zika to three, but that allowed young Wally Petro, a left-leg amputee after he had been involved in a streetcar accident when he was twelve, to shake free and score a game-high sixteen points. The home team avenged their loss to the Gizz Kids and rolled to an unprecedented NWBT three-peat, 30–23.

★ ★ ★

In the spring of 1948, when World War II veterans from Halloran and Cushing hospitals played an exhibition game before some 15,000 fans at Madison Square Garden, wheelchair basketball was considered little more than a niche endeavor. Played exclusively by paralyzed veterans rehabbing at VA hospitals, the sport and its rules were still being formulated. Its future seemed limited.

Five years later, when Tim Nugent staged the 1953 National Wheelchair Basketball Tournament in New York City, the sport had become a recognized and respectable entity. Teams had to qualify or be invited to participate in the tourney; civilians with disabilities other than paraplegia and paralyzed veterans from the Korean conflict had joined the action.

Nugent scored his biggest coup by persuading the Flying Wheels to enter the 1953 NWBT after the conclusion of their annual barnstorming trip. Wheelchair basketball's most storied attraction was reloading at their base in Long Beach with fresh talent, including four veterans from the Korean War. One was Jack Chase, who'd served in the army's occupational forces in Korea before contracting polio. He played for the Gizz Kids at Illinois under Nugent, then moved to Los Angeles to study for the ministry at Life Bible College, founded by Sister Aimee Semple McPherson.

Coached by Jacques Grenier, a noted harness racing trainer, driver, and owner, the Wheels warmed up for the tour by taking on the Harlem Globetrotters at L.A.'s Pan-Pacific Auditorium. Wally Frost was assigned to guard Reece "Goose" Tatum, the "Clown Prince of Basketball," during the abbreviated exhibition.

This time, the Trotters were the laughingstocks. "Goose just went around in circles for five minutes," said Frost, a former medical corpsman, and the Wheels flummoxed the Trotters, 6–2.[11]

The Wheels started their ten-game, seventeen-day trip by beating the national champion St. Louis Rams. They downed their New England PVA rivals, and then scored wins over Bulova and the Jersey Wheelers. Their lone loss came at the hands of the Gizz Kids in a tight 32–30 contest.

During their layover in New York City, the players appeared on the *Strike It Rich* TV program. They donated their $500 winners' check to the National Paraplegia Foundation. The next day, guard Fritz Krauth, injured in 1948 while on the deck of a navy carrier, struck gold on *The Big Payoff* television game show. He won a trip to Europe for himself and his wife, a registered nurse.

There was time for serious business. They visited the new United Nations headquarters, by the East River, and spoke with Mary Pillsbury Lord, U.S. representative to the United Nations Human Rights Commission. On their stopover in Washington, D.C., first lady Mamie Eisenhower greeted them in the White

231

House. Their meeting was brief, but they couldn't get over her graciousness. Then they went out and stomped the Charioteers at Walter Reed Hospital.

The next day, they lunched with Vice President Richard Nixon in the Senate wing of the Capitol. "I am tremendously impressed with you men, especially after you rang up that 67–21 win over the Richmond Charioteers," said the former Whittier College basketball player. "I know many an able-bodied team would like to boast of 67 points for a winning total."[12]

In April, as peace negotiations continued in Korea, the Wheels returned to New York for the fifth annual National Wheelchair Basketball Tournament. The tourney didn't rate Madison Square Garden; the teams faced off at the Columbus Avenue Armory, a massive structure equipped with battlements that resembled a medieval fortress.

The *New York Times* billed the event as "probably the most unusual sports event New Yorkers can see," and noted that "If wheelchair basketball sounds a little mad, there's method to it . . . that if a man can play wheelchair basketball certainly he can 'play' wheelchair bookkeeping, bench assembly, sales."[13]

Thanks to Ben Lipton's diligence, the 1953 NWBT was well organized. Bulova pledged $8,000 to cover expenses, while Harry Schweikert and the PVA designed and published the official program. A nonprofit organization called the 52 Association also contributed. Restaurateur Arnold Reuben, fabled inventor of the Reuben sandwich, had persuaded fifty-two business-owners to chip in $52 per year to host weekly parties for injured servicemen. The 52 Association soon spread throughout the United States with their motto: "The wounded shall never be forgotten."[14]

Scoring at the NWBT was up—way up. Jack Chase set an individual scoring mark with twenty-one points as the Flying

Wheels downed the Brooklyn Whirlaways in the first round, only to see Bronx native John Bianco, a post-polio standout on the New York Spokesmen, tally twenty-three points in a losing cause in the very next game.

Stalking the sidelines, Nugent used a tight rotation of seven players as the Gizz Kids defeated New England in the first round, 45–36, behind Don Seifferth's sixteen points. Then they eliminated the three-time defending champ Rams, 20–19, after the usually accurate Polster went 0–16 from the field.

Nugent anticipated that the Gizz Kids would play the Flying Wheels for the title. But while Fritz Krauth set another scoring record with thirty points, Jack Chase went scoreless on 0–13 shooting, and the experienced Kansas City Pioneers turned back the California crew, 42–40, with Bruce Officer netting seventeen.

The championship game was equally taut. Ben Graham's eleven points carried the Gizz Kids, but they trailed the Pioneers by three points with two minutes remaining. Their star center had just fouled out.

Marv Lapicola, a post-polio freshman, came off the bench with instructions from Nugent "not to shoot." Lapicola, who described his playing style as "a gunner and a shooter," calmly sank two field goals and two free throws to lead Illinois to a come-from-behind victory, 44–41.[15]

The Gizz Kids—the college students who were kicked out of Galesburg—were national champs. Nugent exulted in winning the tournament that he'd created, but already he was looking ahead with typical zeal. He reported that several new teams were taking shape, including the Memphis Rolling Rockets, which he described as "an all-negro paraplegic team from whom we expect great things in the future."[16]

Nugent also revealed that he'd invited a team from Canada to play in the 1954 tourney. The prospect of foreign players competing in the NWBT hinted at one of his long-term dreams: international wheelchair–basketball competition.

In this, Nugent trailed behind Dr. Ludwig Guttmann.

★ ★ ★

As Tim Nugent was expanding wheelchair basketball beyond the community of U.S. paralyzed veterans, Ludwig Guttmann was expanding the breadth of the Stoke Mandeville Games in England. In the summer of 1950, the games featured ten squads, sixty-one athletes, and a third event, javelin, added to archery and netball. The next year, 121 athletes competed in four sports, with snooker added to the mix.

Guttmann's grand aspirations were on display the following year. He'd made numerous entreaties to entice paralyzed veterans from other countries to compete against the British lads. He succeeded at the 1952 Stoke Mandeville Games, when a quartet of paralyzed veterans from the Military Rehabilitation Center in Aardenburg, Netherlands, crossed the North Sea with their medical aides. The World Veterans Federation, an organization that campaigned for the rights of veterans and victims of war, covered their travel expenses.

After noting in his opening speech that the 1952 Olympic Games were underway in Helsinki, Guttmann expressed hope that "one day the paraplegic games would be as international and as widely known in its own sphere as the Olympics."[17]

This seemed unlikely, given that just 130 wheelchair athletes participated in what Guttmann dubbed the "First International Stoke Mandeville Games," while some 4,879 athletes representing sixty-nine countries participated in the Games of the XV Olympiad. But mere numbers did not matter to Guttmann.

Guttmann failed to mention that at least two elite athletes had managed to overcome their disabilities and were excelling at the Helsinki Olympics. Denmark's Lis Hartel was an equestrian champion who developed polio while pregnant. She gave birth to a healthy child, then went through months of physical therapy just so she could lift her arms. She learned to walk with crutches, but was left paralyzed below the knees. She needed assistance to get on and off her horse, Jubilee.

Once mounted in Helsinki, she and Jubilee won the silver medal in individual dressage. The gold medalist, Swedish officer Henri Saint Cyr, assisted Hartel to the victory podium in an emotional moment that intertwined the two athletes and resonated among people with disabilities.

During World War II, American diver Miller Anderson had to bail out of his P-47 fighter plane after catching flak and broke his left thighbone while parachuting. Once on the ground, he was captured by Germans and taken to a POW camp, where his leg was set incorrectly. After Anderson was liberated, doctors told him that they would have to amputate the leg, which had become infected. He protested and, instead, they reset the bones and inserted a metal plate in the knee area. He changed his takeoff approach to accommodate the metal plate and took the silver medal in springboard diving in the 1948 and 1952 Summer Olympic Games.

In 1953, Guttmann proudly introduced swimming to the International Stoke Mandeville Games, with the opening of a forty-two-foot-long hydrotherapy pool on the hospital grounds. He also welcomed the first wheelchair sports team from North America, thanks to the behind-the-scenes effort of William Mackie Hepburn.

Born in Scotland and raised in Canada, Hepburn served with the Black Watch infantry regiment during the war. Afterward, he assisted Canadian paralyzed veterans to organize the country's first wheelchair basketball team under coach Harold Rabin. A reporter from the English-language *Montreal Star* newspaper saw an exhibition game and gushed about the "wonders of the paralyzed." Thus was born the Montreal Wheelchair Wonders. (Hepburn later helped form the Wheelchair Wonderettes, considered to be the first all-women's club.)

The Wonders came equipped with lightweight E&J wheelchairs manufactured in the United States. They wheeled circles around their European opponents, who were ensconced in plush chairs whose speed and maneuverability rivaled that of a sloth. But the Wonders were accustomed to playing wheelchair basketball, not netball. Adjusting to the peculiarities of that sport proved too daunting for the inexperienced Wonders; they fell in the finals to the paralyzed veterans from Lyme Green, an outfit from northwest England that had captured every netball championship at Stoke Mandeville.

Guttmann's crowning achievement was the invention of a distinctive word to describe the wheelchair competition at Stoke Mandeville. "Paralympics" joined the words "paraplegia" (or "paralyzed") with "Olympics." The *Bucks Advertiser & Aylesbury News*, the local paper, was the first mainstream publication to use the word in print: "'Paralympics' of 1953—Just What the Doctor Ordered!" read the headline.[18]

The newfangled term quickly reached American shores. *Paraplegia News* dubbed them the "Stoke Mandeville Paralympics."[19] An article about Guttmann in *Time* magazine, then the most widely read newsweekly in the United States, carried the headline "Paralympics of 1953." Accompanied by a black-and-white photograph of a netball game, the story described Guttmann as "probably the first man to use athletics as paraplegic therapy, and he is one of the most successful."[20]

With the imprimatur of *Time* and the PVA, Guttmann's attempts to couple his homegrown games with the mighty Olympics no longer seemed outrageous. He was probably the only person who wasn't surprised.

"Like the Olympic Games, which were started by a small group of people who believed in sport as a great medium for furthering true sportsmanship and understanding amongst human beings, our Stoke Mandeville Games will, we believe, unite paralyzed men and women of different nations to take their rightful place in the field of sport," he noted in the program for the 1953 Games.[21]

Guttmann went further in an article reprinted in *Paraplegia News*, calling for "the inclusion of teams of paralyzed sports-men in national and international sports tournaments, such as the Olympic Games and Grand National Archery tournament, [whether] in a special section in a specific sport or, in certain sports, on an equal footing with any other competitor."[22]

Fourteen nations sent teams to Stoke Mandeville in 1954. Guttmann scored a major coup with the appearance of Olympic gold medalist David Cecil, famous for being the first person to complete the Great Court Run at Cambridge in less than 43.6 seconds, a feat immortalized (inaccurately) in the 1981 film *Chariots of Fire*. Cecil was now the vice president of the International Olympic Committee. He joined Guttmann as the athletes organized a "wheel-past": grouped together by country, with a banner displaying the name of each nation attached to the back of the lead wheelchair, they rolled together in formation past the reviewing stand, just like in the Olympics.

On this, the tenth anniversary of the opening of the spinal-cord center, Guttmann coupled sports with statistics gleaned from his work. He reported that fewer than 10 percent of the World War II veterans treated at Stoke Mandeville for spinal paraplegia had died, a staggering improvement over the 90 percent mortality rate suffered by veterans paralyzed during World War I.[23]

Guttmann's conclusion: "Victory Over Paraplegia."[24]

The results vindicated Guttmann's unorthodox methods, and the media took note. He was "the genius of the occasion," according to the *Observer*,[25] while the *Manchester Guardian* described him as "a humanist of imagination as well as a neurosurgeon of wide repute."[26]

There was chatter about organizing a "Wheelchair Olympics" for veterans with paraplegia, sponsored by the World Veterans Federation, to be held in the summer of 1954. Harold Russell, the double amputee co-star of *The Best Years of Our Lives,* was named as part of the organizational team. Wheelchair netball, swimming, club swinging to music, table tennis, and badminton were proposed for the program.[27]

The idea never gained traction, primarily because of funding issues. Dr. Ludwig Guttmann's vision of a global, Olympic-style competition for people with paraplegia—the aptly named Paralympics—was never challenged again in his lifetime.

CHAPTER 18

Fighting Polio

Ever since Dr. Ludwig Guttmann launched the Stoke Mandeville Games in 1948, one key element had eluded him. He had not been able to persuade American wheelchair athletes to travel to England. The appearance of a team from the United States, Britain's stalwart ally during World War II and the only other nation to develop sports programs for paralyzed veterans that rivaled Guttmann's, would add prestige and, in his eyes, further legitimize them.

Guttmann worked tirelessly to make this happen. He sent dispatches about the Games to Harry Schweikert for his sports column in *Paraplegia News*. When he traveled to the United States in 1952, he personally urged Ben Lipton to send the Bulova Watchmakers to Stoke Mandeville, to no avail.

Lipton was also eager, in theory at least, to expand adaptive sports internationally. But, as he explained to Guttmann, wheelchair basketball was so dominant among disabled athletes in America that they rarely experimented with other wheelchair sports.

As it turned out, the first American athletes to cross the Atlantic and compete at Stoke Mandeville were a wheelchair basketball team. It wasn't the perennially barnstorming Flying Wheels or

Tim Nugent's Gizz Kids or Lipton's Watchmakers. Rather, it was a squad fashioned from the detritus of an insidious health crisis mixed with a dose of corporate branding.

James McGuire was the head of accounting at Long Island City–based Pan American World Airways, the leading international airline in the United States. He could only watch in horror when his young daughter, Patsy, was stricken with poliomyelitis, a viral infectious disease that spreads "from person to person through contact with fecal waste: unwashed hands, shared objects, contaminated food and water," according to polio scholar David Oshinsky.[1]

Patsy was one of the many unfortunate victims of the polio epidemic that haunted families in postwar America. Transmission peaked in 1952, with 57,000 new cases in the United States, including approximately 21,000 paralytic cases and more than 3,000 fatalities.[2]

At the time, there was no vaccine to combat the deadly menace. In its earliest stages, youngsters whose respiratory systems were compromised were placed in iron lung contraptions to help them breathe. When the virus traveled through the bloodstream and attacked the central nervous system, permanent paralysis often resulted, primarily in the legs.

Marv Lapicola developed polio in the summer of 1950 while attending football camp. He was seventeen years old, a junior at Roosevelt Military Academy in Aledo, Illinois, with aspirations of going to West Point.

"I had about two weeks of 104, 105 temperature," he said. "After the temperature went down, then you were left with the damage. I had therapy, but none of that got the cells in [my] spine to communicate between the brain and the muscles."[3]

Lapicola considered himself "blessed" because his lungs weren't ravaged. One leg was almost completely damaged, while the other one wasn't as badly affected. He used a wheelchair, but after rehabilitation he found that he could also get around with underarm crutches and a leg brace.

His bleak future improved after he enrolled at the University of Illinois at Urbana–Champaign. Like the paralyzed veterans before him, Lapicola found relief by playing wheelchair basketball. "I thought it was the greatest thing in the world because I saw how competitive it was right away," he said. "The opportunity opened up a whole new world for me. It meant a lot."[4]

As Lapicola was finding his way on the basketball court, Dr. Jonas Salk and his staff of researchers at the University of Pittsburgh were racing to develop a vaccine to prevent polio. Salk had spent World War II working with Dr. Thomas Francis Jr., a microbiologist and epidemiologist, to create an influenza vaccine for the army. Their mission was a high priority after the 1918 influenza pandemic killed almost as many U.S. military personnel (about 45,000) as those who died from combat wounds (about 50,000) during World War I.[5]

The army cut through bureaucratic red tape surrounding medical testing so that Francis and Salk could produce a vaccine quickly. Which they did, developing the first modern flu shot that was effective against influenza A and B strains. U.S. soldiers received vaccinations starting in 1945, with civilians able to get their flu shots the following year.

After the war, Salk turned his attention to polio with funding from the National Foundation for Infantile Paralysis, founded by President Roosevelt in 1938 (and later known as the March of Dimes). Using "killed" virus strains derived from the three types of polio, Salk created an injectable vaccine that tricked the body into forming protective antibodies to fight against the infectious agent.

Introduced in a massive national field trial in 1954, this vaccine, as well as the oral version developed by Dr. Albert Sabin using live virus strains, eradicated polio in the United States. (Neither Salk nor Sabin patented their vaccines.)

★ ★ ★

Salk's polio vaccine came too late for Patsy McGuire. She underwent rehabilitation and made slow progress, graduating from a wheelchair to crutches to a cane.

James McGuire's boss at Pan Am was John Sylvester Woodbridge, the company's comptroller. Woodbridge had served as an ambulance driver for the French Army during World War I and was gravely injured fighting with the French Blue Devils. He never forgot his own punishing recovery, and watched Patsy's struggles with compassion.[6]

Beyond Patsy's case, Woodbridge noticed that Pan Am's general accounting office employed several post-polios who also played wheelchair basketball. Many of them competed for the Brooklyn Whirlaways, one of the sport's oldest civilian squads. Their roster was a mix of polio patients from St. Charles Hospital on Long Island and graduates from New Utrecht High School in the Bensonhurst section of Brooklyn.

Joe Vitta, Mario D'Antonio, Pete Acca, Tony Mucci, and Danny Vaccaro formed a tight-knit, aggressive crew on the court, along with Saul Welger, their top scorer, who came down with polio at the age of eight. Even their nickname was memorable, evoking the four-legged stride of the thoroughbred Whirlaway, who'd captured the Triple Crown in 1941.

"They're as tough as Australian goat steaks," the *Brooklyn Eagle* newspaper reported. "The men wear loose-fitting trousers so spectators will watch their ball-handling instead of wasting sympathy on shriveled muscles or missing limbs."[7]

The Whirls were good enough to qualify for the 1954 National Wheelchair Basketball Tournament, sponsored again by the 52 Association. New York City mayor Robert Wagner Jr. received the athletes at City Hall, while Tim Nugent alerted reporters about the first appearance of Canada's Wheelchair Wonders in the NWBT.

The team from Montreal showed potential, but these Wonders weren't ready for the bright lights of the Columbus Avenue Armory. They lost to the Jersey Wheelers, 52–8, and to the Queens Charioteers, 36–13.

Welger and the Whirls trounced Kansas City, 44–29, before nipping St. Louis, 42–40, to reach the finals. Their opponent was a team they knew well from their contests in the Eastern Wheelchair Basketball Association: the Jersey Wheelers.

Anchored by paralyzed veterans Jack Gerhardt, Pete Youakim, and Ray Werner, the Wheelers were a study in perseverance. They were one of the first teams to form outside the hospital setting (and had even flown to Miami in 1949 to demonstrate the sport at an Elks Convention). They'd been using the same core lineup since then, but had never peaked at tournament time.

The finals between the Wheelers and the Whirlaways took place on Palm Sunday. Beforehand, Cardinal Francis Spellman blessed the palms in a forty-minute ceremony at St. Patrick's Cathedral. He then walked to the terrace along Madison Avenue and greeted eighteen wheelchair players, accompanied by their coaches and relatives.

Both teams sought divine intervention during the hard-fought game. Jersey led 23–11 at the half, but Brooklyn drew close, 30–27, after three periods. With the clock winding down, the Whirls committed a foul that sent the Wheelers' Henry Preckajlo to the free-throw line. Preckajlo, who had lost both legs in an artillery burst while fighting with Merrill's Marauders in Burma, converted the opportunity to secure the title, 39–38.

Preckajlo was the game's top scorer with twelve points. His teammate Gerhardt was named to the All-American team, along with Welger of the Whirlaways.

Despite the setback, Pan Am's Woodbridge was impressed by the Whirlaways' tenacity and their ball-handling skills. He also discovered that the players could barely keep the team afloat. They had access only to an outdoor court. They had to borrow wheelchairs from local hospitals or rent them for practice sessions.

A friend who operated a candy store in Brooklyn badgered her customers into dropping spare change into a mason jar to assist the players who wanted to buy their own chairs on installment. They missed games because they couldn't afford to fix the "sprained ligaments on their go-buggies." (That is, they needed new spokes for their wheelchairs.)[8]

During the off-season, Woodbridge and Welger devised a plan that jolted the insular world of the Eastern Wheelchair Basketball Association. The Whirls were folded and, taking a cue from the Bulova Watchmakers, Pan Am stepped in to sponsor a wheelchair basketball team, composed primarily of post-polio employees in the accounting department.

Pan Am purchased new chairs, complete with balloon tires, and agreed to rent the Forest Hills High School gym in Queens for practices. A squad of uniformed cheerleaders, dubbed the "Little Jets," was formed. Bill Condon, a non-disabled junior accountant who'd previously handled publicity for the Whirlaways, was named coach, and he soon filled the pages of *Clipper*, the company's monthly newsletter, with reports of the team's exploits.[9]

Naturally, they were named the Pan Am Jets. Their mascot? None other than Patsy McGuire.

Welger and his teammates scoured the five boroughs for fresh talent. They signed up players from the Bulova Watchmakers and the Queens Charioteers. Mario Galucci, their part-time coach and sometime player, recruited Julius Jiacoppo to the Jets after noticing his affliction at a neighborhood carwash.

Jiacoppo was the son of a barber who had emigrated from Italy and settled near the Brooklyn Navy Yard. He identified himself as a member of "the class of '35," meaning that he was stricken with polio in 1935, when he was two years old. Until he was twelve, he wore braces that went around his waist, all the way down his legs, and clipped to his shoes.[10]

Pan Am and Jiacoppo warmed up with an exhibition match against company employees using wheelchairs. The Jets spotted them fifty points and romped easily, 98–66. They carried that momentum into the 1954–55 regular season and captured the eastern division of the NWBA. They entered the 1955 National Wheelchair Basketball Tournament as one of the favorites.

★ ★ ★

Travel, food, and lodging expenses for the players and coaches at the annual National Wheelchair Basketball Tournament did not come cheap, even with generous underwriting from the 52 Association and other groups that assisted veterans. When these organizations ceased providing such support, Tim Nugent and the fledgling NWBA found it difficult to secure financing for the event. Nugent was on the brink of canceling the seventh edition of the NWBT until, at the last minute, he was rescued by the military.

At the time, the U.S. Armed Forces could legally provide airlifts for needy groups and private individuals that requested such transport. The pilots used the flights as part of their training exercises, and the military accrued some good publicity.

Three weeks before the scheduled tip-off of the 1955 NWBT, Nugent contacted Major General Byron Gates, the commander of Chanute Air Force Base in Rantoul, Illinois, just north of the Urbana-Champaign campus. Nugent persuaded Gates to host the NWBT at Chanute and to assist in the airlift of the seven out-of-state teams (with help from the California Air National Guard).

The teams appreciated the military's involvement because the planes were better equipped than commercial airlines to handle their travel needs. The base at Chanute provided sufficient barracks to house the players, many of whom were veterans, as well as full-service mess halls, gymnasiums, and medical staff. Personnel and staff at the base came out to watch the games and cheer on the athletes.

Four military bases, including El Toro Marine Base in California, hosted the NWBT through 1963, when the U.S. airlift program was halted. "Tim Nugent held the league together when none of us had any money," Jiacoppo later said. "When it was time to find a tournament site, Tim had connections with the military."[11]

At the NWBT in Chanute, Jiacoppo and Pan Am rolled over the Kansas City Pioneers, 39–31, to reach the semifinals. There, they faced wheelchair basketball's original airborne team: the Flying Wheels. And the Wheels were smoking hot.

In February, when they'd embarked on their eighth annual cross-country tour, the Wheels fielded their most talented team to date. Anchored by Gene Haley, Jack Chase, Wally Frost, and

Fritz Krauth, they played a hard, fast style of basketball and didn't lose a game on the seventeen-day trip.

Going undefeated in nine games was one sign of their dominance; their record-setting scoring was another. They twice whipped the Jersey Wheelers, the defending national champs, then downed the Richmond Charioteers, 60–22. They swept through New York, starting with a convincing win over the Jets, 65–53, as Krauth netted thirty points. Routs over the Bronx, 63–17, and the Bulova Watchmakers, 56–35, followed.

As always, the Wheels mixed basketball with business. In Washington, D.C., to play the Charioteers, they decried the paraplegia ward at the Long Beach VA Hospital as a firetrap and lobbied congressional leaders for funds to construct a state-of-the-art facility for paralyzed veterans. (They succeeded in their mission, with the new $8 million center opening in 1959.)

They again visited the White House, where Mamie Eisenhower had received them the previous two years. This time, President Eisenhower himself greeted them in the Conference Room. He shook hands with all twelve athletes, posed for photographs, and chatted with them about the team's nifty record.

They flew to Chicago and, for the first time in three attempts, beat Nugent's Gizz Kids, 46–31, as twenty-two hospitalized veterans from Korea watched courtside from wheelchairs. Art Jurado, who played the muscular pal to Marlon Brando's character in *The Men*, provided the halftime entertainment at the Navy Pier gym by demonstrating his rope-climbing technique. Delayed for five hours by a snowstorm, the Wheels arrived in Kansas City with no time to warm up or eat dinner, but still had enough in the tank to defeat the Pioneers, 46–43.

There was no rest for the weary. Less than two months later, the Wheels boarded a C-47 bucket-seat job, with litter cots strung up inside the plane so the players could lie down, and flew to Chanute for the 1955 NWBT.[12]

With them was a familiar face. Bob Rynearson had not previously accompanied the Wheels on their yearly junkets because his job at the VA, as well as family responsibilities, kept him tethered to Southern California. In 1955, the "James Naismith of wheelchair basketball" used his vacation days to coach the Flying Wheels in Chanute.

In the decade since he wrote the first rules for wheelchair basketball in the cozy confines of the Birmingham Hospital gym, the sport had evolved from an exclusive enclave for paralyzed veterans from World War II to an inclusive sport for amputees, post-polios, civilians, and veterans from Korea; from being viewed as an astounding exhibition of human bravery to being a competitive sport that transcended disabilities; and from a loose confederation of PVA-affiliated teams to an organized league with corporate sponsored teams and a national championship tourney.

The can-do spirit of the first wave of wheelchair athletes still permeated the sport. World War II–era paralyzed veterans like Jack Gerhardt and a good portion of the Flying Wheels' roster continued to play wheelchair basketball at an elite level. But due to a combination of factors—starting with TB 6-60 and the closure of Birmingham and Halloran, as well as the demands of work and family—their numbers and influence were beginning to wane.

With the inclusion of post-polio players like Marv Lapicola and Julius Jiacoppo—and, later, Henry Hampton, who went on to create and produce *Eyes on the Prize*, an award-winning fourteen-hour television series about the civil rights movement—the very nature of the sport was being transformed. Post-polios often retained sensation and even movement below the waist, and their overall muscle function tended to be superior to those with paraplegia. "The paraplegics didn't have the balance [in the chair]," said Jiacoppo. "That was the big difference."[13]

Tim Nugent and the NWBA's rules committee decided to add the "physical advantage" foul—recorded separately from personal and technical fouls—to "keep the game equitable for participants of all types of disabilities." A physical advantage foul was deemed to occur, according to the NWBA newsletter, "if through some means [an athlete] hoists his buttocks off the seat of his chair, uses a foot or a leg where he has control or partial control of same for propelling the chair, stopping the chair, or directing the movement of the chair." (Another new violation was the "use of cushions in excess of four inches of foam rubber as authorized by the Association.")[14]

Rynearson and the Wheels felt rusty entering the tournament, despite their undefeated skein. "Our season usually ends after our annual coast-to-coast trip in February," said Lee Barr, an invaluable reserve, "whereas the season runs through March for the Eastern teams who enjoy regular league competition."[15]

They opened with a decisive victory over the Watchmakers, 47–32. Krauth was fighting the effects of an intestinal flu, but he paced the attack with nineteen points. Next up: the Pan Am Jets in the semifinals.

California took a 28–15 halftime lead. Leading scorers Krauth and Wally Frost got into foul trouble, forcing Rynearson to go to his bench. Bill Fairbanks, a post-polio player who was the only non-veteran on the roster, took up the scoring slack with thirteen points, and Morris Moorhead, an ex-Marine sergeant who'd been injured in Korea, chipped in nine, and they cruised to a decisive victory, 46–35. Only Jiacoppo (thirteen points) and Welger (ten) managed double figures for the Jets.

The Wheels had an unexpectedly easy time in the finale against the St. Louis Rams. Jack Chase broke the individual foul-shot mark by netting twelve out of fifteen, and the Wheels coasted, 44–27. Krauth, Chase, and Frost earned all-tourney honors and were awarded Bulova watches.

Rynearson basked in the Wheels' unprecedented achievement. Not only were they the only team to capture both the PVA title and the NWBT, albeit in different years and with different line-ups, they were the first to complete an undefeated season. They flew home in a style befitting champions: in a plush DC-4 usually assigned to Air Force General Leon Johnson. They took turns holding the gleaming four-foot-high trophy that served as a fitting tribute to the paralyzed veterans who'd gone before them.

The Pan Am Jets flew home to Long Island. Disappointed but undaunted, they had little time to regroup. They were poised to take wheelchair basketball to the Stoke Mandeville Games.

Gene Fesenmeyer, in his U.S. Marine Corps uniform *(Courtesy of Leona Rubin)*

Stanley Den Adel, after returning home from the war *(Margaret Herrick Library, Academy of Motion Picture Arts and Sciences)*

Johnny Winterholler and Dessa Tippetts at the University of Wyoming *(Courtesy of Deborah Harms and the Winterholler family)*

Johnny Winterholler and Dessa Tippetts at the Naval Hospital Corona *(Courtesy of Deborah Harms and the Winterholler family)*

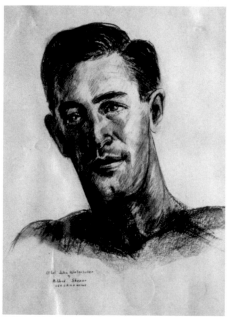

Sketch of Johnny Winterholler, made while he was rehabilitating in the hospital *(Mildred Shearer, Institute on World War II and the Human Experience, Florida State University)*

A wooden wheelchair designed by Thomas Twining, c. 1845. Note the oversize front wheels. *(Wellcome Collection)*

A rare photo of President Franklin D. Roosevelt in his wheelchair at his estate in Hyde Park, New York *(Margaret Suckley, courtesy of the Franklin D. Roosevelt Library)*

Dr. Ernest Bors, head of the paraplegia unit at Birmingham Hospital *(Margaret Herrick Library, Academy of Motion Picture Arts and Sciences)*

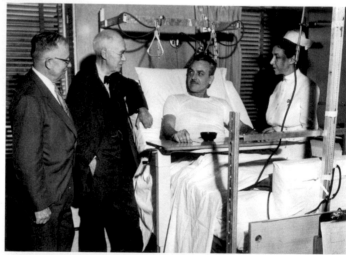

Dr. Donald Munro (second from left) checks on a patient with paraplegia. *(*Boston Herald Traveler *photo morgue, Boston Public Library,* Boston Herald*)*

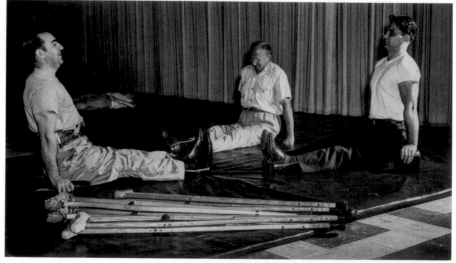

A paralyzed war veteran instructs other veterans in physical therapy. *(Department of Special Collections & University Archives, W. E. B. Du Bois Library, University of Massachusetts Amherst)*

Bob Rynearson at Birmingham Hospital, around the time he created the sport of wheelchair basketball *(Courtesy of the Rynearson family)*

Bob Rynearson (referee) and pioneering wheelchair basketball players practice in the gymnasium at Birmingham Hospital, c. 1946. *(Courtesy of the Rynearson family)*

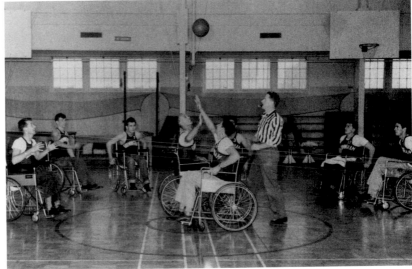

Stan Den Adel (far left) and other paralyzed veterans play water basketball as part of their rehabilitation at Birmingham Hospital. *(Valley Times Collection, Los Angeles Public Library)*

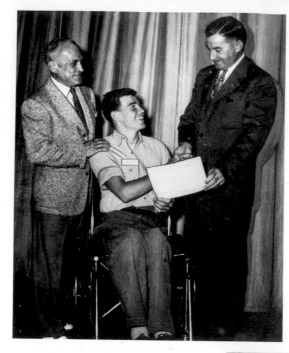

Stan Den Adel (seated) receives a merit award for surpassing the efficiency records of non-disabled fellow workers at Birmingham Hospital. *(Valley Times Collection, Los Angeles Public Library)*

Aerial view of Naval Hospital Corona: at center are the original structures of the Norconian Resort Supreme; at right center are three new ward buildings; at upper right are temporary wards being constructed. *(Courtesy of Kevin Bash)*

The Rolling Devils from Naval Hospital Corona with John Winterholler (center, seated), Gene Fesenmeyer (far right), and Dr. Gerald Gray (left, standing) *(Courtesy of Deborah Harms and the Winterholler family)*

Gene Fesenmeyer touches down as the Rolling Devils prepare to meet the Oakland Bittners. *(Courtesy of the family of Dr. Gerald Gray)*

Louis Largey of the Rolling Devils defends against the Bittners' Jim Pollard. *(Courtesy of the family of Dr. Gerald Gray)*

The crowd at the Oakland Civic Auditorium delights in the Rolling Devils' easy victory. *(Courtesy of the family of Dr. Gerald Gray)*

The Birmingham Hospital team readies for its first cross-country tour in 1948. Stan Den Adel (seated, third from right) met his future wife, Peggy Stapleton, who was the nurse on the trip (standing, middle). *(Courtesy of the Rynearson family)*

Veteran Jack Heller is hoisted aboard as the Birmingham Hospital team leaves on the barnstorming trip. *(Los Angeles Times Photographic Archives. Library Special Collections, Charles E. Young Research Library, UCLA)*

The Clippers team from Cushing Hospital in Massachusetts defeats Birmingham during the opening tour. *(Courtesy of Armand "Tip" Thiboutot)*

Clippers players (from left) Greg Seymourian, Dick Foley, and Howie Tesnow show off their shooting form before a game against college all-stars. (Boston Herald Traveler *photo morgue, Boston Public Library,* Boston Herald)

Halloran Hospital's Selig Boshnack shoots during the game against Cushing Hospital at Madison Square Garden. *(Courtesy of Annette Boshnack)*

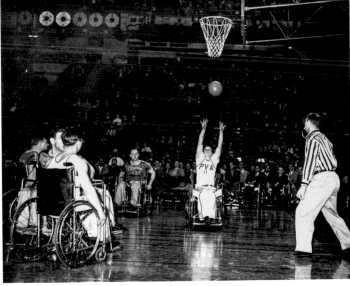

Paraplegia News columnist Harry Schweikert, the first journalist to write extensively about wheelchair sports *(Courtesy of* Paraplegia News, *Paralyzed Veterans of America)*

Ted Anderson (far right) watches as Marlon Brando (foreground) portrays the moment Anderson was injured, while director Fred Zinnemann (seated left) and screenwriter Carl Foreman (middle) consult with him. *(Copyright © Paramount Pictures Corp. All rights reserved.)*

The San Fernando Valley community greets Pat Grissom (seated, far left) and two other veterans after they protested the abrupt closure of Birmingham Hospital. *(Valley Times Collection, Los Angeles Public Library)*

Good luck,
Edith Nourse Rogers

The Flying Wheels take time out from
basketball to lobby for disability rights,
and pose on the Capitol steps with U.S.
Congresswoman Edith Nourse Rogers.
(Courtesy of the Rynearson family)

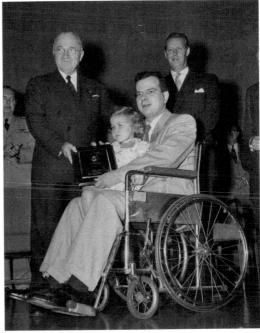

President Harry S. Truman congratulates
veteran and business owner Nils Josefson while
touting the National Employ the Physically
Handicapped Week, 1952. *(Department of Special
Collections & University Archives, W. E. B. Du Bois
Library, University of Massachusetts Amherst)*

President Dwight D. Eisenhower
greets Fritz Krauth and the 1955
edition of the Flying Wheels at
the White House. The team won
the national wheelchair basketball
title. *(National Park Service photo,
courtesy of the Eisenhower Presidential
Library and Museum)*

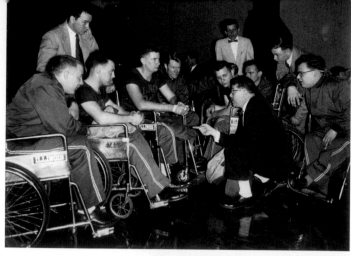

Coach Tim Nugent talks strategy with the Gizz Kids of the University of Illinois. *(Courtesy of the University of Illinois Archives)*

Tim Nugent (center) and two of the kneeling buses created for students with disabilities at the University of Illinois *(Courtesy of the University of Illinois Archives)*

Flyers for the 5th National Wheelchair Basketball Tournament, held in New York City *(Courtesy of the Rynearson family)*

Dr. Ludwig Guttmann (far left) observes the archery competition at the inaugural Stoke Mandeville Games, 1948. *(Photo © IWAS—www.iwasf.com)*

Netball action at Stoke Mandeville Hospital, 1949. Note the oversize wheelchairs, the lowered net, and the lone female athlete (back to camera). *(Raymond Kleboe/Picture Post/Hulton Archive/Getty Images)*

Dr. Roger Bannister readies the tip-off at the 1955 Stoke Mandeville Games, featuring the first appearance of the Pan Am Jets. *(Photo © IWAS—www.iwasf.com)*

Junius Kellogg (center) coaches the Pan Am Jets team, c. 1958. *(Courtesy of Special Collections, University of Miami Libraries)*

Rough-and-tumble action between the Pan Am Jets and the Netherlands at the 1957 International Stoke Mandeville Games *(Courtesy of Bill Mather-Brown, Australian Paralympic Committee)*

Dr. Ludwig Guttmann (far right) escorts Crown Prince Akihito and Crown Princess Michiko at the opening ceremony of the 1964 Tokyo Paralympics. *(Courtesy of the Australian Paralympic Committee)*

Bulova's Ben Lipton (standing, right) and coach Sy Bloom (standing, left) with members of the 1964 U.S. Paralympic team, including Selig Boshnack (far left) and Charles Smith (far right) *(Courtesy of Annette Boshnack)*

Former Dodgers catcher Roy Campanella acknowledges the crowd at the Los Angeles Memorial Coliseum, 1959. *(Tom Courtney,* Herald Examiner *Collection, Los Angeles Public Library)*

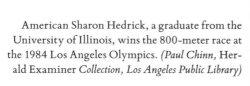

American Sharon Hedrick, a graduate from the University of Illinois, wins the 800-meter race at the 1984 Los Angeles Olympics. *(Paul Chinn,* Herald Examiner *Collection, Los Angeles Public Library)*

Ed Santillanes, the last surviving member of Birmingham Hospital's first wheelchair basketball team, returns to the gymnasium in 2018. *(Gary Leonard)*

CHAPTER 19

Flying Pan Am

On the afternoon of July 26, 1955, eleven wheelchair athletes and coach Bill Condon gathered at New York's Idlewild Airport, passports in tow, and boarded a (what else?) Pan American jetliner for London en route to the Stoke Mandeville Games.

The contingent worried about whether playing outdoors in England's famously fickle weather would disrupt their fast-breaking game. And, because wheelchair basketball had been their solitary focus, they fretted about the other events they were expected to compete in: table tennis, archery, javelin, and swimming. They had practiced for hours at Forest Hills High School and, before leaving, scrimmaged against Ben Lipton's Bulova Watchmakers squad in javelin and archery.

The first wheelchair sports team to represent the United States in international competition also represented a branding opportunity for the airline. Pan Am's name and familiar blue globe logo were plastered on the backs of the players' wheelchairs. Each of the Jets wore a white T-shirt with "USA" and "Pan Am Jets" emblazoned on the front and a gleaming "Pan Am Jets" letterman jacket.

At Stoke Mandeville, sunny skies welcomed them along with

some 279 other competitors from sixteen nations. Dr. Ludwig Guttmann was "very pleased" about the arrival of the Americans, but he was equally relieved that construction of the expanded sports ground at the rear of the hospital had been completed in time for the Games.[1]

Guttmann succeeded in luring two VIPs to Stoke Mandeville. In the summer of 1955, Roger Bannister was perhaps the most famous athlete in the world. The middle-distance runner had finished fourth in the 1,500 meters at the Helsinki Olympics. That disappointing performance was largely forgotten on May 6, 1954, when he took to the Iffley Road track in Oxford and smashed the four-minute barrier in the mile.

It was a feat that many had believed was physically impossible and, like New Zealander Edmund Hillary's ascent of Mount Everest in 1953, buoyed the spirits of people in England and elsewhere in the Commonwealth during the lean postwar years. The achievement earned Bannister the inaugural "Sportsman of the Year" honor from Henry Luce's latest venture, a glossy weekly magazine called *Sports Illustrated*.[2]

Dressed in a dark suit and accompanied by his wife, Moyra, the lanky miler shook hands with wide-eyed fans, signed autographs, and watched the proceedings with a regal bearing that turned to wonderment.

He was also Dr. Roger Bannister, or "Dr. Rogester" as Guttmann mistakenly referred to him.[3] He'd hung up his spikes to attend medical school and was embarking on what was to be a long and distinguished career in neurology. The two discussed diseases of the brain at the scientific meeting about paraplegia that Guttmann convened during the games.

Nearby stood the second celebrity, Geneviève de Galard, wearing sunglasses, a sleeveless white shirt, and binoculars that hung from her neck for use in viewing the archery targets. De Galard had been a flight nurse deployed with the French Air Force during the war between France and the Viet Minh. She had been stranded at Dien Bien Phu, the French fortress in the northwest region of Vietnam, after her medevac aircraft was destroyed in early 1954.

Working in unsanitary and brutal conditions, the sole female nurse on the frontlines dedicated herself to caring for the wounded and comforting the dying even as the Viet Minh furiously bombarded the isolated garrison. One day after Bannister broke through on the cinder oval at Oxford, the Viet Minh overran the remaining defenders to effectively end France's colonial reign in Indochina. De Galard, known by the press in Hanoi as the "Angel of Dien Bien Phu," was flown to safety, given a tickertape parade in New York City, and awarded the Medal of Freedom at the White House. (In November, President Eisenhower dispatched military advisors to Vietnam, marking the beginning of America's involvement in what would become the Vietnam War.)

De Galard accompanied the French team of disabled service-men and civilians to Stoke Mandeville. At Guttmann's invitation, she toured the facilities and observed the work of the nurses. "Since I was [in Vietnam] I have been interested in the rehabili-tation of the wounded from a sentimental point of view," she told reporters, "but soon I am going to take it up seriously."[4]

Jets captain Joe Vitta refused to let the famous personages or the camera crews from British Pathé, the news and documentary service, distract from the team's chief goal: to win the Challenge Shield awarded to the wheelchair netball champion. What was most troubling to Vitta and the Jets was that, while wheelchair netball resembled wheelchair basketball, the two were quite different.

The ball used in netball was larger than a regulation basketball, and the baskets were smaller in circumference. The nets hung about eight feet, four inches from the ground, compared to ten feet in basketball. Netball is customarily played without a backboard; the Jets were fortunate that, for the first time at Stoke Mandeville, backboards were attached to the goals in a hastily arranged accommodation for the visitors.

"Our purpose this year was to combine the techniques of both basketball and netball," Guttmann explained, "although I was aware of the difference of the two sports."[5]

Vitta and the Jets had to make other adjustments. No substitutions were permitted during the games, a quirk that prevented coach Condon from utilizing his deep bench to keep the troops fresh. They were accustomed to playing forty-minute games divided into ten-minute quarters; the games at Stoke lasted thirty minutes, with two fifteen-minute halves. No dribbling was allowed in netball, and each goal counted as one point, not two.[6]

The Jets practiced for two days on the outdoor court, watched the other teams, and tweaked their style. They found that, with the oversize ball and the small basket, making outside shots was extremely difficult. "The rim was about the same size as the ball," Julius Jiacoppo said. "You couldn't take a set shot."[7]

They focused on driving to the basket for layups and shot attempts close to the rim. Their wheelchairs gave them a decided advantage. The E&Js were half as heavy and much more maneuverable than the ponderous chairs used by the European teams. Watching a game between the Jets and one of the European teams was like watching a Mini and a Rolls-Royce traverse an obstacle course.

"The Jets' chairs freewheeled in a straight line once having been pushed, unlike ours and the Dutch front-wheel-drive armchairs, which weighed up to fifty kilos [approximately 110 pounds] and demanded that the hands remain far more on the wheels," recounted George "Ginger" Swindlehurst, a British veteran who had been wounded in Arnhem.[8]

Pan Am's first opponent was the Swindlehurst-led squad of paralyzed veterans from the Lyme Green Settlement House in Macclesfield, a market town sixteen miles south of Manchester. The Red Devils were the New York Yankees of wheelchair netball. They practiced with "military precision" every afternoon, even in the winter, when they had to sweep snow from the court, according to wheelchair basketball historian Horst Strohkendl.[9] They'd won every netball competition held at Stoke Mandeville, a string of six consecutive years, and hadn't lost a game in seven years.

Coach Condon selected the starting five: Saul Welger, Robert Nopper, Pete Acca, Mario D'Antonio, and Tony Mucci. Before a throng of spectators that included Dr. Guttmann, the Jets began slowly. They leaned on their vast experience, honed in Brooklyn when they formed the core of the Whirlaways, and adjusted to netball's peculiarities.

Running pattern plays and the give-and-go to set up their offense, they wrested control of the match and doubled the total of the hitherto invincible Lyme Green, fourteen goals to seven.

"The English had heavy chairs and thought nothing of bumping us around pretty hard," Vitta told the *New York Times*. "They'd say, 'Sorry, old chap,' and then bump us hard again. We decided to avoid contact and just concentrate on speed and finesse."[10]

Coach Condon chose a fresh quintet for the semifinals, later in the day, against war veterans from the Netherlands. This rotation easily outmanned the Dutchmen, eleven goals to two.

On to the finals, where the paralyzed veterans from the Duchess of Gloucester House awaited. Wheeling quickly down the sidelines and passing unselfishly, the Jets dazzled the crowd while motoring past the crew from Middlesex, 21–3.

Three games, three victories, one afternoon: the Jets had outscored their opponents by 46–12. They were the world champions, and it didn't really matter whether the game was called netball or basketball.

They weren't finished. The team cheered on Acca and Mucci as they copped the doubles title in the javelin, and then Welger and Nopper as they took the doubles in table tennis.

After tea, Roger Bannister helped to hand out the prizes. He acknowledged that he was initially "bewildered" and then "overwhelmed" by what he'd witnessed that afternoon. "I felt myself suffering from an acute lack of exercise—I wanted to join in," he told the assembled athletes.

"I regard you," he continued, "as world record holders in your own 'Paralympics.'"[11]

Heartened by the American presence, Dr. Guttmann stated that he wanted a team from the Soviet Union to come to Stoke Mandeville so that disabled athletes from the Cold War powers could meet. Such a challenge might help normalize relations, he surmised.

"I will not be satisfied until there is a match in the Moscow Stadium between the Wheelchair Dynamos and Stoke Mandeville," he said.[12]

The Jets mingled with the other wheelchair athletes and exchanged information regarding training, medical care, and equipment. They promised Guttmann that they would return to Stoke Mandeville to defend their crown, Soviets or no Soviets, and then they boarded a Pan Am airliner with the Challenge Shield in tow.

★ ★ ★

In 1956, as Mickey Mantle was capturing the Triple Crown with the New York Yankees, the Pan Am Jets completed a trifecta of their own. First, they went 10–2 to win the Eastern Wheelchair Basketball Association for the second consecutive season, automatically qualifying them for the National Wheelchair Basketball Tournament.

Using the military airlift system, the teams flew in twin-engine Convairs to Naval Air Station Glenview, located about fifteen miles north of downtown Chicago. Glenview had been the navy's largest training base during World War II, when budding aviators, including future president George H. W. Bush, practiced takeoffs and landings on aircraft carriers (actually, two retrofitted steamships) situated nearby on Lake Michigan. After the war, the facility transitioned to the Naval Air Reserve Training Command headquarters.

Pan Am locked gears with their nemesis, the Flying Wheels, the defending champs, in the first round. The Jets employed a full-court press to grab a 32–19 halftime lead, with Jiacoppo hitting for twenty points, only to have the Flying Wheels cut the advantage to seven in the third quarter.

With three minutes remaining, the stubborn Wheels pulled ahead, 51–50. Coach Condon called a timeout, and the Jets regrouped. Percy Mabee scored three points, while Jiacoppo and Mario D'Antonio chipped in two apiece, and the Jets rallied for the hard-fought victory, 57–53.

Pan Am started slowly in their semifinal match against St. Louis, and the hustling Rams managed a two-point halftime edge. But with Jiacoppo tallying twenty-four points and his teammates relentlessly driving to the basket, they stormed to the finals with a 51–37 thumping. All five starters for St. Louis fouled out trying to stifle the Jets.

Their opponent in the finals was the Jersey Wheelers, captained by Ray Werner, a World War II paralyzed veteran who had been wounded by a sniper in the Solomon Islands. The Wheelers had taken the NWBT title over the Brooklyn Whirlaways in 1954, before Saul Welger and his teammates folded the Whirls to form the Jets.

Two years later, the Jets and six Little Jets cheerleaders came for revenge. The site of the championship tilt shifted from the naval base to a larger, more central venue: the International Amphitheatre on the South Side of Chicago. The Cook County sheriff escorted them from Glenview to the arena in a convoy of four buses, twenty cars, and a cargo truck.

The Jets and the Wheelers rolled onto the court to the strains of "You'll Never Walk Alone," a tune from Rodgers and Hammerstein's hit Broadway musical *Carousel* (and an odd song selection, considering the circumstances). Cubs and White Sox announcer Jack Brickhouse handled the public-address duties before two thousand cheering spectators.

Pan Am led only by four points at halftime as Al Slootsky, a post-polio player, kept Jersey close. The Jets' stout defense, helmed by Mabee, tightened, and behind Jiacoppo's steady scoring and Welger's eighteen points, the Jets took their first NWBT title, 56–36.

The navy band struck up "Anchors Aweigh," the traditional fight song of the Naval Academy (and a more appropriate tune) as the Jets and the other athletes headed for the victory banquet next door at the Stock Yard Inn.

Pan Am's rigorous practice schedule, along with corporate backing and a dedicated coach, had produced a dominant style of wheelchair basketball. Their offensive explosion set or tied eleven national records. Jiacoppo's thirty-two points (eleven field goals and ten free throws) against the Flying Wheels established a new single-game mark, and his tournament total (seventy-six points) shattered the old record of fifty-eight.

"Not a Leg to Stand On, But They're Great!" read the headline in the *Chicago Daily Tribune*.[13]

Back home, the team was fêted at a buffet and cocktail party for Pan Am employees. Olympic-sprinter-turned-sportscaster Marty Glickman featured the Jets and their championship season on *Sports-O-Rama*, his show on the DuMont Television Network. Jiacoppo and company took a short breather before departing for England for their final outing of the season.

★ ★ ★

Dr. Ludwig Guttmann and his two top assistants, Charlie Atkinson and Joan Scruton, reacted to the Jets' overpowering debut in 1955 by switching sides in the basketball-versus-netball argument. With basketball growing ever more popular globally via the Olympic Games, they determined that wheelchair basketball, not netball, would be the future at Stoke Mandeville.

The goals were raised to ten feet. The players began to abandon their obsolete chairs for E&J models (or the European equivalent). When paralyzed veterans from Stoke Mandeville and Lyme Green traveled to Paris's Stade Pierre de Coubertin for the first-ever Britain-France sports meet for athletes with paraplegia, wheelchair basketball—not netball—was one of the two featured events. That demonstration helped spread the sport to other countries, including Italy.

Dr. Guttmann also announced that, with so many post-polio players on the Jets roster, he was splitting the wheelchair basketball competition into two divisions. Post-polios were placed in the "incomplete" category because they tended to have some level of muscle function. Those with severe spinal-cord dysfunction—typically, athletes with paraplegia who'd lost total sensory and motor function below the lesion area—were consigned to the "complete" group. Separating the two, he maintained, eliminated the former's physical advantages and ensured fair play.

The two-tiered system was the first concerted effort to balance competitions involving athletes with different types (or degrees) of disability. The plan, while well intentioned, introduced myriad complications to wheelchair sports. Among other drawbacks, the arrangement was "easy to cheat," according to former player and wheelchair basketball historian Armand "Tip" Thiboutot. "You had individuals with polio that faked that they had total paralysis of their legs."[14]

In addition, the directive essentially limited Guttmann and the Stoke Mandeville Games to athletes with neurological impairments like paraplegia and polio. This restriction diverged from the more inclusive policy of the NWBA; its eligibility rules allowed for "any individual who because of the severity of his leg disability or disability of the lower portions of the body will benefit through his participation in wheelchair basketball and who would be denied the opportunity to play basketball were it not for wheelchair basketball," noted historian Stan Labanowich.[15]

The debate over "classification," as the controversial and complex system came to be known, was just beginning. The rules, and the language of the rules, shifted numerous times during the 1950s, 1960s, and 1970s as the athletes gained greater autonomy over their fate and as people with disabilities other than paraplegia and polio took part in adaptive sports in greater numbers.

In late July, the Jets flew to England accompanied by a full retinue: coach, trainer, publicist, manager, assistant manager, photographer, and camera crew. The flags of eighteen nations and some three hundred competitors greeted them. Guttmann had invited the Soviet Union to send a team of athletes; his efforts yielded a visit by two Russian neurosurgeons.

As they watched the Jets move around the court, they told reporters through their translator, "There are no wheelchair sports as such [in the Soviet Union]...competition between the paralyzed is unknown...We think work should come before games."[16]

One observer thought their absence was a missed opportunity. "If anyone on earth can pull down the Iron Curtain I'm sure it's the disabled, especially the war disabled," he said.[17]

On the court, the Jets could no longer count on the element of surprise. The paralyzed veterans from Lyme Green Settlement House and the Netherlands had replaced their front-wheel-drive chairs with sleeker models made especially for the occasion.

"We were all set to meet our American friends," noted Joan Scruton, Guttmann's chief assistant.[18]

Outfitted in bright-blue jerkins, the Jets were entered in the "incomplete" category instituted by Guttmann. They bullied the Netherlands in the opening match until a nasty collision tumbled Vitta out of his chair. He glared at his opponent and was ready to settle the matter Brooklyn style, until coach Condon called out, "Lay off it there, Joe." The incident ended without fisticuffs.[19]

The Jets' 18–8 victory advanced them to the semifinals against the paralyzed veterans from the Duchess of Gloucester House. Now that they were warmed up, the Americans cruised, 32–8.

Awaiting them were the cagey veterans from Lyme Green. Their lighter, more maneuverable chairs did little to slow down Pan Am. The Jets coasted to a twenty-point advantage at halftime en route to a 36–8 shellacking, their second consecutive international title, and their third major championship of the season.

"They have developed the game into a fine art," the local *Bucks Herald* newspaper reported. "They shout and clown and make the ball do wonders. They are a team of wheelchair-borne Harlem Globetrotters."[20]

Scruton acknowledged the Americans' superiority, but came away convinced that the other teams had begun to close the gap. "We must not let it get us down," she counseled. "After all, there is always cricket!"[21]

The Jets proved to be a popular attraction. After the wheel-past, as athletes, doctors, and spectators socialized on the Stoke Mandeville grounds, the Soviet doctors presented them with souvenir post-cards and a Russian textbook about paraplegia. French and Israeli officials invited them to visit their nations and demonstrate their skills. They respectfully declined the invitations and instead toured the Shakespearean countryside before flying home.

After a seven-minute film about the trip was produced and circulated to much acclaim, the concept of the Jets displaying their wheelchair basketball skills around the world—accompanied by the Pan Am name and logo—began to percolate inside the company's executive suites.

The Jets' first priority was to find a new coach after Bill Condon announced that he was resigning to spend more time with his family. Beyond the obvious time and travel commit-ments, this was a difficult position to fill. The coach had to know basketball as well as wheelchair basketball and had to have experience with disability. Whoever took the job would be following in the tire tracks of the most successful campaign in the brief history of wheelchair basketball, surpassing even the Flying Wheels' unblemished championship season of 1955.

Saul Welger believed he had the perfect candidate in mind.

CHAPTER 20

Junius

The elongated body of Junius Kellogg lay motionless inside the paraplegia ward of the Bronx VA Hospital on Kingsbridge Road. Kellogg was twenty-nine years old and had been an acclaimed basketball standout until an auto accident left him permanently paralyzed.

In other words, he was the perfect candidate to coach the Pan Am Jets.

The story of how Junius Kellogg came to bring his fame to wheelchair basketball has more twists than a Mickey Spillane whodunnit. Kellogg grew up in poverty in segregated Portsmouth, Virginia, the oldest of eleven children. He was drafted into the army just after World War II ended and served three years at Fort Dix, New Jersey.

Kellogg played every sport available—basketball, table tennis, volleyball, swimming, football—and was named the First Army's all-around athlete of the year in 1948. After leaving the army, he became the first African American to earn a basketball scholarship at Manhattan College (and the first in his family to attend college).

In the early 1950s, after the color barrier in professional sports was finally breached, colleges were also drawing from the rich talent pool of black athletes, albeit slowly and only in certain parts of the country. Basketball was no exception.

The six-foot-eight-inch Kellogg appeared to have a bright future with the Jaspers and perhaps in the nascent NBA. He bonded with coach Ken "Red" Norton, himself a veteran, having interrupted his career to serve with the navy during World War II. Norton was a disciple of Clair Bee's innovative program at Long Island University (LIU) in Brooklyn that had won two NIT titles (1939, 1941).

Manhattan, LIU, and the City College of New York (CCNY) transformed the New York metropolitan area into a basketball hotbed at a time when the collegiate version was way more popular than the pros. But beneath the high rankings and championships was a seamy swampland of gamblers and fixers. In January of 1951, during Kellogg's sophomore year, the co-captain from the previous year's team approached Kellogg in his dorm room and offered him $1,000 to "shave a few points" in their upcoming game against DePaul University.

Kellogg reported the bribe attempt to coach Norton. The district attorney of Manhattan, Frank Hogan, was notified, and Hogan enlisted Kellogg to wear a wire to trap the miscreants. The ensuing investigation uncovered the most notorious sports-gambling scandal since members of the Chicago White Sox threw the 1919 World Series; the operation implicated the top programs in the country, including Bee's LIU, Nat Holman's CCNY, and Adolph Rupp's University of Kentucky.

For his integrity, Kellogg was hailed as a heroic whistleblower. He was then called back to the army as a reservist. He donned the uniform again and, as a platoon sergeant, trained draftees bound for Korea. He returned to Manhattan College and graduated in

1953 before starting on his master's degree in physical education at Columbia University.

Kellogg joined the Chicago-based Harlem Globetrotters to stay active and earn a few bucks. Abe Saperstein's barnstorming team was known for its trick shots, fancy dribbling, and side-splitting routines, but the players were well aware that NBA team owners were starting to poach the Trotters' deep roster. Nat "Sweetwater" Clifton, a U.S. Army veteran, had recently left the team to sign with the New York Knicks.

In April of 1954, Kellogg was dozing in the front passenger seat of a car driven by teammate Boid Buie. Three other players were sleeping in the back seat. Buie was delivering them to an exhibition game in Arkansas, near where he was born and raised, while the Trotters were on spring break.

Buie had lost his left arm in an auto accident when he was a youngster. He turned himself into the Pete Gray of the hard-wood: an amputee who was a dribbling and shooting maestro known as "The One-Armed Wonder," the same nickname given to Gray when he briefly played for the St. Louis Browns. (Buie sometimes pitched for the Trotters baseball team.)

As they approached Pine Bluff, Arkansas, a tire blew and Buie lost control of the car, which rolled and flipped several times before coming to rest in a roadside ditch. Buie was hospitalized with a minor injury; the other three men escaped unhurt.

But Kellogg's made-for-basketball body was crumpled. His neck was broken, his spinal column severely damaged. He lay near death for days. "I was in a coma and every once in a while I would wake up for a minute and a doctor would be saying, 'Is he dead yet?'" he later recalled. "And it went on like that for three weeks and most times they couldn't pick up my pulse."[1]

He was transferred to the Bronx VA Hospital, where he

underwent years of grueling therapy and exercise. Initially heart-broken and depressed, he learned how to shave and feed himself while adjusting to being "a paralytic for life," as he put it.[2]

On the day he moved his thumb, he rejoiced. "That was a bigger thrill than the night I scored 32 points in Madison Square Garden against Duquesne," he said.[3]

Saul Welger, the post-polio captain of the Pan Am Jets, visited Kellogg in the hospital and kept encouraging him to stay the course with rehabilitation. Once Kellogg graduated to using a wheelchair, Welger badgered him to watch the Jets in action.

Kellogg saw several games and was impressed. Pan Am comptroller John Woodridge offered him a job in the accounting department as well as coaching duties with the Jets. Kellogg wasn't physically ready to be discharged from the hospital, but he was ready for another chance at basketball.

More than two years after his life-changing accident, at about the same time that Bill Russell and K. C. Jones were leading the U.S. basketball team over the Soviet Union at the 1956 Melbourne Olympics, Junius Kellogg became the first African-American coach of a wheelchair basketball team.

★ ★ ★

To that point, few prominent athletes had seen their sports careers halted because of paraplegia. One was Johnny Winterholler, of course, but his renown occurred before World War II. Almost two decades after his last appearance in a Cowboy uniform, Winterholler was all but forgotten outside of Wyoming.

Jill Kinmont joined this select club in the winter of 1955. Kinmont was a champion skier and U.S. medal hopeful at the 1956 Winter Olympics in Cortina d'Ampezzo, Italy. The eighteen-year-old was skiing in a giant slalom event at Alta, Utah, when she lost control midway through the run and flew off the course. She crashed, spun, tumbled, and cartwheeled on the snowy surface before slamming into a spectator. She broke her neck and was paralyzed from the shoulders down.

A glamorous color photograph of Kinmont, shot by *Sports Illustrated* ace photographer Hy Peskin, had appeared on the magazine's cover just before the accident took place. The portrait began what became known as the *SI* cover jinx.[4]

Junius Kellogg was an army veteran, a college graduate, and a former Harlem Globetrotter. He was a central (and innocent) figure in a scandal that had rocked college basketball; he was now the leader of the nation's foremost wheelchair sports team, based in the media capital of the world and backed by a corporation with global reach.

As such, Kellogg was thrust into the role of de facto expert about sports and disability, even though he had never played wheelchair basketball. The print, TV, and radio journalists who interviewed him—and over the years there were many, including war correspondent Quentin Reynolds for *Reader's Digest*; Milton Gross, syndicated columnist at the *New York Post*; and award-winning writer (and Korean War veteran) Jerry Izenberg of the *Newark Star-Ledger*—invariably mentioned his moral integrity and his courage.

Now he would have to prove that he could coach the world champion Jets, where his own hoop skills meant nothing once the team took the floor.

"Being a coach in wheelchair basketball is totally different," said Jets star Julius Jiacoppo. "You really have to know what a chair can do and what you can do in a chair. It's hard for an able-bodied person to step in and coach a wheelchair team without that know-how."[5]

The Jets delivered for Kellogg during the 1956–57 campaign, beating the Jersey Wheelers, 40–32, to finish undefeated in the Eastern Wheelchair Basketball Association campaign. They skipped defending their crown at the 1957 National Wheelchair Basketball Tournament, held at Scott Air Force Base near St. Louis, because of a corporate commitment for Pan Am.

On April 25, they flew to Brazil and began a barnstorming trip as guests of President Juscelino Kubitschek, a physician, and his wife. At Rio de Janeiro's Galeão Airport, the Jets were met by some 2,000 people, including Ellis Briggs, the U.S. ambassador, and a four-year-old girl with braces on both legs who was holding a bouquet. Kellogg impulsively picked up the child, situated her on his enormous lap, and rolled toward the airport building. Photographs of the incident circulated in newspapers across the country.[6]

Kellogg and the players visited children's hospitals and encouraged the injured to integrate exercise and sports into their rehabilitation. They staged wheelchair table-tennis exhibitions and intra-squad basketball games to demonstrate the savage speed of the sport. (One team was billed as the Jets, the other as the Jatos, which is Portuguese for jet.) They attracted 15,000 spectators to Rio's Maracanãzinho arena and thousands more to São Paulo's newly opened Ibirapuera arena. When fans in Rio demanded that "Kelloggo" take the court, Junius left the sidelines and tallied one basket to a roaring ovation.[7]

Adding to their historic debut at the Stoke Mandeville Games, the Jets were the first group of wheelchair athletes to tour Brazil. They were, in effect, following in the tradition started by the Rolling Devils and the Flying Wheels: spreading the gospel of wheelchair basketball and rehabilitation to the world.

★ ★ ★

The crowd that greeted Kellogg and the Jets at their next outing was much smaller than the throngs they'd encountered in Brazil. On this sunny June day in 1957, on the tree-lined campus of Adelphi College on Long Island, wheelchair basketball was an afterthought.

Ben Lipton was now positioned to see the entire world of wheelchair sports. He was the director of the Joseph Bulova School of Watchmaking as well as the guiding force behind the Watchmakers team. Lipton had an important ally in General Omar Bradley after the former head of the VA was appointed chairman of the board of Bulova Research and Development Laboratories in 1954. According to Lipton, General Bradley took constant interest in the disabled veterans being trained at the school.

Lipton also networked with the most astute minds in the medical sector regarding paraplegia and recreation: Dr. Howard Rusk, now running the Institute of Medical Rehabilitation at New York University; Dr. Arthur Abramson, now chair of the Department of Rehabilitation Medicine at the Albert Einstein College of Medicine in the Bronx; and Dr. Henry Kessler at the Kessler Institute for Rehabilitation in West Orange, New Jersey. When Dr. Ludwig Guttmann traveled to the United States to lecture and observe paraplegia centers, Lipton met with him to discuss the future of the Stoke Mandeville Games.

From his vantage, Lipton noticed a massive void. Wheelchair basketball had become so dominant in America that, besides bowling and archery, other wheelchair sports had gained little traction. This was especially noticeable at the Stoke Mandeville Games, which now featured nine different sports.

On June 1, 1957, Lipton took a trailblazing step to repair that deficit. With underwriting support from Bulova and the PVA, he launched the first National Wheelchair Games. Like Tim Nugent's maiden wheelchair basketball tournament and Dr. Guttmann's inaugural Stoke Mandeville Games, the size of the competition was small: just sixty-three men, most of them hailing from New York, along with four members of the Wheelchair Wonders from Montreal.

At Adelphi College, Lipton worked with two students, Charles Ryder and Joe Crafa, to draw up the rules of the competition and to ready the site, conveniently located near his home. The athletes were divided into two categories: Class 1, for those with injuries above the tenth thoracic vertebra, and Class 2, for those below T10.

Participation was open to a "much broader group" than the Stoke Mandeville Games, Lipton maintained. He deemed anyone with "significant permanent disability (spinal cord disorder, poliomyelitis, amputation, etc.) who will benefit through his participation in sports and who would be denied the opportunity to compete were it not for the wheelchair utilization" as eligible for the NWG.[8]

Basketball was deliberately kept off the program and left under the purview of Nugent and the NWBA. Instead, the National Wheelchair Games hewed to the broader-based format of Guttmann's Stoke Mandeville Games, with offerings of archery, javelin, table tennis, and darts.

Lipton broke ground by concocting a new sport, wheelchair racing, to supplement the Olympic-like arrangement of the games. It transformed the most basic question of athletics—who's the fastest?—into who's the fastest on four wheels?

Two races debuted: the 60-yard dash and the 240-yard relay.

Bulova's Alonzo Wilkins streaked down the straightaway to take the 60 in sixteen seconds among the high-lesion group, while Pan Am's Tony Mucci won in thirteen seconds in the Class 2 category. The Jets, coached by Kellogg, defeated Bulova in the relay.

Led by Wilkins, the Watchmakers won the team competition on aggregate points and took home to Queens the Arde Bulova Trophy. Proceeds from the event went to the National Paraplegia Foundation for spinal-cord research.

The modest success of the NWG encouraged Lipton to stage the games every year, with assistance from the PVA and Bulova, and with official recognition from the Amateur Athletic Union. In short order, he created the National Wheelchair Athletic Association as the governing body for all wheelchair sports except basketball (with himself as chair of the NWAA). He encouraged states to organize their own versions of the wheelchair games, with the top qualifiers meeting at the nationals.

Paraplegia News sports columnist Harry Schweikert applauded Lipton's effort to offer a diverse program of events because "they permit an outlet for others who cannot qualify for the rough sport of basketball. The variety also permits the participation of many ages and many disabilities. It is a very healthy thing...We can only advise these groups who are interested in keeping alive our wheelchair sports that they work hard to create these Wheelchair Games in their section of the country."[9]

★ ★ ★

Later that summer, Junius Kellogg and the Pan Am Jets flew to England in search of a wheelchair basketball three-peat at the Stoke Mandeville Games. They rolled to easy victories in the "incomplete" category of the competition, first dispatching a young team from Argentina, 36–0, despite a summer rainstorm that interrupted play on the outdoor court. Then they beat the veterans from Duchess of Gloucester House, 34–2.

The feel-good atmosphere gave way to discord when Pan Am faced the Netherlands in the finals. Players from the two teams had almost come to blows the previous year; this game was physical from the opening whistle.

There were numerous spills and mounting frustration by the Dutch as the Jets took a comfortable lead. The team's manager, identified in the *Bucks Herald* newspaper as "Mr. G. Tromp," complained that the American style of play resembled rugby, not basketball.

Late in the second half, with the Jets well ahead 14–4, Mr. Tromp abruptly removed the Dutchmen from the court. When they didn't return, Kellogg assumed that they'd conceded defeat or defaulted.

The Jets left the court to ready for the wheel-past parade before the trophy ceremony. To their surprise and dismay, they learned that Mr. Tromp had filed an official protest concerning their rough play, and that Guttmann had ruled in favor of the Netherlands and relegated Pan Am to second place.

"It was weird," Julius Jiacoppo stated some sixty years later. "We were disqualified because we were too good. We were light years ahead of the teams from Europe."[10]

The controversy didn't disappear after they flew home to the States. In the pages of *Paraplegia News*, Harry Schweikert lambasted the circumstances surrounding the verdict. What rankled the Jets, he wrote, was that "some individual had ruled against them for there was only one game official and no Rules Committee to decide controversial decisions! . . . Somewhere someone has boo-booed, but no one is giving out public apologies."[11]

Guttmann fired back a rebuttal. He claimed that Schweikert gave "a distorted version of the events [and] has actually made quite untrue statements." He decried that "such a vicious and quite unfounded report was allowed to be published without first checking that the statements were correct.

"Immediately after the Netherlands were called off the field," Guttmann argued, "the referee was instructed by me, as the responsible organizer and leader of the Games, to call together the managers of both teams, and a full investigation was held immediately. It was with great regret that, after considering all the evidence and from my own personal observation of the game, I had to make the decision of disqualification of the Pan Am Jets. It is, therefore, quite untrue to report that the Jets knew nothing about the disqualification until everyone had congregated for the prize-giving."[12]

The back-and-forth didn't wane. In *Paraplegia News*, an anonymous U.S. "observer" charged that Guttmann could not have seen the game because he was "busy most of the time showing the Duchess of Gloucester around the Center.

"I still believe that the Jets were not notified of their disqualification until the 'wheel-past' ceremony," the observer continued. "I was with them when they were told, and if they had known of it previously, they certainly fooled me at the time. And, though they accepted the decision (what else could they do?) they certainly did not agree with it. In my opinion the entire incident occurred because of the incompetence of the officials at the game. I submit that the reason they were incompetent was due mainly to the ineffectual and skimpy rules."[13]

If there was any positive outcome to the contretemps, a minor ruckus that turned into a torrid trans-Atlantic row, it was that the spat led to reform. Guttmann and Stoke Mandeville officials agreed to appoint a three-person tribunal to decide any future disputes in which the teams involved did not accept the referee's decision. They also resolved to align the rules of the Stoke Mandeville Games as closely as possible to the international rules of each sport.

"Anything as basically good and as basically important as the Paralympics cannot but be improved through a bit of controversy," contended the editor of *Paraplegia News* in the same issue that reported the dispute. "We would not be guilty of doing anything which would jeopardize the chances of the Paralympics continuing and becoming constantly better."[14]

Guttmann was already looking ahead. He started a fund-raising campaign to expand the sports facilities at Stoke Mandeville and received enthusiastic support from Dr. Roger Bannister and Dr. Arthur Porritt, a surgeon with the Royal Army Medical Corps during World War II. Porritt won the bronze medal in the 100 meters at the 1924 Paris Olympics, the climactic race depicted in *Chariots of Fire*. His other job involved serving as New Zealand's representative to the International Olympic Committee (IOC), a post he'd held since 1936.

Porritt found himself so enthralled by Dr. Guttmann's endeavor that he nominated the Stoke Mandeville Games for the Sir Thomas Fearnley Cup. Fearnley was a Norwegian shipping magnate and an honorary member of the IOC. He had donated the trophy to pay tribute to amateur sports clubs for distinguished merit in the name of Olympism.

During the 1956 Melbourne Olympic Games, the IOC awarded the Fearnley Cup to Guttmann's Stoke Mandeville Games. It was the first time that a sports group dedicated to athletes with disabilities received official recognition from the IOC. "The spirit of these Games goes beyond the Olympic Games spirit," Porritt said. "You compete not only with skill and endurance but with courage and bravery too."[15]

Guttmann proudly accepted the Fearnley Cup and once again used the opportunity to align his efforts with those of the Olympic movement. "I hope that this is only the beginning of a closer connection between the Stoke Mandeville Games and the Olympic Games," he said. "In the last few years I have always emphasized that the Stoke Mandeville Games have become the equivalent of the Olympic Games."[16]

With the Summer Olympics scheduled for Rome in 1960, Guttmann began planning how to make the connection between the two competitions even stronger.

★ ★ ★

In the early morning hours of January 28, 1958, Brooklyn Dodgers star catcher Roy Campanella was driving to his home on the North Shore of Long Island. It had snowed during the night. The roads were slick.

Campanella hit an icy patch on a curve. The Chevy sedan he was driving skidded across the road into a telephone pole and turned over, trapping the thirty-six-year-old inside. Police arrived and took him to a local hospital. He had fractured two cervical vertebrae, and his spinal cord was all but severed. He was paralyzed from the chest down.

The son of an African-American mother and an Italian-American father, Campanella had started his professional career in the Negro Leagues at the age of fifteen. He joined the Dodgers in 1948, the season after Jackie Robinson's rookie campaign. Campanella was an All-Star from 1949 to 1956, and a three-time National League Most Valuable Player for one of baseball's most successful and high-profile teams. All of Brooklyn celebrated after Da Bums clinched the 1955 World Series over the Yankees, their hated cross-borough rivals.

In 1958, when the franchise was readying to uproot for Los Angeles, Dodgers owner Walter O'Malley was counting on Campanella and other esteemed veterans to ease the transition and attract a fresh fan base. But instead of catching southpaw phenom Sandy Koufax at spring training in Vero Beach, Florida, Campanella was lying on a Stryker bed—a special frame that held him in place during traction—his neck and head immobilized within a bulky metal brace.

Campanella was transferred to the Institute of Rehabilitation Medicine in New York City, under the care of Dr. Howard Rusk and Dr. Donald Covalt. Exercise and physical therapy helped him regain some movement in his hands and fingers; he learned to feed himself and handle other basic chores.

The media chronicled every detail, every twist in his rehabilitation. He was featured on the cover of *Life* magazine; the *Saturday Evening Post* published a two-part feature about him. He appeared on NBC's *Today* show and was photographed alongside Junius Kellogg, who offered him invaluable advice about life as a former athlete. When the Flying Wheels landed in New York on their annual cross-country tour, the players sent him a telegram wishing him a speedy recovery.

Campanella was reminded daily that fame did not shield him from privation, as occurred when the Yankees invited him to watch a World Series game. "When it came time to put my wheelchair in the aisle, they found the aisle wasn't wide enough for the chair," he recalled in his autobiography. "Before I knew what was happening, a couple of husky firemen lifted me out of the chair and carried me down the aisle. For just that first minute,

I felt like some sad freak. It was the most embarrassing thing that ever happened to me. I felt ashamed. It was awful."[17]

Other times, Campanella basked in the outpouring of affection. The Dodgers threw him a coming-out party on May 7, 1959, disguised as an exhibition game against the Yankees. Shortstop Pee Wee Reese wheeled Campy onto the infield grass at the Los Angeles Memorial Coliseum before the largest crowd ever to witness a baseball game—93,103 spectators, including a couple of rows of fans sitting in wheelchairs. Proceeds from the emotional evening helped pay for his medical bills.

To baseball fans, Campanella represented a modern tragedy. To the disability community, he represented hope. Here was a Major League Baseball star—someone way more famous than Junius Kellogg or Jill Kinmont or Johnny Winterholler—who in an instant had become the face of paraplegia. They envisioned him coalescing public and financial support so that researchers could "unlock the secret of spinal cord regeneration," as the *Paraplegia News* put it, for "all of us with damaged spinal cords."

"We need a champion for our cause," the editorial continued. "We need you, Roy. We need your ability. We need your sense of showmanship. We need your organizing potential. We need your sports contacts to help us raise money...Scientists have already begun to turn the key in the lock, which when opened will release us from the chains that bind us...They need more penetrating oil to loosen the stubborn parts. That oil is money."[18]

Campanella never hid his condition. He was photographed in his wheelchair during his annual visits to spring training, oftentimes alongside the Dodgers' latest crop of catching prospects. His autobiography, *It's Good to Be Alive*, published the year after his injury, is a moving account of his hardscrabble upbringing and the physical and emotional hurdles he experienced after the accident. The book received much publicity, educated many people about disability and rehabilitation, and, in 1974, was turned into a well-received made-for-TV movie starring Paul Winfield and Ruby Dee.

But the former Hall of Famer was not the game-changer that many hoped he'd be. He didn't devote his life to paraplegia research nor did he spearhead fund-raising campaigns for the cause. He was content to be Campy, one of the eternal boys of summer.

CHAPTER 21

Rome 1960

Ever since he created the Stoke Mandeville Games for paralyzed war veterans, Dr. Ludwig Guttmann linked the competition to the Olympics, implicitly and explicitly. The first edition was held on the same day as the opening ceremony of the 1948 London Olympics. He invited paralyzed veterans from other countries so as to make the games an international event; he hosted members of the International Olympic Committee to observe the athletes in person. He introduced emblems and ceremonies that echoed similar concepts in the Olympic movement—including, most obviously, the name: Paralympics. The IOC's Fearnley Cup, awarded to Guttmann in 1956, recognized his relentless efforts.

Guttmann saw a golden opportunity to conjoin the two events with the approaching Rome Olympics of 1960. One of his many disciples in the treatment of paraplegia was Dr. Antonio Maglio, who had served as a medical officer along the Balkan front during World War II. Afterward, the Cairo-born neurologist was named director of the Paraplegic Center, an institution run by the Italian National Association for Injured Laborers (INAIL) in the seaside town of Ostia, just outside of Rome.

Maglio   followed   Guttmann's   rehabilitation   model   and incorporated sports into the treatment of spinal-cord patients at the clinic. In 1956, the tall, bespectacled Maglio took Italy's first wheelchair-sports team to the International Stoke Mandeville Games. His motto: "The patient first of all."[1]

Not long after the IOC, in 1955, selected Rome as host city of the 1960 Olympics, Guttmann and Maglio came up with a masterstroke: to hold the Paralympics in the Eternal City immediately after the conclusion of the Olympic Games.

The idea was outrageous. At a time when no single entity governed wheelchair sports for people with disabilities, how was Guttmann going to persuade teams from around the world to compete? How many athletes would show up? Who was going to pay for this? And, would the IOC resent Guttmann and the Paralympics encroaching on their turf?

Undaunted, Guttmann rallied support among participating countries from past Stoke Mandeville Games. He dispatched his chief aide, Joan Scruton, to Italy to handle preliminary arrangements and organize the event schedule. He persuaded officials with the World Veterans Federation to fund travel for the teams, while Maglio persuaded INAIL to help with accommodation costs. They negotiated with Italian authorities to use the Olympic venues for the Paralympics and the Olympic Village to house the athletes and support staff.

Charged with leading the U.S. effort was Ben Lipton. Arde Bulova, his boss and primary benefactor, had died in 1958. For financial backing, Lipton leaned on contacts within the Paralyzed Veterans of America, the National Wheelchair Athletic Association, the Bulova Foundation, family, and friends.

In early June of 1960, he convened the fourth National Wheelchair Games at Bulova Park to determine America's representatives for the Paralympics. He added swimming events to the program, as well as the 100-yard dash and the 70-yard slalom to the track events. Competitors were divided into three classes: spinal paraplegia above T10; those with spinal paraplegia below T10; and all other disabilities.

Tim Nugent and his Gizz Kids made their first appearance at the NWG. (Scheduling conflicts with final exams had prevented them from traveling to New York in previous years.) They'd never competed in track and field, but a few weeks of practice under coach Casey Clarke and his at-the-ready stopwatch had them prepared. They chartered a bus and rode straight through to New York, with a Pony-Express system of drivers.

Fighting through a hard, driving rain in the late afternoon, the eighteen Gizz Kids swept through the 115-athlete field with sixteen firsts and seventeen seconds in forty events. Ron Stein, a hulking post-polio, won five individual medals, while teammate Paul Sones, paralyzed in a plane crash while attending the Air Force Academy, dominated the swimming events.

Hamstrung by budgetary and scheduling constrictions, Lipton was able to select only twenty-four athletes for the U.S. team. Wheelchair basketball, the granddaddy of adaptive sports, was expected to be the marquee event at the Paralympics. But personnel sacrifices had to be made, and so Lipton was forced to cobble together a roster of athletes who could compete in basketball as well as other sports.

Neither the Junius Kellogg–coached Pan Am Jets, an experienced crew with multiple competitions at Stoke Mandeville under their belts, nor the famed Flying Wheels was chosen to represent the United States in basketball. Instead, the slapdash rosters of the two American hoops squads were drawn from the twenty-four-man pool.

Eight selectees from the Gizz Kids, including Stein and Sones, made up fully one-third of the team. Saul Welger and Percy Mabee from the Pan Am Jets made the cut, as did Alonzo Wilkins from Bulova and the Flying Wheels' Bill Johnson, the only Californian on the squad.

All were top-notch wheelchair basketball players, of course, but they were not chosen solely on the basis of their basketball ability. "We need more money to sponsor Paralympic squads," Junius Kellogg complained. The United States is sending "a composite team" for basketball.[2]

No women were chosen to represent the United States at the 1960 Paralympics. Female athletes with disabilities faced twin barriers of exclusion in America. No woman had ever competed at the National Wheelchair Games—and there were no wheelchair basketball teams for women. This was an embarrassing omission considering that many countries had been sending female athletes to the Stoke Mandeville Games. It would be many years before gender inequality in adaptive sports—and non-disabled sports, for that matter—was addressed in the United States, much less corrected.

★ ★ ★

Against the backdrop of the Cold War, the United States and the Soviet Union turned the 1960 Rome Olympics into the sports version of the space race. Legend-in-the-making Cassius Clay (later known as Muhammad Ali) whipped Russian Gennady Shatkov and then out-decisioned another Iron Curtain rival, Poland's Zbigniew Pietrzykowski, to win the gold medal in boxing's light heavyweight division. Led by future Hall of Famers Oscar Robertson, Jerry West, Jerry Lucas, and Walt Bellamy, the U.S. basketball team easily handled the Soviets, 81–57, in the semifinals en route to the gold medal.

Victories by athletes large and small, from gymnast Larisa Latynina to shot put champ Tamara Press to weightlifter Arkady Vorobyov, allowed the USSR to capture the overall medal count, 103–71, "a resounding victory for Soviet Russia," according to *New York Times* columnist Arthur Daley. "The Red brothers beat us in total medals and in unofficial total points."[3]

America's brightest star in Rome was twenty-year-old Wilma Rudolph. Born two months premature, one of twenty-two siblings, she contracted scarlet fever, double pneumonia, and polio by the age of five, leaving her partially paralyzed. Her impoverished family struggled to provide adequate medical care to combat her polio. She wore a brace on her weakened left leg until, after several years of treatment and four-times-a-day massages, she could walk—and then run and then sprint—unaided.

Rudolph's first love was basketball. She was persuaded to run by her mentor, Tennessee State University coach Ed Temple. Her leggy gracefulness, powerful stride, and charming smile belied the adversity she'd overcome. On the track at Rome's Stadio Olimpico, she swept the 100- and 200-meter sprints and anchored the victorious 4-x-100-meter relay team, beating the Russians, the Germans, and everybody else.

Her journey from polio patient to three-time gold medalist was a heartwarming saga of recovery and grit: the Tigerbelle from Tennessee State blossomed into "La Gazella Nera" ("The Black Gazelle") and "La Chattanooga Choo-Choo." The CBS network, which had paid a whopping $394,000 for the television rights, the first time that the Summer Games were broadcast in the United States, trumpeted her success. Later, she was invited to the White House, where President John F. Kennedy congratulated her in the Oval Office.[4]

A week after the closing ceremony of the 1960 Olympics,

a small group of wheelchair athletes and their aides arrived in Rome. CBS did not stick around to televise their exploits; no athletes were invited to the White House afterward. Their legacy, however, would rival that of Wilma Rudolph.

★ ★ ★

America's maiden Paralympic team assembled in New York City around the same time that the Rome Olympics were wrapping up. The athletes worked out for several days at the Bulova gym before departing Idlewild Airport for Rome. Outfitted in snappy black blazers, gray trousers, and white caps, the twenty-four men "truly looked like an Olympic team," related Charles Ryder, one of the two U.S. coaches, in *Paraplegia News*.[5]

"Crippled Athletes to Hold Olympics," read the send-off headline in the *New York World-Telegram* newspaper.[6]

Authorities at Ciampino Airport extricated the athletes from their DC-8 by means of a forklift truck. Team director Lipton and the competitors soon discovered that, despite Guttmann and Scruton's best-laid plans, they were not treated with the respect and care that the Olympic athletes had received.

They were supposed to be housed in apartments with elevators at the Olympic Village. Instead, they were delivered to two-story flats built on stilts. Escorts worked in pairs to haul the men up the stairs, until Italian soldiers and musclemen were enlisted to facilitate the process.

"All the rooms were up two flights of stairs," coach Ryder noted. "The Italians had built ramps over the stairs but failed to consider the angle of the steps themselves. Needless to say, the ramps were useless."[7]

So, too, the bathrooms within the apartments were inaccessible for regular-size wheelchairs. The hosts worked overtime to supply special wheelchairs for bathroom use.

Guttmann and Scruton were promised that the main events would take place in Acqua Acetosa, a sports training complex that was convenient to where the athletes were staying. Without explanation, every event except for the opening ceremony was shifted to the Tre Fontane grounds, necessitating long and bothersome bus rides.

The athletes reacted with typical gallows humor to the sheer absurdity of the situation and made the best of the subpar arrangements. They requested their bus driver take a different route to the field every day so they could see a different part of the city.

Exactly one week after tens of thousands of spectators filled Stadio Olimpico for the closing ceremony of the Olympics, several thousand curious onlookers gathered inside the Acqua Acetosa stadium to watch the opening ceremony of the 1960 Paralympics. Approximately 350 athletes with spinal-cord disabilities, representing twenty-one nations from five continents, paraded around the track in their wheelchairs, with the British team at the front and host Italy bringing up the rear.

The moment was magical for Ludwig Guttmann, despite the organizational miscues. "I have for many years cherished a dream that these Games for the paralyzed would one day be held in close connection with the Olympic Games," he said. "This day has now become a reality, and the 1960 Stoke Mandeville Games in Rome represent an historic event not only in the field of sport but also in the sphere of humanity."[8]

Nine sports were featured on the program, including the multisport pentathlon (archery, swimming, and athletics). Thanks to Dr. Maglio's efforts, Italy entered more athletes than any other country and easily won the medal count. The home team's Maria

Scutti emerged as the Wilma Rudolph of the Paralympics, earning fifteen medals (ten gold) in athletics, fencing, swimming, and table tennis. The Americans didn't have to worry about meeting the no-show Soviets and finished fifth in medals.

Guttmann and Scruton again divided the wheelchair basketball competition into two categories: "complete" athletes who'd lost sensory and motor function below the neurological level (Class A), and "incomplete" athletes with some function below the affected area (Class B). The games were contested on an outdoor clay court at Tre Fontane that, on the one day of foul weather, was covered from the elements. Certain features from Stoke Mandeville remained in effect; the American basketball players had to deal with a heavier ball, a smaller hoop, dribbling restrictions, and two fifteen-minute halves.

The composite arrangement of the teams, the long-distance international travel, and the unfamiliar rules and surroundings mattered little to the two U.S. basketball squads. Pan Am stalwart Saul Welger and a host of Gizz Kids, including Ron Stein and Paul Sones, powered the Class B squad. They beat Belgium, 37–6, before easily handling Australia, 23–7. In the final round, they downed Britain, 20–12 and dismantled the Netherlands, 21–9, to clinch the victory.

Sones, who battled a severe cold during the games, was amazed by the variety of wheelchairs on display. "I vividly remember a South Rhodesian athlete with a chair that was chain-driven by hand cranks and a Belgian athlete who played basketball in an upholstered chair that looked like something you would find in your living room," he said. "I can't imagine how heavy that one must have been and how hard it must have been to maneuver."[9]

Pan Am alum Percy Mabee paced the Class A team, with offensive wizardry supplied by the Flying Wheels' Bill Johnson, who unleashed an array of no-look passes that amazed spectators and baffled opponents. Johnson scored fourteen points as the United States trounced Austria, 32–10, in the opener. They overcame Israel, 18–8, before defeating Britain's paralyzed servicemen from Lyme Green, 18–14, in the finals.

"You are as good as if you were not playing in wheelchairs," Guttmann marveled.[10]

Guttmann orchestrated an award ceremony every evening. As the moon rose, the first-, second-, and third-place finishers mounted the wooden podium in their wheelchairs by means of a small ramp. Naval officers hoisted the three appropriate flags as the national anthem of the winner played.

Afterward, the athletes celebrated with a rowdy party in the U.S. quarters, despite differences in wheelchairs and languages, and everyone in attendance toasted the budding romance between Saul Welger and Christa Zander, a post-polio athlete and winner of seven medals (six gold). The two had met at the 1958 Stoke Mandeville Games and rekindled their friendship the next year. A long-distance romance developed between the Pan Am accountant and the West German factory supervisor.

Perhaps the highlight of the Paralympics came when the entire contingent journeyed to Vatican City. Pope John XXIII met privately with Dr. Guttmann and then, speaking in French, addressed them from a balcony above the San Damascus Courtyard.

"Recently, we welcomed at St. Peter's Square athletes from all parts of the world, who came for the Olympic Games," he said. "How much more moving for our hearts is the spectacle you offer to our eyes today!... You have shown what an energetic soul can achieve, in spite of apparently insurmountable obstacles imposed by the body. Far from letting yourselves be overcome by misfortune, you have overcome it with a wonderful optimism. You challenge performances apparently reserved only for the fit."[11]

The Pontiff's appearance ensured worldwide media attention. Lipton noted that the U.S. participation in the Paralympics "was the biggest publicity boon for wheelchair athletics."[12]

Coverage in one U.S. newspaper, however, demonstrated that societal ignorance about disabilities had not disappeared. The headline in the *Baltimore Sun* read: "Pope Praises Ill Athletes."[13]

★ ★ ★

Guttmann returned to England ecstatic. The experiment to travel the Paralympics had survived glitches and inconveniences, an accomplishment he characterized, with some embellishment, as being "held at the Olympic Stadium following the Olympic Games and under Olympic Games condition."[14] He devoted the entire issue of *The Cord*, the magazine he published about paraplegia, to the Paralympics and sent a copy to Avery Brundage, the American president of the IOC.

Amid calls to expand the breadth of the Paralympics, Guttmann urged caution. "It is quite impossible to open the Stoke Mandeville Games to other forms of disability, such as amputees and the blind," he commented. "This really would be at the expense of the paraplegic sportsman, as it would immediately reduce the number of paralyzed competitors who could be accommodated at the Games."[15]

Post-Paralympics coverage in the United States focused more on the athletes than on the event itself. Newspapers spotlighted Dick Maduro, "from sunny Madeira Beach, Florida," and his gold medals in basketball and swimming;[16] Gizz Kid Jack Whitman and the archery triumph achieved on his thirtieth birthday; and Vincent

Ward, a navy pilot during World War II, and his swimming medals. (Ward was one of five former servicemen on the U.S. team.)

Ron Stein received the most attention. Stein was a prospect with the Chicago White Sox organization when he was stricken with polio. He enrolled at the University of Illinois and was introduced to Tim Nugent and wheelchair sports. When he returned to his hometown outside St. Louis after graduation, he joined the Rolling Rams squad. He was married with one child and another on the way.

In Rome, the muscular, crew-cut blond earned the moniker of the world's greatest wheelchair athlete by winning the pentathlon with more than 3,000 points, an astounding total for the new event. He took home three other gold medals: in basketball (incomplete), club throw, and shot put.

Reporters in California touted Bill Johnson as another super-star. When he joined the Flying Wheels after the Korean War, he added a dash of vigor to the Long Beach squad. His outside shot was uncannily accurate, his passing touch divine. He'd roll down the court, stop on a dime by jamming his thumb against a tire, and skip a no-look pass to an open teammate.

"He did things in a chair that you just shook your head at," said fellow Paralympian Marv Lapicola. "You'd say, 'How did he pass the ball behind his back like he did and balance-wise not fall out of his chair?'"[17]

For nearly a decade, the Flying Wheels existed as the only wheelchair basketball team west of Kansas City. In 1956, core veterans on the Wheels roster decided to split up and organize new teams so as to expand the competition. The formation of the Los Angeles Jets, the Santa Monica Western Wheels, and the Garden Grove Bears opened up opportunities for more wheel-chair athletes and gave the Wheels strong local opposition.

In January of 1960, months before the start of the Rome Paralympics, the Flying Wheels were informed that there were no longer sufficient funds for their annual barnstorming tour. A tradition that had begun in 1948 at Birmingham Hospital, a twelve-year exodus that took them to the bright lights of New York City, the halls of power in Washington, D.C., the paraplegia wards in VA hospitals, and into the sports sections of hundreds of newspapers, quietly ended.

Johnson and his teammates were determined to keep the Wheels churning. After going undefeated in league play, they scraped together enough money to send an eight-man team to the 1960 National Wheelchair Basketball Tournament at Chanute Air Force Base.

With Johnson on point, the shorthanded Wheels whipped the Gizz Kids, 52–30, and Brooklyn, 45–34, to reach the finals. The Bulova Watchmakers stayed close, but the Flyers closed them out, 48–43, for the championship as Johnson was named to the All-American first team.

"National Paraplegic Kingpins," crowed the *Long Beach Press-Telegram*. "Boston may have its Celtics, but Long Beach has its Flying Wheels, and it couldn't be more proud."[18]

Johnson's magic jumpstarted a dynastic run that brought five consecutive NWBT titles to Long Beach. Their lineup was a finely tuned four-wheeled juggernaut that featured mercurial John Cheves, a single-leg amputee who "commanded the floor like no one else," according to historian Stan Labanowich. "His play was so effortless, so precise, it was like watching a ballet."[19]

Center Earl Gerard didn't allow any easy shots under the rim, and Larry Eaks was a scoring machine. Unselfish Gil Ortiz was a charter member from the Birmingham days and an infantry veteran from World War II; coach Russ Churchman dubbed him

"Super Mex" and lauded his steadying influence on and off the court.[20] Fritz Krauth, another vintage member and navy vet, was considered the Bob Cousy of wheelchair basketball for his passing skills.

The last title of their five-year streak may have been the most satisfying. They entered the sixteenth National Wheelchair Basketball Tournament at Queens College after their rivals in Southern California, the Garden Grove Bears, had snapped their two-year unbeaten streak.

Seeded fourth, the Wheels blitzed Kansas City, 56–41, then downed the Chicago Sidewinders, 54–39, as Cheves scored fourteen points and grabbed nineteen rebounds.

In the finals, they upset the undefeated and top-seeded Indianapolis Crossroad Olympians, 45–40. Johnson and Cheves made first-team All-American.

"Johnson refused to lose," recalled Greg Churchman, the coach's son. "That's why he's still to this day considered the Michael Jordan of wheelchair basketball. The best that ever played. He kept everybody in synch."[21]

Johnson and several Wheels teammates were later enshrined in the Wheelchair Basketball Hall of Fame. So, too, is coach Russ Churchman. The non-disabled navy veteran, who was stationed on the USS *Mansfield* during the Korean War, ably carried on the legacy of Bob Rynearson into the 1960s.

"I was lucky to come back healthy from the war," coach Churchman later said. "Some men—they didn't come back whole."[22]

★ ★ ★

Tom Knowles was serving with the Royal Air Force when he crashed the Vampire fighter jet he was piloting and was paralyzed. He subsequently rehabbed at Stoke Mandeville under Dr. Guttmann. When he returned to his native South Africa, he was appalled by the lack of expert care available there for people with paraplegia.

The handlebar-mustachioed Knowles heard about Tim Nugent's program at the University of Illinois. He visited the campus at Urbana-Champaign and, impressed, invited Nugent to export a group of wheelchair athletes to Africa in the summer of 1962.

To raise funds for the "Wheelchair Safari," Knowles propelled himself by wheelchair from Pretoria to Durban, a distance of some 452 miles. He was said to have refashioned his wheelchair so that he could stash a case of long-necked beer bottles beneath the seat for refreshment.

The lone American reporter to cover the month-long trip was Roger Ebert, a native son of Urbana, the editor of the *Daily Illini*, the student newspaper, and the future Pulitzer Prize–winning film critic for the *Chicago Sun-Times*. He watched thousands of people line the main street of Port Elizabeth as Dick Maduro, Fritz Krauth, Paul Sones, Carl Cash, and thirteen other wheelchair athletes paraded past in their E&J chairs.

At Johannesburg's Wembley Stadium, the athletes gave a two-and-a-half-hour demonstration of wheelchair basketball and wheelchair square dancing. On a continent with little experience in paraplegia rehabilitation or adaptive sports, the exhibitions showed "a person in a wheelchair can lead a full, normal, productive life," Ebert wrote, and "hiring the handicapped, and accepting them as full members of society, makes good sense."[23]

The safari, while well intentioned, revealed a lapse in judgment. In 1962, the same year that Nelson Mandela was arrested and imprisoned on charges of sabotage, the world was well aware that South Africa's racist apartheid system denied equal rights to the black majority population. The country's virulent brand of discrimination extended to sports, where only white athletes were permitted to represent South Africa in international competitions like the Olympics.

That policy turned the country into a sports pariah. The governing body of soccer, the Fédération Internationale de Football Association (FIFA), suspended South Africa from international play in 1961. The IOC followed suit and barred South Africa from the 1964 Tokyo Olympics. (The Olympic sanction lasted until 1992.)

By consenting to the tour and creating sympathetic press about South Africa, the traveling party was, in effect, supporting apartheid. Ebert later wrote that he "kept getting into political arguments until the tour leader took me aside and informed me firmly that there was a time and a place for everything."[24]

Gizz Kid alumnus Tom Jones noted that Nugent wanted to send Henry Bowman to South Africa. Bowman was one of the Tuskegee Airmen from World War II, the first black football and basketball official in the Big Ten, and an employee at the Rehab Center. He also was president of the NWBA Rules Committee.

Bowman was not allowed to make the trip. According to Jones, Nugent was told that "it would not be possible for an outside black to enter South Africa."[25]

At Stoke Mandeville, Dr. Ludwig Guttmann treated numerous paralyzed veterans from South Africa, including Knowles, and felt loyalty to his patients. Beginning in 1962, wheelchair athletes from South Africa were permitted to compete at the Stoke Mandeville Games (and at every Paralympic Games through 1976). Ultimately, Guttmann and Nugent chose to support athletes with paraplegia, no matter their birthplace or political viewpoint, over the fight against apartheid.

CHAPTER 22

Tokyo 1964

The approach of the 1964 Tokyo Olympics, less than twenty years after the end of World War II, revived memories of Pearl Harbor and the vicious battles in the Pacific theater. Japan's proximity to Korea, the Philippines, and Vietnam offered a sobering reminder about the U.S. military's presence in the region, especially in light of the Gulf of Tonkin incident in August that escalated the conflict with Vietnam.

While Japan couldn't erase the past, local organizers wanted the Olympics, the first to be held in Asia, to spotlight a revitalized, modernized nation that was moving forward, not looking backward. Sparkling new venues designed by the likes of respected architect Kenzo Tange and the unveiling of the *shinkansen*—bullet train—were transforming the country's image. Satellites were employed for the first time to broadcast the games live around the world; the first electronic computers used at the Olympics rapidly recorded, processed, and transmitted the results of each event.

The youthful athlete selected to light the cauldron during the opening ceremony of the Olympics symbolized Japan's recovery from the ashes of the war. Yoshinori Sakai was born just outside of Hiroshima on August 6, 1945, two hours after an atomic bomb demolished the city and effectively ended World War II.

For Dr. Ludwig Guttmann, exporting the Paralympics to Tokyo was a far more daunting task than taking them to Rome had been. People with disabilities in Japan were treated as outcasts; many were hidden in institutions or confined to bed. Families resisted "admitting publicly [to] the incidence of a handicapped member," noted one newspaper columnist, and "Japanese employers seem intractable in refusing anyone even with a slight handicap."[1]

Guttmann broke through the cultural divide with help from Dr. Yutaka Nakamura. In 1960, Nakamura received a grant to study at Stoke Mandeville Hospital and spent three months observing Guttmann's spinal-cord unit. The orthopedic surgeon from the southern city of Beppu became a convert to the concept of incorporating sports into the rehabilitation of people with disabilities while also training them for employment.

When he returned home, Nakamura organized the Oita Prefecture Sports Games for the Physically Disabled in 1961, Japan's first such event. The following year, Prime Minister Hayato Ikeda toasted Nakamura and two wheelchair athletes as the trio left for England to make Nippon's debut at the Stoke Mandeville Games.

Nakamura's initiative encouraged Guttmann and his chief assistant, Joan Scruton, to broach the idea of Japan hosting the Paralympics with the country's representative at the World Veterans Federation. They recruited the Japanese Red Cross Society for the effort and received backing from the local government. A crucial piece to the puzzle fell into place when Crown Prince Akihito and his wife, Princess Michiko, threw their support behind the event.

Bartenders placed boxes inside watering holes to solicit donations for the estimated ¥90 million budget (the equivalent of $4.5

million today). The Lions Clubs International pledged to cover the expenses of visiting competitors and their escorts. Student volunteers were enlisted, buses equipped with lifts were made available, translators were trained and hired, and posters were printed. According to the English-language *Japan Times* newspaper, six hundred members of the Self Defense Forces offered to "act as mothers to the participants, helping them in their meals [and] bathing."[2] Nearly three hundred men and women with disabilities climbed Mount Fuji to highlight the coming Paralympics.[3]

Ben Lipton again headed the American team. He organized the Wheelchair Sports Fund and enlisted General Omar Bradley, as chair of the board of directors, to bolster an ambitious $50,000 fund-raising drive. Lipton produced a fifteen-minute documentary about the Paralympics and hosted nearly three hundred athletes at Bulova Park in the eighth National Wheelchair Games.

He was able to take sixty-six athletes to Tokyo, nearly triple the number who had gone to Rome. In a historic breakthrough, twenty women were included. One was already well known in Paralympic circles: Christa Zander Welger, the West Berliner who'd met Pan Am Jets star Saul Welger at the Stoke Mandeville Games. After the two married, she moved to Brooklyn and began competing for the United States.

Another newcomer was Rosalie Hixson. She was raised on a three-hundred-acre farm in Crystal Springs, Pennsylvania, where she drove a tractor, milked cows, and helped with the plowing. Hixson had to relinquish her Olympic dreams in track and field when she was stricken with polio, but she proved adept at wheelchair sports once given the opportunity.

The U.S. team arrived at Tokyo's Haneda Airport and faced a mass of Nikon flash cameras. Paratroopers carried them from the plane. Several pairs of hands were required to lift the nearly seven-foot frame of basketball coach Junius Kellogg.

"His long body with a bunch of legs under it looked like a giant black centipede," U.S. team members later related.[4]

This time, the hosts were well prepared. The Paralympians bedded down in Yoyogi Olympic Village in cottages originally built for U.S. military dependents after World War II. "There were these long ramps for the players to access their rooms," wheelchair basketball star Marv Lapicola recalled. "Everything worked out okay."[5]

On Sunday, November 8, approximately 370 athletes from twenty-one countries (including South Africa) woke to colorful chrysanthemums in bloom. Crown Prince Akihito and Princess Michiko braved chilly winds to open the Paralympics at Oda Field, complete with flag-bearers, fireworks, and a marching band that segued into the hit song "Sukiyaki" when the fifty-three Japanese athletes wheeled onto the track in their maroon-colored gear.

With Dr. Nakamura standing behind him, Shigeo Aono, a forty-two-year-old veteran from the Sino-Japanese War, took the Athletes' Oath. Some five hundred white doves were released into the cloudless blue sky.

Lapicola was impressed that, after the formal proceedings, the royal couple left the reviewing stand and mingled with the competitors. "They seemed to love the idea that disabled athletes were competing in all sports," he said.[6]

Both American wheelchair basketball teams swept to victory without losing a game in the round-robin competition. The Russ Churchman–coached incomplete squad, led by Lapicola and eighteen-year-old phenom Ed Owen, the sport's first dominant big man, dispatched Argentina, Japan, Britain, Israel, and Italy to earn the gold medal.

The Junius Kellogg–coached complete squad featured veterans Alonzo Wilkins, Bill Johnson, and Fritz Krauth as well as Selig Boshnack, the lone paralyzed veteran from World War II on the roster. They had to overcome one close call, against Israel, a rising wheelchair basketball power. Florida's Dick Maduro rushed over from the weight-lifting competition at halftime, and he carried the U.S. to a 45–18 victory.

Lapicola called the experience "a whirlwind." One hundred forty-four contests in nine sports were crammed into a four-and-a-half-day schedule that ended with the United States atop the medal standings, thanks to Rosalie Hixson's six gold medals and Ron Stein's seven. Italy carried its momentum from 1960 to finish second, followed by Britain and South Africa.

"The greatest thrill I have had in wheelchair sports," Saul Welger later told author Harriet May Savitz, "is to stand on the first-place pedestal at the Paralympics and hear 'The Star-Spangled Banner' being played and see the American flag being raised because I have performed well for my country."[7]

Princess Michiko handed out the trophies and medals at the closing ceremony before the athletes gathered together for a rousing version of "Auld Lang Syne." They embraced and made plans to meet in Mexico City in four years.

The 1960 and 1964 Paralympics were small in scale, sparsely attended, and untelevised. The talent level of the athletes was uneven, and logistical problems and budgetary concerns bedeviled Dr. Guttmann and his staff. But in transplanting the International Stoke Mandeville Games to the corresponding Olympic settings, Guttmann established the Paralympics as a legitimate quadrennial competition on a global scale.

In 1966, he retired as head of the National Spinal Injuries Center at Stoke Mandeville. His adopted country used the occasion to honor his two decades of life-saving and life-enhancing work concerning spinal-cord injuries and paraplegia and his pioneering contributions to sports for people with disabilities. He was elected as a Fellow of the Royal Society and knighted by Queen Elizabeth II. The German-born, Jewish neurologist was now Sir Ludwig Guttmann.

He forged ahead with long-gestating plans to raise £350,000 to build a complex for disabled sports on property next to the hospital. The spectacular showpiece, the first of its kind designed exclusively for athletes with disabilities, opened in 1969 to rave reviews and the attendance of the queen. Dressed in a mimosa yellow coat and a matching ruched hat trimmed with ostrich feathers, she spent the afternoon admiring the wheelchair athletes in action on the indoor basketball court as Guttmann beamed proudly.[8]

The day's most poignant moment came when the queen met Abebe Bikila from Ethiopia. Bikila established himself as a sports legend by winning back-to-back Olympic marathons in Rome and Tokyo, the former while running the 26.2-mile course barefoot.

Shortly after dropping out of the marathon at the 1968 Mexico City Olympics, Bikila was paralyzed in a car accident in Ethiopia. He joined the short list of elite athletes whose sports careers were ended by paraplegia: Winterholler, Kellogg, Kinmont, and Campanella.

Bikila was eventually flown to Stoke Mandeville Hospital for rehabilitation. The marathoner whose triumphs foreshadowed the supremacy of distance runners from sub-Saharan Africa was now working to master wheelchair table tennis and wheelchair archery.

★ ★ ★

Wheelchair sports began in the United States and in England as the exclusive domain of paralyzed veterans. They constituted the "para" in Paralympics. In their wake came amputee and post-polio civilians who yearned for the same opportunity: to play wheelchair sports and, if they had the opportunity, to compete against the world's best.

Increased participation was a positive development, of course, and an alphabet soup of groups formed to serve previously underrepresented athletes, including the International Blind Sports Federation (IBSA); the Cerebral Palsy International Sports and Recreation Association (CPISRA); the International Committee of Sports for the Deaf (ICSD, formerly CISS); the International Sports Federation for Persons with Intellectual Disability (INAS, formerly INAS-FMH); and the International Sports Organization for the Disabled (ISOD) for amputees and *les autres* (literally, all others).

Advocates also began getting children with disabilities involved in sports and exercise. Eunice Kennedy Shriver, the sister of the late president, focused her work on youth with special needs. Shriver started a summer day camp before launching the Special Olympics in Chicago in 1968.

The one-size-doesn't-fit-all nature of sports for people with disabilities raised questions that Ludwig Guttmann, Tim Nugent, and Ben Lipton hadn't considered in depth in the 1940s and 1950s. What classification system works best for each disability? How do you prevent coaches and athletes from cheating? Should one umbrella organization oversee the entire disability sports universe, or should each group govern independently?

As the founding fathers of wheelchair sports grappled with

these issues, displeasure about the power structure bubbled to the surface. The athletes didn't question the integrity of Guttmann, Nugent, and Lipton—or their passion for aiding veterans and civilians with disabilities. But they also chafed at the patronizing leadership style of the non-disabled elder statesmen.

When the grassroots origins of wheelchair sports encountered the more politicized era of the 1960s and 1970s, on the heels of the civil rights and feminist movements, athletes with disability demanded more input about the direction of adaptive sports.

For years, Nugent resisted adding a women's division to the NWBA. At Illinois, he relegated women to wheelchair cheer-leading and square dancing. His decree was never questioned because so many of the sport's players, coaches, referees, and administrators had been his students or protégés.

Organizers of the 1968 Paralympics ignored Nugent's stance and added women's wheelchair basketball to the program, with Israel winning gold. A makeshift American team scrambled to take third. (In this, the Paralympics was years ahead of the Olympics, which did not introduce women's basketball until the 1976 Montreal Games.)

In the spring semester of 1971, female students at Illinois formed a wheelchair basketball team they christened the Ms. Kids. They practiced once a week at local church gyms and scrimmaged against non-disabled teams using wheelchairs. A legitimate opponent emerged at Southern Illinois University, located some two hundred miles away from the Urbana-Champaign campus. In February 1974, the Ms. Kids journeyed to Carbondale and defeated the Squidettes, 31–14, in the nation's first intercollegiate women's wheelchair basketball game. (They also won the rematch, 25–8.)

"We're not doing it for blood," said forward Nan O'Connor,

president of Illinois's Disabled Students Organization. "We're just doing it for ourselves."[9]

Another major flashpoint was the categorization system that Guttmann devised for international wheelchair basketball. Until 1966, athletes with spinal-cord injuries were divided into two classes: "complete" and "incomplete" (which included post-polios). Then came a new classification system for the Stoke Mandeville Games, which, at the time, included only those with spinal-cord disabilities.

Players were divided into five classes based on muscle tests performed on an examination table: A, B, C, D, S. An "A" athlete was worth one point; "B" and "C" athletes, two points; "D" and "S," three points. Each team was restricted to a maximum of twelve points for the five players on the floor. The system was designed to balance the lineups and encourage the participation of those with the severest injuries.

This model infuriated many athletes. They contended that Guttmann "did not provide a democratic forum" and instead "relied heavily on the opinions of the medical establishment that populated the movement," according to historians Stan La-banowich and Armand "Tip" Thiboutot. During the exams, the athletes "found themselves prone, looking up at the authoritative medical personnel, the very portrait of loss of individual auton-omy. Their athletic destiny was determined by the decisions of doctors and therapists, some of whom possessed little knowledge of wheelchair basketball."[10]

Their protests produced substantial reforms, starting with the creation of a "functional evaluation" system based on on-court criteria, such as "a player's balance, or lack thereof, while shooting, rebounding, and pushing the wheelchair." That change repre-sented a "triumph of sport over an autocratic and condescending view of rehabilitation controlled by medical personnel," according to Thiboutot, a longtime player and coach with the Boston Mustangs.[11]

Philip Craven was sixteen years old when he was paralyzed in a rock-climbing accident near his childhood home in Bolton, England. He recovered to become one of the top wheelchair basketball players in his country, and the world, but often found himself at loggerheads with "Poppa" Guttmann and his "paternalistic approach."

"He came over [from Germany] and had to take on the antiquated view of the medical fraternity in Britain with regard to: once you broke your back, you were dead meat as far as they were concerned," said Craven, who represented Britain in five Paralympic Games. "So, he had to be a tough guy. He was a dictator. But he couldn't make the transition from sport being a wonderful rehabilitation tool to it being about high performance and us wanting to be the best athletes we can be."[12]

Craven and other athletes with disabilities took control of their fate to change the paradigm of adaptive sports. Loral "Bud" Rumple was a standout post-polio wheelchair basketball player who happened to be a skilled welder. He looked at the E&J wheelchairs, the standard model since the invention of wheelchair basketball twenty years previous, and saw an outmoded clunker that was as poorly designed for sports as the horse and buggy.

With help from supporter Joseph Jones, Rumple engineered and custom-made high-performance sports wheelchairs. He eliminated conventional features, like armrests, that were useless for sports, and incorporated aluminum to reduce weight. The box frame, non-foldable design featured angled rear wheels and repositioned casters for greater stability and maneuverability.

"Speed is a big advantage," said Rumple, whose Detroit Sparks teams used his chairs to claim four NWBT titles between 1967 and 1971. "That's what's important. Building the chair is like building a car. The easier it handles, the better it goes. If you get one that runs like a tank, it won't do you any good."[13]

Cliff Crase was a navigator in the U.S. Air Force. Days before his twenty-first birthday, he was serving stateside when he sustained a spinal-cord injury in an automobile accident. He went on to graduate from the University of Illinois. He became a standout swimmer and track-and-field athlete before taking over the sports columnist chores at the PVA's *Paraplegia News*.

Every month, Crase would end up with reams of leftover material that he couldn't cram into his prescribed space. With support from his wife, Nancy, a graphic designer, he launched *Sports 'n Spokes*, a magazine exclusively about wheelchair sports. The first issue, all of sixteen pages, came out in May of 1975. Thanks to the couple's diligence, *Sports 'n Spokes* turned into an essential resource that informed, entertained, and gave voice to the growing disabled-sports community. (Later, after Crase was hired to edit *Paraplegia News*, the PVA purchased *Sports 'n Spokes*.)[14]

Around the time Crase published the first issue of *SnS*, Duncan Campbell and four others with quadriplegia were rehabbing at a small gym in Winnipeg, Manitoba. When the therapist who managed their exercise sessions didn't show one night, they started tossing around a volleyball, according to Campbell. They soon developed a new sport that combined elements of basketball, handball, rugby, and ice hockey.

"Murderball," as they dubbed the aggressive, full-contact sport, quickly spread across Canada and to the States (where it's known as quad rugby). The collisions on the court were violent—the rugged chairs look like they were created for the *Mad Max* movies—but athletes with quadriplegia found that the sport was better suited for their reduced arm and hand function than basketball.

"It gives them increased independence and mobility because they're stronger," Campbell said. "It opens up the world for them."[15]

★ ★ ★

Daunting tests lay ahead for the Paralympics after Tokyo, even as the number of competitors climbed into the thousands and the menu of sports choices expanded—including Alpine and Nordic skiing at the first-ever Winter Paralympics in Örnsköldsvik, Sweden, in 1976.

Mexico City, the host of the 1968 Summer Olympics, broke from Rome and Tokyo and refused to accommodate the Para-lympics, as did Munich (1972), Montreal (1976), and Moscow (1980). This forced organizers to secure other locales, sometimes in different countries from where the Olympics were held.

In 1979, Ludwig Guttmann suffered a heart attack. He died the next year at the age of eighty. His was a remarkable life of persecution and resurrection, of vision and perseverance. His groundbreaking research and clinical work, his prolific writing and ceaseless proselytizing, and his embrace of wheelchair sports and rehabilitation medicine forever changed the way physicians approached and treated paraplegia.

His most lasting sports legacy, the Paralympics, survived his death, although not without further travails. In 1984, the Summer Olympics returned to American soil for the first time in fifty-two years. As the co-originator of adaptive sports, the United States was ideally positioned to honor Guttmann's memory.

A seemingly perfect marriage was arranged for two locales. The seventh Paralympics for spinal-cord-injured athletes was scheduled to take place on the University of Illinois campus in Urbana-Champaign, with its abundant accessible facilities and well-established roots in disability sports. Timothy Nugent, the "Father of Accessibility" and the country's foremost expert on wheelchair sports, was selected to lead the endeavor.

Meanwhile, Ben Lipton persuaded a friend and neighbor, Nassau County Executive Francis Purcell, to hold the International Games for the Disabled on Long Island. This event was intended for amputees and people with visual impairment, cerebral palsy, dwarfism, and related disabilities.

Momentum surged after the United Nations proclaimed 1981 to be the International Year of Disabled Persons (IYDP) and advocated for full participation and equality for the estimated 450 million people worldwide with disabilities. Two IYDP ambassadors, University of Illinois grad student George Murray and Vietnam War veteran Phil Carpenter, wheeled themselves 3,400-plus miles across the United States in a singular, gutsy "Continental Quest" to raise awareness for the campaign. Murray and his wheelchair later appeared on the familiar orange boxes of Wheaties cereal, the "Breakfast of Champions."[16]

Nugent and Lipton also anticipated that wheelchair athletes would have a significant presence at the 1984 Olympics after the International Olympic Committee expressed interest in staging wheelchair basketball and racing exhibitions in Los Angeles.

But the auspicious push fizzled. A dispute with the U.S. Olympic Committee forced organizers to drop the name Paralympics in favor of the World Wheelchair Games, a move that stanched the marketing plans of previously interested corporations. Fundraising efforts fell woefully short of the multi-million-dollar target, and the University of Illinois canceled its contract. In the end, the British Paraplegic Society transplanted the World Wheelchair Games to the familiar grounds of Stoke Mandeville in a magnanimous last-minute effort.

It was a "pathetic situation," wrote journalist Harriet May Savitz, author of several books about disabled athletes.[17]

Sports 'n Spokes editor Cliff Crase lamented the "dark days for wheelchair sports in the United States."[18]

"I can't believe, don't understand, and certainly can't appreciate what has happened," a crestfallen Nugent wrote to one would-be contributor. "It is a genuine embarrassment to our entire nation and a real disappointment to the athletes around the world who worked so hard to qualify for these Games."[19]

Lipton, too, faced pushback despite having exported wheelchair sports to Mexico and having helped create a wheelchair sports section within the regional Pan American Games. He'd ruled the National Wheelchair Athletic Association since founding the group in the late 1950s. But after a proposal was made that the NWAA chair be elected rather than self-appointed, Lipton complained that he had been "pushed out" of the organization.[20]

Committee member Stan Labanowich told reporters that Lipton's presence had stifled the NWAA. "We wanted to bring our membership the democratic process. Ben Lipton was too dogmatic."[21]

Lipton did play an advisory role in the run-up to the International Games for the Disabled, which went on as planned one month before the start of the 1984 Los Angeles Olympics. President Ronald Reagan arrived by helicopter at Mitchel Field to open the Games for the 1,300 competitors from forty-five countries.

"There's something each of you understands that no one else can ever fully appreciate, something that has to do with courage, with willpower, and with the utter refusal to give up that has enabled you to rise above your disabilities and compete," the president said. "By competing in these games, each of you is sending a message of hope throughout the world. You're proving that a disability doesn't have to stand in the way of a full and active life, and you're showing all of us just how far a man or woman can go if only they have the dedication and the will."[22]

Later that summer, disabled athletes received a burst of publicity in Los Angeles, starting with the appearance of the first competitor with paraplegia to compete in the Olympics: Neroli Fairhall, an archer from New Zealand, who finished in thirty-fifth place.

Local organizers rejected the proposal for a wheelchair basketball tournament. They opted instead to hold two wheelchair contests at the venerable Los Angeles Memorial Coliseum while the Olympic competition was taking place: a 1,500-meter race for men and an 800-meter race for women that, with some exaggeration, the *Los Angeles Times* dubbed "the most important event in modern wheelchair sports history."[23]

In front of a sold-out house of about 80,000 spectators, and a worldwide TV audience of billions tuning in to see if Carl Lewis would win his fourth gold medal, the athletes didn't disappoint. Belgium's Paul van Winkel sped to the front and took the men's division in under four minutes, while American Sharon Hedrick, a wheelchair basketball star at the University of Illinois, won the women's race in record time.

Only in 1988, in Seoul, did the Olympics and the Paralympics finally converge again in the same city. Seoul marked the first Paralympics to include the major disability groups in the same competition: spinal-injured along with amputees, those with visual impairment and cerebral palsy, and *les autres*.

These Paralympics were no gratuitous second act. Some 3,000 athletes from sixty-one countries competed inside the Olympic Stadium and other venues, and they stayed in a specially designed village of apartment blocks, with accessible ramps. Cheering spectators packed the stands daily, and little expense was spared in the spectacular opening and closing ceremonies.

"From now on, disabled competition will be seen as athletic competition," said Ian Jaquiss, the U.S. gold medalist in the 50-meter breaststroke. "To me, the most important aspect of the Seoul Paralympics was finally being recognized as athletes—first by the International Olympic Committee and then by the crowds. These Games set the standard for future disabled meets."[24]

The creation of the International Paralympic Committee (IPC) to govern the competition led to a more formal alliance between the Olympics and the Paralympics. The two quadrennial events are now conjoined, in summer and winter, with the agreement requiring Olympic cities to host the Paralympics signed in 2001.

In 2012, the Summer Olympics returned to London for the first time since the post–World War II Games of 1948. The Paralympics followed immediately afterward in the same state-of-the-art facilities used by the Olympians. Of the 227 American athletes, twenty were service members or veterans of the U.S. Armed Forces.[25]

Each event got its own individual mascot. Mandeville was the character name of the Paralympics mascot, in tribute to Stoke Mandeville's historic role in the invention of adaptive sports.

Dr. Ludwig Guttmann would have been pleased.

CHAPTER 23

Legacy

Ron Kovic joined the marines right out of high school and volunteered to fight in Vietnam. In 1968, on his second tour of duty, he was shot twice during a firefight with the North Vietnamese Army on the northern bank of the Cua Viet River.

The first bullet hit Kovic, a staff sergeant, in the foot. The second bullet struck him in the right shoulder and smashed his spinal cord. He was flown to the intensive care ward in Da Nang, where a doctor told him that he was paralyzed from the waist down and would never walk again.

Kovic was one of the 8.7 million Americans who served during the Vietnam War, including an estimated 3.4 million deployed in Southeast Asia, according to the Department of Defense. Some 58,000 U.S. deaths were reported in battle and in theater, but overall mortality rates fell thanks to lessons acquired during World War II and in Korea.[1]

Prompt emergency treatment by medics at the location where the injury occurred proved vital. Helicopters medevaced Kovic and other wounded personnel from remote jungle locales directly to combat hospitals. Soldiers who likely would have perished in previous wars survived because trauma surgeons were able to treat them more quickly.

Wounded or not, Vietnam veterans received a far different reception from the rapturous welcome that Americans had extended to returning World War II veterans. Some were spat on, others were heckled as "baby killers." There were no joyous parades.

Kovic was overseas when he first heard about the anti-war marches happening across the United States. "I didn't want to believe it at first—people protesting against us when we were putting out lives on the line for our country," he wrote in his memoir *Born on the Fourth of July.* "The men in my outfit used to talk about it a lot. How could they do this to us?"[2]

The stark contrast between the two eras was reflected in Hollywood. Post–World War II movies like *The Men* and *The Best Years of Their Lives* championed veterans for dealing with their injuries and reintegrating into society. An "overcoming" narrative prevailed, one that valued sacrifice and emphasized hope and renewal.

Some thirty years later, the most acclaimed films about the Vietnam War—*Coming Home, The Deer Hunter, Apocalypse Now,* and the big-screen adaptation of Kovic's *Born on the Fourth of July*—focused on the veterans' postwar problems while striking a decidedly anti-war bent.

Another difference was the post-battlefield medical treatment received by the 150,000 Vietnam veterans who required hospital care in the States. A harrowing story in *Life* magazine, accompanied by graphic photographs, revealed the neglectful conditions inside ward 2-B of the Bronx VA.

"A man hit in Vietnam has twice as good a chance of surviving as he did in Korea and World War II, as support hospitals perform miraculous repairs on injuries that tend to be more devastating than ever before," reporter Charles Childs wrote. "But having been saved by the best field medicine in history," servicemen encountered the "bleak backwaters [of a] medical slum...disgracefully understaffed, with standards far below those of an average community hospital. Many wards remain closed for want of personnel and the rest are strained with overcrowding."[3]

The Senate investigated the under-financed and ill-equipped VA system that strained to handle the tsunami of maladies from Southeast Asia: exposure to the toxic chemical Agent Orange; the psychological phenomenon formerly known as "battle fatigue" and now identified as post-traumatic stress disorder (PTSD); the sheer number of soldiers who needed further treatment. Outrage over the scandal forced Donald Johnson, the VA's top administrator and a World War II veteran, to resign his post.

Sports again offered a measure of solace for veterans like Kovic. He began to heal from his body "having been devastated," as he put it, after Carlos Rodriguez, a Korean War veteran and a vocal leader within the Paralyzed Veterans of America, rolled his wheelchair next to Kovic's bed at the Bronx VA and talked about his experiences playing for the Brooklyn Whirlaways and competing at the Stoke Mandeville Games.

"He was a tough New Yorker with a big heart," Kovic recalled. "I was wondering if I could make it to the next day, and here's this guy telling me he'd been in a chair for nearly twenty years and inspiring me to keep going."

Kovic's personal journey from standout high school athlete to gung-ho marine to anti-war activist briefly detoured to the basketball court. "When I would shoot baskets [at the Bronx VA], it would bring me back to when I was whole, when I was on my feet, when I could still function fully as a human being," he said.

"My favorite shot was a hook shot. I had this great sky-hook. Occasionally it would go in."[4]

"Playing with the Rolling Dutchmen [wheelchair basketball team] allowed me to get my mind around the fact that I was paralyzed," he continued. "To transcend, if but for a brief time, the suffering of what I was going through. Once I started moving, it was exciting. I almost forgot I was in the chair. It was liberating. Afterward I was much more talkative, excited about living life, much more positive. It opened me up socially. Eventually, I was able to see myself as a whole person."[5]

Wheelchair sports programs assimilated the latest crop of wounded veterans. Armand Thiboutot sustained a high-level spinal-cord injury and an above-knee amputation of the left leg while he was serving in the army in the late 1950s. As player-coach of the Boston Mustangs, Thiboutot tutored several paralyzed veterans from Vietnam after they rehabbed at Brockton VA hospital in Massachusetts.

One of Thiboutot's recruiting pitches was that veterans can play wheelchair basketball for a long time. "Many good players are in their forties, and one guy in last year's tournament was fifty-three," he told *Boston Globe* reporter Bob Ryan. "Think about it. What's the first thing that usually goes in an athlete? The legs. We don't have to worry about that."[6]

Jim Winthers served with the 10th Mountain Division during World War II. The legendary ski troopers fought the Germans in wintry conditions in the north Apennine Mountains of Italy. Like many 10th Mountain alumni, Winthers devoted his postwar life to skiing and physical education.

At the Donner Ski Ranch, located in the Sierra range of northern California, past the glittery resorts of Reno and Tahoe, the non-disabled Winthers taught amputee war buddies to ski

313

using the "tri-track" system gleaned from travels in Austria. He started the National Amputee Skiers Association (NASA) in 1953, around the same time that Bob Engelien, an ex-paratrooper and Korean War veteran, opened the American Amputees Ski School near Big Bear in southern California.

"Skiing eliminates barriers," Engelien said. "When an amputee finds he can ski, confidence floods back and he knows that a bigger and better world is before him."[7]

During and after the Vietnam War, with large numbers of amputees rehabbing at San Francisco's Letterman Army Hospital and Oakland's Oak Knoll Naval Hospital, Winthers persuaded them to hit the slopes. One-legged veterans were soon carving down mountain trails supported by "outriggers," poles fashioned from forearm crutches with ski tips attached to their ends.

Winthers's grassroots initiative spread across the country and grew beyond skiing into a nonprofit group called Disabled Sports USA, which provides sports rehabilitation for people with disabilities. "We use sports as a vehicle to help them come through the traumatic experience they have had," he said. "They learn that it is a matter of inconvenience but that they can do it. Then they realize they can do anything."[8]

Eugene Roberts was a high school runner from Baltimore. He joined the marines and had been in Vietnam for about a month when he stepped on a land mine in Da Nang in 1966. After he was taken to Clark Air Base in the Philippines, he discovered that he was a double amputee. One leg was amputated below the knee, the other above the knee. He rehabbed at the Philadelphia Naval Hospital.

Roberts unofficially entered the 1970 Boston Marathon. He left almost an hour before the runners did, with his brother at his side, and muscled his hospital-issued wheelchair across 26.2

miles of blacktop and up Heartbreak Hill. He finished at Copley Square in about seven hours.

Five years later, Bob Hall became the Boston Marathon's first sanctioned wheelchair racer when he rolled to the starting line at Hopkinton. The post-polio athlete was the fastest player on Thiboutot's Boston Mustangs; he completed the storied marathon course in under three hours and shattered any myths about whether wheelchair athletes are hardy enough to handle endurance sports.

Hall and others, including post-polio athlete Marty Ball, went on to design aerodynamic racing chairs that dusted the E&Js. These new models were aligned for maximum push-rim thrust and shifted the center of gravity to "where it belongs: under the center mass of your body," said Ball in an interview with the LA84 Foundation.[9] The functional innovations significantly lowered the athletes' times and advanced wheelchair sports equipment into the twenty-first century.

★ ★ ★

Tom Brown was not a veteran. In his own words, he was a "birth defect baby" born with two stumps for legs. He was put up for adoption shortly after entering the world.[10]

As a youth, he embraced wheelchair sports. By the seventh grade, he was playing wheelchair basketball against adult men and holding his own. "Tim Nugent said to me, 'You need to come to the University of Illinois,'" Brown recalled. "You don't argue with Tim Nugent."[11]

Brown enrolled at Illinois and steered the Gizz Kids to two consecutive national titles. He could do anything and everything on the basketball court: "reverse layups, incredible hook shots, behind-the-back passes," according to one teammate. Not to mention, he was "the greatest shooter in the world," with dead-eye range from thirty feet.[12]

He didn't stop playing the sport he loved even after graduating with a master's degree in recreational therapy. He enjoyed stints with the Baltimore Ravens and teams in Richmond and San Antonio. "Being disabled all my life, basketball has made me feel like I was part of a team," he said. "It was the single most important rehabilitation I have had in my entire life."[13]

In 1981, Brown was working as a recreational therapist for the VA. To commemorate the UN's International Year of Disabled Persons, Brown and two colleagues co-founded the National Veterans Wheelchair Games (NVWG). They wanted "to get our veterans out of the hospital, back into society, back into the community, showing them things that maybe because of their injury they thought they couldn't do anymore," he said. "We're here to show them that the impossible is possible."[14]

Some seventy-four veterans from fourteen states competed in the inaugural NVWG on the grounds of McGuire VA Hospital. The games were initially planned to be a one-time affair, but Brown saw that they filled an urgent need and they "snowballed from there," he said.[15]

The NVWG is now an annual event that rotates to cities across the country. Co-sponsored by the VA and the Paralyzed Veterans of America, the games attract every type of veteran: old and young, male and female. Their success has kicked off a throwback trend of sporting events for military personnel only: the Warrior Games, funded by the U.S. Department of Defense; the National Veterans Golden Age Games (for seniors); and the National Disabled Veterans Winter Sports Clinic (co-presented by the VA and the Disabled American Veterans).

In 2013, on a visit to the United States, England's Prince Harry took in the Warrior Games in Colorado Springs. He returned home and launched the 2014 Invictus Games for injured servicemen and women, both active duty and veterans, to "harness the power of sport to inspire recovery, support rehabilitation and generate a wider understanding and respect for those who serve their country," according to the foundation's website.[16]

Brown has since retired from the VA and from running the NVWG. He said that being disabled himself gave him "a kind of advantage" when he worked with wounded veterans and exposed them to adaptive sports.

"I think people could relate to us because they saw that we were the same as they were," he said. "We were not only telling them, but showing them."[17]

★ ★ ★

In 1964, when Ludwig Guttmann took the Paralympics to Tokyo, a wealthy American ex-pat named Justin Dart Jr. was working in Japan. He'd been infected with polio when he was eighteen and used a wheelchair to get around.

Dart was the grandson of the founder of the Walgreens drugstore chain and the son of the president of the Rexall-Dart Industries conglomerate. His father's holdings included Tupperware, and the younger Dart had been installed to run the company's Tupperware division in Japan.

During the Tokyo Paralympics, Dart donated wheelchairs to the athletes and was drawn to watch the action. He was impressed by the athleticism of the U.S. wheelchair basketball teams and, in particular, the play of Dick Maduro, who helped the complete squad win the gold medal. Dart compared Maduro's muscular arms to "the legs of a horse."[18]

Afterward, Dart started a program to hire people with disabilities to work in the company warehouse. He persuaded Maduro and his wife to move from Florida and coach a wheelchair basketball team sponsored by Japan Tupperware.

Maduro had become paralyzed in a motorcycle accident in the 1940s, when he was living in Massachusetts. He learned about wheelchair basketball from the World War II veterans who helped invent the sport while rehabbing at Cushing Hospital in Framingham. After he recovered and moved to Florida, Maduro formed the Free Wheelers, a short-lived wheelchair basketball team featuring other paralyzed veterans and post-polio players.

In Japan, Maduro spent two years as player-coach as the team gave exhibitions around the country. The team once played the non-disabled Japanese Olympic team on national television. According to Dart, after Tupperware took a huge lead at halftime, he was approached by his public relations representative and advised to "let the Olympic players make a comeback in the second half" so as not to lose the sympathy of the audience.

"I told him an unprintable thing," Dart said. "You tell them to go blank themselves. You tell them that we've been trying for hundreds of years to lose *sympathy* and gain *respect*. And if they want to make a comeback, let them come out and do it, but we are not going to pull any punches."[19]

Tupperware won easily, although the Olympians did manage to make one basket. "They looked upon us as cripples and as hospital patients," Dart said. "They were shocked when we played the game like it was tank warfare."[20]

After Dart and his wife, Yoshiko, settled in Texas in the late 1970s, they became involved in the disability rights movement that was seeking to end discriminatory practices in housing, education, employment, and transportation. Or, as one wheelchair demonstrator bluntly declared, referencing the protests of the civil rights movement, "I can't even get to the back of the bus."[21]

Dart's father was a major donor to the Republican Party and one of Ronald Reagan's closest advisors. In 1981, President Reagan named Dart Jr. vice chair of the National Council on the Handicapped (now known as the National Council on Disability).

In his trademark cowboy hat and boots, Dart toured the country to speak with everyone with a stake in the issue of disability, including activists aligned with the "independent living" movement (some of whom were graduates of the University of Illinois); families and caregivers; doctors and health professionals; government and VA officials; educators and students; and members of the Paralyzed Veterans of America and other veterans' groups.

Out of this effort came a concerted push for comprehensive federal legislation to end discrimination against people with disabilities. With his seat at the political table, Dart hit the road to campaign for the Americans with Disabilities Act (ADA), a bill cosponsored by Senator Tom Harkin (D-IA), whose brother was deaf, and by Representative Tony Coelho (D-CA), who had debilitating epileptic seizures.[22]

When the bill stalled amid pressure from business interest groups, among others, advocates abandoned their crutches and wheelchairs and pulled themselves up the steep marble steps leading to the Capitol building in Washington, D.C. The dramatic protest of the "Capitol Crawlers" won the day, quieted the lobbyists, and led to passage of the ADA.

On July 26, 1990, President George H. W. Bush signed the ADA in a ceremony on the South Lawn of the White House. Sitting next to the president was Justin Dart Jr., in his wheelchair.

"America welcomes into the mainstream of life all of our fellow citizens with disabilities," said Bush, a former navy pilot who flew fifty-eight combat missions during World War II. "We embrace you for your abilities and for your disabilities, for our similarities and indeed for our differences, for your past courage and your future dreams.

"Let the shameful wall of exclusion finally come tumbling down," he concluded.[23]

For the estimated 61 million Americans (one in four adults) who live with mobility, cognition, hearing and vision, and self-care disabilities, passage of the ADA "has not fully assured disability justice" according to Rosemarie Garland-Thomson, professor of English and bioethics at Emory University and co-director of the school's Disability Studies Initiative. But the ADA has brought about "a change in attitudes, a lessening of the stigma . . . We were no longer hidden or shut away because of someone else's sense that our ways are inept or our presence shameful."[24]

★ ★ ★

The legacy of the paralyzed veterans from World War II begins with their military service. Men like Johnny Winterholler, Stan Den Adel, and Gene Fesenmeyer sacrificed their physical well-being, in the prime of their youth, for their country. They returned home to show that what was thought of as a condition leading to certain death was treatable. Of the estimated 2,500 U.S. paralyzed veterans from World War II, more than 1,700 were alive in 1968—and 1,400 were employed, according to Dr. Howard Rusk. "This time they did not die," he said.[25]

Their demonstration of the efficacy of rehabilitation established that branch of medicine as totally essential. Then they daringly and matter-of-factly wheeled their chairs onto the basketball court and declared that they had nothing to hide. They created a novel kind of recreation and, like Jackie Robinson breaking into baseball's major leagues, their presence expanded the possibility of sports. Efforts here and in England led to the invention of the Paralympics, the National Wheelchair Basketball Tournament, and countless other previously unimaginable events and activities once the gymnasium doors were thrown open to people with all manner of disabilities, including intellectual disabilities.

Not only did they reduce the stigma of disability, they were among the first people to be applauded for their condition, the first to be considered as something other than freaks or damaged goods. If paralyzed veterans in wheelchairs could play an exciting and exacting brand of basketball—basketball!—they couldn't possibly be "wheelchair-bound." Given the chance, they could do everything and anything non-disabled veterans could do: drive a car, hold down a job, buy a home, get married and raise children, and, yes, pay taxes.

They also had the support of the government, starting with the GI Bill, and the backing of the military, via the Veterans Administration, which summoned vast resources to repair their bodies and souls. Hospitals were built and paraplegia wards were opened; doctors, nurses, and physical therapists were hired; special equipment designed, manufactured, and purchased; medical studies undertaken and academic papers written.

They were allowed years to recover. Their inspirational heroism and their vulnerability were applauded in newspapers, magazines, and Hollywood movies. Salvaged from the wreckage of war, their resilience, courage, and spirit helped the country move forward after the horrors of war.

Finally, as their health and self-respect improved, they rallied themselves into the Paralyzed Veterans of America. They formed a beachhead from which to tend to their unique needs—and fired opening salvos in what has become a protracted fight for disability rights. They raised money for scientists to research paraplegia; lobbied politicians for legislation that addressed accessibility, employment, housing, and transportation; published articles and op-eds about their plight; advocated for the principles of independence and self-determination; and stated loudly and eloquently that they didn't want to be treated as objects of pity. Then they visited VA hospitals and persuaded service members returning from Korea, Vietnam, and other war zones to follow in their well-worn wheelchair tracks.

The saga of the revitalization of the paralyzed veterans—yet another legacy of the Greatest Generation—could not have happened without the commitment of innovative physicians and unsung coaches and sports advocates. Drs. Donald Munro, Ludwig Guttmann, Ernest Bors, Howard Rusk, Gerald Gray, and others collaborated with the veterans to advance research and treatment of spinal-cord injuries. Bob Rynearson, Timothy Nugent, Ben Lipton, and other non-disabled allies (including the leaders of the Bulova and Pan Am corporations) didn't allow longstanding societal prejudice against people with disabilities to deter their enthusiasm for creating and growing wheelchair sports.

Together, they preached a hard-fought but deceivingly simple lesson: what mattered most wasn't disability, but ability.

EPILOGUE

Whatever Happened to . . .

Johnny Winterholler

Dessa and Johnny Winterholler enjoyed a quiet life after they moved to the Oakland area and built a wheelchair-accessible ranch home in Lafayette. They adopted two children: a girl, Deborah, and a boy, David.

Johnny was able to walk using the shorter Canadian crutches, but he preferred to get around with his manual wheelchair. A friend had a pool installed so that, after work and on weekends, John could soak himself. "He'd put his arms up and his legs out in front of him and he'd sit there and kick his legs to try to exercise them," recalled his son, David.[1]

Johnny handled the business affairs for Dr. Gerald Gray and his plastic surgery practice—bookkeeping, scheduling appointments, taxes—and shuttled between Dr. Gray's office in the Pill Hill area of Oakland and his Tenacre Ranch in Walnut Creek.

"He is my right hand," Dr. Gray told a reporter in 1964. "I couldn't get along without him. I do work on birth defects, and I do cosmetic work too. I talk to patients when they first consult me and decide what can be done. They want to know what it will cost. I send them to John. They always leave with a smile.

"He is completely adjusted—more cheerful than most people who have no handicap at all," Dr. Gray said.[2]

They played dominoes every day at lunchtime and were members of the same hunting club. Once, when they went hunting near Santa Cruz, Johnny was stationed on a promontory while Dr. Gray and the rest of the party went off to track deer. They returned hours later empty-handed, only to see that John had gotten his buck.

Johnny stayed in touch with Major Walter Hinkle, who had helped carry him out of Bilibid Prison after they were liberated. He kept smoking cigarettes, a habit he picked up in the POW camps, although a stint in the hospital in the early 1970s forced him to stop. He kept one souvenir from the war: a sapphire ring, inlaid in gold with a pagoda on one side and a dragon on the other, given to him by a fellow marine. He wore it until the day he died.[3]

He never discussed at length his wartime experiences with his two children; any anger and bitterness that remained was kept hidden. "If he had problems, they weren't problems anymore when we came along," his daughter said. "He was part of the generation that didn't talk about things like that. He was tough as nails. He was The Colonel."[4]

What resentment lingered was expressed in one word. He referred to people of Japanese descent as "Japs," although he refrained from using the word in public.

In 1964, *Sports Illustrated* honored Winterholler and twenty-four other collegiate football players from the class of 1940 for "their significant contributions to their times."[5] That same year, Johnny and Dessa flew to Laramie as guests of the University of Wyoming for "Johnny Winterholler Day." Along with fellow

honorees Governor Clifford Hansen and writer Olga Moore
Arnold, he received the school's Distinguished Alumni Award
at the Memorial Fieldhouse. Warm applause greeted his brief
words of gratitude for the university, Laramie, and the people of
Wyoming.

To mark the fortieth anniversary of the end of World War
II, the town of Lovell threw a two-day bash. Lovell High
School used the occasion to dedicate the "John Winterholler
Gymnasium." At the ceremony, attended by Representative Dick
Cheney (R-WY), Winterholler said that moving to Lovell had
changed his life for the better because that was where he met
Dessa. Several years later, he was inducted into the University of
Wyoming Athletic Hall of Fame.

His brief but significant role in establishing wheelchair basketball as a popular and legitimate sport has been long overlooked,
probably because the Rolling Devils weren't around for long
and never participated in the National Wheelchair Basketball
Tournament or in the Paralympics. Recently, Winterholler and
the entire Rolling Devils team were nominated for induction
into the National Wheelchair Basketball Hall of Fame.

Dessa passed away in 1996. Colonel John Winterholler died in
2001 at the age of eighty-five.

★ ★ ★

Stan Den Adel

Peggy and Stan Den Adel resided at the wheelchair-accessible
ranch home he designed and built in Northridge. He used the GI
Bill to finish the college education he'd started at Cal Berkeley
during the war. He enrolled at UCLA and graduated with a

master's degree in business administration in June of 1953. Not long afterward, he and Peggy adopted a girl, Christina.

Before Stan's father passed away, he gave his son one piece of advice: do not become a banker. Almost immediately after college, Stan started working for Bank of America. After two years, he was promoted to assistant cashier and headed a thirty-eight-person shift in the bank's central office in Los Angeles. He then became the bank's manager of computer operations, in charge of nearly one thousand people. When he retired in 1979, he was vice president and manager of Bank of America's Data Processing Center in Los Angeles.[6]

He never stopped advocating for veterans and civilians with disabilities. He was a member of the Mayor's Committee on Employment of the Handicapped in L.A. and a board member with the L.A. chapter of the National Rehabilitation Association. He was the winner of the national Outstanding Disabled Veteran award in 1972.

"We've come a long way," he said, "but we're still one of the most discriminated against minorities."[7]

Stan and Peggy were married for sixty years. Sergeant Stan Den Adel died in 2009 at the age of eighty-six. Peggy died in 2012.

★ ★ ★

Gene Fesenmeyer

Gene Fesenmeyer made good on his vow not to let paraplegia get in the way of living life to the fullest.

He was married three times, worked in electronics for Hughes and other companies, and was an avid CB-radio operator. He learned to fly a small airplane and loved driving fast. At various times, he owned a Cadillac, an all-terrain vehicle, and a tricked-out van. When he visited his younger sister Leona in Iowa, he'd take her on the back of his specially equipped motorcycle and drive "like a bat out of hell," as she put it.[8]

Gene gravitated to warm-weather locales. He lived for many years in Southern California and Hawaii. He moved to Guadalajara, Mexico, and joined other American veterans with paraplegia and quadriplegia who'd sought out the balmy temperatures, modest cost of living, and party-time atmosphere in the beer halls and brothels. (So many wounded veterans settled there that they nicknamed the city "Quadalajara.")

"I went where I wanted and did what I wanted to do," he said. "I wanted to do some living."[9]

He eventually settled in Rio Hondo, Texas, by the Gulf of Mexico. He lived on a three-acre lot, with a river flowing behind his well-equipped mobile home, and twenty-four-hour homecare provided by a rotating platoon of aides.

He had one regret: that he didn't take advantage of the GI Bill and go back to college. "I didn't think I was smart enough," he said, "which was a big mistake because, as somebody told me later, that's where you go to get smarter."[10]

Fesenmeyer said he wanted to live "to hit 100." Corporal Gerald Gene Fesenmeyer died in 2018 at age ninety-one.

★ ★ ★

The Washington, D.C.-based Paralyzed Veterans of America continues to advocate for its members. In 1971, a long-sought goal was achieved when the PVA was granted a Congressional Charter, an extremely rare distinction for a nonprofit organization. The PVA still publishes *Paraplegia News* and *Sports 'n Spokes*.

Jack Gerhardt, who appeared on the cover of *Newsweek* after leading the Halloran Hospital team to victory in Madison Square Garden, died in 1965. He was elected to the National Wheelchair Basketball Hall of Fame in 1973. Today, the Jack Gerhardt Award is given to the "Athlete of the Year" in wheelchair sports by the PVA.

In 1966, Dr. Donald Munro received the PVA's "Speedy Award," the organization's highest honor, for outstanding contribution to the field of paraplegia. Dr. Munro died in 1973.

The Ernest Bors Spinal Cord Injury Center opened at the Long Beach VA Medical Center in 1990, the same year that Dr. Bors died. Since 1994, the *Journal of Spinal Cord Medicine* has awarded the Ernest Bors Award for Scientific Development.

Bob Rynearson worked for the U.S. Veterans Administration his entire professional life. He retired in 1980 after thirty-five years of service. In 1975, he received the PVA's Speedy Award, honoring his pioneering work in wheelchair sports. He was inducted into the National Wheelchair Basketball Hall of Fame in 1997. He died in 2002.

Dr. Gerald Gray became president of the California Society of Plastic Surgeons and, at Oakland's Highland Hospital, was chief of plastic surgery. He treated any World War II veteran whom he'd helped at Corona for free, including Gene Fesenmeyer, whenever they came to see him in Oakland. The avid outdoorsman and member of the Rancheros Visitadores riding crew died in 1982.

Tim Nugent died in 2015. The "Father of Accessibility" and the "Abner Doubleday of wheelchair sports" added to his many honors by being posthumously elected to the U.S. Olympic & Paralympic Hall of Fame in 2019. He joined such luminaries as Duke Kahanamoku, Wilma Rudolph, and the 1960 U.S. Olympic basketball team.

The men's wheelchair basketball team at the University of Illinois eventually changed its name from the Gizz Kids to the Fighting Illini. The women's team, formerly the Ms. Kids, is also now known as the Fighting Illini.

Ben Lipton received the PVA's Speedy Award in 1962, and was elected to the NWBA Hall of Fame in 1974. He died in 1991. The Joseph Bulova School of Watchmaking closed its doors in 1997 (although the building still stands). The Bulova Watchmakers no longer exist.

Junius Kellogg worked for New York City's Community Development Agency for more than thirty years. His alma mater, Manhattan College, awarded him an honorary doctor of laws degree in 1998. He died that year at age seventy-one. The Pan Am Jets played their last game in 1964.

Naval Hospital Corona, which reopened during the Korean War, closed in 1957. The property today houses U.S. Navy operations, a state prison, and Norco College. The original buildings of the Norconian Resort Supreme still stand, including the gymnasium built by the navy that is recognized as the site of the first organized wheelchair basketball game. Sadly, despite being listed on the National Register of Historic Places, many of the original buildings have been neglected. Led by Norco mayor pro tem Kevin Bash, community leaders are seeking to add the former naval hospital to the National Register.

The Long Beach Flying Wheels remain active. They are the oldest continuously playing wheelchair basketball team. They won their last NWBT championship in 1964.

Many of the buildings of Birmingham Hospital in Van Nuys were demolished years ago, although the gymnasium in which the first edition of the Flying Wheels played and practiced still stands. It is now the site of Birmingham High School.

In 1980, Bob Rynearson, Stan Den Adel, Pat Grissom, Fred Smead, and other Birmingham Hospital alumni returned to the campus to dedicate a stone plaque in honor of the veterans, doctors, and aides who pioneered research about spinal-cord injuries.[11] The plaque reads: "On this site of Birmingham Hospital 1943–1950, veterans returning from World War II were given renewed confidence and hope by the dedicated personnel who cared for them. Their legacy of pride and courage remains here as an incentive for all who now share these grounds."[12]

ACKNOWLEDGMENTS

This book came together from interviews with the participants in this story and their families and via research at libraries and archives in the United States and in England.

I want to thank Gene Fesenmeyer for sharing his life experiences with me. We spoke many times on the phone before his death in 2018, and I treasure the time I spent visiting with him (and his caretakers and his pets) at his home in Rio Hondo, Texas. He even let me drive his adapted van that, thankfully, didn't crash when the steering mechanism malfunctioned. After his death, Fred and Jerry Paul Fesenmeyer were kind enough to speak with me about their brother, with assistance from Jerry Paul's wife, Beverly. His younger sister, Leona Rubin, was especially helpful, with assistance from her daughter, Brenda Dehmer. Thanks also to Jon King, a son of one of Gene's wives. Major thanks to the family of Johnny Winterholler—daughter Deborah Harms and son David Winterholler—for sharing memories of their father and mother and for supplying background information, letters, and photographs. I also want to thank the family of Stan Den Adel—sister Shirley Garthwait and daughter Tina Den Adel— for entrusting me with their remembrances and with personal material written by Stan himself. I could not have written this book without their help.

The family of Bob Rynearson provided much support and encouragement. It was a pleasure to speak with Diane Forbes and Bob Jr. about their father; Bob Jr. was incredibly generous in supplying invaluable background material about their father's unsung contributions to wheelchair basketball, including a personal scrapbook from the team's cross-country trips. (I have to thank Bob Rynearson Sr. for having the foresight to save priceless documents, photos, and mementos from the 1940s.) Thanks also to Susan Rynearson, Kevin Rynearson, and David Rynearson and his family for their patience. Also, special thanks to the children of Dr. Gerald Gray: Celia Gray Cummings, Alice Gray Coelho, and Gerald Gray. I appreciate that they took time to speak with me and share stories about their father and to share photographs from the Rolling Devils scrapbook.

I couldn't begin to appreciate the long history of wheelchair basketball without the assistance and knowledge of Armand "Tip" Thiboutot, a veteran and the co-author of *Wheelchairs Can Jump!* Tip patiently explained the nuances of the sport and supplied excellent guidance and wisdom, ably assisted by his wife, Patricia. The writings of Stan Labanowich, Tip's late co-author, were particularly helpful.

Kevin Bash, the mayor of Norco, helped me at every stage of this project. His voluminous research about the Norconian Resort Supreme and the Rolling Devils showed the way, and he graciously shared articles, photographs, scrapbooks, and rare material and answered countless questions. He and the city of Norco now host an annual wheelchair basketball tournament that pays homage to the Rolling Devils, and he's been a community bulwark in efforts to preserve the structures of the Norconian and the Naval Hospital. Historical research by Bill Wilkman, commissioned by the city of Norco, was very useful.

Ed Santillanes is, at this writing, the oldest surviving original wheelchair basketball player; he was gracious enough to share stories about his World War II service and adventures at Birmingham Hospital. Many thanks to Ed's stepdaughter, Cindy Koellisch, for arranging our meeting and follow-ups. Marv Lapicola related his experience surviving polio as well as his education at the University of Illinois and his stint in the Paralympics. Julius Jiacoppo recounted his experience surviving polio and his time with the Pan Am Jets; he sent me an amazing scrapbook about the team via his daughter, Liz Mines. Sir Philip Craven was gracious enough to speak with me about Dr. Ludwig Guttmann and his own Paralympic experience. Kevin Foley spoke with me about his father, Dick Foley, and the Cushing Clippers/New England PVA teams. Greg Churchman spoke with me about his father, Russ, and the Flying Wheels of the 1950s. Tracy Nugent took time from his busy schedule to chat about his father, Timothy Nugent. Mark Boshnack provided details about the extraordinary life and career of his father, Selig Boshnack. Tom Brown talked to me about his life and the National Veterans Wheelchair Games. Ron Kovic's unique and sobering perspective about healing from war was extremely helpful. Thanks as well to Jack Tumidajski and his memories of "Quadalajara."

Many thanks to Tom Fjerstad, the current editor of *Paraplegia News* with the Paralyzed Veterans of America. Tom answered my numerous emails, steered me toward vital material about PVA history, shared priceless archival material, and encouraged my efforts. I want to acknowledge the work of the late Harry Schweikert and Cliff Crase; their lively reportage for *Paraplegia News* and *Sports 'n Spokes* provided the first draft of history about wheelchair sports.

Many superlative institutions facilitated my research. The Wellcome Library in London holds the archives of Dr. Ludwig Guttmann as well as a treasure trove of medical literature and books. Staff (including Simon Demissie, Nicola Cook, and Alexandra Milne) was, ahem, welcoming and professional during my visits. Not far from the Wellcome is the British Library and its brilliant holdings (thanks to Karen Waddell of the News Reference Team, among many helpful staff). The tireless, accommodating personnel at the National Archives and Records Administration in St. Louis (including James Hébert and Donna Noelken) facilitated research about veterans even while navigating a fire drill (and Dean Gall was kind enough to retrieve my forgotten glasses). Thanks, too, to Lori Miller (Redbird Research) for her research efforts at NARA, and thanks to Tom Pescatore at National Archives at College Park. The Archives Research Center at the University of Illinois holds the Timothy Nugent Papers; staff there, particularly Christopher John Prom and archivist Ellen D. Swain and reference librarians at the school's main library, efficiently handled queries and requests. The holdings at the National Library of Medicine at the National Institutes of Health in Bethesda, Maryland, are a national treasure; thanks to Stephen Greenberg in the History of Medicine division, among others. Thanks to Martin Meeker at the Oral History Center, The Bancroft Library, University of California, Berkeley. I'm forever grateful to Shirley Ito, Michael Salmon, and Wayne Wilson—and give props to their knowledge, enthusiasm, and imagination—at the LA84 Foundation.

I spent many eye-straining hours fiddling with microfilm knobs, filling out request forms, feeding coins into the copy machines, and using the digital resources of these fine institutions: New York Public Library; Brooklyn Public Library; Queens Public Library (thanks to librarian Judith Todman); St. Louis Public

Library; Cincinnati Public Library; Oakland Public Library; and numerous public libraries in southern California: Beverly Hills, Glendale (Adams Square branch), Long Beach, Los Angeles (thanks to Rosemarie Knopka with the Rare Books Room at Central and to staff at the Lincoln Heights and Van Nuys branches), Pasadena and South Pasadena, and the L.A. County Library (City Terrace branch).

I accessed material from the following libraries and museums and/or their websites: the Library of Congress; the James Naismith Collection with the Duane Norman Diedrich Collection at the William Clements Library, the University of Michigan (thanks to Jayne Ptolemy and Louis Miller); the Pritzker Military Museum and Library; the National World War II Museum (hat-tip to Tanja Spitzer); the U.S. Army Medical Department Office of Medical History; the Arthur and Elizabeth Schlesinger Library; the Clarinda Public Library (thanks to Andrew Hoppmann); the J. Willard Marriott Library (thanks to Robert Behra); Special Collections at the University of Miami; the Imperial War Museum in London; the Alfred Gray Marine Corps Research Center at the Marine Corps University Research Library; the Society for Military History; the American Heritage Center at the University of Wyoming; and the Munger Research Center at the Huntington Library, Art Museum and Botanical Gardens (thanks to Morex Arai). Thanks to the scholars/historians/academics who corresponded with me and/or sent me their writings and dissertations: James Deutsch ("Coming Home from 'The Good War'"); Jack Hourcade ("Special Olympics: A Review and Critical Analysis"); David Legg (Paralympic Games); Ian Brittain and Tony Sainsbury (Paralympic Games); and Dr. John Silver (treatment of spinal injuries and Dr. Ludwig Guttmann). Special thanks to Dr. Brian Shaw for explaining the complexities of the human spine.

This book started as a short feature for *Los Angeles* magazine; thanks to Ann Herold, Matt Segal, Eric Mercado, and Amy Feitelberg. Thanks to Norman Bussell for insight on POWs and PTSD from World War II; Tommy Gelinas at Valley Relics Museum; Patty Everett at *Leatherneck* magazine; Rob Soto with the current edition of the Flying Wheels; Molly Josette Bloom with the Shield Maidens; Bruce Wolk for sharing his research and encyclopedic knowledge of Junius Kellogg; director Nick Spark, who shared his knowledge about World War II documentaries; Volker Kluge, Bill Mallon, and David Wallechinsky with the International Society of Olympic Historians; Carl Rosen and Julia Maher Loftus with Bulova; Frederic Wallace at the Framingham History Center for his groundbreaking history of Cushing Hospital; Michael Negrete and Mike Guilbault with the New England PVA; Greg Edelbrock for speaking with me about his father, Dr. Harold Edelbrock; Christi Wilkinson for speaking with me about her father, Tex Schramm; and Michael Hamel about the Boston Celtics promotions.

Photographs: Thanks to the Bob Rynearson family; the John Winterholler family; the Dr. Gerald Gray family; the Stan Den Adel family; Leona Rubin and the Gene Fesenmeyer family; Annette and Mark Boshnack; Armand "Tip" Thiboutot; Christina Rice, head librarian of the photo collection at the Los Angeles Public Library; Gary Leonard; Jeanie Braun, Allison Francis, and Faye Thompson, photograph archive coordinator at the Margaret Herrick Library; Larry McCallister at Paramount Pictures; Aaron Schmidt, librarian at the Boston Public Library; Jim Mahoney, Chris Christo, and Marc Grasso at the *Boston Herald*; Patrick Fahy, archives technician at the Franklin D. Roosevelt Presidential Library; Mary Burtzloff, audiovisual archivist at the Eisenhower Presidential Library and Museum; Laurie Austin, audiovisual archives, Harry S. Truman Library; Tom Fjerstad and Sherrie Shea with the Paralyzed Veterans of America; Nicola Hellmann-McFarland and Yvette Yurubi at Special Collections, the University of Miami Libraries, Otto Richter Library; archivist Mike Kasper and G. Kurt Piehler, director of the Institute on World War II and the Human Experience, Florida State University; Kyle Boyd and staff with Special Collections and University Archives, W. E. B. Du Bois Library, University of Massachusetts; Molly Haigh, Library Special Collections, Charles Young Research Library, UCLA; Leona Manasturean, digital artist at Samy's; Katie Nichols, archives program officer, Archives Research Center, University of Illinois at Urbana-Champaign; Hanna Soltys, reference librarian at the Library of Congress, and Marc Bauman; Erik Huber, photo archivist at the Queens Library; Deborah Tint, special collections cataloger at Brooklyn Public Library; Peter Corina, reference specialist, Cornell University; Ellen Embleton at the Royal Society; Clair Sim, grant operations and data manager at the Wolfson Foundation; Lucy Dominy with IWAS; Wendy Wergeles. Also, thanks to staff at Vidéothèque in South Pasadena for help with World War II movies.

A huge shout-out to the pros in my corner: author-editor Glenn Stout, who championed the book proposal; attorney extraordinaire Orly Ravid; accountant Bob (and Rosemary) Reinhardt; literary agent Rob Wilson of Wilson Media, whose unflagging support buoys me; Kate Hartson, Sean McGowan, Katie Broaddus, Patsy Jones, Rudy Kish, Eliot Caldwell, Anjuli Johnson, Becky Maines, Tom Watkins, Laura Hanifin, Ed Crawford, and Jaime Coyne with Hachette Book Group; producer Dennis Nishi; staff at the Authors Guild.

Thanks to friends, family, and colleagues who provided comfort, inspiration, and encouragement: Jonathan Abbott, Donnell

Alexander, Bruce Bebb, Vince Beiser, Donna Davis, Sally Berman, Greg Burk, Kateri Butler, Terry and Mary Cannon, Regino Chavez, Mark Cirino and family, Tonio Cirino, Curtis Claymont and Denise Lento, Dan Cooper and Lynn Bechtold, the Davis family (Susan, Rick, Ina, David, and my uncle, the late Mort Davis, a World War II veteran), Roberto De Vido, the ERB crew, Paul Feinberg and Patty Nomura, Michael X. Ferraro, Lynell George, Emily Green (thanks again for the ride to Bethesda), Jean Guccione and Robert Levins, Adam, Julie, Liz, and Ned Hazen, Tom Hoffarth, Amy Inouye and Stuart Rapeport, Lucy Ito and Rob Corn, Shirley Ito, Michael Kaplan, Steve Kettmann, Pamela Klein and the late Bob Giacose, Jason Levin, Alec Lipkind, Steve Lowery, Kate Maruyama and family, Connie and Giles Moore, Tricia Nickell and Rob Reichman, Ed Odeven, Barry Petchesky, Kit Rachlis, Ron Rapoport, Mack Reed and family, Jeremy Rosenberg, Julian Rubinstein, Susan Reifer Ryan, John Schulian, the Shaw family (Daniel, Diana, Tony, and Dr. Brian), Joan Spindel, George Stephens, Steve Tager, Karen Wada, Don Wallace, and Dewey Wigod.

I lean on my immediate family in ways great and small. Thanks to Orleans, Figueroa, Dexter, and Ranger for keeping me sane. Thank you to my sister, Jennifer Hall, and her children: Delaney, Chloe, and Gavin. Thanks especially to my parents, Jessie and Andy Davis, who are always there for me, in good times and bad. And a toast to the boss of me: Flora Ito. I could not have done this without you.

BIBLIOGRAPHY

Select Books

Adler, Jessica. *Burdens of War: Creating the United States Veterans Health System*. Baltimore: Johns Hopkins University Press, 2017.

Algren, Nelson. *The Man with the Golden Arm*. New York: Seven Stories Press, 1999.

Alperovitz, Gar. *The Decision to Use the Atomic Bomb and the Architecture of an American Myth*. New York: Alfred Knopf, 1995.

Ambrose, Stephen. *Band of Brothers: E Company, 506th Regiment, 101st Airborne from Normandy to Hitler's Eagle Nest*. New York: Simon & Schuster, 2001.

Arnaz, Desi. *A Book*. New York: William Morrow and Company, 1976.

Bailey, Steve. *Athlete First: A History of the Paralympic Movement*. London: Wiley and Sons, 2008.

Barlow, John Perry. *Mother American Night: My Life in Crazy Times*. New York: Crown Archetype, 2018.

Barton, Betsey. *The Long Walk*. New York: Duell, Sloan and Pearce, 1948.

Bash, Kevin, and Brigitte Jouxtel. *The Navy in Norco*. Charleston, SC: Arcadia Publishing, 2011.

Bash, Kevin, and Brigitte Jouxtel. *The Norconian Resort*. Charleston, SC: Arcadia Publishing, 2007.

Berkow, Ira. *The Corporal Was a Pitcher: The Courage of Lou Brissie*. Chicago: Triumph Books, 2009.

Bohman, Charles Frederick. *A Study of the Recreation Programs in Veterans Hospitals* (masters thesis). University of Utah, 1950.

Bradley, Omar. *A General's Life: An Autobiography*. New York: Simon & Schuster, 1983.

Brando, Marlon, with Robert Lindsey. *Songs My Mother Taught Me*. New York: Random House, 1994.

Brittain, Ian. *From Stoke Mandeville to Stratford: A History of the Summer Paralympic Games*. Champaign, IL: Common Ground Publishing, 2012.

Brittain, Ian, and Aaron Beacom (eds). *The Palgrave Handbook of Paralympic Studies*. London: Springer, 2018.

Bussel, Norman. *My Private War: Liberated Body, Captive Mind: A World War II POW's Journey*. New York: Pegasus Books, 2008.

Caddick-Adams, Peter. *Snow and Steel: The Battle of the Bulge, 1944–45*. New York: Oxford University Press, 2014.

Callahan, John. *Don't Worry, He Won't Get Far on Foot: The Autobiography of a Dangerous Man*. New York: William Morrow and Company, 1989.

Campanella, Roy. *It's Good to Be Alive*. Boston: Little, Brown and Company, 1959.

Catapano, Peter, ed., and Rosemarie Garland-Thomson. *About Us: Essays from the Disability Series of* The New York Times. New York: Liveright Publishing Corp., 2019.

Childers, Thomas. *Soldier from the War Returning: The Greatest Generation's Troubled Homecoming from World War II*. Boston: Houghton, Mifflin, Harcourt, 2009.

Cole, Hugh. *The Ardennes: Battle of the Bulge*. Washington, D.C.: U.S. Army, 1977.

Conference on Spinal Cord Injuries. Army Service Forces, 1945. Accessed online: https://collections.nlm.nih.gov/bookviewer?PID=nlm:nlmuid-23810670R -bk#page/1/mode/2up.

Cowdrey, Albert. *Fighting for Life: American Military Medicine in World War II*. New York: The Free Press, 1994.

Cozzens, James Gould. *Guard of Honor*. New York: Harcourt, Brace and Co., 1948.

Crase, Nancy, ed. *Cliff Crase: The Editorials from* Sports 'n Spokes, *1975–2007*. Phoenix: Paralyzed Veterans of America, 2015.

Croizat, Victor. *Journey Among Warriors: The Memoirs of a Marine*. Shippensburg, PA: White Mane Publishing, 1997.

Cushing, Harvey. *From a Surgeon's Journal, 1915–1918*. New York: Little, Brown, 1936.

Daws, Gavan. *Prisoners of the Japanese: POWs of World War II in the Pacific*. New York: William Morrow and Company, 1994.

Dettloff, William. *Ezzard Charles, A Boxing Life*. Jefferson, NC: McFarland and Company, 2015.

Deverich, Linsey. *Wandering through La La Land with the Last Warner Brother*. Bloomington, IN: AuthorHouse, 2007.

Donovan, William. *P.O.W. in the Pacific: Memoirs of an American Doctor in World War II*. Wilmington, DE: Scholarly Resources, 1998.

Dower, John. *War without Mercy: Race and Power in the Pacific War*. New York: Pantheon Books, 1986.

Dyess, Lt. Col. William E. *The Dyess Story: The Eye-Witness Account of the Death March from Bataan and the Narrative of Experiences in Japanese Prison Camps and of Eventual Escape*. New York: Van Rees Press, undated. Viewed online. https://archive.org /stream/dyessstory007009mbp/dyessstory007009mbp_djvu.txt.

Ehrlich, Gertrude. *The Solace of Open Spaces*. New York: Penguin Books, 1985.

Ellsworth, Scott. *The Secret Game: A Wartime Story of Courage, Change, and Basketball's Lost Triumph*. New York: Little, Brown and Company, 2015.

Else, Jon. *True South: Henry Hampton and* Eyes on the Prize, *the Landmark Television Series That Reframed the Civil Rights Movement*. New York: Viking, 2017.

Eltorai, Ibrahim. "History of Spinal Cord Medicine," in *Spinal Cord Medicine: Principles and Practice*. New York: Demos Medical Publishing, 2002.

Feuer, A. B., ed. *Bilibid Diary: The Secret Notebooks of Commander Thomas Hayes, POW, the Philippines, 1942–45.* Hamden, CT: Archon Books, 1987.

Frankel, Glenn. *High Noon: The Hollywood Blacklist and the Making of an American Classic.* New York: Bloomsbury, 2017.

Fussell, Paul. *Wartime: Understanding and Behavior in the Second World War.* New York: Oxford University Press, 1989.

Gellhorn, Martha. *Point of No Return.* New York: Open Road Integrated Media, 2016.

Gerber, David, ed. *Disabled Veterans in History.* Ann Arbor: The University of Michigan Press, 2012.

Glusman, John. *Conduct Under Fire: Four American Doctors and Their Fight for Life as Prisoners of the Japanese.* New York: Viking Penguin, 2005.

Goodman, Jack, ed. *While You Were Gone: A Report on Wartime Life in the United States.* New York: Da Capo Press, 1974.

Goodman, Matthew. *The City Game: Triumph, Scandal, and a Legendary Basketball Team.* New York: Ballantine Books, 2019.

Goodman, Susan. *Spirit of Stoke Mandeville: The Story of Ludwig Guttmann.* London: William Collins Sons and Co., 1986.

Gowdy, Curt. *Cowboy at the Mike.* Garden City, NY: Doubleday & Company, 1966.

Gray, Dr. Gerald. "Whatever Happened to Johnny Winterholler?," in Ralph McWhinnie, ed. *Those Good Years at Wyoming U.* Laramie, WY: The University of Wyoming, 1965.

Guttmann, Ludwig. *Textbook of Sport for the Disabled.* Aylesbury, UK: HM+M Publishers, 1976.

Guttmann, Ludwig. "Unpublished Autobiography," viewed at the Wellcome Collection, London.

Guttmann, Ludwig. "Victory Over Paraplegia," in I. Fraser, ed. *Conquest of Disability: Inspiring Accounts of Courage, Fortitude and Adaptability in Conquering Grave Physical Handicaps.* London: Odhams Press, 1956.

Hager, Thomas. *The Demon under the Microscope: From Battlefield Hospitals to Nazi Labs, One Doctor's Heroic Search for the World's First Miracle Drug.* New York: Harmony Books, 2006.

Halberstam, David. *The Coldest Winter: America and the Korean War.* New York: Hyperion Books, 2007.

Hallas, James. *Killing Ground on Okinawa: The Battle for Sugar Loaf Hill.* Westport, CT: Praeger, 1996.

Hampton, Janie. *London Olympics: 1908 and 1948.* Oxford, UK: Shire Publications, 2011.

Hanes, Roy et al., eds. *The Routledge History of Disability.* Abingdon, UK: Routledge, 2018.

Harris, Mark. *Five Came Back: A Story of Hollywood and the Second World War.* New York: Penguin Press, 2014.

Hedrick, Brad, et al. *Wheelchair Basketball.* Washington, DC: Paralyzed Veterans of America, 1994.

Heinemann, Larry. *Paco's Story.* New York: Farrar, Strauss and Giroux, 1986.

Heller, Joseph. *Catch-22.* New York: Scribner Paperback, 1996.

Hersey, John. *Hiroshima.* New York: Vintage Books, 1989.

Hersey, John. *Men on Bataan.* New York: Alfred A. Knopf, 1942.

Hillenbrand, Laura. *Unbroken: A World War II Story of Survival, Resilience, and Redemption.* New York: Random House, 2010.

Ibuse, Masuji. *Black Rain.* John Bester, trans. Palo Alto: Kodansha International/USA, Ltd., 1970.

Jackson, Col. Calvin G. *Diary of Col. Calvin G. Jackson, M.D.* Ada, Ohio: Ohio Northern University Press, 1992. Accessed online. https://babel.hathitrust.org/cgi/pt?id=wu.89095872677.

James, D. Clayton. *The Years of MacArthur, Volumes One and Two.* Boston: Houghton Mifflin, 1970 and 1975.

Jennings, Audra. *Out of the Horrors of War: Disability Politics in World War II America.* Philadelphia: University of Pennsylvania Press, 2016.

Jones, Tom. *The Real Tom Jones: Handicapped? Not Me.* Lincoln, NE: iUniverse, Inc., 2003.

Juette, Melvin, and Ronald Berger. *Wheelchair Warrior: Gangs, Disability, and Basketball.* Philadelphia: Temple University Press, 2008.

Kentner, Robert. *Kentner's Journal: Bilibid Prison, Manila, P.I. from 12-8-41 to 2-5-45.* Washington, DC: U.S. Army Medical Service, 1946. Accessed online: https://archive.org/details/KentnersJournal/page/n3.

Kerr, E. Bartlett. *Surrender and Survival: The Experience of American POWs in the Pacific 1941–1945.* New York: William Morrow and Company, 1985.

Kessler, Henry. *The Crippled and the Disabled.* New York: Columbia University Press, 1935.

Kinder, John. *Paying with Their Bodies: American War and the Problem of the Disabled Veteran.* Chicago: The University of Chicago Press, 2015.

Kovic, Ron. *Born on the Fourth of July.* New York: McGraw-Hill, 1976.

Kramer, Stanley. *A Mad, Mad, Mad, Mad World.* New York: Harcourt Brace & Company, 1997.

Labanowich, Stan. *Wheelchair Basketball.* Danbury, CT: Capstone Press, 1998.

Labanowich, Stanley. *Wheelchair Basketball: A History of the National Association and an Analysis of the Structure and Organization of Teams* (doctoral thesis). University of Illinois at Urbana-Champaign, 1975.

Labanowich, Stan, and Armand Thiboutot. *Wheelchairs Can Jump! A History of Wheelchair Basketball.* Boston: Acanthus Publishing, 2011.

Layton, Robin. *Hoop: The American Dream.* New York: powerHouse Books, 2013.

Le Clair, Jill, ed. *Disability in the Global Sports Arena: A Sporting Chance.* London: Routledge, 2014.

Lepore, Jill. *These Truths: A History of the United States.* New York: W. W. Norton & Company, 2018.

Lukacs, John D. *Escape from Davao: The Forgotten Story of the Most Daring Prison Break of the Pacific War.* New York: Simon & Schuster, 2010.

Macrakis, Kristie. *Surviving the Swastika: Scientific Research in Nazi Germany.* New York: Oxford University Press, 1993.

Maisel, Albert. *Miracles of Military Medicine.* New York: Stratford Press, 1943.

Manchester, William. *Goodbye, Darkness: A Memoir of the Pacific War.* Boston: Little, Brown and Company, 1980.

Manso, Peter. *Brando: The Biography.* New York: Hyperion, 1994.

Maraniss, Andrew. *Games of Deception: The True Story of the First U.S. Olympic Basketball Team at the 1936 Olympics in Hitler's Germany*. New York: Philomel Books, 2019.

Maraniss, David. *Rome 1960: The Olympics That Changed the World*. New York: Simon & Schuster, 2008.

Marble, Sanders. *Rehabilitating the Wounded: Historical Perspective on Army Policy*. Washington, DC: Office of Medical History, 2008.

Maudlin, Bill. *Back Home*. New York: William Sloane Associates, 1947.

McBee, Fred, and Jack Ballinger. *Continental Quest: First Wheelchair Crossing of North America*. Tampa: Overland Press, 1997.

McCracken, Alan. *Very Soon Now, Joe*. New York: Hobson Book Press, 1947.

McGee, John. *Rice and Salt: Resistance, Capture and Escape on Mindanao*. San Antonio, TX: The Naylor Company, 1962.

Miller, J. Michael. *From Shanghai to Corregidor: Marines in the Defense of the Philippines*. From the Marines in World War II Commemorative Series, produced by the Marine Corps History and Museums Division. Accessed online: https://www.nps.gov/parkhistory/online_books/npswapa/extcontent /usmc/pcn-190-003140-00/index.htm.

Miller, Merle. *That Winter*. New York: William Sloane Associates, 1945.

Miller, Thomas, ed. *The Praeger Handbook of Veterans' Health: History, Challenges, Issues and Developments*. Santa Barbara: ABC-CLIO, LLC, 2012.

Morris, David. *The Evil Hours: A Biography of Post-Traumatic Stress Disorder*. New York: Houghton Mifflin Harcourt, 2015.

Murphy, Robert. *The Body Silent*. New York: W. W. Norton, 1990.

Newell, Rob. *From Playing Field to Battlefield: Great Athletes Who Served in World War II*. Annapolis, MD: Naval Institute Press, 2006.

Nichols, David, ed. *Ernie's War: The Best of Ernie Pyle's World War II Dispatches*. New York: Random House, 1986.

O'Farrell, Elizabeth Kinzer. *WW II: A Navy Nurse Remembers*. Tallahassee, FL: CyPress Publications, 2007.

Ornoff, Anita Bloom. *Beyond Dancing: A Veteran's Struggle—A Woman's Triumph*. Silver Spring, MD: Bartleby Press, 2003.

Oshinsky, David. *Polio: An American Story*. New York: Oxford University Press, 2005.

Ossad, Steven. *Omar Nelson Bradley: America's GI General, 1893–1981*. Columbia: University of Missouri Press, 2017.

Owen, Ed. *Playing and Coaching Wheelchair Basketball*. Urbana, IL: University of Illinois Press, 1982.

Pelka, Fred. *What We Have Done: An Oral History of the Disability Rights Movement*. Amherst, MA: University of Massachusetts Press, 2012.

Poore, Carol. *Disability in Twentieth-Century German Culture*. Ann Arbor: The University of Michigan Press, 2010.

Pyle, Ernie. *Brave Men*. New York: Henry Holt and Company, 1944.

Rampersad, Arnold. *Jackie Robinson: A Biography*. New York: Alfred A. Knopf, 1997.

Reaume, Geoffrey. *Lyndhurst: Canada's First Rehabilitation Centre for People with Spinal Cord Injuries, 1945–1998*. Montreal: McGill-Queen's University Press, 2007.

"Report on American Prisoners of War Interned by the Japanese in the Philippines," prepared by the Office of the Provost Marshall General, Nov. 19, 1945. Accessed online: http://www.mansell.com/pow_resources/camplists/philippines /pows_in_pi-OPMG_report.html.

Rusk, Howard A. *A World to Care For.* New York: Random House, 1972.

Savitz, Harriet May. *Wheelchair Champions: A History of Wheelchair Sports.* New York: Thomas Y. Crowell, 1978.

Schrijvers, Peter. *Those Who Hold Bastogne: The True Story of the Soldiers and Civilians Who Fought in the Biggest Battle of the Bulge.* New Haven: Yale University Press, 2014.

Schweik, Susan. *The Ugly Laws: Disability in Public.* New York: New York University Press, 2009.

Scott, James. *Rampage: MacArthur, Yamashita, and the Battle of Manila.* New York: W. W. Norton, 2018.

Scruton, Joan. *Stoke Mandeville: Road to the Paralympics: Fifty Years of History.* Brill, Aylesbury, UK: The Peterhouse Press, 1998.

Shapiro, Joseph. *No Pity: People with Disabilities Forging a New Civil Rights Movement.* New York: Crown, 1993.

Sidrer, Ethel. *The Development of Wheelchair Athletics in the United States* (master's thesis). Pennsylvania State University Graduate School, College of Health, Physical Education and Recreation, 1971.

Sledge, E. B. *With the Old Breed at Peleliu and Okinawa.* New York: Ballantine Books, 1981.

Spoto, Donald. *A Girl's Got to Breathe: The Life of Teresa Wright.* Jackson, MS: University of Mississippi Press, 2016.

Stafford, George. *Sports for the Handicapped.* New York: Prentice-Hall, 1947.

Stark, Douglas. *Wartime Basketball: The Emergence of a National Sport during World War II.* Lincoln: University of Nebraska Press, 2016.

Stockman, James. *The First Marine Division on Okinawa: 1 April–30 June 1945.* Washington, DC: Historical Division, U.S. Marine Corps, 1946. Accessed online: https://archive.org/details/firstmarinedivis00stoc/page/n5.

Strohkendl, Horst. *The 50th Anniversary of Wheelchair Basketball.* New York: Waxmann Publishing, 1996.

Szyman, Robert. *The Effect of Participation in Wheelchair Sports* (dissertation). University of Illinois at Urbana–Champaign, 1980.

Tate, Loren, and Jared Gelfond. *A Century of Orange and Blue: Celebrating 100 Years of Fighting Illini Basketball.* Champaign, IL: Sports Publishing, 2004.

Timberg, Robert. *Blue-Eyed Boy: A Memoir.* New York: Penguin Press, 2014.

Tobin, James. *The Man He Became: How FDR Defied Polio to Win the Presidency.* New York: Simon & Schuster, 2013.

Tomizawa, Roy. *1964: The Greatest Year in the History of Japan: How the Tokyo Olympics Symbolized Japan's Miraculous Rise from the Ashes.* Carson City, NV: Lioncrest Publishing, 2019.

Truman, Harry. *Harry S. Truman: Public Papers of the Presidents of the United States.* Washington, DC: U.S. Government Printing Office, 1966.

Tumidajski, Jack. *Quadalajara: The Utopia That Once Was.* Binghamton, NY: Brundage Publishing, 2005.

Valens, E. G. *The Other Side of the Mountain.* New York: Warner Books, 1977.

Van Ells, Mark D. *To Hear Only Thunder Again: America's World War II Veterans Come Home.* Lanham, MD: Lexington Books, 2001.

Vonnegut, Kurt. *Slaughterhouse-Five.* New York: Dell Publishing, 1969.

Wallace, Frederic. *Pushing for Cushing in War and Peace: A History of Cushing Hospital, 1943–1991.* Framingham, MA: Damianos Publishing, 2015.

Wallechinsky, David. *The Complete Book of the Summer Olympics.* New York: The Overlook Press, 2000.

Waugh, Evelyn. *Sword of Honour.* Boston: Little, Brown and Company, 1961.

Weinstein, Alfred. *Barbed-Wire Surgeon.* New York: The MacMillan Company, 1948.

Wheeler, Kevin. *We Are the Wounded.* New York: E. P. Dutton & Company, 1945.

Wilkman, Bill. "Norconian Property: Historic Resources Survey & Evaluation, Hospital Era (1941–1957)." Draft Report, 2015.

Williams, Ted. *Rogues of Bataan.* New York: Carlton Press, 1979.

Wolfe, Don, ed. *The Purple Testament: Life Stories of Disabled Veterans.* Harrisburg PA: Stackpole Sons, 1946.

Wouk, Herman. *The Caine Mutiny.* New York: Doubleday, 1979.

Wright Jr., John. *Captured on Corregidor: Diary of an American P.O.W. in World War II.* Jefferson, NC: McFarland & Company, 1988.

Yost, E., and L. M. Gilbreth. *Normal Lives for the Disabled.* New York: Macmillan, 1944.

Zinnemann, Fred. *A Life in the Movies: An Autobiography.* New York: Charles Scribner's Sons, 1992.

Zupan, Mark, and Tim Swanson. *Gimp.* New York: HarperCollins, 2006.

Select Articles from Newspapers, Magazines, Journals, and Websites

Abrahamson, Alan, and Wayne Wilson. "Marty Ball: An Oral History." LA84 Foundation, Jan. 10, 2019.

"America's Wars," published by the U.S. Department of Veterans Affairs. Viewed online: https://www.va.gov/opa/publications/factsheets/fs_americas_wars.pdf.

Anderson, Julie. "'Turned into Taxpayers': Paraplegia, Rehabilitation and Sport at Stoke Mandeville, 1944–56." *Journal of Contemporary History*, July 2003.

Anderson, Ted. "Meet Gil Moss." *Paraplegia News*, November 1956.

Anderson, Ted. "Meet Pat Grissom." *Paraplegia News*, March 1958.

Anderson, Ted. "The Men." Unpublished account of his military service in the Fred Zinnemann Collection, the Academy of Motion Picture Arts and Science Library.

Anderson, Ted. "Paraplegia in Review." *Paraplegia News*, February 1957.

Anderson, Ted. "Paraplegic GI." *Los Angeles Times*, February 26, 1950.

Baker, Michael. "Military Medical Advances Resulting from the Conflict in Korea, Part 1." *Military Medicine*, Vol. 177, April 2012.

Baldwin, Hanson. "The Fall of Corregidor." *American Heritage*, August 1966.

Barton, Betsey. "23,000,000 Disabled: A Challenge to Us." *New York Times*, January 19, 1947.

Baum, Geraldine. "He Goes to Bat for Disabled Athletes." *Newsday*, April 29, 1984.

Bedbrook, Sir George. "The Development and Care of Spinal Cord Paralysis (1918 to 1986)." *Paraplegia* 25, 1987.

Bedbrook, Sir George. "Ludwig Guttmann: Man of an Age." International Medical Society of Paraplegia, First Ludwig Guttmann Memorial Lecture. *Paraplegia* 20, 1982.

Bors, Ernest. "Regeneration of the Spinal Cord." *Paraplegia News*, December 1955.

Bors, Ernest. "Spinal Cord Injuries." *Veterans Administration Technical Bulletin* 10, December 15, 1948.

Bors, Ernest. "The Spinal Cord Injury Center of the Veterans Administration Hospital, Long Beach, California, U.S.A.: Facts and Thoughts." *Spinal Cord*, November 1967.

Bors, Ernest. "Urological Aspects of Rehabilitation in Spinal Cord Injuries." *Journal of the American Medical Association*, May 19, 1951.

Brando, Marlon. "Thirty Days in a Wheel Chair." *Varsity Magazine*, April 1950.

Breu, Giovanna. "Tim Nugent Helps Disabled Students at Illinois." *People*, November 28, 1977.

Brittain, Ian, et al. "The Genesis and Meaning of the Term 'Paralympic Games.'" *Journal of Olympic History*, Vol. 27, No. 2, 2019.

Brodner, Donald. "A Pioneer in Optimism: The Legacy of Donald Munro, MD." *The Journal of Spinal Cord Medicine*, August 2009.

Bull, Albert. "Sir Ludwig Guttmann: From a Grateful Patient." *Paraplegia* 17, 1979.

Cantwell, Robert. "An Era Shaped by War." *Sports Illustrated*, November 30, 1964.

"Champions—Yet Not." *Paraplegia News*, September 1957.

Christensen, Jeanne. "Meet Junius Kellogg." *Paraplegia News*, October 1960.

Clausen, Christopher. "The President and the Wheelchair." *Wilson Quarterly*, Summer 2005.

Comarr, A. Estin. "Reconstructive Surgery in Spinal Cord Injuries." *Journal of the American Medical Association*, May 19, 1951.

Connor, Joseph. "Let There Be Light: How a Film on PTSD Worried the Army." *World War II Magazine*, March–April 2017.

Crewe, Nancy, and James Krause. "Spinal Cord Injury," in *Medical, Psychosocial and Vocational Aspects of Disability*, Martin Brodwin et al., eds. Athens, GA: Elliott & Fitzpatrick, 2009.

"Data on Veterans of the Korean War," published by the Office of Program and Data Analyses, June 2000. Viewed online: https://www.va.gov/vetdata/docs/SpecialReports/KW2000.pdf.

Den Adel, Stanley, "Wheelchair Basketball Team Makes Nationwide Tour," in *PVA News Bulletin*, March 26, 1948.

Donovan, William. "Spinal Cord Injury—Past, Present, and Future." *The Journal of Spinal Cord Medicine*, Vol. 30(2), 2007.

"'Dummy' Hoy." *Deaf Life Magazine*, November and December 1992.

"Famous Negro Athlete Conquers Paralysis." *Performance*, May 1958.

Flanagan, Steven, and Leonard Diller. "Dr. George Deaver: The Grandfather of Rehabilitation Medicine." *The American Academy of Physical Medicine and Rehabilitation*, May 2013.

Florescu, Steve. "Tokyo and Back." *Paraplegia News*, January 1965.

Flury, Bob. "Sports Shavings." Monthly columns and reports in *Paraplegia News*, 1958–1961.

Fraley, Oscar. "Wounded War Veterans." *Daily Herald*, February 3, 1948.

Frost, Dennis. "Tokyo's Other Games: The Origins and Impact of the 1964 Para- lympics." *International Journal of the History of Sport* 29 (4): 2012, 619–637.

Garland-Thomson, Rosemarie. "From Medical Condition to Political Condition: The Story of the ADA." *Los Angeles Review of Books*, February 22, 2017.

Glusman, John. "Heroes and Sons: Coming to Terms." *The Virginia Quarterly Review*, Autumn 1990.

Groth, John. "Hanging in There." *Paraplegia News*, May 2017.

Guttmann, Ludwig. "Claim Made That PN & Sports Editor Are Irresponsible." *Paraplegia News*, December 1957.

Guttmann, Ludwig. "Coming-of-Age of the National Spinal Injuries Centre." *The Cord*, Winter 1964–65.

Guttmann, Ludwig. "Competitive Sports and Physical Medicine." *Paraplegia News*, November 1953.

Guttmann, Ludwig. "New Hope for Spinal Cord Sufferers." *Paraplegia*, 1979 (17). (Originally published in *Medical Times*, November 1945.)

Guttmann, Ludwig. "Looking Back on a Decade." *The Cord*, 6 (4): 1954(a), 9–23.

Guttmann, Ludwig. "Married Life of Paraplegics and Tetraplegics." Papers Read at the 1964 Scientific Meeting, *Paraplegia*, 182–188.

Guttmann, Ludwig. "Message to the Competitors in the Stoke Mandeville Games." Program for the Rome 1960 Paralympics, published in *The Cord*, Fall 1960.

Guttmann, Ludwig. "'Olympic Games for the Disabled.'" *World Sports*, October 1952.

Guttmann, Ludwig. "Oral History." Imperial War Museums. Interviewed by Margaret Brooks, February 18, 1980. Accessed online: https://www.iwm.org.uk/collections /item/object/80004556.

Guttmann, Ludwig. "The Value of Sport for the Severely Handicapped," and "Development of Sport for the Spinal Paralyzed," parts 1 and 2, *Olympic Review*, Nos. 109–111, n/d.

Guttmann, Ludwig. "Statistical Survey on One Thousand Paraplegics." *Proceedings of the Royal Society of Medicine*, Joint Meeting, Vol. 47, 1954.

Hamburger, Philip. "The Boys in Maroon." *The New Yorker*, September 25, 1943.

Hamowy, Ronald. "Failure to Provide Healthcare at the Veterans Administration." Independent Policy Reports, The Independent Institute, 2010.

Heimburger, Robert. "The Paralyzed Veterans of America: Eyewitness to History." *Paraplegia News*, March 2006.

"'Herald Man,'" *Bucks Herald*, August 3, 1956.

Hohmann, George. "Obituary: Ernest H. J. Bors, MD (1900–1990)." *Paraplegia* 29, 1991.

Holmes, Oliver Wendell, and Supreme Court of the United States. *U.S. Reports: Buck v. Bell, 274 U.S. 200*. 1926. Viewed online: https://www.loc.gov/item /usrep274200.

Howard, Tom. "Lovell Honors Veterans of World War II." *Billings Gazette*, June 30, 1985.

Izenberg, Jerry. "Jerry Izenberg at Large." *Syracuse Post-Standard*, June 11, 1965.

Jackson, R. W. "Sport for the Spinal Paralysed Person." *Paraplegia* 25, 1987.

Jares, Joe. "A Baker's Dream Needs Dough." *Sports Illustrated*, September 7, 1970.

Jefferson, Robert. "'Enabled Courage': Race, Disability, and Black World War II Veterans in Postwar America." *The Historian*, September 2003.

"Joseph Bulova School." Company History. n/d.

Kahn, Roger. "Success and Ned Irish." *Sports Illustrated*, March 27, 1961.

Kamenetz, Herman. "A Brief History of the Wheelchair." *Journal of the History of Medicine*, April 1969.

Keefer, Louis. "Birth and Death of the Army Specialized Training Program." *Army History*, Winter 1995.

Labanowich, Stan. "A Brief History of the National Wheelchair Basketball Association: The First 25 Years, 1948 to 1973." *Palaestra*, Summer 1995.

Labanowich, Stan. "The Physically Disabled in Sports: Tracing the Influence of Two Tracks of a Common Movement." *Sports 'n Spokes*, March–April 1987.

Labanowich, Stan. "Wheelchair Basketball Classification: National and International Perspectives." *Palaestra*, Spring 1988.

Laird, Lulu. "I Married a Paraplegic." *Coronet*, May 1950.

Lehman, Milton. "The War's Not Over for Them." *Saturday Evening Post*, February 28, 1948.

Level, Hildegard. "The Miracle of Ramp C." *Hygeia*, September 1949.

Linker, Beth, and Whitney Laemmli. "Half a Man: The Symbolism and Science of Paraplegic Impotence in World War II America." *Osiris*, 2015.

Lipton, Benjamin. "Bulova School of Watchmaking 12 Yrs. Old." *Paraplegia News*, July 1957.

Lipton, Benjamin. "The Role of Wheelchair Sports in Rehabilitation." *International Rehabilitation Review*, Vol. XX1, No. 2, 1970.

Mathers, Carol. "Recreation Is Important." *News-Gazette*, March 8, 1972.

Maurer, David. "Veteran Remembers 'the Forgotten War.'" *Daily Progress*, November 22, 2010.

"Meet Dr. Bors." *Paraplegia News*, October 1955.

"Meet Dr. Rusk." *Paraplegia News*, August 1956.

"Meet the Editor." *Paraplegia News*, April 1955.

"Meet H. A. Everest." *Paraplegia News*, December 1955.

"Meet Ted Anderson." *Paraplegia News*, June 1955.

Miller, Bob, et al. "In Grateful Memory of Dr. James Naismith." Letter in the James Naismith Collection, Duane Norman Diedrich Collection, William L. Clements Library, University of Michigan. November 6, 1948.

Morris, S. W. "Sports Heal War Neuroses." *Recreation Magazine*, October 1945.

Mosby, Aline. "Cycle of Films," *Daily Worker*, August 23, 1949.

Moss, Robert. "To Paraplegics of the Korean War." *Paraplegia News*, June 1951.

Munro, Donald. "Thoracic and Lumbosacral Cord Injuries: A Study of Forty Cases." *Journal of the American Medical Association*, Vol. 122, No. 16, August 14, 1943.

Murdock, Lorinda. "Veterans Dedicate Plaque." *Valley News*, December 16, 1980.

Murray, Jim. "Better Half." *Los Angeles Times*, September 30, 1964.

Mydans, Carl. "The Rescue at Cabanatuan." *Life*, February 26, 1945.

National Wheelchair Basketball Association annual tournament programs, 1949–1964.

"The New Kind of Veterans' Hospitals." *Woman's Home Companion*, February 1947.

Nicosia, Angelo and Lynn Phillips. "An Overview . . . with Reflections Past and Present of a Consumer." From "Choosing a Wheelchair System," in *Journal of Rehabilitation and Development Clinical Supplement #2.* Department of Veterans Affairs, September 1992.

Nugent, Timothy J. "Founder of the University of Illinois Disabled Students Program and the National Wheelchair Basketball Association, Pioneer in Architectural Access," interview conducted by Fred Pelka, 2004–2005, Regional Oral History Office, The Bancroft Library, University of California, Berkeley, 2009.

Nugent, Timothy. "Let's Look Beyond. . ." n/d. Viewed online: https://archives.library.illinois .edu/erec/University%20Archives/1606018/Box2/1606018_002_059_001_nugent _look_beyond_meaning.pdf.

Nugent, Timothy. "Reflections: From Nothing to Something and What It's Meant." Paper presented at the Seward Staley Symposium, March 15, 1984.

"An Observer Answers Dr. Guttmann." *Paraplegia News,* December 1957.

Ochmann, Sophie, and Max Roser. "Polio." *Our World in Data.* Viewed online: https://ourworldindata.org/polio.

"An Oral History of the Paralyzed Veterans of America." PVA, 1985. Accessed online: https://www.azpva.org/wp-content/uploads/2017/07/history_oral.pdf.

"Our Champion." *Paraplegia News,* March 1959.

"'Paralympics' of 1953," *Bucks Advertiser & Aylesbury News,* June 26, 1953.

"Paralympics of 1953," *Time,* August 17, 1953.

"Paraplegics: The Conquest of Unconquerable Odds." *Newsweek,* March 22, 1948.

Paul, John. "Thomas Francis, 1900–1969: A Biographical Memoir." National Academy of Sciences, 1974.

Pollak, Lisa. "The Other Ravens." *Baltimore Sun,* September 1, 1996.

Price, John. "Meet Harry Schweikert." *Paraplegia News,* February 1957.

"A Promise Kept." *The Link,* October 1953.

Rademeyer, Cobus. "Guttmann's Ingenuity: The Paralympic Games as Legacy of the Second World War." *Historia,* May 2015.

Reagan, Leslie. "Timothy Nugent: 'Wheelchair Students' and the Creation of the Most Accessible Campus in the World," In Frederick Hoxie, ed. *The University of Illinois: Engine of Innovation.* Champaign: University of Illinois Press, 2017.

Reagan, Ronald. "Remarks at the Opening of the 1984 International Games for the Disabled." June 17, 1984. Viewed online: https://www.reaganlibrary.gov /research/speeches/61784a.

"Recreation in Veterans Administration Hospitals." *Recreation Magazine,* May 1951.

"The Rehabilitation of Junius Kellogg." *Newsday,* January 29, 1978.

"Remarks of President George Bush at the Signing of the Americans with Disabilities Act." July 26, 1990. https://www.eeoc.gov/eeoc/history/35th/videos /ada_signing_text.html.

"Repair Shop for Heroes." *Popular Mechanics,* November 1944.

Robertson, Fyfe. "Making New Men." *Picture Post,* September 3, 1949.

Robinson, Elsie. "Lest We Forget," from her "Listen, World!" column, *The Evening News,* May 20, 1947.

Rodney, Lester. "Vets Who Score the Hard Way." *Daily Worker,* February 4, 1948.

"Roger Bannister: Sportsman of the Year." *Sports Illustrated,* January 3, 1955.

Rogers, Jane. "Ray Werner: Wheelchair Basketball Pioneer." *Smithsonian*, February 5, 2016.

Roosevelt, Eleanor. "My Day: April 28, 1943." Digital edition at George Washington University. Accessed online. https://www2.gwu.edu/~erpapers/myday/display doc.cfm?_y=1943&_f=md056482.

Rusk, Howard. "Living with What's Left," *American Journal of Surgery*, November 1949.

Rusk, Howard. "Physical Handicaps Helped by Psycho-Social Services." *Paraplegia News*, May 1949.

Rusk, Howard. "Rehabilitation." *Journal of the American Medical Association*, May 21, 1949.

Ryan, Bob. "These Guys Wheel, Deal." *Boston Globe*, n/d.

Ryder, Charles. "The 1960 Paralympics." *Paraplegia News*, November 1960.

Sailors, Kenny. "Oral History." University of Wyoming, American Heritage Center. Interviewed by William Schrage and Dennis Dreyer, February 26, 2011. Accessed online: http://digitalcollections.uwyo.edu/luna/servlet/detail /uwydbuwy%7E91%7E91%7E1895033%7E258372:Oral-History-Interview -with-Kenny-S.

Saltman, Jules. "Paraplegia: A Head, A Heart, and Two Big Wheels." New York: Public Affairs Pamphlet, 1960. Accessed online: https://hdl.handle.net/2027 /uiug.30112059892965.

Schweikert, Harry. "The History of Wheelchair Basketball." Appeared in *Paraplegia News,* May 1954, and in the annual programs of the National Wheelchair Basketball Tournament.

Schweikert, Harry. "The Paralyzed Veterans of America 25 Years Later." *Paraplegia News*, July 1971. Accessed online: https://www.azpva.org/wp-content/uploads /2017/07/history_25years.pdf.

Schweikert, Harry. "Sports Highlights" and "The Handicapped in Sports." Monthly columns and articles in *Paraplegia News*, 1948–1958.

Scotch, Richard. "'Nothing About Us Without Us': Disability Rights in America." *OAH Magazine of History*, July 2009.

Scruton, Joan. "The Legacy of Sir Ludwig Guttmann." *Palaestra*, Spring 1998.

Shaplen, Robert. "The Freeing of Bilibid." *The New Yorker*, March 3, 1945.

Silver, John. "History of the Treatment of Spinal Injuries." *Postgrad Medical Journal*, 2005.

Silver, John. "Ludwig Guttmann's Memorandum." *Spinal Cord Series and Cases*, 2017 (3). Viewed online: https://www.ncbi.nlm.nih.gov/pmc/articles/PMC5550927/.

Silver, John. "Ludwig Guttmann (1899–1980), Stoke Mandeville Hospital and the Paralympic Games." *Journal of Medical Biography* 20, 2012.

Silver, John. "The Making of Ludwig Guttmann." *Journal of Medical Biography*, July 15, 2013.

Silver, John. "The Role of Sport in the Rehabilitation of Patients with Spinal Injuries." *Journal of the Royal College of Physicians of Edinburgh* 34, 2004.

Silver, John, and Weiner, M-F. "George Riddoch: The Man Who Found Ludwig Guttmann." *Spinal Cord*, 2012. Viewed online: https://www.nature.com/articles /sc2011117.pdf?origin=ppub.

Sobocinski, André. "History of Wheelchair Basketball." *Navy Medicine*, Summer 2013.

Smead, Fred. Speech given at Birmingham High School, December 15, 1980.

Smith, Helena Huntington. "They're Still the Same Inside." *Woman's Home Companion*, October 1945.

Smith, Marcia. "Dad's Deeds Left an Impression." *Orange County Register*, June 18, 2006.

Spears, Ethel. "Jets Wheel to Victory." *Journal of Rehabilitation*, July 1, 1958.

Stavis, Barrie. "'We Will Walk.'" *Saturday Evening Post*, March 30, 1946.

Sullivan, Ed. "Little Old New York." *The Morning Herald*, January 2, 1948.

Summar, Polly. "Ms. Kids." *Daily Illini*, April 10, 1974.

Sussillo, Jerry, and Phil Faustman. "We Live in a VA Hospital." *Coronet*, September 1949.

Taaffe, Dorothy. "Working at Play." *Recreation Magazine*, December 1947.

Talbot, Herbert. "A Report of Sexual Function in Paraplegics." *Paraplegia News*, November 1950.

"Teaching the Crippled to Walk." *Life Magazine*, May 5, 1947.

"Ted Anderson Dies in Van Nuys Home." *Paraplegia News*, November 1958.

"They Walk Again." *Newsweek*, September 24, 1945.

"38 Years of Progress and a Look into the Future for the Disabled." An interview with Timothy Nugent. *Accent on Living*, Summer 1985.

"Tupperware of Japan Sponsors W/C Basketball." *Paraplegia News*, September 1965.

Tweedie, Neil. "The Olympic Hero They Kept in Hiding." *London Telegraph*, July 4, 2012. Accessed online: https://www.telegraph.co.uk/sport/olympics/9373096/The-Olympic-hero-they-kept-in-hiding.html.

"U.S. Exec Here Leads Campaign for Crippled." *Japan Times*, February 13, 1965.

Valiunas, Algis. "Jonas Salk, the People's Scientist." *The New Atlantis*, Summer/Fall 2018.

Van Dyck, Dave. "Tim Nugent Recalls Lean, Fun Times in Wheelchairs. *News-Gazette*, March 31, 1970.

"We Are Responsible." *Paraplegia News*, December 1957.

"Wheelchair Sportsmen." *Bucks Herald*, August 5, 1955.

Whitteridge, D. "Ludwig Guttmann: 3 July 1899–18 March 1980." From *Biographical Memoirs of Fellows of the Royal Society*, Vol. 29, November 1983.

Williams, Pat. "The Man Who Turned Broken Men into Winners." *Daily Mail*, n/d. Viewed at Wellcome Collection.

Wolff, Alexander. "The Olden Rules." *Sports Illustrated*, November 25, 2002.

Zaks, Rich. "Nugent, Abner Doubleday of Wheelchair Sports." *Champaign-Urbana Courier*, June 21, 1970.

Zelazny, Jon. "The Dawn of Brando: Richard Erdman Remembers 'The Men.'" Eight Million Stories.com, Feb. 6, 2010, accessed via The Hollywood Interview.com, September 2008.

Select Films

Act of Violence. Dir. Fred Zinnemann. MGM, 1949. Viewed on DVD.

Attack. Dir. Robert Aldrich. United Artists, 1956. Viewed on DVD.

Back to Bataan. Dir. Edward Dmytryk. RKO Radio Pictures, 1945. Viewed on DVD.

Backfire. Dir. Vincent Sherman. Warner Bros., 1950. Viewed on DVD.

Bad Day at Black Rock. Dir. John Sturges. MGM, 1955. Viewed on DVD.

Band of Brothers. Dir. Phil Alden Robinson, et al. HBO, 2001. Viewed on DVD.

Bataan. Dir. Tay Garnett. MGM, 1943. Viewed on DVD.

Battle Cry. Dir. Raoul Walsh. Warner Bros., 1955. Viewed on DVD.

Battle of the Bulge. Dir. Ken Annakin. Warner Bros., 1965. Viewed on DVD.

Battleground. Dir. William Wellman. MGM, 1949. Viewed on DVD.

The Best Years of Our Lives. Dir. William Wyler. Samuel Goldwyn Productions, 1946. Viewed on DVD.

The Big Red One. Dir. Samuel Fuller. United Artists, 1980. Viewed on DVD.

The Blue Dahlia. Dir. George Marshall. Paramount, 1946. Viewed on DVD.

Body of War. Dirs. Ellen Spiro and Phil Donahue. Film Sales Company, 2007. Viewed on DVD.

Born on the Fourth of July. Dir. Oliver Stone. Universal Pictures, 1989. Viewed on DVD.

Bright Victory. Dir. Mark Robson. Universal Pictures, 1951. Viewed on TCM, November 18, 2018.

Coming Home. Dir. Hal Ashby. United Artists, 1978. Viewed on DVD.

Corregidor. Dir. William Nigh. Producers Releasing Corp., 1943. Viewed on DVD.

Crossfire. Dir. Edward Dmytryk. RKO Pictures, 1947. Viewed on DVD.

Debt of Honor: Disabled Veterans in American History. Dir. Ric Burns. PBS, 2015.

Destination Tokyo. Dir. Delmer Daves. Warner Bros., 1943. Viewed on DVD.

Dive Bomber. Dir. Michael Curtiz. Warner Bros., 1941. Viewed on DVD.

The Fighting Sullivans. Dir. Lloyd Bacon. 20th Century Fox, 1944. Viewed on DVD.

Five Came Back. Dir. Laurent Bouzereau. Netflix, 2017. Viewed on DVD.

Flying Leathernecks. Dir. Nicholas Ray. RKO Radio Pictures, 1951. Viewed on DVD.

Guadalcanal Diary. Dir. Lewis Seiler. 20th Century Fox, 1943. Viewed on DVD.

Gung Ho! Dir. Ray Enright. Universal Pictures, 1943. Viewed on DVD.

Hacksaw Ridge. Dir. Mel Gibson. Summit Entertainment, 2016. Viewed on DVD.

Hail the Conquering Hero. Dir. Preston Sturges. Paramount, 1944. Viewed on DVD.

Hangmen Also Die! Dir. Fritz Lang. United Artists, 1943. Viewed on DVD.

Home of the Brave. Dir. Mark Robson. United Artists, 1949. Viewed on DVD.

Ice Warriors: USA Sled Hockey. Dir. Brian Knappenberger. PBS, 2014.

It's a Wonderful Life. Dir. Frank Capra. Republic Pictures, 1946. Viewed on DVD.

Let There Be Light. Dir. John Huston. U.S. Army, 1946. Viewed online. https://www.filmpreservation.org/preserved-films/screening-room/let-there-be-light-1946.

Letters from Iwo Jima. Dir. Clint Eastwood. DreamWorks Pictures, 2006. Viewed on DVD.

Lifeboat. Dir. Alfred Hitchcock. 20th Century Fox, 1944. Viewed on DVD.

Listen to Me Marlon. Dir. Stevan Riley. Passion Pictures, 2015. Viewed on DVD.

The Longest Day. Dirs. Ken Annakin, Andrew Marton, and Bernhard Wicki. 20th Century Fox, 1962. Viewed on DVD.

The Man in the Gray Flannel Suit. Dir. Nunnally Johnson. 20th Century Fox, 1956. Viewed on DVD.

A Matter of Life and Death. Dirs. Michael Powell and Emeric Pressburger. Eagle-Lion Films, 1946. Viewed on DVD.

The Men. Dir. Fred Zinnemann. Republic Pictures, 1950. Viewed on DVD.

Mrs. Miniver. Dir. William Wyler. Metro-Goldwyn-Mayer, 1942. Viewed on DVD.

Never Fear. Dir. Ida Lupino. Eagle-Lion Films, 1949. Viewed on DVD.

The Pacific. Dir. Tim Van Patten, et al. HBO, 2010. Viewed on DVD.

Patton. Dir. Franklin Schaffner. 20th Century Fox, 1970. Viewed on DVD.

Pride of the Marines. Dir. Delmer Daves. Warner Bros., 1945. Viewed on DVD.

The Purple Heart. Dir. Lewis Milestone. 20th Century Fox, 1944. Viewed on DVD.

Run Silent, Run Deep. Dir. Robert Wise. United Artists, 1958. Viewed on DVD.

Saboteur. Dir. Alfred Hitchcock. Universal Pictures, 1942. Viewed on DVD.

Sands of Iwo Jima. Dir. Allan Dwan. Republic Pictures, 1949. Viewed on DVD.

Saving Private Ryan. Dir. Steven Spielberg. DreamWorks Pictures, 1998. Viewed on DVD.

So Proudly We Hail. Dir. Mark Sandrich. Paramount Pictures, 1943. Viewed on DVD.

The Story of G.I. Joe. Dir. William A. Wellman. United Artists, 1945. Viewed on DVD.

The Stratton Story. Dir. Sam Wood. MGM, 1949. Viewed on DVD.

Submarine Command. Dir. John Farrow. Paramount Pictures, 1951. Viewed on DVD.

They Were Expendable. Dir. John Ford. MGM, 1945. Viewed on DVD.

Thirty Seconds Over Tokyo. Dir. Mervyn LeRoy. MGM, 1944. Viewed on DVD.

This Land Is Mine. Dir. Jean Renoir. RKO Radio Pictures, 1943. Viewed on DVD.

Till the End of Time. Dir. Edward Dmytryk. RKO Pictures, 1946. Viewed on DVD.

Tora! Tora! Tora! Dirs. Richard Fleischer, Kinji Fukasaku, and Toshio Masuda. 20th Century Fox, 1970. Viewed on DVD.

Twelve O'Clock High. Dir. Henry King. 20th Century Fox, 1950. Viewed on DVD.

The Undefeated. Dir. Paul Dickson. Worldwide Pictures, 1950. Viewed online via Wellcome Library on December 24, 2018.

Wake Island. Dir. John Farrow. Paramount Pictures, 1942. Viewed on DVD.

Walk in the Sun. Dir. Lewis Milestone. 20th Century Fox, 1945. Viewed on DVD.

Wing and a Prayer. Dir. Henry Hathaway. 20th Century Fox, 1944. Viewed on DVD.

With the Marines at Tarawa. Dir. Louis Hayward. U.S. Marine Corps Photographic Unit, 1944. Viewed online, March 14, 2018.

Select Short Films

Diary of a Sergeant. Dir. Joseph Newman, 1945. Army Pictorial Service Signal Corps. Viewed on June 18, 2018. https://www.youtube.com/watch?v=xp1E5smfSDI.

Half a Chance. Department of Defense, 1946.

Meet McGonegal. Army Service Forces Signal Corps, 1944. Viewed on June 18, 2018. https://www.c-span.org/video/?322505-1/1944-film-meet-mcgonegal.

No Help Wanted. Wilding Pictures Production, n/d. Viewed on June 18, 2018. https://www.youtube.com/watch?v=xtMPWv-9W8A.

Out of Bed into Action. First Motion Picture Unit, Army Air Forces, 1944. Viewed on June 18, 2018. https://www.youtube.com/watch?v=23_OLZqOGl4&feature=youtu.be.

Toward Independence. Dir. George L. George. U.S. Army, 1948. Viewed on June 18, 2018. https://www.youtube.com/watch?v=MDzkxHZC-VI.

Voyage to Recovery. Department of the Navy. Viewed on June 26, 2018. https://www.youtube.com/watch?v=epo3W1aGL1U.

Welcome Home. The War Department, 1947. Viewed on June 26, 2018. https://www.youtube.com/watch?v=Jflu_JLP7RY.

What's My Score? The Veterans Administration, 1946. Viewed on June 26, 2018. https://www.youtube.com/watch?v=AnUqoLQcyRk.

NOTES

Chapter 1

Background about Johnny Winterholler's life, his time in
Lovell, and his athletic career at Wyoming was culled from
newspaper articles, published texts (yearbooks, oral histories,
books), his Official Military Personnel File (OMPF), and
author interviews with family members. The section about
Stan Den Adel's life is based on historical newspaper accounts, published interviews with Den Adel, his own written
accounts, his OMPF, and interviews with his sister. The
section about Gene Fesenmeyer's life is based on numerous
interviews with the author, his OMPF, and conversations
with his siblings. All of his quotations, here and elsewhere
in the book, were from interviews conducted by the author,
except as noted.

1 Curt Gowdy, *Cowboy at the Mike* (New York: Doubleday &
   Company, 1966), 33.
2 "Lovell Honors," *The Billings Gazette*, June 30, 1985, 34.
3 Ibid.
4 Loudon Kelly, *Rocky Mountain News, Casper Star-Tribune*, June
   6, 1939, 6; *Billings Gazette*, June 30, 1985, 34; author interviews.

5 From an oral history by Kenny Sailors, accessed online: http://digitalcollections.uwyo.edu/luna/servlet/detail/uwydbuwy%7E91%7E91%7E1895033%7E258372:Oral-History-Interview-with-Kenny-S.
6 Letter from Arthur Crane dated May 29, 1940. From Winterholler's OMPF.
7 Ibid.
8 John Hersey, *Men on Bataan* (New York: Alfred A. Knopf, 1942), 288–89.
9 *Clarinda Herald-Journal*, December 4, 1941, 4.

Chapter 2

The section about the war in the Pacific theater and Winterholler's POW experience in the Philippines is based on his OMPF, author interviews with his children, newspaper articles, and eyewitness and historical accounts, including Miller's *From Shanghai to Corregidor*; Jackson's *Diary of Col. Calvin G. Jackson, M.D.;* Gray's "Whatever Happened to Johnny Winterholler?"; Glusman's *Conduct Under Fire*; James's *Years of MacArthur*; Daws's *Prisoners of the Japanese*; Donovan's *P.O.W. in the Pacific*; Cowdrey's *Fighting for Life*; Kerr's *Surrender and Survival*; Weinstein's *Barbed-Wire Surgeon*; Feuer's *Bilibid Diary*; Williams's *Rogues of Bataan;* Lukacs's *Escape from Davao*; Baldwin's "Fall of Corregidor"; Dower's *War without Mercy*; Dyess's *The Dyess Story*; McGee's *Rice and Salt*; McCracken's *Very Soon Now*; Wright's *Captured on Corregidor*; Scott's *Rampage*; Shaplen's "Freeing of Bilibid"; Kentner's *Kentner's Journal*.

1 Letter dated November 17, 1941.
2 Letter dated March 26, 1941.
3 Letter dated October 23, 1941.
4 Quoted in J. Michael Miller, *From Shanghai to Corregidor* (Diane Pub Co., 1997).
5 "Splinters," *Casper Star-Tribune*, May 13, 1942, 7.

6   John A. Glusman, *Conduct Under Fire* (New York: Viking Penguin, 2005), 183.

7   "Whatever Happened to Johnny Winterholler," 236.

8   "Testimony of John Winterholler," OMPF file; other accounts vary slightly.

9   Ibid.

10   Ibid.

11   *Twin Falls Times*, April 30, 1945, 6.

12   John D. Lukacs, *Escape from Davao* (New York: Simon & Schuster, 2010), 160.

13   Sailors' Oral History; newspaper accounts.

14   Calvin G. Jackson, *Diary of Col. Calvin G. Jackson, M.D.* (Ada, Ohio: Ohio Northern University, 1992),159–160, 172.

Chapter 3

The section about Stan Den Adel's military career is based on his written remembrances, his OMPF, and author interviews with his sister. Many excellent histories and accounts of the Battle of the Bulge have been published, including Ambrose's *Band of Brothers*, Cole's *The Ardennes*, and, most recently, there's Caddick-Adams's *Snow and Steel* and Schrijvers's *Those Who Hold Bastogne*.

1   From Fifty Questions and Answers on Army Specialized Training Program, quoted in Keefer's "Birth and Death," *Army History*.

2   Den Adel written account.

3   Ibid.

4   See Peter Schrijvers's *Those Who Hold Bastogne* (New Haven: Yale University Press, 2014).

5   Den Adel written account.

6   Ibid.

7   Estimates on casualties vary depending on the source. Viewed online: https://history.army.mil/html/reference/bulge/index.html.

8   Den Adel's written account; OMPF.
9   Den Adel's written account.

Chapter 4

The section about Gene Fesenmeyer's military service is based on numerous interviews with the author and his OMPF. All quotations from Fesenmeyer were taken from interviews conducted by the author except as noted. Perspectives on Okinawa came from (among others) Hallas's *Killing Ground*; Cowdrey's *Fighting for Life*; Stockman's *First Marine Division*; Sledge's *With the Old Breed*; Nichols's *Ernie's War*.

1   Albert E. Cowdrey, *Fighting for Life* (New York: The Free Press, 1994), 315.
2   *Time*, July 23, 1945.
3   *Fighting for Life*, 306.
4   Ernie Pyle from *Ernie's War,* ed. David Nichols (New York: Random House, 1986), 403.
5   Ibid., 404.
6   John Groth, "Hanging in There," *Paraplegia News*, May 2017, 31.
7   The author wrote about this incident and quoted Fesenmeyer in *Los Angeles Magazine*, September 2016.
8   Quoted in David Lawrence, "American Strategy on Southern Okinawa Open to Challenge," *Casper Star-Tribune*, May 31, 1945.

Chapter 5

Details about the injuries and medical care of Winter-holler, Den Adel, and Fesenmeyer came from their written remembrances, their OMPFs, and newspaper accounts. All quotations from Fesenmeyer came from interviews with the author, except as noted. Historical material and descriptions of the spinal cord, spinal-cord injuries, and paraplegia came from medical journals, including books, journal articles, and oral histories from Drs. Cushing, Bors, Munro, Donovan, Silver, Eltorai, Guttmann, Bedbrook, Tribe, Shaw, and Dick. Statistics related to wartime wounds and deaths came from "America's Wars," published by the U.S. Department of Veterans Affairs.

1   Den Adel's written account, OMPF.
2   *Pella Chronicle*, July 19, 1945, 4.
3   Letter dated February 10, 1945.
4   "Winterholler's Marriage," *Casper Star-Tribune*, March 21, 1945, 5.
5   "Winterhollers Hold Reunion," *Casper Star-Tribune*, September 25, 1945, 4.
6   John A. Glusman, *Conduct Under Fire* (New York: Viking Penguin, 2005), 3, 466.
7   Donovan's "Spinal Cord Injury," 85–86.
8   Ibid., 86–87.
9   Ibid.
10 Howard A. Rusk, *A World to Care For* (New York: Random House, 1972), 97.
11 Treves, *American Journal of Care for Cripples,* quoted in David Gerber's *Disabled Veterans in History* (Ann Arbor, Michigan: University of Michigan Press, 2012), 324.
12 Most sources phrase Rusk's quotation this way; a slightly different version appears in Rusk's "Convalescence and Rehabilitation," in the *Proceedings of the American Philosophical Society*, September 1946, 271.

Chapter 6

Biographical information about Drs. Bors and Munro drawn from interviews and articles in both mainstream newspapers and scientific journals, including *Paraplegia* and *Paraplegia News*. Background on the GI Bill and the VA from government documents, *Congressional Record*, American Legion accounts, newspaper and historical accounts.

1 "Meet Dr. Bors," *Paraplegia News*, October 1955, 4.
2 Ibid., 11.
3 Quoted in Jules Saltman's "Paraplegia," 19–20.
4 Ibid., 19.
5 George Hohmann, "Obituary," *Paraplegia*, 1991, 278.
6 Jill Lepore, *These Truths* (New York: W. W. Norton & Company, 2018), 527.
7 Steven L. Ossad, *Omar Bradley* (Columbia: University of Missouri Press, 2017), 342.
8 FDR letter to Henry Stimson, dated December 4, 1944, quoted in Marble's *Rehabilitating*, 49.
9 Quoted in Ossad, *Bradley*, 334.
10 Jessica L. Adler, *Burdens of War* (Baltimore: Johns Hopkins University Press, 2017), 258.
11 Quoted in Ossad, *Bradley*, 356.
12 Rusk, *A World to Care For*, 85; "Living," 551.
13 Holmes, *Buck v. Bell*, 274 U.S. 200.
14 James Tobin, *The Man He Became* (New York: Simon & Schuster, 2013), 166–67, 242.

Chapter 7

Details about Den Adel's rehabilitation and Birmingham Hospital came from his written remembrances, his OMPF, and author interviews with his sister Shirley, Ed Santillanes, Gene Fesenmeyer, the family of Bob Rynearson, and the Rynearson papers.

1 Linsey Deverich, *Wandering Through La La Land with the Last Warner Brother* (Bloomington, IN: AuthorHouse, 2007), 6.
2 From speech given by Smead, December 15, 1980, from Rynearson papers.
3 Frank Anderson, "Hippocrates Would Swear," *Long Beach Independent*, January 13, 1969, 22.

4   Both quotations found in the Fred Zinnemann Papers at the Margaret Herrick Library, Los Angeles.
5   Anderson, "Hippocrates Would Swear," 25.
6   Bors, "Spinal Cord Injury Center," 128.
7   Den Adel written remembrances.
8   Author interview.
9   Rusk, *A World to Care For*, 111.
10   Truman, *Public Papers*, 559.
11   Quotes from the films *No Help Wanted, What's My Score?, Welcome Home*.
12   *Birmingham Reporter*, n/d, from Rynearson papers.
13   *Birmingham Reporter*, n/d, from Rynearson papers.
14   Barrie Stavis, "We Will," *Saturday Evening Post* (March 30, 1946); "They Walk Again," *Newsweek* (September 24, 1945); "Teaching the Crippled," *Life* (May 5, 1947).
15   Stavis, "We Will," *Saturday Evening Post*, March 30, 1946, 14.
16   Den Adel written remembrances.
17   Ibid.
18   "Meet H. A. Everest," *Paraplegia News*, December 1955, 4.
19   Ibid., 4, 10.
20   Den Adel written remembrances.

Chapter 8

Biographical details about Bob Rynearson came from his papers, newspaper articles, and author interviews with his children (Bob Jr. and Diane Forbes). Background about James Naismith and the history of basketball came from, among others, Ellsworth's *Secret Game*; Stark's *Wartime Basketball*; Maraniss's *Games of Deception*; Wolff's "Olden Rules." Wheelchair basketball history background came from, among others, Rynearson papers; Nugent papers; Den Adel's writing; Labanowich and Thiboutot in *Wheelchairs Can Jump!*; author interviews with Thiboutot; Strohkendl's *50th Anniversary*; and Schweikert's articles in *Paraplegia News*. Biographical background of the pioneering wheelchair basketball players came from the Rynearson files, Nugent papers, program notes, newspaper articles, and author interviews. Background about Cushing Hospital and their players from Wallace's *Pushing*; newspaper articles; and author interviews.

1 Hildegard Level, "Miracle," *Hygeia*, September 1949, 626.
2 "Basketball Plays," *Life*, January 22, 1945, 53.
3 Scott Ellsworth, *The Secret Game* (New York: Little, Brown and Company, 2015), 84–86.
4 Rynearson papers.
5 Ibid.
6 Labanowich and Thiboutot's *Wheelchairs Can Jump!,* pp 11–12.
7 Author interview, 2018.
8 *Birmingham Reporter*, November 29, 1946, 1.
9 Ibid.
10 Braven Dyer, "The Sports Parade," *Los Angeles Times*, January 14, 1947, 8.
11 Den Adel written remembrance.
12 "Medically Speaking," from Rynearson's files.
13 Roe Laramee has also been identified as "Rod Laramie," "Romeo Laramee," and "Larami Roe."
14 Frances Burns, "Wheelchair Basket Ball Teams Clash. . .," *Boston Globe*, November 15, 1946, 2.
15 *Framingham News*, December 6, 1946. Background also from http://www.michaelhamel.net/promotions/Celtics1947.htm and Seth Washburne's http://thirsty13th.com.

Chapter 9

Description and history of the Norconian, Naval Hospital Corona, and the Rolling Devils came from author interviews with Kevin Bash; Bash and Jouxtel's *Navy in Norco* and *Norconian*; Wilkman's "Norconian Property"; newspaper articles;

author visits to Norco. Background on Dr. Gray from author interviews with Dr. Gray's children and newspaper articles. Background on Johnny Winterholler from his OMPF file and interview with his children. All quotations from Fesenmeyer came from interviews with the author, except as noted.

1 Author interviews with Kevin Bash; Wilkman's "Norconian."
2 "My Day, April 28, 1943," from *The Eleanor Roosevelt Papers*, Digital Edition, at The George Washington University. Viewed online: https://www2.gwu.edu/~erpapers/myday /displaydoc.cfm?_y=1943&_f=md056482.
3 Letter reprinted in *Clarinda Herald-Journal*, n.d., from Fesenmeyer papers.
4 Author interviews; *Oakland Tribune* articles, 1947–1982.
5 Author interviews.
6 Letter to Rynearson, dated July 24, 1947.
7 *Salt Lake Tribune*, September 30, 1945, 12.
8 *Casper Star-Tribune*, October 10, 1945, 10.
9 Letter dated February 10, 1945.
10 Winterholler's OMPF.
11 *Robesonian*, December 26, 1945, 6.
12 *Argus-Leader*, February 4, 1951, 30.
13 This is the date given by Rynearson; other sources state the game occurred on February 7 and March 18.
14 *Birmingham Reporter*, March 7, 1947.
15 *Oakland Tribune*, May 20, 1947, 1.
16 *Birmingham Reporter*, March 7, 1947.
17 O'Farrell, *Navy Nurse*, 53.
18 Letter to Rynearson, dated July 24, 1947.
19 Ibid.

Chapter 10

Description of the Rolling Devils trip came from author interviews with Fesenmeyer; *Oakland Tribune* articles; articles from various Corona, Pomona, and Riverside newspapers; Kevin Bash collection; Wilkman's "Norconian Property." Details about the PVA's formation came from back issues of *Paraplegia News*, newspaper and magazine articles about the PVA; interviews with Fesenmeyer; "Oral History of the Paralyzed Veterans of America"; Schweikert's "25 Years Later"; author interviews. All quotations from Fesenmeyer came from interviews with the author, except as noted.

1   *Atlantic News-Telegraph*, April 25, 1947, 6.
2   *Evening Star*, April 25, 1947, A-20.
3   *Oakland Tribune*, May 18, 1947.
4   *Oakland Tribune*, May 11–29, 1947.
5   Lee Dunbar, *Oakland Tribune*, May 15, 1947.
6   *Oakland Tribune*, May 11–29, 1947.
7   *Oakland Tribune*, May 24, 1947.
8   *Oakland Tribune*, May 20, 1947.
9   *Oakland Tribune*, May 27, 1947.
10 Larry Birleffi quoted in *Corona Daily Independent*, July 4, 1947.
11 Elsie Robinson, "Lest We Forget," *Evening News*, May 20, 1947.
12 Ibid.
13 *Orlando Evening Star*, January 24, 1948, 6.
14 *Paraplegia News*, September 1961; newspaper articles about Price; Schweikert's "25 Years Later."
15 From speech given by Smead, December 15, 1980; Smead in *California Paralyzed Veterans of America Bulletin*, n/d, from Bob Rynearson papers.
16 "Oral History," PVA, 1.
17 Smead, undated statement, from Rynearson files.
18 Letter to Rynearson, dated July 24, 1947.
19 *Los Angeles Times*, June 15, 1947, A8.
20 *New York Daily News*, July 21, 1946, 37.
21 *Oakland Tribune*, May 22, 1947.

Chapter 11

Details about Birmingham's first cross-country trip came from the Rynearson papers and scrapbook (many of the newspaper clippings were unidentified in the scrapbook); Den Adel's personal accounts; newspaper articles by John Old; magazine articles; program notes; film clips.

1   Level, "Miracle," 648.
2   Ibid.
3   John Old, *Herald-Express*, February 17, 1948.
4   *Pasadena Independent*, February 17, 1948.
5   Den Adel written remembrances.
6   Claude Newman, *Valley Times*, February 19, 1948, 14.
7   *New York Times*, February 17, 1948, 34.
8   *Handicap*, September 1947.
9   *Birmingham Reporter*, July 18, 1947, 1.
10 From "The Bucket," a Birmingham Hospital newsletter, n/d.
11 Level, "Miracle," 648.
12 Ibid., 649.
13 Ibid.
14 Quoted in William Dettloff, *Ezzard Charles* (Jefferson, North Carolina: McFarland and Company, 2015), 55.
15 *New York Times*, February 27, 1948, 20.
16 Oscar Fraley, *Daily Herald*, February 3, 1948, 6.
17 Will Cloney, *Boston Herald*, February 24, 1948.
18 *New York Times*, February 25, 1948, 32.
19 Letter reprinted in *Paraplegia News*, April 1949.
20 Den Adel, "Wheelchair Basketball," in *PVA News-Bulletin*, March 26, 1948, 4.
21 *New York Times*, February 26, 1947, 13.
22 *PVA News-Bulletin*, March 26, 1948, 5.
23 *Evening Star*, February 28, 1948, A-12.
24 *PVA News-Bulletin*, March 26, 1948, 5.
25 *Popular Mechanics*, April 1948, 54–55; *Daily Worker*, various

columns by Rodney, 1948; Helena Huntington Smith, "They're Still the Same Inside," *Women's Home Companion*, October 1945, 32; Lulu Laird, "I Married a Paraplegic," *Coronet*, May 1950, 28–30.

26   *Newsweek*, March 22, 1948, 50.

27   *New York Times*, February 27, 1948, 20.

28   Claude Newman, *Valley Times*, January 7, 1947.

29   "Pedally...," *The Record*, January 23, 1953, 20; "veterans...," *Atlanta Constitution*, January 26, 1948, 16; "They play. . ." *Nashua Telegraph*, March 23, 1949; "invalids' basketball. . ." *Asbury Park Press*, March 16, 1958, 21; "whole-bodied opponents. . ." *S.F. Chronicle*, May 26, 1947; "They'd love...," *Daily Independent*, February 3, 1948, 2.

30   "Legless," *Salt Lake Tribune*, January 29, 1948; "Laughs," *Bismarck Tribune*, April 25, 1947, 8; "Useless," *Rotarian Magazine*, November 1946; "Crippled," *Oxnard Press-Courier*, April 13, 1948, 4.

31   *Nashua Telegraph*, March 9, 1949, 11.

32   *Daily Press*, January 30, 1949, 12.

33   *Newsweek*, March 22, 1948, 56.

Chapter 12

Background on the Madison Square Garden game came from newspaper articles, coverage from *Newsweek*, film clips, and interviews. Background about Paul Helms and the Helms Athletic Foundation came from the LA84 Foundation archive and newspaper articles. Background about paraplegics' housing and P.L. 702 came from *Paraplegia News* and the *Congressional Record*. Background about African-American wheelchair basketball players came from programs and newspaper articles. Background about Executive Order 9981 came from the Truman Library's archives; background about Jackie Robinson's military service came from Arnold Rampersad's biography (among others).

1 Ed Sullivan, "Little Old New York," *Morning Herald*, January 2, 1948, 4.

2 Ibid.

3 Oscar Fraley, *Daily Herald*, February 3, 1948, 6.

4 Lester Rodney, *Daily Worker*, February 4, 1948, 14.

5 *Newsweek*, March 22, 1948, 50.

6 Ibid.

7 John Price, "Meet Harry Schweikert," *Paraplegia News*, February 1957, 4–5.

8 Schweikert, *Paraplegia News*, April 1948, 8.

9 Schweikert, *Paraplegia News*, February 1949, 8.

10 Schweikert article, n/d, in Rynearson papers.

11 Author interview.

12 *New York Times*, January 17, 1948, 30.

13 Henry Talbot, "Report on Sexual Function in Paraplegics," *Journal of Urology*, February 1949. Reprinted in *Paraplegia News*, November 1950, 3–5. Ernest Bors, et al., "Fertility in Paraplegic Males," *The Journal of Clinical Endocrinology & Metabolism*, April 1950, 381–398.

14 Lulu Laird, as told to Kate Holliday. "I Married a Paraplegic," *Coronet*, May 1950, 29–30.

15 Author interview.

16 Rodney, *Daily Worker*, February 4, 1948, 14.

17 *Paraplegia News*, July 1948, 1; PVA oral history, viewed online: https://www.azpva.org/wp-content/uploads/2017/07/history_oral.pdf.

18 *Paraplegia News*, August 1951, 3.

19 *Valley Times*, April 7, 1950, pg. 1–2.

20 Executive Order 9981: https://www.trumanlibrary.gov/library/executive-orders/9981/executive-order-9981.

21 Arnold Rampersad, *Jackie Robinson* (New York: Alfred A. Knopf, 1997), 82–112.

Chapter 13

Background on 1948 Olympics came from the IOC's Official Report and Hampton's *London Olympics*. Background on Dr. Ludwig Guttmann and the early Stoke Mandeville Games from his archives, papers, and writings housed at the Wellcome Collection in London (including his unpublished memoir); oral history by Guttmann at Imperial War Museums (viewed online); Scruton's *Stoke*; newspaper and magazine articles in England and the United States; medical literature about spinal-cord injuries, written by Guttmann and about Guttmann; articles in *Paraplegia News*, *The Cord*, and *Paraplegia*.

1   "Ray Lumpp," *New York Times*, January 17, 2015.
2   *Wembley News,* quoted in Janie Hampton's *London Olympics*, 24.
3   Quoted in Hampton, *London Olympics*, 24.
4   Neil Tweedie, "Olympic Hero," *London Telegraph*, July 4, 2012.
5   Pat Williams, "Man Who Turned Broken Men," *Daily Mail*, n/d.
6   Ludwig Guttmann, unpublished memoir, 33.
7   Ibid., p 33–34.
8   Ludwig Guttmann, "Oral History with the Imperial War Museums," part 1. Viewed online: https://www.iwm.org.uk /collections/item/object/80004556.
9   Ibid., part 3.
10 John Silver and M-F Weiner, "George Riddoch," *Spinal Cord*, 2012 (50), 88–93. Also: Silver's article viewed online: https://www.ncbi.nlm.nih.gov/pmc/articles/PMC5550927/.
11 Ludwig Guttmann, "Looking Back," *The Cord*, 1954, 12.
12 Joan Scruton, *Stoke Mandeville* (Aylesbury: The Peterhouse Press, 1998), 12.
13 Quoted from a speech given to the National Paraplegia Foundation, April 4, 1970. From the Timothy Nugent Papers, Folder 28.

14 "Making," *Picture Post*, September 3, 1949, 31.

15 "Sir Ludwig Guttmann," *Paraplegia*, 1979 (17), 16.

16 "Married Life," from Guttmann's paper read at the 1964 Scientific Meeting, *Paraplegia*, 188.

17 COB, "I Watched My Chair . . ." *The Cord*, 1952, 25.

18 Ludwig Guttmann quoted in Ian Brittain, *From Stoke Mandeville to Stratford* (Champaign, Illinois: Common Ground Publishing, 2012), 3.

19 Ludwig Guttmann, *Textbook of Sport for the Disabled*, 22–23.

20 Guttmann, "New Hope," *Paraplegia*, 13.

21 Guttmann quoted in Susan Goodman, *Spirit of Stoke Mandeville*, 150.

Chapter 14

Background about the Flying Wheels trips came from the Rynearson files, newspaper and magazine articles. Background about Timothy Nugent from the Timothy Nugent archives at the University of Illinois, Urbana-Champaign; Nugent's oral history with Fred Pelka; articles and interviews; author interview with his son. Background about the first NWBT came from program notes; NWBA newsletters; Nugent's papers; and newspaper articles in Illinois.

1 "'Flying Wheels' Complete Tour," *Paraplegia News*, April 1949, 1.

2 Bob Miller quoted in Labanowich, *Wheelchair Basketball* (thesis: Capstone Press, 1997), 37.

3 Bob Miller, et al., Letter "In Grateful Memory," November 6, 1948.

4 Rusk, *A World to Care For*, 109.

5 Letter to Ray Mitchell, February 27, 1949, Rynearson files.

6 Letter to Howard Hughes, March 16, 1949, Rynearson files.

7 *Daily Oklahoman*, March 19, 1949.

8 "Flying Wheels," *Paraplegia News*, April 1949, 1.

9 Hedda Hopper, "Looking at Hollywood," *Chicago Tribune*, April 14, 1949, 34.

10 Fred Pelka, Nugent Oral History, 2004–2005, 8.

11 Ibid., 10.

12 Ibid., xiii.

13 Rick Zaks, "Nugent, Abner Doubleday of Wheelchair Sports," *Champaign-Urbana Courier*, June 21, 1970.

14 Fred Pelka, *What We Have Done* (Amherst: University of Massachusetts Press, 2012), 96.

15 Nugent interview with Stan Labanowich, July 10, 1974. Nugent Papers, Box 1, Folder 3.

16 *News-Gazette*, March 31, 1970, 12.

17 Vance quoted in Loren Tate and Jared Gelfond, *A Century of Orange and Blue* (Champaign, IL: Sports Publishing LLC, 2004), 34.

18 Paul Bergman, profile published November 16, 1979. Nugent Papers, Box 1, Folder 2.

19 Nugent interview with Labanowich.

20 Minutes of the First National Wheelchair Basketball Tournament, NWBA, 1949.

21 Article in *Citizens Tribune*, n/d, from Nugent Papers, Box 34, Folder 8-1, scrapbook 8.

22 Fred Pelka, Nugent Oral History, 45.

23 *Parade*, April 8, 1962.

24 *News-Gazette*, March 31, 1970, 11.

25 *Chicago Tribune*, January 26, 1963, 139.

26 *St. Louis Post-Dispatch*, April 8, 1962, 224.

27 Harry Schweikert, *Paraplegia News*, November 1949, 8.

Chapter 15

Background research about *The Men* came from The Margaret Herrick Library of the Academy of Motion Picture Arts and Sciences, in particular the Fred Zinnemann

Papers there; newspaper and magazine articles; coverage in *Paraplegia News* and in the Birmingham Hospital newsletter; autobiographies and biographies of the principal participants; repeated viewings of the movie as well as other war-related movies; author interviews; the Rynearson papers.

1 Stanley Kramer quoted in Glenn Frankel, *High Noon* (New York: Bloomsbury USA, 2017), 58.

2 Susan King, "The Method," *Los Angeles Times*, March 31, 2005.

3 Ted Anderson, "Paraplegic GI," *Los Angeles Times*, February 26, 1950, D3.

4 Deverich, *Wandering Through La La Land*, 9.

5 Anderson, "Paraplegic GI," *Los Angeles Times*, February 26, 1950, D3.

6 Darr Smith, *Daily News*, May 12, 1950.

7 Aline Mosby, "Cycle of Films," *Daily Worker*, August 23, 1949, 10.

8 Hedda Hopper, *Los Angeles Times*, November 24, 1950, B18.

9 Fred Zinnemann, "On Using Non-Actors," *New York Times*, January 8, 1950, 87.

10 Marlon Brando, "Thirty Days in a Wheel Chair," *Varsity Magazine*, April 1950, 32.

11 Brando in *Listen To Me Marlon*, Passion Pictures, 2015.

12 Ibid.

13 Gladwin Hill, "Grim Masquerade," *New York Times*, October 16, 1949, X4.

14 Author interview.

15 Hill, *New York Times*, October 16, 1949, X4.

16 Philip Scheuer, "Paraplegic Film Role," *Los Angeles Times*, October 23, 1949, D1–2.

17 Ted Anderson, "I Will Not Walk Again—So What?," essay in Zinnemann Papers; *Daily News*, November 11, 1949.

18 Scheuer, *Los Angeles Times*, October 23, 1949, D2.

19   Jon Zelazny, "The Dawn of Brando: Richard Erdman Re-
     members *The Men.*" Viewed online: http://thehollywood
     interview.blogspot.com/2010/03/dawn-of-brando-richard
     -erdman-remembers.html

20   "The Brilliant Brat, *Life*, July 31, 1950, 49–58.

21   Hedda Hopper, *Los Angeles Times*, May 7, 1950, D1.

22   Stanley Kramer, *A Mad, Mad, Mad, Mad World* (New York:
     Harcourt Brace & Company, 1997), 52.

23   "The New Pictures," *Time*, July 24, 1950.

24   Bosley Crowther, *New York Times*, November 12, 1950, 183;
     July 21, 1950, 15.

25   Robert Moss, *Paraplegia News*, July 1950, 7.

26   *Daily News*, May 12, 1950; *Daily News*, November 28, 1949.

27   Fred Zinnemann, *A Life in the Movies: An Autobiography* (New
     York: Charles Scribner's Sons, 1992), 85.

28   Ted Anderson, *Los Angeles Times*, February 26, 1950, D3.

29   "13-Year Struggle," *Los Angeles Times*, October 5, 1958.

Chapter 16

Background about the Joseph Bulova School of Watchmaking
and the Watchmakers basketball team came from newspaper
and magazine articles; company reports; interviews given by
Ben Lipton; General Omar Bradley's autobiography; Savitz's
Wheelchair Champions; Sidrer's *Development*; Labanowich's
Wheelchair Basketball; team rosters at the NWBT; *Paraplegia
News*.

1   "A Promise Kept," *The Link*, October 1953, Vol. 11, No. 10.

2   Ibid.

3   Howard Rusk, *New York Times*, August 15, 1955, 17.

4   *New York Times*, October 10, 1946.

5   Lipton quoted in Robert Szyman's dissertation entitled "The
     Effect of Participation in Wheelchair Sports," 1980. Nugent
     Papers, Box 6, Folder 15.

6 Benjamin Lipton, "The Role of Wheelchair Sports," *International Rehabilitation Review*, 1970.

7 Geraldine Baum, "He Goes to Bat," *Newsday*, April 29, 1984, 19.

8 Red Smith, "Views of Sport," *Lancaster New Era*, February 9, 1950, 36.

9 Harry Schweikert, *Paraplegia News*, January 1950, 8.

10 Harry Schweikert, *Paraplegia News*, January 1951, 8.

11 Labanowich, *Wheelchair Basketball*, 42.

12 John Wessells, "Paralyzed Vet's House," *Richmond Times-Dispatch*, July 17, 1949.

13 John Archibald, "Loss of Use," *St. Louis Post-Dispatch*, November 3, 1949, 27.

14 Bob Miller, "From the Past President," *NWBA Bulletin*, 1950–51, 4.

15 *Los Angeles Times*, April 28, 1950, A7; Birmingham newsletter, Rynearson papers.

16 "VA Told to Shift," *Los Angeles Times*, May 4, 1950, 4.

17 "Warren Aids," *Los Angeles Times*, May 17, 1950, 2.

18 Rosemarie Mullany, "Paraplegic Cites," *Tucson Daily Citizen*, May 31, 1950, 21.

19 "VA Plans New Hospital Here," *Los Angeles Times*, May 23, 1950, 1.

20 Joseph Hearst, "3 Wheel Chair," *Chicago Daily Tribune*, May 31, 1950, 18; *Paraplegia News*, June 1950, 7.

21 Ernest Bors, "Spinal Cord Injury," *Spinal Cord*, November 1967, 127.

Chapter 17

Background on the Korean War came from President Truman's papers and writings; President Eisenhower's papers and writings; *Paraplegia News*, Halberstam's *Coldest Winter*, newspaper articles. Background on NWBA and NWBT came from newspaper articles, "Bulletins," Labanowich and Thiboutot writing, Schweikert columns, and author interviews. Background on Stoke Mandeville came from newspaper and magazine articles, *The Cord*, *Paraplegia News*, Brittain's books and essays.

1 David Halberstam, *The Coldest Winter* (New York: Hyperion, 2007), 630.

2 "America's Wars," published by the U.S. Department of Veterans Affairs. Viewed online: https://www.va.gov/opa/publications /factsheets/fs_americas_wars.pdf. Also, "Data on Veterans of the Korean War," published by the Office of Program and Data Analyses, June 2000. View online: https://www.va.gov/vetdata /docs/SpecialReports/KW2000.pdf.

3 Halberstam, *The Coldest Winter*, 2.

4 John Power, "Cushing's Musings," *Paraplegia News*, September 1950, 7.

5 "'Pill Hill' Blood Drive," *Oakland Tribune*, June 2, 1953, 14.

6 Michael Baker, "Military Medical Advances," *Military Medicine*, April 2012, 423–429.

7 David Maurer, "Veteran Remembers 'the Forgotten War,'" *Daily Progress*, November 22, 2010.

8 Robert Moss, "To Paraplegics of the Korean War," *Paraplegia News*, June 1951, 1.

9 *NWBA Bulletin*, 1950–51, 417.

10 *Paraplegia News*, July 1952, 8.

11 *Los Angeles Times*, January 23, 1953, 89; *Independent Press-Telegram*, January 23, 1955, 110.

12 Sam Schnitzer, "Nixon Praises 'Wheels," Los Angeles Examiner, February 11, 1953, Sec. IV, 3.

13 *New York Times*, April 16, 1953.

14 Arthur Mulligan, "52 Association," *Daily News*, February 29, 1948, 362.

15 Author interviews with Lapicola.

16 *NWBA 1953–54 Bulletin*, 8.

17 Quoted in Brittain, *From Stoke Mandeville to Stratford*, 13.

18 "'Paralympics' of 1953," *Bucks Advertiser & Aylesbury News*, June 26, 1953, 10. Also see: Ian Brittain, et al., "The Genesis and Meaning of the Term 'Paralympic Games,'" *Journal of Olympic History*, Vol. 27, No. 2, 2019.

19 "Stoke Mandeville Paralympics," *Paraplegia News*, November 1953, 5.

20 "Paralympics of 1953," *Time*, August 17, 1953, 42.

21 Quoted in Brittain's *From Stoke Mandeville to Stratford*, 15.

22 Ludwig Guttmann, "Competitive Sports and Physical Medicine," *Paraplegia News*, November 1953, 6.

23 Ludwig Guttmann, "Statistical Survey on One Thousand Paraplegics," *Proceedings of the Royal Society of Medicine*, Vol. 47, 1102.

24 Ludwig Guttmann, "Victory Over Paraplegia," in Fraser, Ian (ed.), *Conquest of Disability* (London: St. Martin's Press, 1956).

25 John Gale, "Wheel-chair Sportsmen," *The Observer*, August 1, 1954, 8.

26 "Sports Meeting," *Manchester Guardian*, August 2, 1954, 8.

27 "Paraplegic War Veterans," *New York Times*, April 4, 1954, S8.

Chapter 18

Background about polio epidemic came from Oshinsky's *Polio*; medical journals and newspaper articles; author interviews. Background about the Whirlaways and the Pan Am Jets came from newspaper and magazine articles; NWBA and NWBT program notes; Pan Am Clippers newsletters; research about Junius Kellogg by Bruce Wolk; Savitz's *Wheelchair Champions*; *Paraplegia News*; author interviews. Background about the airlifts came from NWBA and NWBT notes; author interviews; Labanowich and Thibotout's *Wheelchairs*.

1 David M. Oshinsky, *Polio* (New York: Oxford University Press, 2005), 8.

2 Polio incidence rates from various sources including "Polio,"

by Sophie Ochmann and Max Roser, from "Our World In Data." Viewed online: https://ourworldindata.org/polio.

3   Author interviews.

4   Ibid.

5   John Paul, "Thomas Francis, 1900–1969: A Biographical Memoir." http://www.nasonline.org/publications/biographical -memoirs/memoir-pdfs/francis-thomas.pdf.

6   "Stricken Basketball Star Finds a New Life," *Negro Digest*, September 1963, 19–23. (Reprinted from *Industrial Bulletin*.) Also, Harriet May Savitz, *Wheelchair Champions* (John Day Co., 1978); Wolk's writing and research.

7   *Brooklyn Eagle*, December 18, 1952, 7.

8   Ibid.

9   Pan Am's *The Clipper*, Vol. 1, No. 11, April 1954; and subsequent issues. Viewed online: https://merrick.library.miami.edu /cdm/search/collection/asm0341.

10   Author interview.

11   Ibid.

12   John Old, "'Wheels Wing East," *Los Angeles Herald & Express*, n/d. Rynearson files.

13   Author interview.

14   "NWBA 1953–1954 Bulletin," 11–12.

15   Old, "'Wheels Wing East," *Los Angeles Herald & Express*, n/d. Rynearson files.

Chapter 19

Coverage of the Stoke Mandeville Games came from Guttmann and Scruton's writings; local newspaper reports; *The Cord*; Brittain's Paralympics history. Pan Am Jets background came from the company's *Clipper* newsletter; player scrapbook; newspaper articles; and author interviews.

1   Ludwig Guttmann letter to Dr. Howard Rusk, October 14, 1955.

2 "Roger Bannister: Sportsman of the Year," *Sports Illustrated*, January 3, 1955.

3 Scruton, *Stoke Mandeville*, p. 76.

4 "Wheelchair Sportsmen," *Bucks Herald*, August 5, 1955.

5 Guttmann letter to Rusk.

6 Labanowich and Thiboutot, *Wheelchairs Can Jump!*, pp. 20; Welger quoted in *Paraplegia News*, September 1956.

7 Author interview.

8 Strohkendl, *50th Anniversary*, pp. 60-61.

9 Ibid., p. 58.

10 "Wheel Chair Unit," *New York Times*, August 3, 1955, p. 16.

11 "Wheelchair Sportsmen," *Bucks Herald*, August 5, 1955.

12 "'Herald Man,'" *Bucks Herald*, August 3, 1956.

13 *Chicago Tribune*, April 9, 1956, p. 71.

14 Author interviews.

15 Labanaowich, "Wheelchair Basketball Classification," *Palaestra*, Spring 1988, p. 14.

16 "'Herald Man,'" *Bucks Herald*, n/d.

17 Ibid.

18 Scruton, *The Cord*, n/d.

19 *Bucks Herald*, August 3, 1956.

20 *Bucks Herald*, August 3, 1956.

21 Scruton, *The Cord*, n/d.

Chapter 20

Background on Junius Kellogg and the Pan Am Jets came from newspaper and magazine articles; NWBA program notes; Pan Am *Clipper* newsletters; research and writing by Kellogg biographer Bruce Wolk; Savitz's *Wheelchair Champions*; *Paraplegia News*; author interviews. Background about Stoke Mandeville Games came from *The Cord*; Guttmann's writings; Scruton's book; newspaper and magazine articles; *Paraplegia News*. Background about Roy Campanella and his car accident from

Campanella's autobiography; Roger Kahn's *Boys of Summer*; newspaper articles; *Paraplegia News*.

1   Jerry Izenberg, "Jerry Izenberg at Large," *Syracuse Post-Standard*, June 11, 1965, 23.
2   Ibid.
3   Quentin Reynolds, "Nobody's Better Off Dead," *Reader's Digest*, March 1958, quoted in "Famous Negro Athlete Conquers Paralysis," *Performance*, May 1958, 6.
4   *Sports Illustrated*, January 31, 1955.
5   Author interview.
6   "Famous Negro," *Performance*, 13.
7   Pan Am *Clipper* newsletter, viewed online: https://merrick .library.miami.edu/cdm/search/collection/asm0341.
8   Ethel Sidrer, *Development of Wheelchair Athletics*, 40.
9   Harry Schweikert, "The Handicapped in Sports," *Paraplegia News*, August 1957, 16.
10 Author interview.
11 Harry Schweikert, "Champions—Yet Not," *Paraplegia News*, September 1957, 16.
12 Ludwig Guttmann, "Claims Made," *Paraplegia News*, December 1957, 10–11.
13 "An Observer Answers Dr. Guttmann," *Paraplegia News*, December 1957, 11.
14 "We Are Responsible," *Paraplegia News*, December 1957, 12.
15 *Bucks Herald*, August 3, 1956, 9.
16 "They Set Example," *Bucks Herald*, August 2, 1957.
17 Roy Campanella, *It's Good to Be Alive* (Boston: Little, Brown and Company, 1959), 241.
18 "Our Champion," *Paraplegia News*, March 1959, 1.

Chapter 21

Background on the 1960 Paralympics came from newspaper and magazine articles; Pan Am *Clipper* newsletters; Savitz's

Wheelchair Champions; *Paraplegia News*; author interviews; *The Cord*; Guttmann's writings; Scruton's writings; *Paraplegia News*; Maraniss's *Rome 1960*; Brittain's *From Stoke Mandeville to Stratford*; Labanowich and Thiboutot's writings; Official IOC Olympic Report. Background on South Africa trip from Jones's *Real Tom Jones*, Ebert articles.

1   INAIL newsletter, viewed online: https://www.inail.it/cs /internet/comunicazione/news-ed-eventi/news/news-premio -antonio-maglio-2018.html.
2   Jeanne Christensen, "Meet Junius Kellogg," *Paraplegia News*, October 1960, 5.
3   Quoted in David Maraniss, *Rome 1960* (New York: Simon & Schuster, 2009), 384.
4   Maraniss, *Rome 1960*.
5   Charles Ryder, "The 1960 Paralympics," *Paraplegia News*, November 1960, 20.
6   Quoted in Labanowich and Thiboutot's *Wheelchairs Can Jump!*, 280.
7   Ryder, "1960 Paralympics," *Paraplegia News*, November 1960, 20.
8   Ludwig Guttmann, "Speech of the President," *The Cord*, 1960.
9   *Wheelchairs Can Jump!*, 46.
10 Anna Brady, "Pope Praises Ill Athletes," *Baltimore Sun*, September 26, 1960.
11 "Benediction of His Holiness Pope John XXIII," *The Cord*, 1960.
12 Quoted in Sidrer, *Development of Wheelchair Athletics*, 52.
13 Brady, "Pope Praises Ill Athletes," *Baltimore Sun*, September 26, 1960.
14 Ludwig Guttmann, *Sport for the Disabled*, 24.
15 Ludwig Guttmann, "Editorial," *The Cord*, 1960, 6.
16 Dick Maduro, *St. Petersburg Independent*, September 29, 1960, 12-A.

17 Author interview.

18 *Long Beach Press-Telegram*, March 28, 1960, 17.

19 Quoted in article by Errol Willett, in *Spinal Network Extra* magazine, Fall 1990. From Timothy Nugent Papers, Box 12, Folder 15.

20 *NWBA Newsletter*, November 10, 1992, 15–16.

21 Author interview.

22 Marcia Smith, "Dad's Deeds Left an Impression," *Orange County Register*, June 18, 2006.

23 *News-Gazette* articles by Roger Ebert, July 1962, in Timothy Nugent Papers.

24 Roger Ebert, Foreword to *The Real Tom Jones*, xii.

25 Tom Jones, *The Real Tom Jones* (iUniverse, 2003), 33.

Chapter 22

Background on the 1964 Paralympics came from newspaper and magazine articles, particularly *Japan Times* (English-language); *Clipper* newsletters; Savitz's *Wheelchair Champions*; *Paraplegia News*; author interviews; *The Cord*; Guttmann's writings; Scruton's *Stoke Mandeville*; Goodman's *Spirit*; Labanowich and Thiboutot's writings; Brittain's *From Stoke Mandeville to Stratford*; Roy Tomizawa's *1964* (and https://theolympians .co/?s=1964+paralympics).

1 "Athletes in Wheel Chairs," *The Times* (London), November 9, 1963, 9.

2 *Japan Times*, October 8, 1964, 5.

3 *Japan Times*, July 16, 1964, 4.

4 Cliff Crase, Editorials from *Sports 'n Spokes*, 178.

5 Author interview.

6 Ibid.

7 Savitz, *Wheelchair Champions*, introduction.

8 Scruton, *Stoke Mandeville*, 123–24.

9 Polly Summar, "Ms. Kids," *Daily Illini*, April 10, 1974.

10 Labanowich and Thiboutot, *Wheelchairs Can Jump!*, 78–79.

11 Ibid., 192; author interview.

12 Author interview.

13 Labanowich and Thiboutot, *Wheelchairs Can Jump!*, 246–47; *Detroit Free Press*, October 5, 1979, 61.

14 Crase, Editorials, *Sports 'n Spokes*.

15 Andrew Wright, "Rolling with the Hits," *Forward Sports*, December 5, 2016. Viewed online. https://forwardsportsmagaz .wixsite.com/home/single-post/2016/12/05/Rolling-with -the-Hits.

16 Fred McBee and Jack Ballinger, *Continental Quest: First Wheelchair Crossing of North America* (Overland Press, 1984).

17 *Mount Carmel Daily Republican*, February 7, 1984.

18 Crase, Editorials, 56.

19 Letter to William Greener, April 24, 1984, from Timothy Nugent Papers.

20 Geraldine Baum, "He Goes to Bat," *Newsday*, April 29, 1984.

21 Ibid.

22 Ronald Reagan, "Remarks at the Opening," June 17, 1984. Viewed online: https://www.reaganlibrary.gov/research /speeches/61784a.

23 Bob Cuomo, "Seven Nations," *Los Angeles Times*, August 12, 1984, H33.

24 Ian Jaquiss, "Reception in Seoul," *Los Angeles Times*, February 14, 1989.

25 Statistics from the U.S. Department of Defense.

Chapter 23

Background about Ron Kovic's military service came from *Born on the Fourth of July*, published accounts, author interviews. Background of more recent wheelchair sports: author interviews, newspaper articles, columns in *Paraplegia News* and Crase's articles in *Sports 'n Spokes*.

1   "America's Wars," published by the U.S. Department of Veterans Affairs. Viewed online: https://www.va.gov/opa/publications /factsheets/fs_americas_wars.pdf.

2   Ron Kovic, *Born on the Fourth of July* (New York: McGraw-Hill, 1976), 119.

3   Charles Childs, "Assignment to Neglect," *Life*, May 22, 1970.

4   Author interview.

5   Ibid.

6   Bob Ryan, "These Guys Wheel," *Boston Globe*, n/d.

7   Ethel Van De Grift, "Ski Slants," *Los Angeles Times*, n/d.

8   Harriet Stix, "Sportsmen in the Valley," *Los Angeles Times*, March 9, 1975, L1.

9   "An Oral History: Marty Ball," interviewed by Alan Abrahamson and Wayne Wilson. LA84 Foundation, 6–7.

10 Author interview.

11 Ibid.

12 Lisa Pollak, "The Other Ravens," *Baltimore Sun*, September 1, 1996.

13 Robin Layton, *Hoop: The American Dream* (New York: power-House Books, 2013), 117.

14 Brian Grimmett, "36th National Veterans Wheelchair Games," www.kuer.org, June 27, 2016.

15 Author interview.

16 Invictus Games Foundation website: https://invictus gamesfoundation.org/foundation/story/.

17 Author interview.

18 *Japan Times*, January 25, 1965.

19 Pelka, *What We Have Done*, 169.

20 Ibid.

21 Protest sign, 1990. Viewed online: https://everybody.si.edu /media/889'.

22 "National Council on Disability: 20 Years of Independence." Viewed online: https://ncd.gov/publications/2004/July262004.

23 "Remarks of President George Bush at the Signing of the Amer-

icans with Disabilities Act," July 26, 1990. https://www.eeoc.gov /eeoc/history/35th/videos/ada_signing_text.html.

24 Figures from the Centers for Disease Control and Prevention; Rosemarie Garland-Thomson, "From Medical Condition," *Los Angeles Review of Books*, February 22, 2017.

25 Howard Rusk quoted in "Proceedings of the Panel on the International Scene," The President's Committee of Employment of the Handicapped, May 1969, 7.

Epilogue

1 Author interview.

2 *Oakland Tribune*, October 30, 1964, 6.

3 Author interview.

4 Author interview.

5 Robert Cantwell, "An Era Shaped by War," *Sports Illustrated*, November 30, 1964.

6 *Performance*, September 1968; *Van Nuys News*, July 27, 1973.

7 Jan Meier, "National Day Winner," *Los Angeles Herald Examiner*, July 4, 1972.

8 Author interview.

9 Ibid.

10 Ibid.

11 Lorinda Murdock, "Veterans Dedicate Plaque," *Valley News*, December 16, 1980, 14.

12 Author visit.

INDEX

NOTE: *Italic page references* indicate photo insert.